Diplomacy and Persuasion

Diplomacy and Persuasion

How Britain Joined the Common Market

Uwe Kitzinger

Thames and Hudson · London

*Printed in Great Britain by
The Camelot Press Ltd,
London and Southampton*

ISBN 0 500 01080 3

Contents

List of Tables and Diagrams

Acknowledgments

For typing a voluminous correspondence and the bulk of the text I should like to thank my secretary, Margaret Bett, and for helping to take the overload at crunch week-ends also June Harris of Standlake.

To Harriet Macandrew, my research assistant until April 1972, I owe vast files of press cuttings and also the computer breakdowns set out in the Appendix 1; her successor Dov Zakheim read the popular press and tabulated the opinion polls. I am grateful to both for checking innumerable details, for holding the fort during my frequent absences, for their patience with me, and for their unfailing support. Thanks are also due to John Hawkins who drew the graphs, and to John Goulding who prepared a difficult typescript for the printer.

For permission to reproduce the opinion polls set out mainly in Chapter 12 and Appendix 3, I am grateful to the Opinion Research Centre and Louis Harris Research Ltd, Social Surveys (Gallup Poll) Ltd and NOP Market Research Ltd.

My greatest debt of all is due to the Warden and Fellows of Nuffield College. It is just ten years since I became one of their number. I could not have hoped for a happier comradeship of endeavour.

The friends who were neglected, burdened with portions of the draft, or both, shall remain nameless. It is to the closest of them that the book is dedicated.

For Sheila

Preface: Some Headaches of Contemporary History

Seek not to present a perfect work
  The Lady Julian of Norwich

This is a tale of three cities: Paris, Brussels and London. It is made up of several strands. In Franco-British relations it starts at the nadir with the Soames affair – when French civil servants found it difficult to accept even dinner invitations at the British embassy – and ends with the Queen's visit to Paris, welcomed by President and people alike. Over British entry into the EEC it starts with Harold Wilson's conversion to accession to the Rome Treaty, and ends with his fight in the House of Commons against an alien system of law. In British domestic politics it begins with the difficulties faced by the newly elected Conservative government and the danger for the Conservative Party of splitting over the Common Market: it ends with a deep rift in the Labour Party over the issue, with the government on that issue happily in the clear. In the realm of public opinion and its formation, it begins with a 71 : 12 majority in favour of entry in 1966 and via a 17 : 63 majority against entry in 1971 ends with a more balanced but still unfavourable division of view. It describes both the Goliaths of the hidden and overt persuaders in favour of entry, and the embattled Davids fighting their tactical rearguard action against, from which a strategic counter-offensive may yet emerge.

Several of these themes thus have their own dramatic unity. Others, however, form part of the continuing themes of British politics: the reassessment of Britain's role in the world, the up and down (and stop and go) of her economic tides of fortune, the conflict between tradition and modernization in the Conservative Party, between Left and Right, and between Parliamentary Party and trade unions on the Labour side. These strands implicitly run through the story as the continuing warp that began long before it, and may well continue – changed and conditioned, no doubt, by these events – into the future.

To that extent what this book seeks to describe is certainly a test case in the political process, but also one that is too atypical to constitute a representative example. Even if it is not representative, however, it can be an exception that 'proves' the rule: the working of the British political system in unusual circumstances can serve to throw unusual light on its normal nature. Moreover, the events described in this book undoubtedly have to be regarded as sufficiently special to be worth remembering historically for their own sake – and for the way they may prove to have affected the future of the system. What the book does not attempt to do explicitly is to sort out which are the general rules, which the particular accidents. That is a task which it is in many ways too early for either historian or political scientist to perform – which is why the book ends without any presumptuous attempt at a chapter of summary 'conclusions'.

One could, of course, have waited another six months, until more people had been interviewed, more alleged facts cross-checked, more points of view considered. One could have waited four or five years, until the memoirs of some of the principal present actors begin to sprout on the bookshelves. (Those of Harold Wilson, George Brown, Couve de Murville and some other actors in the 1967 attempt are already available.) One could have waited thirty years, when the official archives will allow us to distinguish in detail the attitude of a key civil servant in one week from his reactions three weeks later. One could wait until, at some as yet indeterminate date, some major phase of European integration appears to be concluded, then to put Britain's entry and subsequent events into historical perspective. At each of these points the story will have to be re-written, no doubt from different points of view. With each re-writing it will become more complete in one sense – but also perhaps less 'true' in another.

The present essay thus does not set out to be a cathedral. It constitutes at most a quarry. (The fact that Marketeers and anti-Marketeers alike may use stones from it to throw at one another is a different matter.) The cathedral – if it can ever be accomplished – will have to be constructed with stone from many quarries. Moreover, this particular way of telling the story will no doubt provoke the publication of further material. In that sense it is itself a tool of research, a means for others to gather further material before it is too late, for future treatment in more traditional historical style or future use in more systematic political analyses.

The contemporary chronicler – and the bulk of this book was written in early 1972 – certainly has some advantages over the traditional historian; but he also faces in particularly acute form problems which impinge rather less on those writing of a remoter period. Four problems in particular have troubled me, and on each of them I owe the reader some kind of explanation of what I have tried to do. The four problems are those of objectivity, of reliability and completeness of evidence, of 'political discretion', and of the chronicler's own concept of the structure of political events. The four problems tend to become intimately intertwined.

Classical historians either spontaneously see, or more consciously reinterpret, events of a previous epoch in terms of their own images of the world as it is or ought to be. The contemporary chronicler or political analyst would have to be a peculiar creature indeed if he were at once sufficiently interested to work in detail on public events and yet devoid of any personal views on those events or on the political framework in which they take place. I happen to have been an advocate of world-wide and hence also European political integration since my schooldays, and an active participant on the side of the 'Marketeers' for many years. Rather than pretend to any impartiality, to which I would lay little claim, I can only warn the reader of my open bias. As one of my informants put it: 'On this issue, silence would have been the only neutrality.'

This bias obviously affects the overall framework in which I see the story. It would be understandable for an anti-Marketeer to wait before recounting the same events until Britain has re-extricated herself from this monstrous Continental entanglement. For him 1 January 1973 cannot be a natural terminal point for a sub-division of the story, but only the most farcical episode in it. Nonetheless, I hope that before too long there will be an account of these events written from the opposite point of view to set against mine. In turn, of course, both points of view may seem irrelevant, or beside the real point, to historians or political scientists dealing with the same period but with a different focus.

The reliability of the evidence in writing an almost immediate chronicle is not necessarily less than in the more classical forms of writing. Some of my worst sources have been published ones. Some of my best informants have been my friends. Yet memory is fallible. A colleague recalls having been given by five informants four different names for the chairman of an important meeting.[1] I have also met strident contradictions and, given the limitations on time to triple-check information, I have no doubt succumbed to unnecessary and painful

[1] David Butler and Michael Pinto-Duschinsky, *The British General Election of 1970*, Macmillan, London, 1971, p. xiii.

inaccuracies. But in addition I have, for example, had categorical denials from different sources of the presence or involvement of a certain civil servant in one set of events, a certain politician in another, a certain diplomat in a third – each denial countered from other sources with detailed descriptions of their behaviour or regularity of attendance; and I have had written denial of four statements in international minutes from the man responsible for these minutes, which will no doubt form a source for the classical historian. Some of the means of checking will become available to later historians, others will be irretrievably lost to them. Our work, once again, is not so much competitive as complementary.

It is on the completeness of the evidence that the contemporary historian – certainly when he is dealing with as complex and inter-national an event as this – inevitably falls short of the classical. I have interviewed several hundred people and read several thousand press reports, but am conscious of having had to leave untapped a great many further possible sources. It will be apparent that I have inter-viewed widely in London, a good deal in Paris, a little in Brussels, and not at all in Bonn, Rome, The Hague, Washington or other relevant cities. This was for obvious logistic reasons. My thanks go to all who were willing to give me of their time and counsel, quite a few of them by writing memoranda or commenting on draft chapters no less than by long conversations. It is part of my thanks, particularly to some of those to whom I am most grateful, that I mention none of them by name.

This leads to the consideration of my third problem – that of political discretion. Almost inevitably any contemporary chronicler knows more than he feels he can tell. Some facts are acquired by being oneself involved in events, and are therefore not available for use in a different capacity. Some facts are given off the record for academic purposes as background material to help interpretation but not for use. Some facts are supplied for use but only on condition that their source cannot be identified – but it then proves impossible to state the facts accurately in such a way as to obscure the source. Some facts are not given but obtrude themselves within a context of implicit confidentiality.

These are the easy cases. But there are other facts specifically given to me for use on the record, either immediately or else after a certain lapse of time, the publication of which might, however, itself affect either the further progress of the events described, or the actors in them, or even other historians' access to future information. In some cases the repercussions would most probably be trivial, while the historical relevance of the events is appreciable; in others the detail may be incidental to the story, while repercussions on those involved might be unhappy. These are not simply questions of balancing probabilities: in these cases issues of principle arise. On the one side is the role of academic work in relation to the long-term development of the polity as a whole; on the other, the personal loyalties and the immediate political causes in which any individual academic happens to be involved. The separation of personal from professional life is a general problem of social role in which there are general standards, however ill-defined, both as to the use of information and as to the treatment of individual cases (including one's personal friends) in an impersonal fashion. It is here that the privileges of academic life impose their heaviest responsibilities.

The problem arises both in that part of the story which concerns diplomacy and in that concerning domestic persuasion. How far, in either case, does one go in the naming of civil servants who played important roles, and did so for reasons and in ways which showed them clearly to be rather more significant individuals than mere interchange-able cyphers doing no more and no less than executing their political masters' bidding? How relevant on the domestic side is the exact source of a sum less than £5,000 spent on a particular public relations exercise? How far does one go – on the diplomatic side of the story – in tracing disagreements between the Permanent Representation of the French Republic in Brussels, different schools of thought in the Quai d'Orsay, and thinking in the Elysée? To what extent and in what detail is a 'conflict' or 'difference of emphasis' within the British official machinery on French intentions, or on tactics of co-operation with the so-called 'friendly five' rather than with the French, a fit subject of anecdote and of comment? How relevant to the establishment of a tactical line by the British delegation was a conversation between two civil servants in a taxi or the absence of a Minister in Mexico at a certain moment? How crucial was a particular dinner in a Brussels restaurant attended by French and British delegates? How far in fact is anything that happens at an official meeting ever decisive – or even at the unofficial preparative meeting or in telephone calls before these – compared with the plans laid in his study or while driving to the office by the man whose ideas happen on that occasion to be adopted? Is it not in this private rumina-tion or where two or three cabal together that the roots of history lie? It is here that the questions of discretion mingle with those of the level

of historical and political discourse, as it reflects both the detail of the
evidence available, the minutiae to which one can subject a reader and
– more important – the underlying catagories of causality in decision-
making.

More and more as I look at the political process – and this is even
truer for international political processes than for national ones, a point
that many would no doubt think of major topical political importance
– it turns out to be constructed like Peer Gynt's onion. There will be
history books in the future which sum up the four hundred pages of
this volume in the four words 'Britain joined in 1973 . . .'. In so doing
they will with perfect accuracy portray the blue outer skin of the
onion. Sir Con O'Neill has been writing an official history for the
Foreign Office considerably longer than this book, which deals it would
seem essentially with the topics here sketched in a mere two or three
chapters. Long newspaper articles have already appeared about, and
future memoirs will deal in massive chapters with, topics here skated
over in a paragraph or so. This book sets out to deal with the middle
layers of the onion.

But it is not really the level of description that raises the problem,
uneven as it has to be. The real problem lies in the levels of causal
explanation which the descriptions may seem to imply. In one sense
Jean Monnet a quarter of a century ago, and future historians a quarter
of a century hence (if that is how things finally turn out), may agree
that British participation in West European unity was historically
inevitable: it was in the nature of things, it was predestined by geography, or it was the result of ineluctable global forces of population
and technological (and hence political) evolution. President de Gaulle's
vetoes were nothing but a temporary delaying factor, and once 1968
had undermined his power base the rest naturally followed. Approaching the picture a little more closely, others might say it all depended on
Georges Pompidou. If he said 'no', no it would be, whatever all the
busy Brussels bureaucrats might put in their interminable papers, and
even Edward Heath could not have changed his mind. If he said 'yes' –
to quote one of my friendliest and fiercest critics – 'Soames' chauffeur
could have done the rest'. Yet when and why he said yes, only Pompidou's psycho-analyst could tell us (if, incongruously, he consulted
one) and most probably not even he. Similarly – in domestic affairs – at
one level, provided the British government decided, Parliament and
people were bound to follow – so only Edward Heath mattered. At
another level of explanation, personal relationships going back to

student days, the generosity of a rich backer for a movement, a round of drinks in a politician's home after the formal meetings were over, a flash of inspiration to a civil servant on a technical solution, or the contingency planning which a party manager made in his bath-tub one Sunday morning (to quote actual examples given to me) were all significant factors *sine qua non*, perhaps *non*. A great many horses had to be shoed, and in the end none of the nails that did get lost lost the battle. Indeed one senior negotiator very seriously attributes the success of the negotiations to that least explicable of causal forces – luck.

We are thus dealing with factors that range from secular world trends to those of the order of Cleopatra's nose. All one can say is that there are thousands of people whose political activities are motivated by the belief that the long-term global forces all point the opposite way, and will prove British signature of the Rome Treaty to have been a reactionary aberration. Others are by no means convinced that history did (or in the future will) take the course it ought inevitably to take, but believe it needed their personal efforts not just to hasten its timing and shape its modalities, but for 'good' to triumph over 'evil' as they see it, with no divine predestination to take their individual responsibility from their shoulders. For those who have faith in historic inevitability, I have sought to trace at any rate the how and the when. Personally I must confess to feeling that too much has happened in the world that was pointless and even 'inconceivable', that too much of what was imperative and 'inevitable' has failed to materialize, not to believe that even the 'predestined' needs a possible time and a possible way for human agents to bring it about.

What I would, however, more and more doubt is that there can, by the nature of this story, be any single 'inside' version of it. There may be an 'inside' version from the point of view of the European Move-ment, from that of Britain's Paris embassy, or from that of the Com-mission's negotiating task-force; there may be one from the point of view of the Labour Marketeers, from that of Keep Britain Out, or from that of the Independent Television News. But each of these is a different story. Any attempt at putting them all in a common perspective must remain a subjective exercise, and therefore any 'definitive' version of 'how things actually happened' is in principle inconceivable. Not only do we have to weave about between layers on the onion. In the end, the onion has no heart.

Whereof one cannot speak, thereof must one be silent? I think not.

For a book of this kind is concerned not simply with the elusive heart of the onion, but with the search for it and with the intrinsic character of its different parts in their different layers. The purpose of telling the story – and telling it at particular different levels in different parts – is not simply to explain how Britain acceded to the Rome Treaty. This chronicle is concerned just as much or more with an attempt to explain how in one instance the process of decision actually worked. It is meant, in other words, as a quarry not simply for the historian, but also for the political scientist, or (to use a more modest description) the student of politics as a system of regulating society.

Certainly, agreed, the instance here described is atypical in two respects. For one thing, within Britain it cut right across the established party lines. Whether the demands of modern social problems will produce an increasing number of such cross-party divisions it is too early to say with certitude, but there are signs that this will not be an isolated instance. Moreover, both in the diplomatic and in the domestic aspects of the story we are dealing with a complex case that does not fall into any single text-book category. But it is a type of decision-making into which we are more and more being pushed by events, whether we like it or not. Decisions have more and more to be taken and implemented in multiple dimensions: in different countries simultaneously; in national, international and 'supranational' spheres; by a degree of concurrence between politicians, diplomats, civil servants, economic power-holders, opinion-formers, and various elements of the public; and on matters that transcend the frontiers of law and economics, of social and political life. In that sense, though historic truth is impossible, and obviously the task needed far more time, for me not to publish now would have been to commit *la trahison des clercs*.

Standlake Manor, Oxfordshire
September 1972

Introduction: Time-Lags in Political Psychology

There is one thing you British will never understand: an idea. And there is one thing you are supremely good at grasping: a hard fact. We will have to build Europe without you: but then you will come in and join us

Jean Monnet

This book focuses on the years 1970–72, when the government of Britain negotiated her accession to the three European Communities, and Parliament made that accession legally possible. The present Introduction, therefore, briefly sketches the reasons why the six Continental countries formed their Communities in the first place, and why Britain stood aside at that time. The answer to the first question must be sought largely in the years leading up to the Schuman Plan of 1950. The answer to the second differed in two successive phases – the decade of the 'fifties when Britain, though urgently pressed to join, refused to do so, and that of the 'sixties when successive British governments, now anxious to join, were prevented from doing so.[1] Only in 1971 did the will and the power appear at last to coincide for Britain: and even then the contemporary chronicler cannot take it for granted that the conclusion of the constitutional process entails the final settlement of the political issue.

The Mainsprings of the European Movement, 1945–50

The political impetus for the unification of Europe effectively dates from the closing stages of the Second World War. Those were the years when leading statesmen all over the world, following the principles laid down in the Allies' war aims, sought to create a far stronger League of Nations, a United Nations, even a federation of the world. Shocked by the legal and illegal crimes against humanity which they had witnessed in the previous decade, both in the pre-war dictatorships and during the war itself, appalled by the vast problems of hunger and want facing every part of the world at the end of that conflict, the

[1] In retelling this story I have naturally drawn on my earlier accounts of the same periods, notably in *The Challenge of the Common Market*, Blackwell, Oxford, 1961, and in the Introduction to A. Moncrieff (ed.), *Britain and the Common Market 1967*, BBC, London, 1967.

World Federalist movement took as its main aim the abolition of physical force as a method of diplomacy, the abatement or abolition of national sovereignty, and the creation of a body of international law in the full sense of the term, pronounced and sanctioned by a world authority.

The San Francisco Conference of 1944 did not fulfil these hopes. It produced a United Nations which has certainly shown itself stronger than the old League, but is still not even a confederation of states, let alone a world government. Its General Assembly remains an assembly of governments exercising their sovereignty – not one of representatives of the people deliberating in common for the common good. The final contradiction of these dreams of the war years was to be found in the national right of disobedience to any UN majority decision, formally recognized by the right of veto given to the five nations then regarded as big. So hopes for a world government were dashed to the ground.

By 1947 it was clear that more intensive international co-operation was possible only on a less extensive front. A tighter bond could be forged only between a smaller number of nations. Failing progress on a world scale, the countries of Europe (for which the federalists in Europe felt they had the most immediate responsibility) were to set an example to the world. For some idealists at least, European unity was thus not simply a regionalist approach for its own sake but a pilot project for something to come on a wider scale: any abdication of sovereignty, even on a regional basis, seemed better than allowing the nation state to consolidate itself once more after its great moral and material bankruptcy.

It was in Britain in particular that the World Federalist strain was intertwined with the ideal of European federation. The result was not entirely happy. Since federalists were among the most active in post-war relief and in international meetings, Europeans (who could not always tell an English crank from a normal Englishman) overestimated their strength in Britain. The moral absolutism and salvationist dogma of many of the early post-war federalists stemmed from their belief that federation was a technical prerequisite for translating the Sermon on the Mount into practice in the twentieth century. But because in their preoccupation with ultimate aims many federalists seemed starry-eyed, British observers were tempted to write off the federalists on the Continent as equally cranky and unrepresentative. For a very long time British policy was affected by this image of federalists as outsiders who were not to be taken quite seriously. All the greater was

British surprise when they did succeed in pulling off some of their curious plans.

There was indeed a profound difference in outlook and psychology on the two sides of the Channel. In her finest hour Britain had stood alone. She was undefeated, she had escaped occupation, she had not known bitter internal cleavages, she had no feelings of guilt, but came through with greater self-confidence, greater pride in her national virtues and national institutions, than she had known for years. The Continent, on the other hand, had just passed through the worst ordeal of its history. Almost every family had experienced the effects of nationalism run riot, almost every country had been subjected first to national defeat and then to enemy occupation. Their national self-confidence, their national institutions had been shattered. Starting from the ruins, it was imperative to develop new conceptions and more radical ideas that would make any future civil war between European brother nations impossible. In Continental Europe, a federal surrender of sovereignty thus seemed more feasible than in many as yet less disillusioned parts of the globe.

Common opposition to the Hitler regime had brought Resistance fighters and exile governments of different nationalities closer together: against Hitler's new order for a united Europe under Nazi domination, the men from the *maquis* and other underground movements set an alternative ideal. As activists of nine European Resistance movements expressed it in July 1944: 'Federal Union alone can ensure the preservation of liberty and civilization on the Continent of Europe, bring about economic recovery, and enable the German people to play a peaceful role in European affairs.'[1] For, if common fear of a third wave of German aggression seemed a bond that could unite many nations for some time, the more far-sighted also knew that it would be impossible to discriminate against Germany for ever. Any such attempt would fail and breed just what it was designed to prevent. If German policy was to be subjected to international controls, and if Germany was to be an equal member in the European family of nations, then there was only one way out of the dilemma – other nations must abdicate to supranational bodies the same measure of sovereignty which they intended Germany never to regain.

Winston Churchill, then Leader of the British Opposition, saw much

[1] 'Draft Declaration by the European Resistance Movements, July 1944', reprinted in Kitzinger, *The European Common Market and Community*, Routledge, London, 1967, pp. 29–33.

the same problem: in Zurich in 1946, he called for European unity to be based on 'something that will astonish you . . . a partnership between France and Germany'. But Britain was not included in this concept of 'a kind of United States of Europe' which Churchill advocated: 'France and Germany must take the lead together. Great Britain . . . America, and I trust Soviet Russia . . . must be the friends and sponsors of the new Europe'[1] – its friends, but not part of it. Indeed the notion of a partnership with Germany proved a far more unpopular one for far longer in Britain than it did in Belgium, Holland or France, who were closer to Germany geographically, had been under occupation, in some ways had had to differentiate between Germans on other than purely national criteria, and wanted more quickly to forget experiences which were not always of their proudest. In Britain, on the other hand, emotions about Germans as such had remained less challenged by concrete experience, and were cherished by a whole generation – all the more so as the country increasingly found herself almost needing the memory of a dragon to recall her heroic role as St George. Not perhaps till the emotionalism had – temporarily – swung almost too far in the other direction at the time of the Queen's visit to Germany in 1965 did this mistrust from the past cease to be an appreciable factor in British attitudes towards building a joint future together with Germany and France.

World federalism in general, and the specific European problem of Germany, thus formed the first two mainsprings of West European integration. Soon, however, the memories of the last enemy became less real than the fear of a new aggressor. Armed Soviet Communism had advanced to the Elbe and beyond, and French and Italian Communism was showing its strength in parliamentary and direct action as far as the Channel and the Pyrenees. The year 1948 saw the Communist *coup* in Prague and the beginning of the Berlin blockade. In the face of this immediate common threat of terrifying proportions, national differences loomed less large, and some important Continental countries hoped to shore up the instabilities in their own political systems by being contained in a broader-based framework. Common defence, a common front in foreign policy, and political solidarity at home seemed the only way for non-Communist Europe to survive the new pressures applied to it from within as well as without.

Here, too, things looked rather different from the other side of the Channel. There was no domestic Communist menace worth mention

[1] For the bulk of the text of this speech see Kitzinger, op. cit., pp. 33–7.

either under the Labour government of 1945–51 or thereafter. And the external menace was not one of being overrun in a matter of hours by Soviet land troops, but of air and, in due course, nuclear strikes and longer-term pressures. It was hardly surprising if, given a lesser menace and one which took a somewhat different form, Britain chose, instead of integrating politically with the exposed countries to the south and east of her, to remain turned westwards whence her salvation had come in the two World Wars, and where by the 'forties and early 'fifties the only credible counterpoise and deterrent to Soviet conventional forces were to be found. It was in the special relationship with the United States that she sought protection and a certain guiding influence on the evolution of the balance of world power.

Fourthly, a number of the Continental countries were troubled over the relative position of Europe in the world, not simply *vis-à-vis* Russia (and the United States), but also with regard to the rest of the globe. The rise of the countries of Asia and Africa to a new influence and a new power in world affairs occupied much of federalist thought. Their idealization of European tradition forced some of the older European federalists of the time to take a gloomy view of mankind's prospects in this imminent shift in the configuration of world power. European political unity would not stem the tide. But some (particularly French) circles hoped it would at least buttress the 'civilizing presence' of Europe overseas, while others, faced with the same situation at one remove, felt unity was desperately needed to rehabilitate Europe morally in the eyes of world opinion, and to mark the abandonment of the national concept by the very nations that had served as the model for national-ism overseas. Given the rate of expansion of the Afro-Asian countries, economic unity might produce a margin of economic manœuvre that would allow Europe to provide more aid to those countries and thereby cushion and guide, even as it accelerated, their progress to positions of world power.

Here, too, things looked very different from Westminster. The contrast for Britain seemed not to be between national policies and European ones, but between Europe and the Commonwealth. Both to the Labour government, which saw the multi-racial Commonwealth as a potential world-wide bridge between the rich and the poor, the black, the brown and the white, and to Conservatives, who valued it in terms of the proven loyalty of the white Dominions in two World Wars, Europe could be at most a complement, but never a rival to the Commonwealth concept. Britain, as Winston Churchill put it in

1950, stood at the intersection of three overlapping circles – the English-speaking world, the Commonwealth, and Europe. It was by her unique position within all three that she would still, even after the Second World War, have an opportunity of playing a unique world role. Therefore none of these three bonds, and certainly not that with Europe, could afford to be tightened to the extent that they might damage the other two.

To support the common defence effort, the common political influence, and the joint positive enterprises within Europe for the future, it seemed essential on the Continent to reconstruct the devastated national economies, not separately, but by co-operation: only common efforts could make the best use of the scant resources available. Thus on the Continent economic unity was advocated by free-trade liberals who wished to diminish the restrictive effects of political boundaries and the influence of national governments on economic life. Yet among its foremost champions there were also those who regarded the national economy as too small an entity for effective planning, and who strove to set up supranational authorities to direct production and trade on a vaster international scale.

On the Continent the European Movement thus cut right across the domestic political disputes in economic affairs. In Britain the same was true, but in the opposite sense. In the late 'forties and early 'fifties British standards of living, British income per head, and the strength of the British economy had seemed – indeed, at that time were – greatly superior to those of most of the Continent (see page 29 for the 1950 figures). While Britain was prepared to make some sacrifices in the immediate post-war period (introducing bread rationing after the war to help feed defeated enemies), there seemed little to be gained from economic integration with nations suffering from such economic difficulties – quite apart from their social problems and their political instability. The Labour government up to 1951 wanted to set up a welfare state, if not actual Socialism, in one country; after 1951 the Conservative government wanted to 'set the people free'. Neither party wanted to load itself with the burden of open-ended economic commitments to the Continent and of compromising their own economic policy with the ideas of the Continentals – interpreted by one side as high capitalism, by the other as dirigist planning. So on this fifth count, too, the same type of reasoning which on the Continent had led to the conclusion that Western Europe must integrate, on the other side of the Channel also led to the corollary that Britain must keep

away from any supranational integration that involved a formal surrender of sovereignty, and go no further than co-operation between
national governments – at least unless the United States was equally
involved.

It was here that the 'functionalists' (to use the phraseology of the
period), who were most strongly represented by the British and
Scandinavian governments, parted company with the 'federalists', who
were well represented in the governments of France, Italy and the
Low Countries. It was the hallmark of the 'federalist' that he sought
joint action not least as a means for obtaining more effective common
political institutions, whereas the 'functionalist' attempted to set up
only that minimum of political institutions that was indispensable in
order to direct the common action that was most urgently required.
While the federalist may be accused of concentrating excessively on
legal formalities, the functionalist may have underrated the handicap
imposed on effective everyday co-operation by the survival of national
vetoes. Federalists and functionalists in the late 'forties failed fully to
understand each other, and the federalists – not by accident, but for
good historical reasons – were able to sway the policy of six and only
six of the countries of Western Europe. What they achieved was
something less than a United States of Europe, though Jean Monnet's
Action Committee for a United States of Europe retained a more
maximalist title. Yet though the terminology, the fervour and the
time-scale of objectives changed with the passage of time, this
original contrast and even conflict between federalists and functionalists
was to mark the whole history of post-war Europe.

But there were divergencies even within the federalist camp. The
United States' insistence on European co-operation had been one of
the conditions of Marshall Aid. The United States was welcomed as
an ally by most of those who sought to unite Europe; yet they were far
from agreeing on the policy which Europe was to pursue towards the
United States once it had been united. The campaign for European
unity as such was thus, in fact, neutral between two sets of corre-
lative political and economic concepts. Political unity was advocated as
tending to enhance European freedom of movement – whether towards a more equal partnership within a strong Atlantic alliance or
towards a more independent position in the world as a third force.
Whichever way that decision might go, only unity, it was argued,
could make it effective.

There was a parallel ambivalence or mixture of economic aims.

Economic unity, with its advantages of larger markets and greater specialization of production, was advocated as a means of redressing the balance of dollar payments. But for some the first objective was to form a regional bloc embracing only Europe and the countries associated with it overseas, while others saw the discriminatory removal of economic barriers (between the countries of Europe, but not yet against the rest of the world) as a tactical move to strengthen the economies of Europe for full convertibility and non-discriminatory trading relationships with the world as a whole.

Even the historic cleavage of clericals and anticlericals was bridged by the European idea. Certainly three of the men in the van of the movement were devout Catholics born in Lothair's middle kingdom, an area where the liberal conception of the world and its denizens as naturally divisible into neat nation states appears unsophisticated in the extreme: Robert Schuman, a German during the First World War and then Prime Minister of France; Alcide de Gasperi, a Deputy in the Vienna Diet while Austria-Hungary was at war with Italy, and then Prime Minister of Italy; and Konrad Adenauer, the non-combatant anti-Prussian mayor of Cologne who flirted with the idea of separating the Rhineland from Prussia after the First World War. To them, the restoration of Charlemagne's empire of a thousand years before, with the cultural unity it implied, had an emotional appeal. But the stalwarts of the movement came also from the ranks of the anticlerical Left, organized, in the early post-war years, in the Socialist Movement for a United States of Europe. The Socialist Paul-Henri Spaak, a former Belgian Prime Minister, provided the personal driving force in the drafting of the Rome Treaties, and the French Socialist leader Guy Mollet was Prime Minister during the critical phases of the Common Market negotiations and secured the votes of 100 out of the 101 French Socialist deputies in favour of their ratification.

The European idea was thus originally neutral in foreign policy between a third-force concept and the Atlantic Alliance, undecided in trade policy between regionalism and multilateralism, ambivalent in its attitude to the problems of emergent nations in Africa and Asia, silent in cultural and educational matters between Catholicism and anti-clericalism, and neutral also in economic policy between *laissez-faire* liberalism and Socialist planning. Approached from very diverse points of view, European unity seemed to make sense to Continental leaders, to small but highly articulate pressure groups, and to many of the war and post-war generation. It would give greater scope to Europe for whatever policy aims were envisaged. A sudden realization of Continental federation could have produced sharp conflicts over the use to which unity was to be put; as it was, the long common struggle and the course of post-war events softened the contrasts of ultimate aim and produced not merely international but also inter-party understanding. Only the Communists in every parliament of the Six consistently voted against integration.

Britain and the Communities, 1950–70

The story has often been told of how, in 1950, six countries and six only sought to advance beyond the looser and wider organizations of NATO, the Organization for European Economic Co-operation, and the Council of Europe (in all of which Britain was a member). They set up their Coal and Steel Community as a first step to a general common market and economic community, and they worked out detailed blueprints for a defence community, and for a political community to overarch the rest. Though they failed with the last two, they then succeeded with the EEC and Euratom. Britain's various attempts – through Western European Union, through the Free Trade Area proposals, and by various other arrangements – to get the best of both worlds, as both 'in' and yet not 'of' the emergent Europe, are equally familiar. What is relevant to the theme of this book are the reasons for which, by 1961, the British government had completely changed tack and made its application for negotiations to see if terms could be found on which she could, after all, join the endeavours she had cold-shouldered only five years before.

There were five milestones on that road to Damascus. The first came as early as 1956 with the Suez disaster: even in a traditional sphere of influence, even acting together with an ally, nineteenth-century gunboat tactics had proved humiliatingly self-defeating, and thus the first crack appeared in British post-war self-confidence. With angry young men challenging social smugness and the Campaign for Nuclear Disarmament challenging Britain's image of her place in the world (let alone the forms which military power was assuming in that world), self-questioning became a little more widespread.

Then came the fateful year of 1960, in which the abandonment of Blue Streak on technical and financial grounds represented the abandonment of Britain's claim to any truly independent military deterrent; the collapse of the Paris summit meeting, the last occasion on which a British Prime Minister attempted to play a major role at the top table of world diplomacy; and the first of that series of sterling crises which was to dog the British economy right through the 'sixties, though successive governments of both political parties sacrificed domestic economic growth to the maintenance of the dollar-sterling rate of exchange. Fifthly, there was the demand for faster economic growth at home. Performance indicators on the Continent appeared to be startlingly superior (see the table on p. 29, which shows the comparative dynamism of the Six in almost every one of its sections). Though the Labour Party had in 1959 drawn attention to the 'growth league tables' in which the British economy was shown to have performed substantially worse than most of those on the Continent, the Conservative government had shrugged them off with the slogan 'You've never had it so good'; it was only in 1960-61 that the government began to ponder seriously the slow rate of growth in Britain's national product, and turned simultaneously to a form of indicative planning modelled on the French and to the concept of a 'bracing cold shower' of competition through entry into the EEC.

It was much at the same time that there spread among policy-makers in Britain a certain scepticism as to the future of those two other overlapping circles, the Anglo-American special relationship that had been the hub of Churchill's 'English-speaking world', and the Commonwealth. In the 'fifties the Commonwealth had still looked like giving Britain increased economic scope and additional leverage in the world. In the 'sixties it became obvious that the overseas sterling area was the most stagnant sector of British exports (its share of total British exports diminished from 48% in 1950 to 30% in 1960 and then 27% in 1970) and that, so far from increasing Britain's political freedom of action, the Commonwealth tended if anything to restrict it. The notion that the Commonwealth would somehow be a means of exporting the Westminster model of parliamentary democracy and adding to the peace of the world by the sort of internal regimes it would propagate had long been abandoned in the face of experience in Africa. By the 1971 Singapore conference of Commonwealth Prime Ministers many felt that Britain almost needed liberating from a grouping that stood her in the dock and judged her according to some superior moral standard over Rhodesia – the judges being people whose own racial policies (whether in Biafra, over East African Asians, or, not much later, in Bangla Desh) were far more lacking in liberalism and human brotherhood than Britain's own. There remained a general argument about helping the underdeveloped world – a criterion of useful world citizen-

		UK	The Six	USA
Population (millions)	1950	50	157	152
	1958	52	165	174
	1970	56	190	205
Gross national product	1950	47	75	318
($ billion)	1958	65	163	455
	1970	121	485	993
GNP per head ($)	1950	940	477	2040
	1958	1258	955	2613
	1970	2170	2557	4760
Industrial production				
(1953=100)	1950	94	80	82
(1953=100)	1958	114	144	102
(1958=100)	1963	119	142	135
(1963=100)	1970	125	151	135
Gross fixed asset formation	1958	15·1	20·4	16·9
(% of GNP)	1970	18·0	25·0	17·0
Imports	1950	7·2	11·2	8·7
($ billion)	1958	10·5	22·9	13·3
	1970	21·7	88·4	40·0
Exports	1950	6·3	9·4	10·1
($ billion)	1958	9·3	22·8	17·9
	1970	19·4	88·5	43·2
Exports to (other) EEC	1950	0·8	3·0	1·6
countries	1958	1·3	6·9	2·4
($ billion)	1970	4·2	43·3	8·4
Official reserve assets	1950	3·4	2·9	22·8
($ billion)	1958	3·1	11·8	20·6
	1970	2·8	29·8	14·5
Development aid				
(net official flow $ billion)	1958	0·3	1·3	2·4
	1970	0·4	2·1	3·1

Sources: United Nations Statistical Year Books, OEEC and OECD monthly Statistics, and Development Assistance Committee annual reports.

ship in which the Six could claim a recent record by no means inferior to Britain's; there remained also one or two specific economic problems arising out of the Commonwealth sugar agreement or the New Zealand butter trade; but the Commonwealth as an alternative power configuration had virtually disappeared from British policy-makers' minds.

Much the same was true from the early 'sixties as far as the 'special relationship' was concerned. There could be little doubt that, whatever had been true under Dwight Eisenhower's presidency, under the Kennedy administration the relationship between Washington and Bonn was coming to be in some ways at least as 'special' as that between Washington and London. The Kennedy 'grand design' of Atlantic partnership quite explicitly involved a relationship between a United States of America on one side of the Atlantic, and a fast unifying single economic and power complex on the other. Though some were surprised when it became even more obvious in late 1962, the failure of Skybolt was for President Kennedy 'the grand opportunity to terminate the special relationship and force Britain into Europe'.[1] Yet it was largely by reference to that special relationship that President de Gaulle, in early 1963, vetoed Britain's application.

Whatever the realism of looking upon the European Community as a replacement of the other two 'circles' or as a new lever for British political influence, by the end of the 'sixties the arguments had changed. The possibility that the United States might withdraw from Western Europe – a realization of the old slogan of 'US go home' – raised fears of a void in West European security which only much closer military and logistic collaboration between West European nations could convincingly fill. The spectre of 'collusion' between the United States and the Soviet Union, both of them more concerned with the pressure of China than with the dangers they once seemed to spell for each other, became an argument for diplomatic and political collaboration between Europeans anxious not to have their fate settled over their heads.

In international economics, there was a triple concern: over the comparative lack of autochthonous European technology to set against the USA's lead in research and development; over the 'American challenge' of multi-national but basically American-dominated companies spreading over Europe while remaining largely free of any

[1] Arthur M. Schlesinger, Jr, *A Thousand Days. John F. Kennedy in the White House*, Deutsch, London, 1965, p. 734.

effective political supervision and control; and finally over the world's monetary problems, exacerbated by the mass of footloose and uncontrolled 'Eurodollars' and the weakness of the United States balance of payments, which threatened to thrust monetary responsibilities on the Community long before it was really equipped to face them.

On Western Europe's internal problems, too, the arguments began to change once more at the very beginning of the 'seventies. In the late 'fifties and early 'sixties, economic growth as reflected in gross national product statistics had been regarded as a cardinal indicator of success; now economic growth (compounded by population increase) was continuing at such a rate that it began on the one hand to be seen more for what it is – a prerequisite for achieving social objectives which have to be politically defined – and on the other hand to be viewed with suspicion for its environmental, social and psychological costs which could not be measured in the economic dimension alone. There might be little hope that the problems of inflation (rampant at different rates in different countries) could be greatly eased at any early stage by Community action. But over as vital a problem as environmental deterioration the Community, it was argued, could act far more effect-tively than nation states on their own (with the Common Agricultural Policy one possible ingredient in its action). If the original inspiration was the fear that Western Europe might be crushed with a bang, new tasks were now discovered in preventing it from stifling itself with a whimper.

Similarly, within Britain, the argument had also changed. Where in the early 'sixties the Community was still largely a thing of hope and aspiration to be shaped by its participants, with each member and possible member reading into its potential those policies which corres-ponded to his own needs, by now detailed policies had taken shape on barley prices and on value added tax, on lorry-axle pressure and on food additives. Tailored to suit the six member states, yet for obvious political reasons impossible to nullify and rejig all over again, these policies could not be expected to be optimal for late entrants who had refused to join at the beginning. The combination of an agricultural policy and a fiscal system which taxed imports from outside the Community (on which Britain had hitherto been heavily dependent) for the benefit of farmers (of whom Britain had relatively few) would put a substantial tax burden on Britain; and the combination of high food prices and a value added tax less selective than British consumer taxation was liable to result, unless offset in other ways, in a less progressive tax system within Britain. The consequent additional obstacles to economic growth and difficulties for social policy were potent arguments against entry, at least in the short term. At the same time, particularly in 1972, the constitutional problems were very clearly displayed. The British Parliament had to take over lock, stock and barrel forty-two volumes of legislation passed by Community institutions – whose legitimacy as democratic representatives (even of the citizens of the original Community) seemed obscure. Worse still, Parliament entered into an open-ended commitment to incorporate into British law all future Community legislation and make it virtually unamendable by the domestic Parliament. The democratic legitimacy of Community institutions may or may not be a problem that can be solved once Britain is inside the Communities. The relegation of the Westminster Parliament in matters where the Community has competence was not so much an unfortunate accidental disadvantage as inherent in the essence of the Community as such, and thus part and parcel of the aim of entry.

We thus touch on the core problem of Community-building: how far the larger unit with which men identified in politically relevant ways remained overwhelmingly the nation state, and how far both smaller subnational and wider supranational units became co-ordinate frames of reference: how far in particular the political use of the word 'we' referred to West Europeans rather than to the British people.

Nothing perhaps illustrates more convincingly the difference between the British public and the population of the Six in their identification with a wider than national group, and their view of the need for wider institutions to take decisions for that group, than the opinion polls commissioned simultaneously in seven countries in early 1970 by the EEC itself. (Their results are set out on page 33.) Whereas on the Continent every single question elicited a clear preponderance of 'Europeans', in Britain the 'Europeans' remained on every single question in a minority. While Continental political leaders could thus count on a fair degree of popular support for their attempts at further integration, the lag between the British public and the Continental public, the British public and the British political leadership, posed serious problems of domestic persuasion, and no doubt also helped make more difficult the problems of foreign diplomacy.

There thus remained profound differences: differences of attitude between the Continent and Britain; acute conflicts in Britain between long-run and short-run, political and economic objectives; divergencies

A Comparative Poll in Seven Countries

Are you in favour of, or against, Britain joining the European Common Market?

	Holland	Luxem- burg	West Germany	France	Belgium	Italy	EEC	Britain
In favour	79	70	69	66	63	51	64	19
Against	8	6	7	11	8	9	8	63
Don't know	13	24	24	23	29	40	28	18

Assuming that Britain did join, would you be for or against the evolution of the Common Market towards the political formation of a United States of Europe?

	Holland	Luxem- burg	West Germany	France	Belgium	Italy	EEC	Britain
For	64	75	69	67	60	60	65	30
Against	17	5	9	11	10	7	9	48
Don't know	19	20	22	22	30	33	26	22

Would you be in favour of, or against the election of a European parliament by direct universal suffrage; that is a parliament elected by all the voters in the member countries?

	Holland	Luxem- burg	West Germany	France	Belgium	Italy	EEC	Britain
In favour	59	71	66	59	56	55	59	25
Against	21	10	9	15	11	6	11	55
Don't know	20	19	25	26	33	39	30	20

Would you be willing to accept, over and above your own government, a European Government responsible for a common policy in foreign affairs, defence and the economy?

	Holland	Luxem- burg	West Germany	France	Belgium	Italy	EEC	Britain
Willing	50	47	57	49	51	51	53	22
Not willing	32	35	19	28	19	10	20	60
Don't know	18	18	24	23	30	39	27	18

If a President of a United States of Europe were being elected by popular vote, would you be willing to vote for a candidate not of your own country – if his personality and programme corresponded more closely to your ideas than those of the candidates of your own country?

	Holland	Luxem- burg	West Germany	France	Belgium	Italy	EEC	Britain
Willing	63	67	69	61	52	45	59	39
Not willing	18	20	20	22	24	19	18	41
Don't know	19	13	19	17	24	36	23	20

of tactics between British policy-makers; and not least a gulf between policy-makers and people. It is really with the attempts to bridge all these gaps more or less at one and the same time that this book is concerned. Its first part is devoted to the problems of diplomacy posed for the government abroad; its second to the tasks of persuading the public at home of what the policy-makers had decided was the best road for the country to take.

PART ONE

1 The General Begins to Shift?

La guerre des guerres, le combat des combats, c'est de l'Angleterre et de la France; le reste est épisode

Jules Michelet

Rival Theories

On 27 November 1967, Charles de Gaulle, in an almost boisterous press conference, vetoed British entry for the second time. Less than three and a half years later, on 21 May 1971, his successor, Georges Pompidou, all smiles at an Elysée banquet, spoke of 'two peoples . . . trying to find each other again to take part in a great joint endeavour' and claimed a 'complete identity of view on the working and development of the Community'. President Pompidou himself recognized the paradox, the total reversal of policy, in his opening sentence affirming 'friendship and warmth': 'What could be more normal? And yet, today, what could be more spectacular?'

Here in Paris, far more than anywhere else, lay the crux of the issue whether Britain's accession to the EEC would or would not be possible. Had French foreign policy on the issue really veered by 180 degrees? Until May 1971 this remained the riddle of the Sphinx. So the question of just what happened, when, and why, to eliminate France's veto is the most central problem in explaining the difference between failure in 1963, failure in 1967 – and finally success in 1971.

The trail for an explanation naturally leads to Paris. And in Paris responsible senior officials close to the personalities and events of our story give totally contradictory answers as to both the timing and the motivation of the process. What is certain is that – as in the case of the Labour Party in Britain – answers as to the past are inevitably influenced by attitudes in the present: as always, history serves as a political weapon for ongoing battles and to prepare positions for the future.

Let us set out the two extreme theories to be heard on the other side of the Channel. Obviously there is a whole gamut of alternative explanations on the (not entirely one-dimensional) scale between them. But the two extremes will serve to define the area within which we must look for the most likely story.

On the one side is what one might call the 'hard' theory. The decision to allow Britain in was not taken until spring 1971, after genuine attempts by the French to resist the British initiative. It was only taken when there was no longer any viable alternative: when the pressure of the 'other five', culminating in blackmail from Willy Brandt and Emilio Colombo, forced Pompidou to give way. Germany and Italy threatened retaliation bordering on the break-up of the EEC; but the Community had become vital to France, and her national interests would have been hurt more by keeping Britain out than by letting her in. Only then did Pompidou, like a good diplomat, suddenly consent to see Heath, turn on the charm, and reap what credit he could both from the other five and from the applicant nations.

At the opposite end of the scale is the 'soft' theory. President de Gaulle started it all himself, and Pompidou was only continuing along the course which his illustrious predecessor had himself begun to steer. Had not de Gaulle, on 4 February 1969, received Christopher Soames and spoken to him honeyed words designed as a first step towards drawing Britain into the construction of a political Europe after all? If, when the British behaved so intolerably afterwards, nothing more came of it in the remaining weeks of de Gaulle's tenure of office, that was hardly his fault. Pompidou asserted at his very first presidential press conference in July 1969 that there was no objection of principle to British entry, and if it still took another two years to consummate that policy – well, major changes cannot be achieved in a hurry.

Clearly there are psychological and political advantages for different sets of people in each of these lines of explanation. The Quai d'Orsay worked hard on a tough negotiation (which might have made the British Prime Minister give up in despair of ever obtaining terms that could get through the House of Commons). Naturally they may not want to believe afterwards that they were expendable pawns pushed forward by a political master who intended to let the British through in any case, and to make them look ridiculous in having to reverse their negotiating positions overnight later on. It is not surprising that they should give Pompidou credit for having been faithful for as long as he could to the consistent French position that they fought to defend right through the 'sixties. Conversely it must suit the book of the Gaullist party managers to represent Pompidou as faithful throughout, and even now, to the General: and to argue that it was de Gaulle who had already come to the conclusion that Britain either could not be kept out or else positively ought at some stage to be brought in – in other words, that the vital decisions had already been taken or prepared as early as the winter of 1968–69.

There is no alternative to going over the period between the two dates with both these theories in mind, looking for clues.

The General's Vetoes

President de Gaulle's public reasoning on 27 November 1967 differed slightly from that of 14 January 1963, the time of the first veto.[1] The emphasis in 1963 was on Britain's overseas relationships: 'England is, in effect, insular, maritime, linked through its trade, markets and food supply to very diverse and often very distant countries.' He stressed the fear that if Britain (and, in her train, other European countries) entered the Community 'in the end there would appear a colossal Atlantic Community under American dependence and leadership which would soon completely swallow up the European Community'. De Gaulle went on to discuss Nassau, rejecting the offer of Polaris missiles and noting in passing that, in the building of submarines and warheads, the British had received privileged assistance from the Americans which had never been offered to – or asked for by – France. He then invited a question on Germany to stress that France and Germany 'in thought, philosophy, science, the arts and technology are complementary' and declared himself 'overwhelmed by the elemental and extraordinary outbursts of enthusiasm displayed in favour of the friendship of Germany and France, of the union of Europe as they both wish it and of their common action in the world' and 'touched to the very depths of my soul and strengthened in my conviction that the new policy of Franco–German relations rests on incomparable popular support' It was basically a contrast of Anglo-Saxons against Continentals, free traders against builders of a tight community, a choice in favour of Germany as against the Americans' Trojan horse.

[1] For the relevant passages from the two press conferences see Kitzinger, op. cit., pp. 182–94 and Kitzinger, *The Second Try*, Pergamon Press, Oxford, 1968, pp. 311–17. The November 1967 press conference had been preceded by the 'velvet veto' of the 16 May 1967 press conference, large parts of which are reprinted in Harold Wilson, *The Labour Government 1964–70: A Personal Record*, Weidenfeld and Nicolson and Michael Joseph, London, 1971, pp. 392–4.

In the November 1967 press conference, after harking back to Britain's earlier opposition to the EEC, he declared what was needed was 'a radical transformation of Great Britain, to enable her to join the Continentals. This is obvious from the political point of view.' But in his detailed argument he concentrated on economics, and particularly on monetary affairs:

The Common Market is incompatible with Great Britain's economy as it stands, in which the chronic balance of payments deficit is proof of its permanent imbalance and which, as concerns production, sources of supply, credit practices and working conditions, involves factors which that country could not alter without modifying its own nature. . . .

The Common Market is further incompatible with the restrictions imposed by Great Britain on exports of capital which, on the contrary, circulates freely among the Six.

The Common Market is incompatible with the state of sterling, as once again highlighted by the devaluation, together with the loans that have preceded and are accompanying it; also the state of sterling which, combined with the pound's character as an international currency and the enormous external debts weighing on it, would not allow the country to be part of the solid, interdependent and assured society in which the Franc, the Mark, the Lira, the Belgian Franc and the Florin are brought together.

Under these conditions it would obviously mean breaking up a Community that was built and operates according to rules which do not tolerate such a monumental exception.

The public record of the time on the General's motivations can now be supplemented with the memoirs of the two British Ministers who then confronted him. Harold Wilson's story of his private meetings with de Gaulle emphasizes the General's worries concerning the effect of enlargement on the Community:

He then went on to a theme which was to become familiar during the year – the nature of the Community as it was, and was becoming, and how the entry of new countries might affect it. The Treaty was not itself a reality – it was simply a treaty – but its application had created certain realities, difficult as that application had been, both in the industrial and economic field and also – and here the difficulties had been very great indeed – in agriculture.[1]

And clearly what worried him most of all in private was still the same as in 1963 – 'the mortal sin of Atlanticism':

[1] Wilson, op. cit., pp. 334–41 and esp. 407–18.

He had always observed, in war and peace, and whether or not Britain really wanted it, that she was linked to the United States. Thus, if Britain joined in her present condition and even if the British Government did not state or think that this was their purpose, Britain would introduce an element that inclined towards an Atlantic type of Community.

Moreover, as I well knew, certain members of the Six were also favourable to it, though possibly less so than Britain. He then proceeded to list them in lofty tones, with the indication that they were only restrained from the mortal sin of Atlanticism by the firmness of the General.

'Les Hollandais' – they were strongly in favour of the Atlantic concept. 'Les Belges' – more or less equally so. 'Les Allemands' – they would be very tempted. 'Les pauvres Italiens' – they, being directly dependent on the United States, could not hope to prevent it.[1]

George Brown, recording his solo encounter with de Gaulle late in 1966, confirms the General's attitude and demonstrates that the Labour government had no evidence of any change in it. But he also adds the General's preoccupation with the EEC's internal balance:

It was very clear that de Gaulle was adamantly against us. He regarded the Continent as France's place and the Atlantic Ocean and the United States as Britain's place. It was at this meeting that de Gaulle made his famous remark about the impossibility of two cocks living in one farmyard with ten hens. He said that he had had a lot of trouble getting the five hens to do what France wanted, and he wasn't going to have Britain's coming in and creating trouble all over again, this time with ten.[2]

It was no doubt in indirect reply to these kinds of thought that Harold Wilson, in the intimacy of 'a small French car, about the size of a British 1100 saloon, . . . the General, somehow, wrapping his legs into the small space available', in June 1967 tried to play the German card when the two men met at Versailles:

In international affairs, surely the one thing he had to fear was an increase in the relative strength of Germany . . . did he not fear that post-de Gaulle France, particularly if his forecast of a period of anarchy and division were realised, would be relegated to second-class status against the power of a strong Germany? . . . This surely was a case he must see for greater British involvement in the political affairs of Europe. He said he was very well aware of these questions. But he would not then have the responsibility. Après moi – probably what was in his mind was what he had said in the afternoon was the

[1] ibid., p. 409.
[2] George Brown, In My Way, Gollancz, London, 1971, p. 220.

determinant: Europe would become 'Atlantic', and while he had the power, he was not going to speed the process.

Certainly the General repeatedly assured his British interlocutors that he had understood certain changes in Britain's position. On the military side, as Wilson puts it, 'We had just decided not to ask for the Poseidon missile in place of Polaris. To that extent I was presenting him not with a new Nassau but a Nassau in reverse. Trianon was the opposite of Rambouillet,' and this was noted by the General. On the other hand in monetary matters 'he had not, he said, found me too explicit about the future role I envisaged for the pound sterling . . . our attitude and policy towards sterling still seemed to be very closely linked with United States financial policy'.[1] But then, since monetary had some time earlier come to replace military affairs as the General's chosen battlefield against the United States, the changes in Britain's defence policy were hardly as decisive in the General's eyes as some might have imagined.

These changes, which President de Gaulle recognized even in his press conferences, were insufficient: what was required was a profound economic and political transformation. What he had said in 1963 he repeated in May 1967 and then again in November: other sorts of trading arrangements might be possible with Britain, but the day for British entry into the Community had not yet come. 'If Britain one day reaches that stage, with what great joy will France then greet this historic transformation.'

So in the communiqué which in effect interred the second try, the EEC Council of Ministers noted 'that no member state raised an objection of principle against the enlargement of the Communities', but France stood out against the rest on two points: 'One state, however, expressed the opinion that this enlargement would modify profoundly the nature and the ways of administering the Communities.' And 'one member state considered that the process of restoring the British economy must be completed for Britain's application to be reconsidered'.[2] The chief overt stumbling blocks were agriculture and sterling, involving Britain's relationship with the United States on the second, and Britain's balance of payments on both the first and the second counts.

[1] Wilson, op. cit., pp. 413, 408, 337.
[2] Communiqué of 19 December 1967 (reprinted in *The Second Try*, ed. cit., pp. 317–18).

The Fateful Last Twelve Months

All that was in 1967. It marks the point of departure, over which there is no disagreement. The record is full, well-corroborated and unambiguous. It is only on what happened thereafter that the theories differ.

In spring 1968 de Gaulle was outwardly at his most self-willed, independent and self-confident ever. The previous year, on top of vetoing British entry, he had been active with deliberate conspicuousness in the most diverse areas. In the Middle East he had taken sides against Israel, as much perhaps in opposition to the United States as from any sympathy for Arabs in general. In North America, he had astounded the world (some claimed, actually, even himself) by his slogan of '*Vive le Québec libre*' – again as much perhaps in opposition to the Anglo-Saxons as in pursuit of linguistic and cultural Frenchdom. He had gone a long way in his monetary *politique du pire*, attacking the dollar exchange standard both directly and through 'the soft underbelly of sterling' – again combining his attack on the Anglo-Saxons with the pursuit of other objectives. Having ended most of his military participation in NATO in 1966, he was content to let speculation run as to whether he would withdraw from the alliance altogether on its twentieth anniversary in 1969, when the Treaty allowed. Early in 1968 he came out in favour of his old idea of military defence against all comers – the logical corollary of his policy of independence from the United States as much as from the Soviet Union,[1] and considered doubling or tripling his nuclear submarine programme or building his own intercontinental ballistic missiles.

This atmosphere of dramatic foreign activity on all points of the compass was accompanied by an appearance of bored quiescence at home. National product had risen, since the General came to power in 1958, by an average of 5% per annum in real terms. Wages had nearly doubled under his presidency while consumer prices had risen by less than half. Unemployment was insignificant. The gold and foreign exchange reserves had risen from $1 billion in 1958 to nearly $7 billion, equal to more than six months' imports, a ratio unparalleled even by the Germans. The French economic miracle was holding its own against the much-vaunted German performance, and *per capita* national product in France was – with the exception of tiny

[1] The doctrine was set out by Charles Ailleret, 'Défense "dirigée" ou défense "tous azimuts"', *Revue de Défense Nationale*, December 1967.

Luxemburg – the highest in the Community. What did it matter that the foundations for this expansion had been laid by the deliberate imposition of sacrifices on the voters of the Fourth Republic by its long-term planners (notably Jean Monnet and Étienne Hirsch)? The fruits in terms of consumer satisfaction were being reaped by the Gaullist regime. Election results, with the one exception of the first ballot in 1965, were satisfactory, the Parliament more or less side-tracked, the society so 'apoliticized' that no clouds on the horizon could be detected, in April 1968, by skilled political observers not a stone's throw from the Boulevard Saint-Germain where, within weeks, the stones were flying.

The events of May 1968, when a mishandled student disturbance discredited authority and triggered off strikes all over France, reducing the country to chaos for almost a fortnight, have been repeatedly analysed from diverse points of view. All that matters here are their effects on the President's stance in foreign policy in general and on Britain's role in Western Europe in particular. The possible effects were two. Directly, the political self-confidence of the General's regime was seriously undermined (in spite of the thumping electoral majority it received on 30 June 1968 in reaction against the disorders). Indirectly, de Gaulle had to count the economic cost first of the strikes and then of the wage-rises and other reforms with which discontent was bought off.

Two further developments, this time outside France, must also be cited for their possible effects on the General's thinking. On 31 March 1968 President Johnson announced not only that he would not accept another term of office, but that he had ordered an end to the bombing of most of North Vietnam, adding: 'We are prepared to move immediately towards peace through negotiations. . . . I am taking the first steps to de-escalate the conflict.' At the end of October all bombing stopped and the National Liberation Front was accepted as a partner in the peace talks. The image of a militarist, imperialist USA was beginning to look less convincing. It was not in itself, perhaps, a major factor in de Gaulle's attitude to the Anglo-Saxons, but it combined with several other twists in international relations.

For in Eastern Europe, that summer, there was a far more dramatic development; if it pointed back to the division of the world along cold-war lines, it yet had in effect parallel lessons for French policy. Czechoslovakia was invaded by Soviet tanks on the night of 20–21 August 1968. De Gaulle's first reaction was to blame it all on Yalta; as an acute observer put it: 'For the next several days the Yalta conference was the subject of nearly as much official comment and attention on the government-managed television news programmes as the invasion itself.'[1] His second reaction was to blame the West Germans for triggering off the invasion through their indiscreet 'opening to the East' – according to one eyewitness, somewhat to poor Chancellor Kurt-Georg Kiesinger's pained surprise. But what had, more seriously, become apparent was that his concept of a Europe 'from the Atlantic to the Urals' had become incompatible with his other principle of national self-determination, the principle he had been upholding in his support for Biafra and Quebec separatism. With the USA attempting to make peace in Vietnam and Brezhnev invading Czechoslovakia his policy of indifference between the blocs looked less appropriate.

So his third reaction, though he does not seem to have admitted this publicly, was his failure to withdraw from the Atlantic Alliance. By spring 1969, no doubt for a combination of financial and foreign policy reasons, General Fourquet, General Ailleret's successor, publicly rejected defence 'tous azimuts', clearly addressed himself only to 'the enemy coming from the East', and accepted the doctrine of graduated response.[2] 'Indeed', writes one authority, 'according to certain sources, Franco-American conversations on possible future collaboration in the field of nuclear weapons are said to have been started at the end of 1968.'[3]

November 1968 also witnessed the currency crisis that was largely an indirect international result of the French domestic events of the previous May. There had, of course, been a flight of suitcases full of money out of France across the borders into Belgium, Germany and Switzerland at the time of the disturbances, curbed by the introduction of severe exchange controls on 29 May. On 4 June France had to draw $745 million from the International Monetary Fund to protect the value of the franc. She did so with the blessing of the United States – a queer twist of fate, since France had twice in the preceding nine months been active in attempting to force a devaluation of the dollar. Then, to meet the bill for the 'Grenelle agreement' that had substantially settled the May strikes by raising the incomes of public employees and

[1] John Newhouse, De Gaulle and the Anglo-Saxons, Deutsch, London, 1970, p. 322.

[2] General Fourquet, Revue de Défense Nationale, May 1969. (This lecture was delivered in March 1969, well before President de Gaulle's resignation.)

[3] Guy de Carmoy, 'The Last Year of de Gaulle's Foreign Policy', International Affairs, July 1969, p. 426.

farmers, the budget had to be sharply increased. Inflation was clearly unavoidable, yet the exchange controls were rescinded on 4 September almost at the same moment as a rise in estate duties was tabled. Hundreds of millions of dollars' worth of francs again left the country in the weeks that followed to be converted – particularly into Deutschmark. The foreign exchange reserves of France fell from $6·9 billion to $4·0 billion and those of Germany rose from $8·5 billion to $10·9 billion between April and November 1968.

So on 20–22 November 1968 the Group of Ten, the inner council of the major industrial countries members of the IMF, was summoned to Bonn. Initially all the pressure was on the Germans to revalue: the Anglo-Saxons and the French – the Allies of the Second World War – were united against Germany on a major issue for the first time in many years. And, for the first time since 1945, the Germans defied them. (It is difficult for other countries to force a revaluation: reserves can always rise still higher. Forcing a devaluation is easier: reserves cannot fall below zero.) So when the Germans said 'no', the pressure was on the French. The foreign exchange markets had been closed since Wednesday, and on Friday the Group of Ten meeting dispersed having issued a communiqué that measures had been agreed to stabilize the situation: in fact, Herr Franz-Joseph Strauss was tactless enough to have himself quoted as announcing the devaluation of the French franc.

Then came the *coup de théâtre*. On Saturday the Elysée abruptly stated that the franc would not be devalued, and on Sunday de Gaulle announced stern penalties to enforce reimposed exchange restrictions, a policy of retrenchment and economies, and wage and price controls. President Johnson wired to assure de Gaulle of his support and $2 billion of credit from the Group of Ten buttressed the franc, which thus remained at its 1958 parity (thanks principally to American support) until after de Gaulle left office. The change of front forced upon the General by economic circumstances was significant. His irritation with the Germans was scarcely veiled. His dependence on the Anglo-Saxons – in whose boat he suddenly found himself with another weakened currency – was also difficult to hide.

The reconciliation with the USA was to proceed during the Nixon visit from 28 February to 2 March 1969: where all previous post-war US Presidents had assumed either that France had virtually disappeared in the war or else ought to disappear into a United Europe, Richard Nixon, fact-finding immediately after his assumption of office, found that France existed, that nation states continued to exist in Europe, that he must deal with them bilaterally, and that it was de Gaulle's leadership which had restored 'this great nation to the true place that she should hold in the family of nations'. If this is slightly to anticipate the chronology, it is only to show that by February 1969 de Gaulle's thinking on his world political strategy had changed substantially, as had his feelings on one of the two Anglo-Saxon powers whom he had in military, in monetary, in economic and in diplomatic ways been so anxious to oppose. And that may be of relevance to our interpretation of the celebrated Elysée lunch just three and a half weeks before the Nixon visit: de Gaulle's conversation with the British ambassador on 4 February 1969.

The Soames Affair

In 1968 George Brown had chosen as the new British ambassador in Paris a former Conservative front-bencher who had lost his seat in the House of Commons in 1966, Christopher Soames. It was, as indeed Brown records himself,

absolutely right. We had a lot to overcome in our relations with France. One problem was to remove a kind of arid frigidity which seemed to have settled down over all official relations between Britain and France. . . . It seemed to me that the Embassy was in all kinds of ways totally out of touch with what was really going on. . . . It needed a man with imagination, a knowledge of and a feel of France and with a particular social flair and, I am afraid, a man with some money.[1]

Soames proved a highly acceptable appointment in Paris. *Le Monde* described him at the lowest point in Franco-British relations as 'Churchill's son-in-law, who has inherited from him his very conservative views, his round shape, and his frankness. A *Croix de Guerre* won at Bir-Hakeim is witness to the long standing of his love for France.'[2]

Soames arrived in September 1968 and presented his credentials to the General, who clearly knew who he was – a politician used to taking the initiative – and what he had come for – to start up a political dialogue between the two countries. Soames set to work to convince his French friends and contacts that relations between the two countries

[1] Brown, op. cit., pp. 131–3. On the 'arid frigidity', however, see Lord Gore-Booth's letter in the *Sunday Times*, 1 November 1970.

[2] André Fontaine in *Le Monde*, 11 March 1969.

could hardly remain as they were. Their mutual hostility was hurting them both, and was hurting Western Europe in its role in the world.

His message did not fall on deaf ears. Michel Debré had replaced Maurice Couve de Murville as Foreign Minister when the latter had replaced Georges Pompidou as Prime Minister in July 1968. Debré was one of the few people capable of insistently pressing his views on the General. And for years he had been anxious not to let the Franco-British relationship deteriorate too far; what is more, he had wanted to see Britain in the Common Market. For this he had two reasons: firstly to redress the balance with the Germans; secondly to ensure that the Community would not become too supranational in character. By the turn of the year he had convinced the General – much against Couve de Murville's opposition – that he should talk to Soames and see if there was not the chance of taking up again some sort of political exchange of views between the two countries. A meeting was originally fixed for 10 January, but Soames had overdone things in his eagerness to get his feet under the table in Paris, and was ill. But on 4 February Soames was one of a small lunch party at the Elysée, and saw the General privately for an hour or so before and another hour or so after the meal.

We do not have de Gaulle's own side of the run-up to the lunch – he did not live to write that part of his memoirs. In Paris it is said that he was himself not over-eager to go into this conversation, saying to Michel Debré that he did not think much good would come of it. What we do have is Couve de Murville's characteristically sparse account – but then since Couve was a faithful voice of his master, this is as authentic a French government view as we can hope to get.

One could not but be saddened by the growing deterioration in Franco-British relations. De Gaulle was the first to regret it, and sought ways to re-open the dialogue. It could not be on the candidature itself, for the positions had hardened too much for any negotiation on that to be envisaged. One had to raise the debate to its real level – the political future of Europe [la politique européenne]. For de Gaulle, if Britain with her followers entered the Community, the latter would be radically transformed and become a free trade area with arrangements for trade in farm products. That might not nevertheless be such a bad thing. The two governments could talk about it, but on condition they also discussed the resulting political association, in which the four principal partners, France, Britain, Germany and Italy, would necessarily play a key role. In reply to a question from the ambassador on NATO (and not on the Atlantic Alliance) the Head of State added that he did not want the United Kingdom to leave it straight away as a precondition [*au préalable*], but that if one day there were a truly independent Europe, then there would no longer be any need for a NATO as such, with America's preponderance and her commanding position in it.

The overture to London was clear, on the basis of ideas that France had frequently expressed before and which could not surprise anyone. It was now a matter of putting politics above economics and of talking frankly about them for the first time. This overture was devoid of *arrière-pensées*, Michel Debré and I know that and can vouch for it; and for that very reason secrecy was asked for until such time as conversations might be started.[1]

There might, in that account, seem at first blush to be two inconsistencies: can you have an initiative on the basis of previously expressed ideas? And, if the dialogue were not on the candidature itself, how could the two governments talk about Britain entering the Community? Both *prima facie* contradictions disappear, however, when one remembers that the initiative lay in the procedure – bilateral talks – and that this new procedure might well be initiated on the basis of previously expressed ideas, whether de Gaulle's, or the British government's, or both. From that wider conversation about Europe's future there might then follow British entry, not through the mechanics of the Brussels candidature as it had been presented in the past, but as naturally falling into place once agreement had been reached as to the sort of political Europe which it was all about.

Soames returned to the embassy and sent a full telegram to London the same afternoon. In view of the importance he attached to the affair, and to be sure there should be no confusion later as to what had transpired, he decided to revert to a nineteenth-century practice not normal these days, and follow Guizot's precept as given to one of Soames' predecessors and quoted in Satow:

It is said that Lord Normanby, when ambassador at Paris, reproduced a conversation of M. Guizot's, which the latter asserted was incorrect, and he pointed out that the report of a conversation made by a foreign agent can only be regarded as authentic and irrefragable when it has previously been submitted to the person whose language is being reported.[2]

So on Thursday 6 February he presented Bernard Tricot, the Secretary-General of the Elysée, with a copy of his telegram: the

[1] Maurice Couve de Murville, *Une Politique Etrangère*, Plon, Paris, 1971, pp. 427-8.

[2] Sir Ernest Satow, *A Guide to Diplomatic Practice* (4th ed.), Longmans, London, 1957, p. 100.

latter according to some accounts could not from what the General had told him confirm the form in which Soames had interpreted the reference to the four principal powers in effect forming an inner council, or the loosening of the Common Market into a free trade area. But he suggested he keep the copy and that Soames should check with Debré, who was then abroad. Debré saw Soames on the Saturday, mentioning the telegram with noises of approval and without any sort of objection or correction at the end of a conversation devoted to other matters.

One could perhaps with hindsight argue that the procedure of a private lunch-time conversation had been less than optimal under the special circumstances. One of the subsequent problems proved to be that London laid great emphasis on the substance of the General's ideas (which were not really new) to the detriment of his willingness to engage in bilateral talks with Britain at all – which would have been a major innovation of form. It may well be that there was a little wool-gathering on the General's part, grand ambiguous sentiments of the kind to be found in his memoirs and press conferences. It may well be too that Christopher Soames asked questions which led the General into paths he had not originally intended to explore, and reported as de Gaulle's cut and dried views what may merely have been rather improvised replies. (This presumably is the implication of Couve de Murville's emphasis in the passage on NATO.) But if this was so, it was up to the French to co-ordinate their diplomatic services some time before the Saturday when Michel Debré met with Soames, to make sure that the impression given was the one they wanted. There is in fact evidence that they were embarrassed at feeling obliged, after the matter had become public a fortnight later, to add to the charges of indiscretion the charge of inaccuracy as well: and that was levied not at Soames' telegram, but at the later Foreign Office summary of it.

At this point, however, the scene shifts to London, where Soames' telegram must have been read at the latest on the Wednesday morning, 5 February. Harold Wilson writes in his memoirs that that week 'we had a report from Christopher Soames, the British ambassador in Paris, who had been granted his long-awaited audience with President de Gaulle. It had been affable and forthcoming, though nothing General de Gaulle said had indicated any greater willingness to see Britain in the Community than he had shown in his long talks with me in Versailles.'[1] Wilson records that neither he, nor, he thought, Soames (nor, as he

[1] Wilson, op. cit., p. 610. Wilson's view of the affair is on pp. 610–13 and 617–18.

later records, Willy Brandt) saw anything new in de Gaulle's ideas on the substance except perhaps for one item that might cause trouble with some of the other five: 'his clear hint that the looser association he proposed would be largely directed by France, Britain, Germany and Italy.'

On the procedure, Wilson records:

He went on to suggest bilateral talks with Britain initially in conditions of great secrecy, on a wide range of economic, monetary, political and defence matters to see whether we could resolve our differences. He said he would like to see a gesture by the British Government proposing that such talks should take place, which he would then welcome. . . . His proposals for bilateral talks I would have regarded as a friendly gesture, subject to our ensuring that they were not used to divide us in either defence or economic affairs from our partners in EFTA and our prospective partners in EEC.[1]

If we were concerned simply with interpreting de Gaulle's mind, this is where we could leave the story. It seems to show readiness on his part, in the context of the changes of the year 1968, to improve his relations with Britain, offer her some alternative political place in Western Europe that might also include EEC membership on the economic side (though the EEC would naturally look different then from the present Community of the Six), and see what would happen. It was, of course, from de Gaulle's point of view a fairly safe thing to do. Just what it really amounted to he did not have to decide until rather later, and in the meantime whether the British accepted or rejected it he would gain some goodwill from trying.

What he had not expected was the sequel, which put an end to all dialogue between the two countries for the remainder of his presidency. To get the story first from the French side (which could see the effect, without being able to disentangle the causes):

Was there a misunderstanding, did London see a trap as people said afterwards (but what trap?), or was it simply that British diplomacy obstinately continued its efforts to drive a wedge [brouiller les cartes] between France and her partners? Whatever the reason, before even replying to our offer or telling us in advance, the Foreign Office sent them a version of the conversation so distorted as to affront them, maintaining for example that de Gaulle wanted a loosening-up of the Community, or that the political association would be confined to the four principal powers. That version was published a few days later, and unleashed a violent press campaign against France.

[1] Wilson, op. cit., p. 610.

It was a 'diplomatic manœuvre' in the best style of bygone centuries. Actually it misled only the naive, and our Brussels colleagues were more embarrassed than irritated with us. But unfortunately the bridges remained cut as badly as they ever had been.[1]

What had happened? In London, the receipt of Soames' telegram caused anxious discussions, both in the Foreign Office and in No. 10 across the way. Harold Wilson was afterwards to blame the Foreign Office for what happened, though as a Prime Minister he was not always – or should not have been – helpless clay in their hands.

The Foreign Secretary and the Office between them in fact had a number of different concerns partly of morality, partly of tactics, partly as to the ends, partly the means. Firstly, Michael Stewart was a convinced supporter of British entry into the EEC and was not prepared to look at any substitutes. He had repeatedly asserted that the only kind of lesser arrangement that Britain could accept would be one that was clearly linked to entry and a prelude to it. In so far as this initiative might lead to entry into the Community, it was obviously to lead into a much looser Community than that of the Six. For de Gaulle this was a fact of life – that, if there were ten, it could no longer be that of the Six but one of Ten – and he was convinced (perhaps it was up to the British to show him wrong) that a wider extension would lead to lesser intensiveness. As far as Michael Stewart was concerned, all de Gaulle had shown was that if de Gaulle really believed that that was all we wanted, then he had not understood what was going on. So this was an unacceptable basis for talks.

Secondly, Michael Stewart had strong views on the political structure of the Community we wanted to enter. It was not one to be dominated by France – nor (if that was what the General seemed now to be retreating towards) by a Franco-British condominium. Britain wanted to enter a Community in which all members had their rightful, constitutional place as befits a democratic body. If de Gaulle thought she wanted to enter to lord it in some sort of directorate over the rest, he was, there too, unfortunately at cross-purposes with her. Thirdly, Michael Stewart was not one of those who believed that entry into the EEC could be secured through Paris directly. To try it that way only meant one was asked for a price one was not prepared to pay – perhaps even a nuclear deal. The only way to get in was to stay close to the

[1] De Murville, op. cit., pp. 428–9.

other five and loyal to the ideal of a Community in which all such decisions have to be taken jointly.

All these three are obviously important points, reflecting credit on the singlemindedness and honour of those who held them. But at the same time one must ask what else they might have expected the General to say. Was it to be expected that an hour with Soames before lunch and an hour after would have converted the General into believing that Luxemburg's place was in its way as important as that of Germany, or that NATO must become a permanent institution in which France would play her part, and that the EEC would remain as it was if it had four new northern members? If not, and if nothing less, however 'affable and forthcoming', would do, then why send in Soames to try to get a dialogue going? In the end it reflected some credit on French cool that they did not try to denounce Soames' attempts to get this conversation as a trap baited for the General to lead him into confidences which could provide ammunition to Britain for denouncing him to the other five.

That, however, leads us on to the questions of procedure. And there, fourthly, the Foreign Office was profoundly suspicious. As one of them said afterwards: 'We had the noose around our neck.' They argued that there must be a trap in it because the French suggested the initiative should seem to come from the British. Yet was the procedure really that fishy? In a sense the initiative had already come from the British in any case. Fundamentally it was they who were asking for a place in Western Europe. Tactically, it was Soames who had been pressing for an audience. Diplomatically it would accord well with French *amour propre* to be seen to accede to rather than to be making a request. And discussion as to who is to initiate a proposal is not such an unusual practice.

Fifthly, there were those in the Foreign Office who believed that the French had before now leaked confidential Franco-British conversations to their partners. They might not do so this time – but the mere implicit threat that they could do so could constitute a form of blackmail. To quote Wilson again, 'They feared – and they were right to emphasize this – that an acceptance by us of the bilateral proposals might be used by the General as an argument, with his colleagues in the Six, that we were not really serious about entry into EEC; indeed that we were having negotiations with him on an entirely separate basis. To do this would not have been out of character, . . .' But Wilson immediately adds what could have substantially removed the threat providing it was done the right way: '. . . and certainly, if we were to enter into bilateral talks, we should have had to make clear to the Five the basis on which we regarded the talks.'[1]

Finally, Michael Stewart himself went rather further. While there were people in the Foreign Office who urged that the French must be consulted or at least warned as to what Wilson might do (and Wilson himself, as we shall see, at one stage said that they had tried to warn the French in advance or at least simultaneously), the Foreign Secretary was adamant not only that the General's proposals must be retailed to the other five, but also that the only honourable course towards the other five was that this should be done unilaterally and without informing the French in advance. As he stated firmly in the House of Commons afterwards: 'It would not have been right to put ourselves in a position where we were in any sense appearing to ask permission to inform our allies of something they had a right to know.' He maintained that 'we never entered into, nor would we have thought it right to enter into, any undertaking to conceal . . . these things from them'.[2] Whether such an undertaking was not implicit in Soames' request for an audience with the General may or may not be another matter. Michael Stewart was later to counter that argument by saying that the General's thinking about the disappearance of NATO and an inner council of the four big powers was a confidence which ought never to have been forced on us – it was as if one of his constituents had confided in him that he intended to commit murder.

What followed was to a certain extent partly an accident of timing. Wilson was due to see Chancellor Kiesinger in Bonn on Wednesday, 12 February, and he relates that 'On the afternoon of my departure for Bonn, Michael Stewart came to see me. . . . It was strongly pressed upon me that if I went to Bonn and did not mention it General de Gaulle might make capital out of that, and succeed in convincing Dr Kiesinger that we were flirting with anti-EEC moves in Paris while supporting EEC legitimacy in Bonn.' Wilson says he did not much like the course of action pressed upon him: 'The way they wanted me to handle it in Bonn seemed designed to discredit the French with their EEC partners, and at the same time present ourselves as a rather priggish little Lord Fauntleroy who had resisted the General's anti-EEC blandishments. I expressed my dislike of the manœuvre, but, as I had to leave within ten minutes, told Michael Stewart that I would

[1] Wilson, op. cit., p. 610.
[2] Hansard, 24 July 1969.

discuss the matter with the senior Foreign Office team who were accompanying me to Bonn.'[1]

But was there really quite such a rush that the whole matter had to be decided on a 'plane, or sitting up late at night in the embassy in Bonn, without cabinet consultation and after only ten minutes with the Foreign Secretary? If so, while sympathizing with the fact that a government has to take a great many decisions simultaneously, one could yet also sympathize with the resignation of the previous Foreign Secretary on 'a really serious issue which has, as you know, been troubling me for some time. It is, in short the way this Government is run, and the manner in which we reach our decisions.'[2] There was a cabinet meeting on Tuesday 11 February, devoted among other things to the farm price review and the Parliament Bill, but there is excellent evidence that several senior cabinet Ministers did not have the problem drawn to their attention until a week after Harold Wilson's return from Bonn. Wilson's account makes it clear that 'we' had had the report the previous week, and not on the Tuesday afternoon. The problem had indeed been under anxious consideration in London – and not without the Prime Minister's knowledge – for six days and a half.

Thus Wilson writes, 'I was anxious to have a fuller assessment from Christopher Soames'. Yet, since transport and telecommunications between the two capitals were uninterrupted throughout that period, one must conclude at the very least that Soames was not sent for to give any such fuller assessment and one may suspect that he received instructions not to come to London. Presumably it was feared that as a political figure in his own right he might seek to influence the use to which his telegram reporting his conversation might be put. And it is, of course, easy for an ambassador to a country to become, as it were, the ambassador for that country and to forget that there are overall policy considerations at stake which are not for him to judge and in comparison with which his position is of subsidiary importance. Wilson concedes that in the event Soames was 'rightly and bitterly upset', though he may have over-estimated the retiring nature of the man in his remark: 'He came over to dine with me at Chequers, but any thoughts he may have had of resigning were dropped.' Having agreed to interrupt his domestic political career to take the Paris embassy and try to shift the log-jam in European affairs, Soames

[1] Wilson, op. cit., pp. 609, 610–11.
[2] Brown, op. cit., p. 169.

seemed determined to bide his time and try again when the opportunity arose. Given that any man had to have a few affairs associated with his name, he was to tell a questioner at the Paris Diplomatic Press Association on 12 March 1969, this was not one of which he need feel ashamed.

It was a pity, from the point of view of the operation on which George Brown had sent Soames out to Paris, that Brown had resigned from the Foreign Secretaryship before Soames ever moved into the Rue de Faubourg Saint-Honoré, so that the partnership which these two colourful characters were hoping to develop in the cause of British entry proved abortive. There is no knowing now how George Brown would have played the ball the General had bowled, but since Brown had persuaded Soames to take the job precisely in order to initiate political conversations, he would hardly have seen the problem in terms described by some as 'a boy scout dilemma'. Was it really impossible to reply immediately that Britain could not be expected to initiate bilateral talks – and that France clearly would not wish to engage in them – without the knowledge of the other five, and that the two countries should therefore forthwith jointly inform the others that they intended to put their heads together? To discuss Europe's political future was after all not tantamount to giving up the attempt to enter the EEC, and that also could have been made clear to the other five. Indeed the reaction of the five only confirmed that they would have welcomed any such development that could start things moving again in Western Europe.

But that was not to be. The rest of the story turned into a muddle of the kind that decisions too long deferred are liable to become. The Foreign Office, having seen the Prime Minister fly off without knowing which way he would decide, had to cover itself against a gamut of contingencies, and warn British ambassadors in the relevant capitals of what might be afoot, telling them to await further instructions. It is at this point that the word 'directorate' appears to have crept into the summary, which was to feed later French accusations of distortion. (What if anything the Foreign Office may at this moment have wired to Paris is, of course, anyone's guess.)

Harold Wilson did not in the event decide till late on the Wednesday morning that he would at least mention the talks-about-talks between de Gaulle and Soames to Kiesinger, so that the German Chancellor could not, if and when he received information later, accuse him of withholding relevant information. He agreed to do it in a few simple sentences without any of the overtones that had been proposed. He continues:

I reached Chancellor Kiesinger's office at four o'clock and asked the Foreign Office team for the brief and anodyne note I had been expecting on the de Gaulle affair. Reading it I found that it was the full works. I made it clear that I was furious; but it was difficult to keep this up in front of the Germans. I therefore made a short statement to Dr Kiesinger of the facts, in as reasoned and unsensational a manner as possible.[1]

The way it actually came over to the Germans was very unfortunate. The Germans got on to their own Paris embassy the same day to get confirmation of the story so as to be able to see it in perspective, but someone from the British embassy in Paris was 'unable to confirm' even the outline of it. The British embassy in Paris had been caught hopping without instructions from London. It was not in fact until around 8.00 p.m. the same day that Christopher Soames was able to arrive at the Quai d'Orsay to see its Secretary-General (who as a result of the late visit, we are informed in a special correction in Le Monde, had to go off to a dinner party in a lounge suit for lack of time to change).[2] Whatever the form in which Soames might have put it, the essence of what he had to say was that the President's confidence had been broken by the Prime Minister, and broken because whatever their Paris ambassador might feel about it, his masters distrusted the President so deeply that they thought he would have betrayed them first.

The final stage of the affair involved its general publication and open mutual recriminations. The French had in any case refused to have any truck with the London meeting of WEU to which Michael Stewart had, on 6–7 February, invited the member states for a discussion of the Middle East on 14 February. Two French newspapers dated Friday 21 February (and published the night before) carried reports of the British diplomatic indiscretion. The Foreign Office that Friday released on an unattributable basis the summary of the Soames telegram that they had sent to British ambassadors. The French countered with accusations of 'diplomatic terrorism', and charges of deliberate distortion (reminiscent of the Ems telegram that had triggered off the Franco-German war of 1870). The coolness between the two countries, which George Brown had sent Soames to thaw, in effect became glacial.

Richard Crossman's hitherto unpublished diary conveys much of the

[1] Wilson, op. cit., p. 611.
[2] 16 March 1969.

atmosphere and also sheds a good deal of light on the affair in the entry dictated on Sunday 23 February:

The first main incident of the week is the de Gaulle explosion.

From my point of view it started when I vaguely noticed in our telegrams there had been an account by the Ambassador, by Christopher Soames, of an interview he had had before lunch with de Gaulle. And at Cabinet on Thursday, in the course of reports by Harold Wilson on his visit to Bonn and Michael Stewart on his visit to the WEU and the manœuvres there, both referred to this conversation. It became clear that Harold Wilson felt compelled to tell Kiesinger in Bonn of the astonishing proposals de Gaulle had made to him, and to pass them on. He felt that in order to prove himself a good boy and a loyal NATO man and a loyal EEC man, he must tell Kiesinger what de Gaulle said to him and of the suggestions de Gaulle made about the future, about the break-up of the EEC and of NATO, and the formulation of the new ideas.

I must admit that during this last Thursday morning I was not attending much. The voice of Michael Stewart is so boringly dull, it goes through your head, it drills into your head, and he goes on and on and on, for twenty minutes or half an hour. He preceded his references to de Gaulle by dealing with four other subjects, and did not suggest it was particularly important. As Roy Jenkins said to me on the 'phone today and as Barbara also said, he has a power of making everything equally unimportant, and he certainly did so on this occasion. Harold Wilson did of course bring it more to one's attention, and then Fred Peart made some observations on whether it was really important for us to make ourselves turn down a proposition for something beyond the Common Market, but he was hardly listened to, so that is how I first heard about it discussed at the Thursday Cabinet.

Well, on Friday evening it became clear that in the course of Friday mid-day a major decision had been taken, and that decision was that the Foreign Office would announce formally that the conversations had taken place and give their version of them. But this of course produced a major Anglo-French crisis which went on booming along in the Saturday and Sunday papers. The decision by the British Foreign Office and the British Foreign Secretary to announce a top secret conversation is of course quite distinct from the decision of Harold Wilson on going to Bonn to tell Kiesinger about it. It's intelligible that he should fear that if he didn't tell Kiesinger and the French did our whole position would be undermined and this was the trap which de Gaulle had laid for him. I don't so much blame Harold for at least telling Kiesinger something about it. But I was very interested as to why on earth on Friday afternoon, though no suggestion had been made to the Cabinet that it should be published, the decision had been taken to publish it. And I took the opportunity this morning, when I was ringing up Harold Wilson about the successor to Stephen Swingler, of asking him about it. And he said: 'Well you know, after we got back from the funeral' (you see, he and I were at Stephen Swingler's funeral at 12.30 and got back into London about 1.30 from the funeral) 'after I got back from the funeral, just before I went off to Ipswich I got this proposal from the Foreign Office to publish in view of the French leaks and we said "Maybe . . .". Of course I didn't want to lay a trap for de Gaulle, but maybe I was wrong.'

I said: 'My God. Do you mean that is how it was fixed?'

He said: 'Yes. I gave my consent then, I am not so sure it was wise.' And then I said, 'What will Christopher Soames do about it? He's coming back today.' And Harold said, 'Well, he'll be in a terrible fury because he will think his honour has been impugned.' And then he explained how he, Harold, had told Kiesinger before Soames had got permission from the French Foreign Office, although the plan had been for Soames to see Alphand on the evening before Harold talked to Kiesinger. It didn't work that way because the interview in Paris was postponed until the next morning and so technically we put ourselves in the wrong by telling the Germans before we got the leave of the French. And now this had been followed up by an announcement by the Foreign Office of the content of the conversations. No wonder the French talk about a crisis.

In the end as it happened the affair did not do lasting harm. President de Gaulle relinquished his office within three months, Harold Wilson within eighteen, and both sides decided to start afresh. (Perhaps neither felt that they had come out of this affair in the best of all possible lights.) On the contrary, the episode came to serve President Pompidou's entourage as a stalking horse to defend British entry in the face of some Gaullist reproaches. But its mythical value today does not on the other hand solve our historical problem. Did de Gaulle – or did he not – start steering French policy into the curve which finally led to the Treaty of Accession?

The answer is partly determined by how one interprets such metaphors. What one can perhaps conclude is this. De Gaulle had from the beginning been aware of the cross-Channel implications of the integration of the Six. (Pompidou – for his own purposes of course – related in 1971 how de Gaulle had years before said to him of the EEC 'Ça va nous brouiller avec les Anglais'.) He was not so obtuse as to fail to see what a really 'European-minded' Britain could add to the construction of a powerful European-minded Europe to offset the larger power of the USA. Like a good politician, therefore, he never said 'never'. What he said was that the British were not ripe, and that the Continentals themselves, in their own construction, were not yet securely enough established to be able to absorb the British without transforming their Community totally. So the British must not come in too early. In particular, the agricultural policy really had to be tied up first before the British came in.

Yet, at the same time, the British must not come into the West European political equation too late either: while de Gaulle himself was alive France could prevail in the Community, but time was on Germany's side, and German power was growing. The events of 1968 speeded up the shift in the relative weight of the two powers, Germany and France. No harm, therefore, perhaps – even if little good could yet come of it – in making a friendly gesture to a new ambassador, in thinking aloud into the future, and, if bilateral talks did begin, in showing the other five that France could talk to Britain, was willing to do so, and was not married exclusively to them. Particularly since, tactician as he was, it would cost him nothing, and just what it was he meant by it he could always decide in the light of later requirements.

Had the Soames affair been merely one of diplomatic ineptitude, even new evidence on what happened would not justify lengthy discussion. In fact, however, the affair did point up several factors that were to take on greater significance later. On the French side, it displayed the unease with which influential people in Paris – even under de Gaulle, and perhaps including de Gaulle – saw the almost pathological enmity between the two countries. On the side of the five, who were embarrassed and unhappy at London's behaviour, it once more demonstrated their concern to have this enmity bridged, even by bilateral procedures. Competent observers in Paris believe, indeed, that to gain credit with the other five was one of the General's motivations. He may well have envisaged a settlement with the British as the price to be paid for the agricultural settlement which he needed in Brussels – precisely the bargain that his successor was to strike at The Hague. And in Britain it illustrated – apart from anything more episodic about individuals – the conflict between the two very different lines of policy: on the one side that of talking – without the French, if need be (as in WEU) – to the other five, and hoping that France's partners would twist her arm into letting Britain in; and on the other side that of seeking secret bilateral negotiations with the French behind the backs, if necessary, of the rest. We shall encounter the two strategies again in considering the bid that was finally successful.

2 Pompidou Keeps his Options Open

Le propre de l'action politique, je l'ai dit à propos d'autre chose, c'est de se
garder les mains libres, et croyez que je tâcherai de me les garder!

Georges Pompidou

The Domestic Constraints

Charles de Gaulle's resignation from the presidency of France occurred
only days before the twentieth anniversary of the Council of Europe on
5 May 1969. The celebrations of the date held in London were notable
for the jubilation of the 'Europeans' at his departure and the reiterated
determination of the British government to accede to the EEC. In the
election campaign that ensued for the French presidency the 'Europeans' (who had very largely supported Lecanuet in 1965) rallied to the
flag of the honest, previously almost unknown and totally uninspiring
Acting President Alain Poher, who among other worthy liberal causes
championed Britain's entry into the EEC.

The Gaullists naturally put up as their candidate Georges Pompidou,
de Gaulle's Prime Minister from 1962 until July 1968, when – after his
cool competence at the time of the May events – the General placed
him 'in the reserve of the Republic'. 'I hope', de Gaulle had written
to him in his letter of dismissal, 'that you will remain in readiness to
carry out any mission and to take up any office which the nation may
one day call on you to assume.' Georges Pompidou's public attitude to
British entry was proclaimed less forthrightly than Alain Poher's, but
it was not hostile. Within a week of the resignation – be it because
that was what he already really believed, because he had not yet found
his feet in international affairs and did not want to have to fight in
defence of the General's foreign policies, because he needed electoral
support, or for a combination of such reasons – he declared his agreement with the policy of Giscard d'Estaing's Independent Republicans
(who had commanded some 61 seats in the Assembly after the 1968
general election): this policy included both the maintenance of the
Atlantic alliance and the enlargement of the EEC. On 9 May 1969
Pompidou told the National Central Committee of the Gaullist party
that he would like to see Europe 'enlarged once the conditions for thi,
are achieved by our potential partners' – still a cautious formulations

but at least cast in a positive (if conditional) rather than a negative form. And he called Britain's exclusion by President de Gaulle 'dramatic' – as if to imply that he was less likely to indulge in such gestures.

Alain Poher obtained 23% against Georges Pompidou's 44% of the votes cast in the first ballot, and 42% against Pompidou's 58% in the run-off in June. On the surface Gaullism appeared to have obtained the chance of continuity beyond the General's reign. It remained to be seen how far anyone but de Gaulle could carry it off, and how far Pompidou for that matter would even wish to do so once he was firmly in the saddle. He himself defined his overall policy as a combination of continuity and 'ouverture' – change. That was a platitude. What he refused to say was where the change would come, in what direction, to what extent, and when.

Let us note that, on taking office, Pompidou had to reckon with quite definite handicaps. He was put up by the Gaullists, and the Gaullists formed the backbone of his support in the country. Yet he was not by nature or record a natural Gaullist himself at all. He had stood aside from de Gaulle's historic struggle for France against the Nazis. He had not met de Gaulle until that struggle was over and the liberated country had to be administered. He was not cast in the heroic soldier's, but in the peasant's and banker's mould. His concern might well be less with the glory of France, more with the well-being of the French: he would be less prone to the dramatic gesture, more to the calculation of economic costs and benefits. Had de Gaulle not chosen him, he would hardly have chosen de Gaulle. And that fact was very well understood by the historic Gaullists, who knew he was beholden to them for his election and were determined to see that he did not betray them once they had put him into the Elysée.

They seemed at the outset to be fairly well placed to do so. With 280 out of 487 seats in the Assembly (the result of the 1968 vote for stability) they felt able to block departures from orthodoxy, and made it certainly more convenient for Pompidou to adopt at least the language of continuity. Though the General himself had declared that he would not interfere again in French politics except in time of crisis (and had absented himself in Ireland during the election campaign), there were always a few people willing to spread the latest word from Colombey in Paris. The fundamentalist wing of the party founded a group to keep the rest on the straight and narrow under the title Présence et Action du Gaullisme. In November 1969 some became associated in a Mouvement pour l'Indépendance de l'Europe determined to preserve the

General's attitude towards the Anglo-Saxons. It has even been argued that the municipal elections of March 1971 (in which nearly 40,000 candidates were standing) were a date the French government preferred to have behind it before seeking a breakthrough in the Brussels negotiations. However that may be, there were certainly faithful Gaullists looking critically over Pompidou's shoulder in the early months of his presidency.

What was then not yet clear was how the balance of the institutions of the Fifth Republic would shift once de Gaulle was gone. Some have argued that de Gaulle constructed the constitution to fit himself. Others have argued that he did not need it: he constructed it to fit his successor. Whatever the intention, the effect has indeed been that France remains under a system of government obviously *sui generis*, but still far closer to the presidential than the parliamentary model. The distinction soon came to be made between the presidential and the parliamentary coalition. The Gaullists could not have elected Pompidou on their own. It had taken Giscard's Independent Republicans and the Centrists of Jacques Duhamel and Maurice Schumann to give Pompidou an absolute majority in the second round. But it also soon became apparent that once elected, and after getting the feel of the system, President Pompidou was no less dominant over the French political scene than de Gaulle had been – indeed was sometimes more in charge than de Gaulle had been, not least because he used a 'low-profile', rather less abrupt and subtler political style.

On the European front it was immediately noted that in the government he chose to install under him Pompidou put into key posts three men with established European leanings: Valéry Giscard d'Estaing at the Ministry of Finance; Jacques Duhamel at Agriculture; and, at the Quai d'Orsay, Maurice Schumann, 'the most European of the Gaullists, the most Gaullist of the Europeans', an Anglophile who looked back to the years spent in London during the war as the 'Voice of Free France' as perhaps the happiest of his life. Yet not too much must be made of the effects of these three appointments. Duhamel as Minister of Agriculture was hardly likely to welcome in the British except on the toughest of material terms. Schumann, however much happier he might feel being nice than being beastly to the British, was to prove an executor rather than a formulator of policy. At most his appointment marked a change of style in foreign relations: after the dour, tough precision of Maurice Couve de Murville (who was dropped altogether) and Michel Debré (who took on Defence, which he could hardly refuse), the genial, talkative Schumann presented an image of good fellowship travelling to all the neighbouring capitals and many a more distant land. In any case all three men were really put there for reasons of domestic, not foreign policy: Giscard, in spite of his difficult relations with Pompidou, because he had an independent parliamentary base within the Gaullist coalition, Duhamel and Schumann because some of the leaders of the Centre (which had by no means always supported de Gaulle, and indeed walked out of his government in 1962) needed to be brought in to consolidate the parliamentary majority after the presidential election.

The idea of a European summit conference was in the air during the election campaign. But it was not until some weeks after his victory that Georges Pompidou, on 10 July 1969, committed himself to it. No such summit could possibly have avoided dealing with the issue of the Community's enlargement. Had Pompidou not wished to put himself into a position where he would have to discuss that issue with the other five, he should not have called for a summit: if the summit was 'imposed' on him as a condition of electoral support, or as one element in an agreement on how to form a presidential majority, then here already was an internal constraint on him which could help balance the Gaullist vigilantes. In other words by entering into an electoral alliance which on the issue of British entry implied 'ouverture' rather than 'continuité' and by honouring that alliance with the appointment of Centrist Ministers, Pompidou was – intentionally or not – already beginning to give himself a margin of manœuvre between opposing wings of his own majority, a margin he could hope to widen and then exploit with time.

The Prime Minister, however, was a Gaullist. Jacques Chaban-Delmas had led the Gaullist group in the National Assembly in the mid-'fifties, held office as a Gaullist in the Fourth Republic first as Minister of Works under Mendès-France, then as Minister of Defence in the cabinets of Mollet and Gaillard, and then presided over the National Assembly of the Fifth Republic until Pompidou, in 1969, moved him to the Hôtel Matignon. The new Prime Minister was a keen supporter of Pompidou during de Gaulle's last months as President after Pompidou had been relieved of the premiership. It was generally thought that Chaban-Delmas was favourable to British entry. Mayor of Bordeaux since 1947 – like so many other French politicians, he retained his local functions though busy on the national level – he comes from a region where the British are liked, in any case.

Yet if any appointment had nothing to do with foreign policy it was his. 'The Prime Minister never meddles in foreign affairs. Indeed it's quite embarrassing. When we want him to visit some foreign country, he tells us he is far too busy doing his job to go abroad.' There is no prize for guessing to which country's foreign office the speaker of that sentence belonged. Perhaps indeed one must beware in the case of the Fifth Republic of translating *premier ministre* as anything but 'first Minister' – the man in charge of relations with the party, the parliament, and (supervising the Minister of the Interior) with the people, absorbing domestic pressures, administering the government at home, to free the President for greater concentration on foreign affairs. 'Pompidou himself hardly ever opened his mouth in cabinet on foreign affairs when he was Prime Minister', one of his colleagues related later. As for Chaban-Delmas it seems that indeed there was at one time a danger of his becoming involved in the British entry issue. February 1971 was the time of the Franco-British rugby international at Twickenham. Chaban-Delmas let it be known that he wanted to come over and see it. Downing Street replied that he was of course welcome, and must stay and use the opportunity to have a chat. But the unfortunate former wing-forward had to be content with watching the match on television. The President of the Republic signified that he was not to go.

In his book *British Politics and European Unity*, Robert Lieber set himself a theoretical task – that of verifying the proposition that 'politicization' causes a decline in the role of sectional pressure groups. Politicization he defines as an increase in the perception and treatment of an issue as one of major national importance; it is indicated by the issue being handled by primarily political ministries, the involvement of the broader public, and the active participation of political parties.[1] However convincing his conclusions may be in the British case, the Fifth Republic does not fit very easily into this kind of treatment. The involvement of the broader public was minimal, and the participation of the political parties marginal. To that extent the issue was 'non-politicized'. Yet the handling at the highest political level was complete, and the role of the pressure groups almost non-existent. To that extent the issue was 'superpoliticized'. Foreign policy in other words is regarded in the Fifth Republic as being of such major national importance (Lieber's definition of politicization) that it cannot be left to the politicians – nor to the political parties and the public. It was and still

[1] Robert J. Lieber, *British Politics and European Unity – Parties, Elites and Pressure Groups*, University of California Press, Berkeley, 1970, pp. 10–13.

predominantly remains the prerogative of the President, regarded almost as being 'above' politics.

At the same time the problem of British entry was no longer as capital an issue of France's foreign policy as it had been. The difference between being and not being a member of the EEC obviously has far greater consequences for a country than the difference between being in an EEC of six or an EEC of ten members. It clearly mattered to the French farmers on just what terms Britain was to come in, if she were to come in. The *Confédération Générale du Travail*, following the Communist line, in so far as it took up any attitude at all was hostile to British entry. The other unions were perhaps not especially interested, but rather favourable: the inclusion of a strong British labour movement in the EEC might help keep business interests in check and revive the social thrust of the whole enterprise. The *Patronat*, which had made detailed studies in 1961–62, did not really trouble to go into the issues involved again this time: broadly speaking they felt that if they could not simply survive, but do extremely well with their exports in competition with German industry, there was nothing to be frightened of in Britain's entry. Indeed, the large firms could see distinct advantages. The *Petits et Moyens Entreprises* were more concerned, since some of their members in certain sectors could expect to suffer. But few of the so-called pressure groups appear to have made any public representations on the issue. They may on average be regarded as having blessed the outcome with benign neglect.

As far as the National Assembly was concerned' as early as November 1969 the foreign affairs debate already revealed a certain change of emphasis. Maurice Schumann's speech remained well within the Gaullist orthodoxy in everything it said – though not perhaps in everything that it omitted. Michel Boscher, as loyal a Gaullist as one could wish, talked of British entry as an accepted fact that France could not oppose for long. Jean de Broglie, chairman of the Foreign Affairs Committee, presented a report in the name of his Committee later in the month asking

If it is in France's interests to secure for Europe an economic potential that allows her to raise herself to the American level, how could one imagine a European currency without the pound sterling, a capital market without the contribution of the City, a Europe of computers without the contribution of the most complex and advanced which are of British manufacture?

And he was quite unequivocal in his pronouncement that 'It is in the political, strategic and economic interest of France that the entry of Britain should come about'.[1]

His report spelled out these interests in detail. As far as the political side was concerned, stereotyped rhetoric took over:

The democratic and parliamentary tradition anchored in the British mentality provides a guarantee for the Community's future that our concepts of individual human dignity will be psychologically reinforced, and that the chances of freedom will have greater eternity in the West. The vagaries [la houle] of the Latin, the sometimes disquieting romanticism of the Germanic spirit will find in contact with the English character a reinforcement that must be regarded as beneficial and reassuring.[2]

But there was also a hardheaded consideration of where British influence would be a lesser evil:

A proper understanding of our interests leads us very much rather to note that in the end the United Kingdom's influence would be much more equivocal and uncontrollable [insaisissable] outside than inside the Community. . . . Britain's non-entry into the European whole would . . . lead the United Kingdom back into the American orbit from which one could never prise her loose, and would induce such a shock and disappointment among some of our partners that the Community would be permanently weakened by it. The notion of Europe's independence would become even more removed from reality.[3]

Maurice Schumann endorsed de Broglie's speech as 'one which could be already a foreign minister's' and it was not surprising that a guardian of the holy grail, de Gaulle's brother-in-law Jacques Vendroux, found it necessary to reiterate:

The upholding of French standpoints is not only a matter of intention but also, and especially, one of firmness. . . . The adventure of broadening the Common Market must not be embarked upon before the completion and consolidation of the Europe of the Six.[4]

But the Gaullist orthodoxy on the point was vanishing fast. By spring 1970 the 'completion' if not the 'consolidation' was after all agreed. Thereafter there never really developed any debate in France on the

[1] Doc. 865 annexed to the National Assembly official proceedings of 5 November 1969, p. 13.
[2] Op. cit., p. 12.
[3] Op. cit., pp. 12–13.
[4] The Times, 6 November 1969.

abandonment of the stand de Gaulle had taken so dramatically and
repeatedly.

Of course the diehards maintained their position. But the very fact
that there was a Gaullist President with a Gaullist Prime Minister at the
helm undermined their practical opportunities of resistance. As
François Bruel put it:

There is growing anxiety among several of the personalities who follow diplomatic affairs that Messrs Pompidou and Debré are committing one of the most
dramatic errors of judgment in history. . . . Europe and France would fall into a
state of complete dependence, through the agency [*truchement*] of Great Britain
acting on behalf of the United States.

Bruel added

Who could have imagined any such total reversal of French foreign policy?. . .
No other parliamentary majority, whether under François Mitterand or under
Alain Poher, could have gone to such lengths in the opposite direction from
General de Gaulle's desire to save France and Europe from such a fate.[1]

The counter-arguments were summarized, just as the 1971 Paris
summit was being fixed, by Jean-Marcel Jeanneney, who had been
three times a Minister under de Gaulle, and who set out 'three reasons
against Britain's entry into the EEC',[2] if the latter was to be a 'European Europe'. The first was the fear of economic dependence on the
USA if Britain were to join. At first sight this seems a paradoxical
argument, considering how much stronger the Community might
become through enlargement. But enlargement, Jeanneney argued,
would provoke a reaction. Third countries, the USA in particular,
'have – not without some regret – been prepared to put up with the
very moderate protectionism of the Six. They could hardly tolerate
that of an enlarged Community. . . . They will seek to make it into a
free trading one, and one must fear that, thanks to the many different
means of pressure the USA has at its disposal, they will succeed.' The
result would be asymmetrical, making Europe incapable of conducting
her own economic policy and in a slump laying her open to foreign
competition with disastrous economic and political results.

The second reason Jeanneney cited was that Britain would impose
on the enlarged Community her own close links with the USA, 'for
Britain would have a determining weight in the Community precisely

[1] *Le Télégramme Economique*, 26 April 1971.
[2] *Le Monde*, 5 May 1971.

because of America's support for her and also because of the great skill her diplomats have always had to divide and rule'.

Thirdly (under the subtitle 'The French language is threatened') he argued that 'in the Community of the Six, no national language can supplant the others . . . thus the linguistic originality and plurality of Europe are preserved, which are an integral part of her culture and contribute to the international linguistic balance which is gravely threatened already. . . . It is essential that Europeans should express their attitudes to life in the languages which are their own.' In all three ways, therefore, France had to guard against getting drawn into 'a vast Atlantic conglomerate, whose control will be out of our hands, and in which we may well fear that our interests will be sacrificed and European civilization in the end dissolve.'

Brilliant in its dialectics though the article was – and it deserves to be read in full (it contains on the one side long-range threats of a Communist take-over in reaction against dependence on America, and on the other side recognition, all too rare anywhere so far, that supranational institutions might well come to serve Britain's interests and policies) – it was the last shot across the bows before the summit. Couve de Murville and Jeanneney found by this time that there were few to maintain the old stand that had determined French policy right through the 'sixties: indeed Jeanneney was to resign from the party later in 1971. The General himself was now dead, Germany in that same month of May flaunted her independence of France and of the freshly agreed steps towards monetary union by floating the Deutschmark, and the tendency of the United States to turn inwards on its domestic problems was becoming more and more apparent. From May 1968 until May 1971 the fallacies on which Gaullist heroics had been based had relentlessly been exposed one by one by events. By the end of the month British entry was taken as a *fait accompli* and hardly a voice raised in protest against the warmth of the Paris welcome.

The domestic limits on Georges Pompidou's freedom of manœuvre were, therefore, eroded during the first two years of his presidency. Probably they were even at the outset not in fact as strong as he feared and supposed – the Gaullist vigilantes did not have either the leverage under de Gaulle's constitution nor the cohesion and driving-force without de Gaulle's leadership that could have opposed Pompidou effectively. They proved men of straw. With his ministerial team more in favour than de Gaulle's had been, a majority of his parliament apparently willing to be in favour at quite an early stage, the interest groups for what they were worth on balance neutral to favourable, and public opinion vaguely favourable also, by May 1971 it was getting at least as easy for him to say 'yes' as to say 'no'.

Nor was this simply the effect of the passage of time and the evolution of outside events. Certainly time was needed to turn the corner in domestic politics. But Pompidou himself had both adapted to and in turn affected the temper of the French political system on the issue. At the outset the tough negotiating position had reassured the Gaullist traditionalists: a softer position would have invited domestic criticism. By the end, the danger of criticism was more on the other side, from those who might have thought French diplomacy too obstructive: and the Paris summit disarmed them in their turn. It was, in terms of internal politics, a very accomplished operation to free himself by judicious timing from the domestic constraints of the past. The decision could be his, and his alone, and it could be taken in almost purely foreign policy terms.

The Road to The Hague

In January 1968, Georges Pompidou had made a bet with a friend, for £10 in sterling, that de Gaulle's second veto would soon be forgotten and before the year was out the Common Market would have got going again. But Britain did not just go away. The other five did not give up trying to get her in. The Common Market's progress was severely held up right through 1968 and 1969, to the point where *Der Spiegel* in Germany just before the Hague summit devoted the core of its issue to 'the break-up of the Common Market'.[1] Progress in European integration had reached stalemate: Pompidou lost his bet, and no doubt paid up.

In considering his own possible future foreign policy, during that period from summer 1968 to summer 1969 when the General placed him 'in the Republic's reserve', Georges Pompidou thus had to consider how far this pressing desire of France's partners – which he had so underestimated before – now had to be met to allow the Community to reach the end of its transition period as planned on 1 January 1970. He seems early on to have come to the conclusion that, having lost his bet, he had to draw the consequences from the facts of the situation. It was during this period, when he had a small staff in the Boulevard de Latour-Maubourg, that a British diplomat came to see him, and – whether to differentiate himself from the General who had dismissed

[1] *Der Spiegel*, 24 November 1969, pp. 124–48.

him, whether touting for support (a most unlikely hypothesis), whether in anticipation of the electoral alliance that was to give him his presidential majority or whether out of conviction – Georges Pompidou was categoric in the winter of 1968–69 that, if he were President, he would try to bring Britain into the Community. He said the same thing quietly to French observers at the same time.

Later, immediately after his election, when friends wrote to him to urge him not to miss the opportunity of bringing Britain into the EEC, they had an oral message back saying it was a chance that he did not intend to miss. Well before the Hague summit, the British embassy in Paris was convinced that, when Pompidou said there was no objection of principle, they were on firm ground in believing that he meant what he said. It was not a feeling that was shared in London. On the night of the breakthrough in Brussels in May, a British diplomat was heard to declare that the Brussels negotiations had been difficult, but more difficult still had been those of the British embassy with the British government to convince the latter that Pompidou would not deliberately aim at producing a breakdown in the attempt.

On his election the first task facing Pompidou in European policy was, of course, not the enlargement of the Community, but the tying up of the common farm policy and the conclusion of a definitive settlement of the issue of financing it. Yet his partners, who went to see him in Paris in the early weeks of his presidency, Brandt and Luns chief among them, impressed on him the need for enlargement. It became clear that a deal of the one for the other was possible, desirable for both sides, and thus perhaps even inevitable. At his first press conference, on 10 July 1969, Pompidou endorsed the call (already voiced, among others, by Brandt before the French elections were over) for a summit conference. This had to be held when the Germans, too, had gone to the polls, as they were due to do at the end of September. And on enlargement he declared: 'We have no objection of principle against a possible accession by the United Kingdom. But we do think it right that the Six should first reach agreement amongst themselves.' By November 1969, he was saying that he actually wished to see a negotiation opened, while Maurice Schumann went further, saying 'We don't simply accept the opening of negotiations, we also hope that they will succeed'.[1] The precondition remained: the agricultural policy had to be settled once and for all before the negotiations with Britain opened. 'Completion' had to come before 'enlargement'.

[1] *L'Express*, 24 November 1969.

The logic here was perfectly overt. On the one side, a continuity of vocabulary with his former master's voice, and on the other side, a gesture of 'opening' towards the other five, and towards Britain, without which the European log-jam could hardly be resolved. In late 1969, it must be remembered, the financial regulations for agriculture needed re-negotiation: and it was the French who wanted it most badly. De Gaulle had sometimes been able to get what he wanted by blackmail. No one, on the other hand, thought Pompidou quite mad enough to carry out the sort of threat with which de Gaulle was willing to play (and with which he had finally and perhaps half-deliberately committed political suicide). 'A long era of visionaries – Winston Churchill, Charles de Gaulle, Adenauer, Stalin and Kennedy – has just come to an end. The hour of the realists has now come', as Arthur Conte put it in the National Assembly debate.[1] And however much Maurice Schumann argued that there could be no question of a deal, since completion was merely the fulfilment of a contract sealed in 1957, while enlargement was something else, in substance the other five to some extent had France over the barrel.

The other five, in fact, largely shared the agnosticism not to say occasional scepticism of the British government as to the sincerity of the French public declarations. One can see why. President de Gaulle himself had declared in May 1967 that there never had been a veto, and that there would not be one then. That had not prevented him from breaking up the negotiations in 1963 and stopping them from ever starting in 1967. A veto by any other name can be equally effective and indeed less expensive in terms of goodwill from one's partners. So what the five required of France was a convincing show of sincerity. The timing of the two elements was such that the other five had to deliver before the French. The risk was that, after having obtained a financial regulation which under the Treaty had to be pretty final in character, the French would then take up an attitude so stiff that they could not absolutely be accused of a new veto – but that they would force the British to draw back from unacceptable conditions, and thus have it both ways. Moreover time was getting short. The Rome Treaty had set 1 January 1970 as the date by which, the twelve years of transition over, all the common policies were to be in operation. And by the time the summit meeting could actually take place, it was 1 December 1969 – just a month away from the end of the transition period.

[1] *The Times*, 6 November 1969.

In the Ridderzaal at The Hague Pompidou's not very lengthy opening speech in which he said the entry negotiations must be taken up 'in
a positive spirit, but without losing sight of the interests of the Community and of its members' fell flat. *Le Figaro*, having somewhat
prematurely featured the headline 'Pompidou Stars at The Hague', had
rapidly to change its tune. 'A de Gaulle without the same talent', was
an Italian diplomat's reaction.[1] *The Times* called it 'deplorable'.[2] It was
eclipsed by the formidable list of precise demands put together by
'Willy Brandt's eager beavers' – to quote a French diplomat's view of
the asymmetry between the opening statements of the two men, both
appearing for the first time in their lives as heads of state or of government in the international arena.

Brandt's speech, from the British point of view, was notable in that
here the Germans were playing the German card themselves. Addressing himself explicitly to Pompidou, Brandt enumerated four reasons
for broadening the Community: first because (a very lightly veiled
threat) 'experience has shown that putting off the question of enlargement threatened to paralyse the Community': in other words – no
financial regulation without a promise of fair play for the applicants.
Second, because enlargement would be useful

at a time when we are endeavouring to bring East and West more closely
together. . . . Third, the Community must grow beyond the Six if it wants to
hold its own economically and technologically with the giants and to meet its
world responsibilities. And I do not hesitate to add a fourth argument: anyone
who fears that the economic strength of the Federal Republic of Germany
could cause an imbalance within the Community ought to be in favour of the
enlargement for this very reason.

Piet de Jong, the Dutch Prime Minister, then proposed that enlargement should be discussed first. Pompidou, in pained surprise, countered
that farming must come first. This was agreed – everyone knew by this
time that that was France's price for lifting the veto. But Brandt and
de Jong countered with an attempt partially to redress the timing
problem. They would agree to sign a financial regulation before the
end of the year: submission to parliamentary ratification, however,
might not be very immediate. It might – they implied – depend on the
spirit France showed in the further discussion of the enlargement issue.

That night, after Queen Juliana's banquet, Brandt and Pompidou

[1] *L'Express*, 6 December 1969.
[2] Editorial of 3 December 1969.

had a private half-hour session together, and next morning Pompidou struck a totally different note. The journalists naturally concluded that there had been some tough talking not far removed from arm-twisting at the Huis ten Bosch palace. But French diplomats insist that the Monday afternoon speech had been a raising, not an answering of questions, as became the convenor and opener of a conference of that kind – above all if trained in the French academic tradition, which tries to see problems in their context and their wider relationships before getting down to shopping lists of detailed solutions. It was in this speech ('to round off' that of the afternoon before) that Pompidou pulled various rabbits out of his hat on the subject of 'deepening' and notably called for a complete economic and monetary union, plans for it to be agreed by the end of 1970. He added that he was favourably inclined to the enlargement of the Community, and that the Six should get their common position on this agreed 'in the most rapid, active and positive manner'. The long final communiqué was drafted in only five hours (Pompidou was particularly concerned that the French delegation should not go too far in the wording on economic and monetary union). Victory all round had been snatched from the jaws of disaster.

By the same token, however, the options were beginning to narrow. Until The Hague it might have been just possible to try to continue broadly, though less rigidly, along the straight paths originally paved by the General. After The Hague, Pompidou had lost that corset. It began to become as difficult for him to veto as not to veto (and possibly more so). The probability of an outright veto was thus reduced. But that still left open the choice between two very different negotiating strategies: one that could have come close to blocking entry *de facto*, insisting on terms so stiff that the British would give up themselves, and the other that of actually having them in.

France's Negotiating Strategy

For Britain there was thus quite a valley to be traversed between the Hague summit in December 1969 and the Paris summit in May 1971. President Pompidou, in a television address to the nation on 15 December, stated the position of his government very fairly. He emphasized that the Hague summit had 'demonstrated the sincerity of the statements I made on taking office when I announced that France would not veto British entry into the Common Market'. (He also stressed that he wished to see 'the traditional links with our American friends and allies' drawn closer – hardly a Gaullist turn of phrase.) But at the same time he threw the onus of what was to happen on to the British. 'I hope the negotiations . . . will prove that Britain really is determined to turn towards Europe.'

His doubts on the matter were not set at rest by the publication in February 1970 of the British White Paper setting out some estimates of the costs of entry – which had *L'Aurore*, a staunch supporter of Britain on the issue, asking in a two-column headline: 'These English – What do they really want?' When he was questioned in the National Press Club in Washington during his official visit to the United States, Pompidou recalled Winston Churchill's phrase which de Gaulle had quoted so often – when Britain had to choose between the Continent and the open seas, she would always choose the open seas. 'Right up to the last moment', he said, 'we cannot be sure of the British determination to enter the Market.'[1]

If that was true from the French standpoint, it was equally true from the British point of view that right until the last moment one could not be sure whether France would allow Britain in or whether she was determined, by one means or another, to keep her out. French diplomacy in fact remained profoundly ambiguous from Pompidou's election in summer 1969 until the spring of 1971. There was no telling whether Pompidou had made up his mind against British entry but resolved to proceed more subtly than the General, whether he was reserving judgment, or whether he had already decided that Britain had to be admitted, but was determined to exact the maximum price.

What was not clear then, but is clear now, was that not only was the world ignorant of his intentions, but that even some of his top advisers were, for most of this period, uncertain in their own minds as to what he really wanted. He is a man, they agree, who plays his cards very close to his chest. He is a man who is slow to take decisions. He talked tough even in the most restricted negotiating councils at the Elysée – but then he had to, as his Foreign Minister was always anxious to please his partners. Yet his closest collaborators also say they never felt they were actually negotiating to fail.

Once the issue of agricultural finance had been settled between the Six in April 1970, and the EEC had thus – even if four months late – successfully completed its twelve-year transition period, one of the preconditions for enlargement had at last been fulfilled. The system had been consolidated in such a form that new members would have

[1] *The Times*, 25 February 1970.

the greatest difficulty in going back on it. This was a matter of general principle. In addition, and in particular, the French had tied down their partners to a system of finance that would for a long time involve transfers in France's favour by helping to pay for agriculture out of the superior productivity of the Community's industries. The other tasks, in early 1970, were therefore twofold: first, to agree on the conditions that the applicant countries had to fulfil in the negotiations with the Six (and the forms the negotiations were to take); and second, simultaneously to continue the Community's progress without slowing down to wait for the new members to catch up and get on board. The fact that such continued impetus might pre-empt choices which the candidate countries might wish to see made differently was at the least irrelevant, and at the most a bonus in that it would force the candidates to give further proofs of Community virtue beyond those demanded at the time of their application.

At The Hague, Pompidou had non-committally let it be known that he did not think the definition by the Six of their common negotiating position – his prerequisite for the opening of negotiations with the candidates – should take more than six months. The French negotiators did not attempt to filibuster. What they did do was to try to obtain the toughest possible terms. In 1961 the Macmillan government had put its head into a rather dangerous noose with the so-called 'London declaration' – which stipulated that all the partners of EFTA must be granted satisfactory terms by the EEC from the same date, as a pre-condition of Britain's (or any other EFTA state's) entry into the EEC. It was a curious notion, which would have given Portugal or Austria a veto that no one thought of according to Australia or India. In 1966–67 the Wilson government had made it clear that the London declaration no longer obtained. But in 1970 the French tried to revive it in reverse, claiming that no state should be accepted as a member unless it proved possible to make satisfactory arrangements for all the other EFTA members at the same time. That was a condition they in the event could not get agreed by their partners. But they raised the sterling problem, to which we shall return in a moment; and they were glad to agree to a fisheries regulation that suited their deep sea fishermen but not their inshore fishing fleets, because they knew that it would cause far greater difficulties for the British and the Norwegians, and would therefore be another trump card should they want to raise the obstacles so high that Britain would jib at clearing them.

The Quai d'Orsay negotiated hard and was determined not only to throw no cards away but to pick up any more they could get to make their position even tougher. No wonder that in London and in the capitals of the other five there were strong suspicions that Pompidou wanted to remain loyal to de Gaulle's political objectives, but felt it wiser to work for them by rather subtler means.

It is here that one further internal factor came in. There were those in the Quai d'Orsay who were willing to say to all who were willing to hear that British entry would be a major setback for France. The spirit of Couve de Murville and the routine of those who had spent a decade in blocking British entry and were not eager to stand on their heads at this stage were factors in the situation. The 'professional Bruxellois' of the Quai and elsewhere knew their dossiers and were well able to look after themselves. As late as early summer 1971 one of them (unnamed) still got himself reported in Le Monde as hoping that if an agreement could be reached in Brussels, it would be thrown out in Westminster. Of course these men were civil servants and not political masters. But their zeal for a tough negotiation came in very useful to the Elysée. So they were given their head – and they enjoyed themselves in the bargaining right up to May 1971.

We shall examine the negotiations as a self-contained system and a procedure for settling minor issues of a transitional character in the next chapter. What matters for the purposes of the only real decision – whether the negotiations were to succeed or not – is not the subjects they were overtly about, but the time they took, the impression they gave outside, and the covert mutual signals of a political content that were contained in the economic and financial haggling.

'I am now an expert on the Barbados and Fiji sugar harvests', one negotiator could justly claim. Obviously all these tonnages were irrelevant. But 'we put up cases just to show how clever we are'. Pompidou himself could tease Maurice Schumann in public about how he seemed to enjoy being bogged down in tedious negotiations in Brussels. The negotiation as a ritual warrior dance behind which the real decisions could be considered, postponed, and finally agreed was a concept almost explicitly understood on both sides. Mr Rippon's frequent remark that the real issues could all be settled over coffee and cognac (unfortunate though its phrasing was in the British domestic context) pointed to the same apparent triviality and relative irrelevance to the core issue of much of the discussion. Rippon's initial offer of 2·6–3% of the budget for the first year and the French demand for 21·5% or more were alike symbolic stances. Pompidou's television address in January 1971 in which he referred to the 3% offer, saying that the British had 'a sense of humour, realism and tenacity – so far we have seen only the sense of humour' were all part of this posturing – as were Geoffrey Rippon's calculated losses of temper. All this ritual was reminiscent of nothing so much as Konrad Lorenz' geese.

Nevertheless there remained a very real danger that the negotiations might have developed their own negative momentum, and that by misjudgment on one side or the other they could have led to a result that neither side really wanted. No one knew exactly what limits there were on the possible terms compatible with a successful outcome. Terms acceptable to one British government might not prove acceptable to another or to Parliament, and terms acceptable to Parliament in one set of political circumstances might not prove acceptable in another. Moreover, specific terms acceptable to the French government in one political climate might not be acceptable in another – much could depend on the overtones of the British candidature. It would therefore be absurd to say that as of May 1968 or November 1968, or April 1969, or December 1969, the battle was really all over bar the shouting. On the contrary, there was no knowing whether there would be any possible overlap at the crucial moment between these two essentially still undefined and indeed elastic areas of terms acceptable to either side. Certainly, at the end of 1970 and in early 1971 there was little sign of any viable agreement in Brussels.

3 The Negotiators Dig In

It was all a gigantic irrelevance
        Conference Diplomat

The Form of the Negotiations

The legal basis of the negotiation was provided by Article 237 of the EEC treaty:

Any European State may apply to become a member of the Community. It shall address its application to the Council, which shall act unanimously after obtaining the opinion of the Commission. The conditions of admission and the adjustments to this Treaty necessitated thereby shall be the subject of an agreement between the Member States and the applicant State.
This agreement shall be submitted for ratification by all the contracting States in accordance with their respective constitutional requirements.

The Euratom Treaty has an identical article (205), and the Coal and Steel Community a corresponding one (98).

On the side of the applicants, while on 9 August 1961 Harold Macmillan had applied only for negotiations 'with a view to joining the Community if satisfactory arrangements can be made to meet the special needs of the United Kingdom, of the Commonwealth, and of the European Free Trade Association', on 10 May 1967 Harold Wilson had applied actually to join:

The Prime Minister   10, Downing Street,
                                                              Whitehall
                                                       May 10th 1967

Mr President,
    I have the honour, on behalf of her Majesty's Government in the United Kingdom of Great Britain and Northern Ireland, to inform your Excellency that the United Kingdom hereby applies to become a member of the European Economic Community under the terms of Article 237 of the treaty establishing the European Economic Community.
    Please accept, Mr President, the assurance of my highest consideration.

                                                       HAROLD WILSON

His Excellency Monsieur R. van Elslande, chairman of the Council of Ministers of the European Economic Community.

Similar applications had been made in May 1967 by Denmark, Eire and Norway. It was these four applications on which, in December 1967, 'there was not, at the present stage, agreement in the Council on continuing the procedure'.[1] Two years later, the Hague summit opened up the chance of agreement between the Six on how to proceed: and the first six months of 1970 thus saw the preparations for the negotiation to open.

At the first British attempt to negotiate entry into the Community, there had been a Conference between the Six member states of the Community and the applicant states. The Commission of the EEC, that of Euratom, and the High Authority of the Coal and Steel Community had the right to speak, and had acted as advisers to the Six in their attempts so far as possible to put common positions to the candidate countries. It had not been a very tidy form of organization. Not only had it provoked a good many accusations that the candidate countries had attempted to split the Six and to exploit differences of view between them: it had also given the candidate countries every opportunity to do so. The British and the other candidates, for their part, had found the free-for-all multilateralism of the proceedings confusing and unhelpful. Neither side wanted to return to this configuration eight years later.

Already in the Hague communiqué what was envisaged was a negotiation not between the candidates and the Six, but between the candidates and the Community. That formula, however, still left open just who would represent the Community. The French, at first sight surprisingly, seemed to favour giving this task to the Commission – an institution which it had for so long been French policy to disparage. The British on the other hand feared that this could lead to a belittling of the negotiations and leave it open for any member state later to repudiate a bargain struck between the candidates and the Commission – so that agreements reached in Brussels might then remain binding on the candidates, but not on each of the Six, any one of whom might later demand stiffer terms. It was the British view – no doubt with all due respect to the Commission – that they did not want to talk to the monkey if they could deal with the organ-grinders themselves.

In fact the Community was still agreed that since Article 237 placed the final responsibility on the member states, it was the Council of Ministers which had to negotiate. But in order to avoid the multi-

[1] Communiqué of 19 December 1967, reprinted in *The Second Try*, ed. cit., p. 319.

lateralism of 1961–63, it was decided that the member states should be represented *vis-à-vis* the four candidate states not individually, as in 1961–63, but through the President of the Council of Ministers. The representatives of the member states would be present at the confrontations with the candidates, but only as silent observers. What the President of the Council was to put to the candidates, however, was to be decided by the Council according to its normal procedures – very largely on the proposals of the Commission.

The result for the formal mechanism was obvious: the President of the Council could read to the candidates a carefully drafted compromise formula evolved between the Six, but he could hardly ever respond spontaneously to any declaration made by the candidates that did not accept the Community's terms: he had to adjourn the proceedings so that the Six could agree a new formula in every new situation. The candidate delegations – each national delegation in turn, never the four together – would sit at the bottom of the long table, perhaps listen to a series of declarations from the President of the Council (which bored the other five to tears since they, after perhaps hours of haggling over the wording, knew it only too well) and then either 'take note' or 'accept' the declaration. (The latter was sometimes possible straightaway, particularly if the candidates had already seen the declaration and been able to ascertain to their satisfaction that it lay within their negotiating positions.) They would read their own statements and, unless they had already managed to obtain prior approval informally, would then withdraw to play bridge or poker on the floor below while the meeting transformed itself upstairs into the Council of Ministers, until the Conference was reconvened by their being asked upstairs to listen to the new agreed position of the Six. The bulk of the formal negotiation was thus in a sense carried on not so much between each candidate and the six member states, but amongst the Six themselves on how (and how far) to meet the differing requirements of the four applicants. Certainly the Six spent far more of the formal sessions talking to each other than talking to the applicant states.

It will give an idea of the style of the hectic all-night negotiations simply to summarize the meetings on 29–30 November 1971 which together made up the 177th Council meeting, the 12th Conference of the Ministers with the United Kingdom, the 8th Conference with Ireland and Norway, and the 7th with Denmark. The Council of Ministers met at 11.00 a.m. on the 29th to hear the Commissioner responsible for the negotiations, Jean-François Deniau, report on the contacts he had had with the candidate countries since the previous meeting of the Council, and the Council decided that a new proposal must be put forward along certain lines. After lunch the Council met in a highly restricted session to agree on such a proposal. At 7.40 p.m. the Ministers met with the Irish, at 8.00 p.m. with the Danes, at 8.30 p.m. with the Norwegians – the problems on the agenda including (over and above fisheries) taxes on table wines in Denmark, veterinary legislation in Ireland, and Norwegian agriculture. At 9.05 p.m. the British were called in, and Geoffrey Rippon, apart from some holding statements on Papua and New Guinea, the Channel Islands and the Isle of Man, objected to the Community's proposals on fish and on veterinary legislation.

So the Council of Ministers had another meeting, starting at twenty minutes past midnight. Deniau reported on his talks, held in the meantime, with the candidates' delegations: the Norwegians wanted the twelve-mile limit for the whole of their west coast, Ireland wanted special rules not merely for salmon and shellfish, but also for herring, the British had now prepared a written reply with alternative counter-proposals, including a ten-year review clause, and Geoffrey Rippon was very anxious to get agreement before the night was out. (He hoped that Jean-François Deniau would be able to sell the proposed review clause to the Six – but in vain.) Jean-Marc Boegner had, however, received telephone instructions from Maurice Schumann that in view of the gap between positions it was not worth trying to reach agreement just then – 'not tonight'.

The British were, therefore, called in again at 2.50 a.m. Geoffrey Rippon refused to give up and urged that at least some progress should be made then and there – citing the bitterness on the issue in the United Kingdom, the circumstances under which the fishing regulations had been agreed between the Six (six hours after the opening of negotiations with the candidates), and insisting that this question could not just be treated as a normal transitional measure. Twenty-five minutes later the Council was back in session, and authorized Deniau to go and talk to the British again. At 4.40 a.m. the Norwegians came back, without any agreement materializing between them and the Community. Ten minutes later the Council heard a report from Deniau on his talk with Rippon, who still wanted either a twelve-mile limit for 95% of the coastline, or a ten-year period that was 'neither transitional nor permanent'. The Dutch and Germans hoped it would be possible to meet the British, but Boegner stood firm. At 6.15 a.m., still before dawn, the Conference started again, with Geoffrey Rippon back in the room, to be told by the Italian chairman that there really was no point in going on – he himself had to leave Brussels that afternoon. But Geoffrey Rippon again insisted on a last try, and Aldo Moro agreed that the Council should meet one more time, after a few hours' interruption (for a bath, a shave and a rest) in the late morning.

So the Ministers met again at 11.30 a.m. The Commission had some suggestions ready which it had discussed at Deputy level with the British delegation between 7.00 and 8.00 a.m. and of which the Italian chairman had been informed – but the French seized the initiative by presenting an amendment of their own, which was immediately adopted. (This amendment made explicit the need for unanimity in the review of the fishing situation after the first ten years.) At 12.40 the British were called in; they felt unable to accept the new formula. At one o'clock the Irish also rejected the latest version. At 1.10 the Council, alone again, heard various Ministers vent their impatience and demand that after all the effort the Six had put into trying to accommodate the candidates, it was now up to the candidates to try to find a formula acceptable to the Six. Having followed their timetable through these twenty-six hours, one can see why at that stage the atmosphere should not have been all sweetness. But then at least they were, by November 1971, almost at the end of their task.

Of course not all problems were treated at the ministerial level. There were only thirteen ministerial meetings of the Conference throughout the negotiations. At the outset they sometimes lasted a bare ten minutes; at 'the crunch', they could go on intermittently for several days. Far more frequent were the meetings at the level of the Ministers' Deputies – the Permanent Representatives of the Six in Brussels, on whom a great deal of the real work of decision-making had come to fall in the fifteen years of the Community's existence. Their role within the Community as Permanent Representatives of the member states was formally recognized in the Treaty signed in Brussels in 1965 which established a single Council of Ministers and a single Commission for the three European Communities. Now, in the negotiations for the Communities' enlargement, they were for the first time given a task that went beyond that of preparing the meetings of the Ministers themselves: as the Ministers' Deputies they were part of the Conference when they met with the British delegation (headed at that level by Sir Con O'Neill) and with the delegations of the other candidates, to conduct negotiations on behalf of the Ministers on mandates which the Ministers themselves did not actually have to have approved in advance. With thirty-eight meetings in the eighteen months or less of serious negotiations, it is obvious that they really were crucial to the progress of the whole negotiation.

The chairman of the Committee of Permanent Representatives, and hence of the Conference meeting at that level, was the representative of the country that occupied the chair in the Council of Ministers for the half-year in question: in the latter half of 1970 under the German Foreign Minister Walter Scheel, his Permanent Representative to the Communities Ambassador Hans-Georg Sachs; in the crucial first half of 1971 under Maurice Schumann, Ambassador Jean-Marc Boegner; in the second half of 1971 (tying up left-over problems and supervising the actual treaty drafting) under the Italian Foreign Minister Aldo Moro, Ambassador Giorgio Bombassei. In many ways it was a helpful accident that the French held the presidency during the most critical stages of the negotiations, being institutionally committed to both the fairness and the success of the proceedings just when it mattered most.

In fact it was during the period when Maurice Schumann was President of the Council that the Committee of Permanent Representatives, deputizing for the Ministers, was itself supplemented by a new forum, the Committee of Deputies' Deputies – those men (second in rank in each Permanent Representation) who had specialized in the problems of the Community's enlargement (as against the many other problems which were simultaneously on the Community's agenda). All the problems, including the minor, but not for that reason always politically innocuous ones, were brought up in that body from the time of its establishment in January 1971.

In the early summer of 1971 and again later in the year, it met several times a week to prepare the meetings of the Permanent Representatives, who themselves met up to three days a week both to solve the problems assigned to them and to prepare the meetings of the Ministers. It was a three-decker system that was itself fed by reports from expert groups studying specific problems, and of course by the proposals of the Commission. At the very outset of the negotiations the British had proposed that there should also be multilateral working parties to clear the ground: but the specific subjects they proposed for such working parties met with some opposition, since there were fears that the multi-lateral clearing of the ground might so easily spill over into, or at least predetermine, actual negotiation. In the end tariff quotas and the final drafting of the Treaty were dealt with on this basis.

So much for the formal mechanism with its three layers. It was more than the tip of the iceberg, but a good deal less than the whole of the structure of the negotiation. For there was also a fourth level – and that in many ways by far the most important one for finding the technical solutions without which even the political will could not have come to any speedy fruition. This was the whole network of the private, informal contacts between members of different delegations, and above all between the Commission's own negotiating task force and each of the national delegations – particularly those of the applicants. This intensive dialogue between the Commission, sitting at the heart of the spider's web, and the national delegations, was a continuous process that started well before the formal opening of negotiations and often continued well after some particular decision had been formally reached.

One of the most time-consuming parts of the proceedings were the preparatory discussions between the Six and the Commission in the first half of 1970, in which the Community defined its negotiating position *vis-à-vis* the candidates' interests – which they were, of course, at that stage already forced to study in detail with the help of the candidates' representatives in Brussels. Where Britain was concerned, the cardinal document remained George Brown's presentation to Western European Union of 4 July 1967, which had raised virtually every problem that was to come up in the negotiations save fish – and that fell under the paragraph dealing with further developments in the Community.[1] And the Commission had, in September that year, sent the Council its detailed Opinion on the problems involved.[2] But the Community had evolved further in the intervening years, and the British economy also had changed; so there was a good deal more work to be done before the Six were agreed on the lines to take in the negotiation.

Once those negotiations had begun, it was again in unofficial off-the-record conversations that the ground was prepared for solutions fed one way or another (and often in alternative versions) into the formal machinery. It was here that the continuity of the process of paring down differences, trying out this formula and that, and the sense of a common intellectual enterprise were at their most marked – and in sharpest contrast to the political tactics, the sullen deadlocks and the sudden visible breakthroughs on the ministerial level at the other

---

[1] Cmnd 3345, reprinted in full in *The Second Try*, ed. cit., pp. 189–203.

[2] Reprinted in translation, ibid., pp. 205–99. The Commission had sent the Council a Supplementary Opinion on 1 October 1969 – before the Hague summit.

end of the scale. It was in such contacts that officials explored the complications of integrating solutions for four candidate countries in four rather different situations. It was by these means that, as early as the autumn of 1970, difficulties over liquid milk and pork meat could be settled with the British at the request of the Six in talks with the Commission.

In so far as the bulk of the matters covered in the three hundred pages of the Accession Treaty could be settled quietly on a technical level, while the really contentious issues take up only a few pages, the bulk of the negotiation clearly took place without the Ministers ever really having to sit and deliberate on them. Moreover, even the dramatically publicized political solutions never came out of the blue: they needed both careful technical preparation and discreet unofficial soundings before they were tabled. In these senses one may say that practically the whole of the negotiation took place outside the formal meetings – through exchanges of memoranda, in inter-office visits, over meals and late-night drinks, even over the telephone. We shall be dealing in the next chapter with one of the most crucial links in the process – which happened, indeed, to be forged right outside the Brussels framework. Within Brussels the network of contacts was so thick that, even if most of it did not inevitably escape the dragnet of the historian, it would be of limited interest to the general reader.

What matters is the overall character of the negotiation, and the types of role played in it by different actors. The set meetings registered agreement and acted as a formal court of appeal where agreement required major substantive differences to be resolved. For the rest – as is so often the case with any kind of set meeting the world over – their function was to act as a catalyst for the 'real' thinking and bargaining behind the scenes. They were no less important for that. But at least the formal bilateralism, cumbrous as it may have seemed, was made tolerable by this complementary set of constant contacts at various levels which anticipated the reactions of either side, and while the legal channels of communication were safeguarded by the Conference framework, these informal exchanges speeded up the work and made an effective meeting of minds possible behind the bargaining postures.

The Delegations

The key delegations in the whole process were clearly the French and the British. Willy Brandt personally and his government constituted a useful fleet-in-being that had to be reckoned with by the French and that could have set sail had it become necessary. But they were not anxious for a row with the French, and for the rest they could really take it easy: after all, whatever the terms for Britain, Germany was getting two tangible national advantages out of the Community's enlargement and the consequent arrangements for the rest of EFTA: the British, Scandinavian and, in particular, the Swiss and Austrian markets for her industry, and a lessening of her share in the burden of Community finance.

Very helpful were the Italians, who were weary of Franco-German hegemony in the Community, and saw Britain's entry, quite apart from its general foreign policy and economic impact, as a way of re-opening the political alignments within the Community. The Dutch, led in the earlier stages by Joseph Luns, were both staunchly in favour of British entry and also, on bread and butter (or rather, fish and tomato) issues, stubborn defenders of their own interests. The Belgians and Luxemburgers did their bit, Pierre Harmel, the Belgian Foreign Minister, very effectively standing up to the French on the budget contribution in May 1971. But of course there were individual differences within national delegations, and agreements and alliances that went across national demarcations.

There was in fact a good deal more overall cohesion between the six member states this time than ten years before; all six for example rejected the British proposal for an 'initiation period' before progressive transition to full membership, and all six found the opening bid for the British budget contribution derisory. But there were big issues over which the British at times felt very conscious of an underlying difference of attitude between the French and the 'friendly five': and the French, however the others might regard them, felt themselves cast in a special role.

The French negotiators saw the other five delegations as in some sense parasites on themselves: the other five had the easy job of being nice to the British, or sitting and watching the proceedings, knowing that the French would fight their battles for them against Britain's attempts at subversion of the Community and against British special interests. It was left to Maurice Schumann at the level of the Ministers (until he became chairman), to Jean-Pierre Brunet, and to Jean-Marc Boegner to stand up against the British and the other candidates in what was for much of the time a dialogue between the two delegations, conducted through an intermediary chairman of the Council before five silent spectators.

The French were well equipped for this purpose. In Jean-Marc Boegner they had a powerful figure who had played a key role in Brussels for a decade, exercised great influence on his fellow Permanent Representatives, and knew his way about. Moreover – in contrast, for example, to his German colleague – he was backed by a 'mission control' in Paris that ironed out inter-ministerial disagreements in Paris instead of letting them erupt, possibly even in front of the other countries, in Brussels itself. He received his instructions not so much from the Quai d'Orsay as from the Secretary-General of the Inter-Ministerial Committee for European Co-operation, Jean-René Bernard, who was in a key position astride three major elements in the French government – instructing Foreign Ministry personnel while combining a position in the Prime Minister's office with a post in the Elysée on the President's staff. This Inter-Ministerial Committee is a vital piece of machinery worthy of serious study as a model in Britain. It clearly gives the French a major advantage over, for instance, the Germans, whose different Ministries – and sometimes Ministers – at times appear in the European arena with openly conflicting policies.

Jean-Marc Boegner, the son of the well-known head of the French Protestant church, Pastor Marc Boegner, was regarded in Brussels as a tough character, and not necessarily friendly to the British. He had after all negotiated against them under President de Gaulle's instructions for many years. By contrast his titular boss, Maurice Schumann, was known to be friendly: he tended to explain himself at length if a British proposal was unacceptable to his government – which Jean-Marc Boegner did not always feel it necessary to do. Gaul being divided, as is well known, into fifty million Frenchmen, the French delegation was of course no more monolithic on the personal level than any other, and tensions between the French Foreign Minister and his aides, and between Jean-Marc Boegner and his mission control, became visible on more than one occasion. But then they had a difficult task during all the months when Paris appeared to have no policy beyond tough negotiating tactics, and the French representatives were left building up and defending 'holding positions' that were occasionally less disturbing than they might have been only because they were so extreme.

The British delegation was led for a brief spell – for the opening session and one ministerial meeting – by Anthony Barber. Then the accident of Iain Macleod's death catapulted Barber into the Chancellorship, and Geoffrey Rippon took over the European negotiations. An almost flamboyant, physically indefatigable, self-made Conservative

QC and businessman, Rippon's first experience of West European integration had come before he was an MP, through the Strasbourg meetings of the Council of European Municipalities. (He had been leader of the Conservatives on the LCC at the age of 33.)

Geoffrey Rippon certainly distinguished himself and commanded enormous limelight in the subsequent negotiations. If some thought that he was occasionally not persistent enough, or appeared to lose his temper for too long or with excessive publicity (and then had to swallow what he had just spat back at the Six), these are differences of view on the art of diplomacy in which no one can really calculate what the detailed outcome of a different personal style might have been. In London, though the Prime Minister himself of course followed things closely, the ministerial group to which Rippon reported and which acted as his overlord was presided over by the Foreign Secretary and included the Chancellor, the Secretary of State for Trade and Industry and the Minister of Agriculture, with Lord Carrington and William Whitelaw also very much concerned on the side of domestic political management.

Geoffrey Rippon was backed by a hand-picked civil service team that won little but praise on the Continent. Sir Con O'Neill – who had withdrawn for a time from the Foreign Office after a well-documented disagreement with George Brown over his not being appointed ambassador in Bonn – could be judicious, smooth and tenacious in excellent German and French (though in the formal negotiations he spoke in English). He had already served as British ambassador to the EEC in 1963–65, and had an excellent understanding of the workings of the Community. His deputy, John Robinson, had been one of Edward Heath's lieutenants in the 1961–63 negotiations, and had remained at the desks dealing with Britain's relations with the EEC ever since. His competence, hard work and ingenuity earned him the highest praise from the other delegations and the staff of the Commission. Sir William Nield of the Cabinet Office was clearly very influential. The Treasury was represented by Raymond Bell, the Board of Trade (Department of Trade and Industry) by Roy Denman, the Ministry of Agriculture by Freddy Kearns; technology was represented by Patrick Shovelton, while Ian Sinclair was again – as ten years before – legal adviser, and James Mellon acted as the Secretary to the Delegation.

In contrast to the team that had to go in and bat in 1961 supported by a Permanent Delegation that had moved to Brussels for the first

time only a year or less before, in 1970 there was a much greater understanding of how the Community in fact operated – and also quite a few
by then long-established personal links which made mutual compre-
hension that much easier. In the event the secret official history which
Edward Heath and his team had written of the 1961–63 negotiations did
not prove all that useful this time round.

Sir James Marjoribanks was British ambassador to the Communities
until the spring of 1971, and after an interregnum his post was filled in
the autumn by Michael Palliser from the Paris embassy. Kenneth
Christophas, who headed the Permanent Delegation during the interregnum, was in charge of dealing with all the secondary legislation – a
mammoth task of translation in the widest sense of the term, not only
linguistically but in terms of concepts, of adaptation to British circumstances, and often of very complicated transitional measures between
all the Ten. But it would be tedious to mention all who contributed to
the whole negotiation. Sir William Nield, Sir Con O'Neill and
Christopher Soames were awarded the GCMG in the New Year's
Honours List of 1972; one of their typists became an MBE. Others no
doubt will be obtaining promotion in accordance with the talents and
efforts they deployed.

For the Commission, at ministerial level, Franco-Maria Malfatti
intervened himself regularly, but the main burden was borne by Jean-
François Deniau, a French career diplomat. In his early thirties at the
time of the 1961–63 negotiations, he had even then played a key role on
the Commission's staff for those talks. Tall, elegant, smooth and clever,
he had been French ambassador to Mauritania from 1963 to 1966,
between leaving the staff of the Commission and returning to Brussels
as a Commissioner himself. His French colleague Raymond Barre was
– perhaps wrongly – considered less friendly to enlargement. A more
committed Gaullist, he was particularly in charge of the financial
and monetary aspects of the problem, and thus not unnaturally concerned to provide for all possible measures to minimize future difficulties
with monetary and economic union arising out of the special position
of the pound sterling. In the end he was to find that his tough position
on the issue had been sold out behind his back by President Pompidou
himself. With Deniau, on the other hand, there was much more of a
sense of dedication to making the negotiations succeed if that were
possible. He played much more of an intermediary's role – dining with
Edward Heath and several Ministers and their wives at Chequers in
January 1971, warning the British against their intransigent opening

bid on Community finance, reporting back to Paris on reactions, and scuttling up and down between the conference room of the Council of Ministers and the suite of offices of the British delegation, suggesting drafts and amendments to drafts. At the level of the Deputies, it was Edmund Wellenstein, a slightly older Dutchman, whose human warmth complemented Deniau's cool intellectual approach and who worked indefatigably and unreservedly for success. There are those who say that without Edmund Wellenstein – as without several other key figures not necessarily in the public limelight – the job could never have been done. Deniau and Wellenstein were in their turn assisted by a task force drawn from the various Directorates-General of the Commission, selected according to their knowledge and abilities rather than their rank, some of whom worked themselves to exhaustion in the first half of 1971 and again in the final phases preceding the signature of the Treaty of Accession.

Problems of Open Diplomacy

One of the problems with Brussels was the publicity of the proceedings. In principle they were always private. But the principle was far removed from the practice. For a start there were far too many people in the room for there to be any chance of keeping very much confidential. Moreover, since there were in effect eight participating parties, the delegations each had an interest in making sure that no one else leaked a distorted version of their stand, and usually, what is more, had an interest in leaking a (sometimes slightly coloured) version themselves. This is a phenomenon only too familiar to observers of, for example, Commonwealth conferences. But while Commonwealth conferences are episodic, and covered largely by an *ad hoc* purely temporary assemblage of journalists from all five continents, the Council of Ministers in Brussels, one way or another, sat almost as permanently as a parliament, and was covered by a permanent corps of Brussels lobby correspondents who could co-operate much more easily than lobby correspondents inside any one country: they were not so much in competition with one another as complementary to one another. It tended to take no more than half an hour after a meeting on the fifteenth floor for the Brussels press corps on the ground floor to have pieced together the essentials of the argument and the prevailing atmosphere from rival accounts given by members of different delegations. From the outset, therefore, everyone realized that few things could be kept really secret for very long. (It was, of course, hopeless to ask the press to keep anything out of the papers, though there were moments when the British delegation was thankful that journalists' researches had not progressed as far as they might have done.)

Given this inevitable instant publicity, it was decided that the Chairman of the Council and the British Minister should give a joint press conference after each meeting at the ministerial level on what had (and had not) been achieved at each stage. The result was a form of semi-open diplomacy, tempered by the discreet network of informal contacts, but still a very much more complex task than the conclusion of open agreements secretly arrived at. For the sake of appearances, quite apart from the negotiating logic itself, each successive stage in the process of reaching agreement thus had to be represented as a fair component package between the participants within what it was hoped would ultimately be a fair overall package deal: and that demand for internal symmetry of the parts as well as of the whole imposed its own limitation on the negotiations and invited deadlock, with neither side prepared to make the first move.

The British delegation, in particular, faced a thorny dilemma. If their opening bid was not very high (or their opening offer not very low) they were immediately accused at home of selling the pass before the battle had even begun. If their opening bid was high (or their offer low), they knew they were liable to have to depart from it, and be accused of having lost the battle. On the whole, they opted for something nearer the second horn of the dilemma, bargained hard from positions quite some way removed from the likely final outcome, and hoped that public opinion at home understood that these were bargaining positions and would not, when the final package came to be tied up, measure their 'betrayal of the national interest' by the distance they had had to go to meet the Six half way.

Thus the British delegation had, as we saw, on 16 December made its opening bid for Britain's share in the gross contributions to the Community budget with a figure of 2·6–3·0% for the first year – perhaps the only time it made a totally unreasonable demand. The stalemate over that issue was to last for months, by which time the British press itself had begun telling the government not to be silly and to come off it: when Geoffrey Rippon, six months later, accepted the figure of 8·64% for the first year, sufficient time had passed and quite enough other issues had taken the limelight for the government to be able to slide off that particular hook without too much trouble.

Perhaps slightly more embarrassing in some ways were the apparent turns and turn-abouts over sugar in May 1971, when Geoffrey Rippon first had the word spread that he had used very tough language to the Six, demanded that this 'dialogue of the deaf must end', and insisted on stronger guarantees being written into the Treaty – when he had nearly got the whole of his negotiating objective. The need to play to the gallery here included not only the audience in Westminster but also that in Suva, Kingston, Port-of-Spain and Port Louis. It was hardly surprising if the public at home and overseas took it, after such language, that the terms finally agreed were unsatisfactory: for only a few hours later Geoffrey Rippon accepted a formula that differed but little from the previous one, and certainly contained no reference to sugar quantities, prices, or even to the sugar industries themselves. (The British negotiators had in fact long ago abandoned the idea of getting any such price and quantitative guarantees into the Treaty.) The negotiators of the Six recall that, later that night (too late to catch next morning's headlines at home), Geoffrey Rippon came close to apologizing for his earlier outburst.

Autonomous factors of public opinion on the general principle of entry also, of course, entered as a factor into the negotiations. The deterioration in the British opinion polls on the question did not go unmarked in Brussels. To some extent it could help the British delegation to point to all the opposition they would have to face at home and argue that entry was only possible if the terms were better – the old use of a government's domestic weakness as a source of diplomatic strength. When they really had to get a big concession from the Six, then the openness of the diplomacy could be a useful card to play. At the same time the timetable of British domestic politics imposed pressures on the negotiation. The Prime Minister was determined not to lose momentum and to have the agreement sewn up in all essentials before the summer recess and before the economic situation, Ireland, Rhodesia or other untoward factors could sour the climate at home.

While these problems were shared by the Irish, Danes and Norwegians, each of whom were to face referenda at home after the full terms were known, it weighed very little on the delegations of the member states themselves. Their publics were generally in favour of the Communities' enlargement, so any concessions could be justified on those grounds: perhaps it was only the French beet-sugar producers who ever really appealed to the public for any particular safeguards against the possible consequences of entry. Though the French delegation occasionally claimed to be under pressure from their farmers, there was little evidence that this presented any real threat to their freedom of manœuvre – and the French press was not used more than might have been expected of it to entrench the delegation in any particular position. In any case, the enlargement of a Community in which one has already lived for over a decade is a much less dramatic event than entering one from the outside – particularly when it has evolved according to its own requirements for fourteen years, and will deeply affect vast areas of national life. So, apart from some specialists and dedicated Europeans, there was substantially less public interest in these negotiations on the Continent than in the applicant states.

The Start of the Marathon

Luxemburg really figures as the fourth city in our tale, for it was here that the negotiations formally began and here, a year later, that the biggest of all its 'crunches' took place. Indeed, both the place and the date of the opening of the negotiations were meant to be significant. Luxemburg had housed the Coal and Steel Community and also several of the joint Community institutions after the EEC and Euratom were set up; when a single Council and Commission were established for all three Communities (parallel with the single European Parliament that watches over all three), it was agreed that Luxemburg should still be the venue for Council meetings in April, June and October. Since it had been informally agreed at The Hague that the negotiations should open before the first half-year was out, the date was fixed for 30 June, and the place therefore Luxemburg.

The formation of a new British government only eight days before might have been a reasonable cause for postponement: but Edward Heath deliberately stuck to the pre-arranged date. He was determined that there should be no delay on Britain's side: the nearer to his election victory it could all be achieved, the greater would his standing – not to use the word mandate – be on this as on other issues. He was also determined that there should be no excuse later for delay on the side of the Six. Besides, the Labour government had prepared a dossier for the opening of negotiations which the Conservative government could pick up as it stood. Anthony Barber's opening speech in Luxemburg was based on the draft prepared for George Thomson. There was no need to change the civil service team that had been formed to negotiate under a Labour government. The negotiating positions, optimal and fall-back, did not have to be changed because of the general election result. Britain was going through a period of European bipartisanship, and the new government could simply carry on where the old one had left off.

The Luxemburg meeting was, of course, formal in one sense, but its purpose was far more than that of taking a 'family photograph'. The two set speeches, Barber's and Harmel's, clearly set out the opening positions on both sides. Barber's was on the whole very well received, though one friend of British entry wrote afterwards: 'One quickly saw that he knew neither his dossier nor the continent. He regaled his audience with a very dry, very cautious, rather pretentious little speech, giving the impression it was jolly good of Britain to go in with the Six.'[1] Granted Anthony Barber was not identical with George Brown, such criticism was not, however, really fair. There had been another veto in the meantime, and quite apart from a somewhat negative British public opinion listening in, the reservations expressed in Barber's speech were not merely a bargaining posture, they were also all too true; and he certainly rehearsed at length the reasons why Britain felt she must now join the Communities (and thereby acknowledged how wrong she had been in the 'fifties). Like George Brown in 1967, he accepted the Treaties, their political objectives, and the legislation made under them in full, only defining the exact problems on which Britain had special requirements for the transition period.

Pierre Harmel, for the Community, set out its position:

A. We assume in principle that your states accept the treaties and their political objectives, all the decisions of every type which have been taken since the treaties came into force and the choices made in the field of development.

These decisions also include the agreements concluded by the Community with third countries.

B. Under these conditions, the Community wishes at the opening of the negotiations to state a certain number of principles which it intends to apply:

1. The rule which must necessarily govern the negotiations is that the solution of any problems of adjustment which may arise must be sought in the establishment of transitional measures and not in changes in the existing rules.

2. The object of the transitional measures will be to allow for the adjustments which prove to be necessary as a consequence of the enlargement. Their duration must be restricted to that required to achieve this aim. As a general rule, they must incorporate detailed timetables and must commence with an

[1] Anne Laurens, *L'Europe avec les Anglais*, Arthaud, Paris, 1971, p. 217.

initial significant mutual tariff reduction on the entry into force of the accession treaties.

3. The transitional measures must be conceived in such a way as to ensure an overall balance of reciprocal advantages.

With this in mind, it will be necessary to ensure an adequate synchronization of the progress of freedom of movement of industrial goods with the achievement of the agricultural common market.

This consideration must be taken into account in respect of the duration of the transitional measures in the industrial and agricultural sectors.

4. In the field of trade, the duration of the transitional period should be the same for all the applicants.

5. In the other fields in which transitional measures prove to be necessary, the duration of such measures could, if possible and desirable, be varied according to their subject matter and the applicants involved. These questions will be examined during the negotiations.

6. The various accession treaties should come into force on the same date.

C. It is the Community's opinion that the accession of new members will lead to the enlarged Community having new responsibilities towards developing countries, which it will have to meet in appropriate ways. . . .

In July the Conference got down to the nuts and bolts of organization, and then, in September, the real substantive work began. At the turn of the year, after three ministerial meetings and nine at the level of the Deputies, certain questions were got out of the way – though on occasion the Ministers urged the Deputies not to announce some of their agreements but to leave them for the Council to announce, so that the Ministers did not have to go to their press conferences empty-handed.

Fortunately some problems did not need any arguing about. Of course every agreement on any one issue was conditional on agreement on all other issues. Subject to that proviso, for example, Britain was to have full voting rights in the institutions from the day of her accession, even though she would not be fulfilling all the duties of membership until after the end of the transition period or periods. That meant that, like the French, Germans and Italians, Britain would have 36 members of the European Assembly, 24 seats on the Economic and Social Council, and provide two members for the Commission and two judges for the Court of Justice, as well as having the right to nominate an Advocate-General to the Court. Assuming the simultaneous accession of Denmark, Norway and Ireland, this meant enlarging the Assembly to 153, bringing the Commission back to 14, enlarging the Court to 11 judges, and so on. Most of these adjustments were pretty straightforward.

ever carefully hedged on the concept of 'fair return', the British delegation was raising the hackles of the Commission.[1]

The British delegation now found itself in a double dilemma. On the one side it was caught between a British public opinion which, while it recognized the opening bid of 3% as a mere negotiating move, was worried about the balance of payments implications – and its consequences on employment and growth, which could conceivably nullify the hoped-for dynamic effects of joining the Communities. Informed critics at home wanted to see, if not fixed absolute sums, then at least fixed percentages of the Community's total budget set as maxima over as long as possible a transition period. (It is to be reckoned to the credit of the British delegation that at no time did it imagine that changes could be negotiated beyond a transition period.) Geoffrey Rippon tried to argue that, even with a 3% gross contribution, Britain would be starting to take some load off the shoulders of the other member states – with increases beyond that kind of figure pure gain to them, and loss to Britain. On the other hand fixed absolute amounts were quite excluded by the Community's annual budget process, which would naturally increase total spending, and – more important – the transition had to be a steady one so as not to leave the British with an impossible jump to make from the last year of the transition period to the first year of the final system – a jump which could provoke demands for an extension of the transition period, or other new special measures that would upset the working of the whole accession process. That was a concern the French, the other five and the Commission shared – and of course it was in the British interest, too. The progression from the first year of the transition period to the first year of the Britain's final integration into the system had to be made smooth enough to be credible.

The second dilemma into which the French delegation appeared to want to put Britain in the early months of 1971 was that between willingness and ability to pay. True, the British balance of payments, after its decisive swing for the better in the closing months of the Labour administration, was holding its own right through 1971. But if the British were not willing to make their full contribution to the Community budget, clearly they did not deserve to enter: yet, if they did try to pay, would their balance of payments stand up under the strain, and would the precarious position of the pound not lead to an outflow of

---

[1] For a proposal to drop the net contribution concept and instead to go, at a political summit, for large industrial, regional and environment funds out of Community resources, see Kitzinger, *The Times*, 26 January 1971.

money from Britain of proportions that would bring the pound sterling down yet again? And if that happened, the foreign exchange cost of the budget contribution would have to be purchased with even more of Britain's real resources – with consequent further domestic economic, social and political strain. It was a dilemma in which, the French could argue, it did not matter if Britain would not or if Britain could not pay: in either case, British entry was impossible.

Just to rub in what they regarded as the absurdity of the British proposal, Maurice Schumann suggested that if the candidate countries were going to have full rights of representation in the Community institutions from the first day of their entry, they might as well pay a contribution equal to their share in the national product of the enlarged Community from the first day. No representation without taxation, as it were. The figure would have stood at around 21%.

So by December 1970 the French had rejected the British formula even as a basis for discussion, demanding that the British make a new, more realistic proposal: yet it was difficult, at that stage, for the British publicly to shift their ground without the Community at least making some counter-proposal other than the French suggestion that Britain should pay her full share (around 21%) from 1973 onwards. This deadlock was to last from December 1970 until May 1971, and to prove surmountable only when the issue of finance was coupled with a rather different issue to which we shall come in a moment.

Some French diplomats later claimed they already had a solution up their sleeve which sought to tackle the whole problem on a somewhat different basis. Avoiding mention of any actual figures in the first instance, they knotted a ladder of algebra to dig the negotiations out of their entrenched positions again. But they were careful to keep that solution to themselves for the moment – quite happy to see other people, like Pierre Harmel, worry about it, and for the Conference atmosphere to deteriorate towards a crunch in which one problem could be linked with another. In fact perhaps their solution was not all that different in character – though it was in presentation – from that of the Commission itself. But what is interesting is that, even after it was all over, some French negotiators insisted that they were not, in early 1971, trying to be helpful.

No progress had at this stage been made on the two major issues which Britain had essentially raised not on her own behalf, but on that of certain Commonwealth countries: New Zealand dairy products, and cane sugar. Of all the manifold Commonwealth considerations that had played so large a part in keeping Britain out of the early West European efforts at unity, and had been the subject of such dogged negotiation by Edward Heath in 1961–63, these two Commonwealth problems were almost the only two that remained.

With deadlock reached on Britain's financial contribution and no progress on dairy products or sugar a fourth question – that of Community preference – now came to occupy the limelight.

What the French delegation was at this time gunning for was a quite specific major commitment from the British in the agricultural domain. On the agenda of the meeting the question figured (among others) under the title of 'transitional adaptation measures for agriculture'. It came to be known as the immediate adoption of Community preference.

The British negotiators always knew – and the Labour government had already accepted the principle in 1967 – that Britain must adopt the Common Agricultural Policy under which the farmers of the Community would tend to have a price advantage over other countries' farmers – including of course an advantage over Britain's traditional suppliers. (This competitive edge is accorded to them by a complicated system of tariffs or variable levies on imports of farm produce.) It was the British negotiators' hope that this system could be introduced gradually in stages, so as to prevent abrupt changes in the traditional currents of trade. To this the French in particular – with most to gain in exports of cereals – said no. The preference must be given in full from 1973 onwards. Britain would then be a member with full rights. She should – at least in this domain – accept full duties as well. The Commission, for its part, was trying behind the scenes to narrow down the problems involved, to fix dates and precise stages of transition.

In reply to the proposals from the Community, presented in early March, Britain could only promise careful study. Then in late April Freddy Kearns of the Ministry of Agriculture replied that if Community preference, instead of being phased in gradually, were suddenly fully applied, it would lead to too sudden a switch of trade from traditional patterns. That could have serious repercussions on overseas suppliers of commodities in which the Community was in surplus or nearly self-sufficient (especially on suppliers who might have few alternative markets to which to switch their sales). It could trigger off problems, too, for British and Community producers. Politely, but quite definitely, he insisted not simply on safeguard provisions to prevent the occurrence of actual damage but also in some cases on agreed arrangements for transition in advance – in other words he rejected the full introduction of Community preference all in one go, and retorted that one really had to find some acceptable methods of cushioning the diversion of trade with progressive this or degressive that. At the end of the seventeenth meeting of the Deputies, therefore, agreement had not been reached on this issue either.

But the most serious aspect of the negotiations in March and April was neither the lack of progress on milk products and sugar, nor the difficulties on Community preference and the wide gap between the parties on the budget contribution. What seemed most sinister during those weeks was the impression that a far more intractable question had been tabled explicitly in order to throw a very large spanner into the works. It became public knowledge on 18 March that Jean-Marc Boegner had officially asked for the future of the sterling balances and the privileged position of the London capital market to be put on the agenda of the Council meeting to be held on 30 March. The procedure for which the French thus opted cut right across a special procedure already set up in January to deal with sterling. But what was perhaps even more surprising was the content of their proposals: that the sterling balances held by overseas countries should – as if they were customs duties – be scaled down by fixed percentages each year. The French were to maintain that position right until the morning of 7 June, though the other five and the Commission (including Raymond Barre) opposed this as an utterly unrealistic standpoint.

Of course no one had ever thought that sterling could be passed over in silence. The Treasury had already answered a questionnaire put to it by the Six on the subject, though some thought its answers provocatively cavalier, containing nothing that any decent research assistant could not have dug up from public sources. Moreover, it had always been acknowledged that sterling must be discussed between Britain and the Six. What Britain had sought to avoid was making it the subject of negotiation at the conference table. Given the multilateralism, given the almost inescapable publicity (to be proved pretty well inevitable again on this occasion), this – the Treasury had felt – was the wrong forum in which to debate matters the mere discussion of which could so quickly influence the financial situation itself. Moreover, the problem concerned a great many states not represented at the Conference at all. It had to be discussed at the International Monetary Fund, in the Bank for International Settlements in Basle, and in other far wider fora: for the rest, in the interests of discretion, it was best to

discuss it bilaterally. Thirdly, sterling was a problem that might need a
decade to be solved. To suggest it as a subject of negotiation – implying
that a solution had to be found as a precondition to the negotiation's
success – was thus to suggest that the negotiation should head for
ineluctable failure. In fact there were, about this time, top secret
talks going on between officials of the French Ministry of Finance and
the Treasury, trying to understand each other's problems; and the
French participants later acknowledged that some of the problems
which they had felt were posed by the position of sterling turned out
to be based on misconceptions, on excessively facile analogies with the
dollar, or on a lack of appreciation of a change in Britain's own attitude
to sterling's special role.

One explanation heard a little later for the way in which the problem
was posed was that this constituted a reprisal for Britain having, in the
peace and quiet of a Basle weekend, got the Basle Agreements renewed
behind France's back – when she must have known how closely those
Agreements, guaranteeing a part of the sterling balances in foreign
exchange terms for their holders, affected the issue on which the two
countries were then locked in such intense, if at times indirect, discussion. The story is one which, as it happens, can even be heard from
some official French quarters. Those closer to the events, however, deny
it. They insist that the way in which this time-bomb was suddenly
heard to be ticking again so loudly was not their doing. The French
had asked for the declaration on the issue to be kept strictly secret. But
the other five had thrown up their hands in horror at this turn of events
– 'the bottom dropped out of their world'; one national delegation
leaked the story, no doubt to alert public opinion, and the press took it
that this 'secret weapon' was being got ready to be exploded right
under the negotiations.

The British delegation on the other hand kept its cool. The French
were embarrassed by the reactions of the other five, and rather pleased
at the calm way the British said that of course sterling had to be discussed. Looking back on it, in fact, it may be that the French judged it
nicely – deliberately increasing the tension in March and April to
increase the satisfactory *dénouement* to come in May. In any case, there is
another clue to be fitted into this puzzle. It does not square easily with
the 'reprisal theory', but at the same time actually makes the sterling
issue seem even more dangerous a potential landmine. Though this
may not be known in all the relevant French official circles, the Bank
of England had taken great care not only to apprise their French

opposite numbers of their intention to get the agreements renewed, but also to urge them to attend the relevant meetings. It was the French who chose to stay away.

Remembering the arguments used by President de Gaulle for his second veto, pro-Marketeers in Britain and champions of British entry on the Continent found this perhaps the most discouraging moment in the whole negotiation. Nora Beloff reported the atmosphere at the time under the headline 'Pompidou's new Market tactics "amount to veto"':

As he left the conference hall, one veteran who had sat through the first round of British negotiations 10 years ago said he had the nightmare impression of having heard the whole thing before. Maurice Schumann sounded like Couve de Murville (de Gaulle's foreign minister) he said, Jean-Pierre Brunet like his predecessor, René Wormser, and Ambassador Boegner like Ambassador Boegner.

The impression, according to her report, was not confined to the tight little world of the negotiators themselves:

France's new approach to the Common Market negotiations has convinced leading politicians in Brussels, Paris and London that – at least for the time being – President Pompidou wants to keep Britain out.

In the view of these observers France's tougher line at last week's talks on British imports of Commonwealth sugar – described by diplomats in the Community as 'mean', 'stingy' and 'obstructive' – plus her sudden demand that the status of sterling be placed on the agenda, amount to an effective veto.

It is argued that the hopes of Mr Heath and Mr Rippon, Britain's chief negotiator, for a quick deal before the summer recess, have certainly been stalled by these tactics. . . . Barring a highly improbably French change of heart, Mr Heath must decide whether to persevere or cut his losses.[1]

[1] *Observer*, 21 March 1971.

4 The Return to Bilateral Secrecy

Voilà la vraie affaire Soames
Georges Pompidou

French Ambiguity and British Impatience

What worried the British in the spring of 1971, therefore, was their inability to decide with certainty between three fundamentally different interpretations of what was happening at Brussels. One interpretation was that France, unwilling to let Britain in, and unwilling also to incur the odium of a third veto, was quietly tying one noose after another in which the negotiations would strangle themselves. The process could take various forms. It might be that the technical difficulties would simply entail so many delays that negotiations could not be concluded before the deadlines demanded by the British domestic timetable: philosophical arguments on budget contributions and Community preference would simply drag on for so long that the British themselves would lose patience, and either make a silly move or else retire of their own accord. Or it might be that agreement could be reached, but on terms so stiff that no British cabinet would accept them. Or perhaps the terms, though acceptable to a cabinet presided over by Edward Heath (who would by agreeing to them in Brussels already have committed himself to swinging his cabinet if he possibly could), would be so distasteful to a sufficient number of Conservative anti-Marketeers and Labour MPs that the cabinet would lose heart and jib at presenting them to Parliament. Alternatively they might try to bull-doze them through Parliament only to be met by a revolt of public opinion and instructions from Parliament to go back and get better terms – in which case the stalemate could be such that either the British or the Six would get so bored with the whole exercise that they would turn their attention to other urgent problems and the re-negotiation would become a perpetual conference (like the Austrian peace treaty talks of the 'forties and early 'fifties, or the Vietnam peace talks in Paris of more recent years). Finally, there was a possibility that Parliament might actually throw the Accession Treaty out, with or without the government to boot: and in either case, again, the problem would either go to sleep or else go away altogether. (As British politicians never tired of assuring the French, if Britain were rejected a third time, she might not come back for a fourth try.) On that hypothesis a lot of things would have to come right very quickly for Britain still to make it.

The second theory was that the French were at least resigned to British entry, or even actually quite ready for it now. That was, after all, what they were saying in public. But then they could hardly say anything else, or their partners would be after them. And the way they were acting was hardly in accordance with what they were saying. But would one expect them to act any other way? If they were too forthcoming, they would be throwing away their trump card: Britain's obligation to prove that she really meant business by making concessions at the negotiating table. On this interpretation what the French wanted was simply the best possible terms: access for their produce, money for their farmers, support for their view of Europe's future evolution. They could get that in return for admitting Britain: no wonder they hesitated to say 'yes' too clearly until they were sure of their price. On this interpretation the French negotiators had been told to sell entry – but to sell it as expensively as possible. Even on this interpretation, however, entry was not assured. For the French could, in ignorance, or on a mistaken calculation of political probabilities, set a price that was higher than Britain could pay – and both sides could get caught in positions from which there was no retreat. Or they could, on a mistaken calculation of the timetable, delay saying 'snap' so long that it was too late for the British. The possibility that it might thus all founder – without anyone actually having decided that it should, indeed with both sides really wanting to succeed but one or the other miscalculating on the terms or on the timing – was very seriously in people's minds in the early months of 1971, and could certainly not be excluded.

But then there was also a third theory. According to this one the French negotiators were, in effect, left without instructions. It was their job to negotiate as toughly as was compatible with cohesion between the Six, to pick up every new card they could find (whether on fisheries or anything else), play the old cards (like sterling) for all they were worth, and put France into the best of all possible positions: a position of wait and see in which she could either prevent success and throw the blame on the British, or else ensure success and claim all the credit herself. On this third interpretation Georges Pompidou, in early 1971, was not yet obliged to have made any choice either way. He did not even, at that stage, particularly have to bend his mind to the problem; it was simply not yet ripe for decision. He could leave his diplomats to fight hard in Brussels, to test out British reactions and the reactions of the other five, while he himself could keep his options open to the last.

It was the timing of this last moment that was now seriously worrying the British. There was a rising sense of urgency due to several mutually reinforcing considerations. First of all there was public opinion. The percentage of those who disapproved of entry was coming close to 70% in March 1971; a feeling of being kept in the antechamber was not exactly warming to British enthusiasm to go in. The colder popular opinion, the less enthusiasm would there be on the Labour benches, and the longer the delay, the greater the temptation for the Labour Party to shift away from its pro-entry stand. Furthermore, if things were not largely tied up before the summer, there might be difficulties at the Conservative party conference in the autumn, and even greater difficulties for the Marketeers at the Labour conference. The parliamentary timetable for the 1971–72 session could run into serious difficulties; inflation and unemployment looked like worsening and would require more attention in any case; and neither government nor business could work indefinitely on two alternative hypotheses – one of being 'in', the other 'out'.

When Edward Heath visited Bonn for the first time as Prime Minister, on 5 April, he made his impatience very clear. He stressed the 'utmost urgency' of a settlement, and warned the French:

The world will not stand still. If Europe fails to seize this opportunity, our friends will be dismayed and our enemies heartened. Soviet ambitions of domination will be pursued more ruthlessly. Our friends, disillusioned by our disunity, would more and more be tempted to leave Europe to its own devices.

Willy Brandt, the weekend before the Prime Minister's arrival, had spoken in public of an exchange of letters he had been having with Georges Pompidou on the subject of British entry, and the Italian Prime Minister had been writing to the French President too. Things were evidently coming to a head. There was some speculation about a Franco-British summit, but as the *Financial Times* reported from Bonn, 'It is stressed that no arrangements have been made and there are perhaps some fears on the British side that such a meeting would be of a "do or die" nature and at this stage is therefore better avoided'.[1] And the

[1] *Financial Times*, 6 April 1971.

Guardian a few days later, in what was clearly an inspired piece under the heading 'Heath losing patience with Market delay', emphasized:

The Government's sense of urgency is now a major factor in Britain's negotiations to join the Common Market. The Prime Minister has good reasons for his haste and believes that recognition of this in Bonn is the major achievement of his talks with Herr Brandt, the Federal German Chancellor.

If the negotiations with the EEC Council of Ministers in May do not produce the progress the Government is demanding Mr Heath will fly to Paris to try to have things out, one way or another, with President Pompidou.

The possibility for misunderstanding in summitry with the French is well understood – after Mr Macmillan's and Mr Wilson's joustings with General de Gaulle – and Mr Heath will neither risk nor waste such a meeting with Monsieur Pompidou until or unless it is vital.

His tactics are reminiscent of de Gaulle, who was at his most unexpected and intransigent when weak.[1]

The Litmus Tests for Britain

So much for British worries. What must have worried the French most in the whole issue were the manifold memories of Britain's choices of the open sea and in particular of the Atlantic as against Continental Europe centred on the Rhine. And for the future what they feared most was that, one way or another, the upshot of the negotiations might turn out in a few years to have implied not so much that Britain had entered the Community, as that the Community had been dragged into or found itself enmeshed in an essentially Atlantic grouping. That had been the fear of the strict Gaullists, and it had been the fear of some of the strict integrationist Europeans too. Both in order to satisfy themselves and to a lesser extent in order also to be able to demonstrate to these two rather disparate groups that Britain really had chosen the Continent, the French government's strategy could be one of making Britain pass certain tests. Some French officials no doubt hoped that Britain would fail them. Others felt that if she did pass, then on the whole her joining would strengthen both the Community and the French purposes to boot. It remained to define the tests by which Britain was to be judged.

The Commonwealth might, ten years before, possibly have been considered as one such test. But if so, it was dismissed this time as an unsuitable one. Given good will on both sides there was no doubt that the problems of butter and sugar could be satisfactorily settled. They

[1] *Guardian*, 10 April 1971.

were minor in any case, and since they concerned not Britain's interests but those of more or less innocent third parties, they were hardly a very good test.

Defence was a more obvious candidate. In 1962 the question of nuclear weapons – which was never mentioned in the multilateral negotiations – had clearly played a capital role in de Gaulle's decision. It is said in Paris today that de Gaulle had been led to expect a clear pledge from Macmillan on that count: Julian Amery had come to Paris and discussed the problem with various people, and being Macmillan's son-in-law had been taken as his unofficial emissary; Peter Thorneycroft had discussed the problem with Messmer, then Minister of National Defence; and Sir Harold Caccia had had conversations on the subject in London with Geoffrey de Courcel, the French ambassador. Some who have seen the British official record of the Rambouillet meeting maintain that de Gaulle accordingly twice opened the door for Macmillan by saying that if there were propositions about rockets that Macmillan would like to make, he would be disposed to consider them: but twice Macmillan failed to give any positive reply, and of course a few weeks later he made the Polaris deal at Nassau. No wonder if the General felt the door had been banged back in his face.

But it would be inadequate to let the record rest there. The notion of a nuclear deal was floated by one of the General's close collaborators in Paris to two visiting Englishmen thought to have Edward Heath's ear at a lunch in early spring 1962, and when The Economist on 28 April 1962 came out with the notion in its first leader it is not impossible that this was in response to similar initiatives from the French side suggesting that here was an area in which the British should come out with an offer. The French may feel they were led up a garden path. But if so it was a path to which they had probably first pointed themselves.

However that may be, by 1970–71 they were no longer regarding defence as a possible test of British intentions. Britain had already increased her forces on the Rhine after her withdrawal from east of Suez. There was little more to be done in terms of conventional defence. In nuclear terms, on the other hand, the French now realized that there was the 1946 McMahon Act and everything else that made it difficult or impossible to share the secrets Britain had had entrusted to her by the Americans. In the autumn of 1971 Jean-François Deniau was to take up the nuclear issue with a suggestion that the McMahon Act should be discussed with the Americans as part of the general use to which the dollar crisis could be put:

To envisage a 'European nuclear weapon' would cause more problems than one could hope to solve by it. But on the other hand greater technical manufacturing co-operation in the nuclear field . . . would have certain financial and then political advantages. . . . Yet any co-operation, however limited, between France and Britain can be stopped not by a French or British ruling, but by an American one.[1]

Secondly there was the dilemma posed within Europe: had the formula of Anglo-French nuclear collaboration been one that in any way included the West Germans, it would have proved unacceptable to the Soviet Union: had it not done so, it might have created difficulties with the Federal Republic which Georges Pompidou was not anxious to raise. There were quite enough causes of tension without raising defence issues as well.

There was certainly also a third factor in the situation, though how conscious the French were of it is another matter – it does not seem to have been very prominent in their minds, though had they chosen to use it it might well have blocked Britain's path: the domestic reactions in Britain if such a nuclear deal had been part of the package. It may well be doubted if a parliamentary majority could have been secured for accession to the Rome Treaty with such a condition attached to it. Perhaps the French did not fully realize this; perhaps they did, but were dissuaded from using it by the international repercussions or because they did not want to exact conditions which they knew to be prohibitive. Most probably different men working on the problem in Paris had different attitudes to it. Suffice it to say that the French decided that nuclear weapons could not provide the test either.

The real tests, therefore, lay neither in Britain's attachment to the Commonwealth nor in her military relations with the United States. The real test took two forms, of which the lesser, almost subsidiary one, was agriculture. And that agricultural test had two aspects – Community preference, and Community solidarity in meeting the costs of the farm policy (which meant the British budget contribution).

Some of the French, indeed, felt that agriculture was so much a subsidiary test that they should not even fight too much on it themselves. High farm prices were not, they maintained, really in the French interest: their farmers would have been better served by somewhat lower prices, which would have driven the more marginal German and Italian farmers out of business and thus handed over a much bigger

[1] *Le Monde*, 20 October 1971, p. 29.

export market to the French. In theory, therefore, they might have left the British to fight out the farm price policy with the Germans, and stood on the sidelines. But in practice they could hardly do so. They had France's own marginal farmers (and their votes) to consider. They did not want to leave the Germans in the lurch. And they would, of course, have lost a lot of their negotiating position if they had in this domain accepted that the rules of the *acquis communautaire* should be changed in the interests of enlargement. But, though the agricultural issue was a secondary one, it would in any case logically lead to what became, was made, or had to be the acid test – that of sterling.

Sterling had, as we have seen, already been made the big argument in de Gaulle's second veto in 1967. His arguments then were not all still relevant, but others had come to join them. Devaluation – which de Gaulle had used as an illustration of the weakness of sterling, since it occurred only days before his press conference – had been an important step in curing Britain's balance of payments deficit for the period of the negotiations. With the British balance of payments stronger than at any time since the war and the gold and dollar reserves of the Bank of England rising towards unprecedented post-war levels, Pompidou could no longer argue that Britain must put her house in order so far as current payments were concerned. At most he could use British fears of a large balance of payments burden arising out of the farm finance arrangements of the EEC to point to the implications of joining as a reinforcement of the need for Britain to watch the current payments position with extreme care.

On the other hand if that was one argument, or half an argument, less than de Gaulle had had at his disposal – and no one should under-estimate the achievement of the Labour government in having re-versed the balance of payments deficit so effectively, nor the sacrifice it made to do so – Pompidou could now point to a coming world money crisis arising out of the accentuated United States balance of payments deficit. Such a crisis could threaten the world system of multilateral trade, could threaten even the cohesion of the EEC itself. It could also force on Britain important choices between an American and a European orientation. Pompidou's advisers argued that an understanding must be reached on sterling so as to free the dollar from having to worry about its soft underbelly, sterling, whose fate was linked with it, and so as to free Britain from the clutches of the inter-national monetary organizations and hence, indirectly, those of the United States. Only thus could one be certain of avoiding a situation where, instead of Britain entering the European Community, the Community would be embroiled in the money maelstrom of the Atlantic area with its Pacific extensions.

Equally, however, there was a cluster of considerations arising nearer home. Particularly if there were to be steps towards monetary union in the EEC, it was vital to free Britain from the economic and financial constraints imposed on a world banker whose short-term liabilities were a multiple of her short-term assets and whose preoccupation, therefore, had to be at least as much with the maintenance of confidence in her currency abroad as with economic growth and full employment at home. At the outset, some of the French negotiators also felt that for Britain to give up this world reserve currency role would be a substantial and therefore politically significant sacrifice. (They admit now that the problem was not well understood at the beginning of the negotiations, and that they learnt a lot in the process of discussion.) Others also felt that the sterling issue would be a two-way test – a test for the British, certainly, as to how far they were prepared to give precedence to their European over their world-wide interests and policies; but also a test for the Six (which it was best to face at the outset, rather than when it was too late) as to what they for their part were prepared to do for Britain.

It was perhaps particularly in the Prime Minister's office at the Hôtel Matignon that this kind of 'litmus test' thinking was developed. The way things actually turned out was, from this point of view, a little disappointing. The Brussels negotiation was very much concentrated, in the earlier phases, on the *défense du bifteck*: the French sought to safeguard the existing system rather than use the opportunity of enlargement for a further advance in the dimension of deepening the Community. The strategy of using enlargement for such deepening might have transcended the trench warfare of the second phase: yet what actually happened in the third phase was that, in May 1971, Pompidou appeared in effect to throw in his hand – in return for what, it may not be quite easy to say. Perhaps, it is said at the Matignon and the Quai in explanation, the Elysée is further removed than they from the concrete problems – from industrial strategy, airbuses, computers, transnational companies and all the rest. Maurice Schumann talked of letting the new members into a fortress that might have external walls, but had not yet succeeded in tracing even the foundations of its internal buildings: the strategy of seeking explicit agreement on the plan was pursued, but – to some minds – not in enough detail and without exacting sufficient public commitment by the candidates to make full use of the golden opportunity enlargement presented. To some extent that disappointment with the President – the notion that he did not play the game hard enough, did not exact a high enough European (as distinct from French) price - depends on how far one believes the President and the Prime Minister went in committing themselves in private. For the rest it depends on the view that France was free to pursue the game further without excessive cost in terms of the cohesion of the Six themselves.

The Soames–Jobert Talks

We saw in the previous chapter the disadvantages of the Brussels framework arising from the multilateral and the largely public character of the proceedings. We looked at them there primarily from the British point of view. But by this time they were also beginning to hamper France. If one wanted to test British long-term intentions on defence matters – certainly on nuclear weapons – it was difficult to do so in public and with the others (including the Germans) sitting round the table. Certainly on sterling, if commitments were required and secrecy of the essence of their implementation, Brussels was the wrong forum in which to do it – it was in some ways too narrow, no less than in other ways too wide. Again, Europe's place in the world – a subject that transcended both defence and monetary affairs – was a matter that the two recently decolonizing powers of world status might want to discuss quietly without having, for instance, the Germans (with their very special interests *vis-à-vis* America and Russia) listening in and interrupting the dialogue. Not that one would want to take decisions behind their backs – but one wanted to ensure complete mutual understanding. Similarly Brussels was hardly the place, and the Benelux countries hardly the partners, if one wanted to ascertain that the British saw the majority voting rules in the same light as the French.

It was thus that the procedure that de Gaulle had suggested in the Soames affair was now taken up at last: bilateral secret talks directly between London and Paris on the political 'gut issues', as the vital preliminary to the bread-and-butter quantitative topics of the Brussels wrangling. What mattered was that these talks should be carried on at the right time, in the right atmosphere, and by the right people in the right way.

Before the end of 1970 was clearly too early. The Brussels negotiations did not delineate the trenches into which both sides were digging themselves until December. It was not until the deadlock had crystallized at the multilateral level, not in other words until France had made clear that it was in her power to insist on conditions which no British government was likely to be willing to accept, that Georges Pompidou could reckon to obtain the maximum advantage from a direct approach by Edward Heath. A great deal of the bargaining manœuvres in the early part of 1971 could thus in a sense be construed as signals to 'come up and see me some time'. It had to be Heath – head of government, not head of state, junior in office, and in any case the applicant, *le demandeur* – who took the initiative. And of course it helped that by the beginning of April Dr Joseph Luns, the Dutch Foreign Minister, had publicly called for just such a summit meeting, and that the other five clearly appeared to be pressing it on Pompidou. So they could hardly be offended by secret negotiations or talks behind their backs. It was just what they, too, felt was required.

By this time in fact the preparations for a bilateral summit had – in the greatest secrecy – already got under way. The interface between Britain and France consisted, not of large teams arriving by fleets of cars and facing each other with a panoply of aides, interpreters and stenographers, but of two men only: Christopher Soames and Michel Jobert. Their venue was an unobtrusive brisk two minutes' walk from the British embassy up the Rue du Faubourg Saint-Honoré, in Jobert's room on the first floor of the Elysée.

Backing up Christopher Soames in the embassy were two career diplomats: John Galsworthy, with ten years' experience of the Continent in Bonn, Brussels and Paris, who had long taken the line, unpopular in much of the Foreign Office, that Britain must enter the Community not against French obstruction but with French support; and Michael Palliser, who had served as Harold Wilson's interpreter to Charles de Gaulle and was to serve Edward Heath in the same capacity with Georges Pompidou. And on his trips to London, fortnightly at first, but then increasing in frequency until he would make the trip two or three times a week, Christopher Soames kept in closest touch with Robert Armstrong in No. 10 Downing Street (not the Foreign Office). 'There would have been no point in having a political ambassador if he didn't use the direct line', as was afterwards said of Christopher Soames: and at the political level he reported to the Prime Minister, obviously, and a small group consisting essentially of the Foreign Secretary and Geoffrey Rippon, the Permanent Under-Secretary at the Foreign Office, Sir Denis Greenhill, Sir Con O'Neill and John

Robinson. Very few of the senior men in the Foreign Office were told of what was afoot.

The man whom Christopher Soames went up the Rue du Faubourg Saint-Honoré to see, Michel Jobert, was the Secretary-General of the Elysée, a civil servant of about fifty, himself married to an Anglo-Saxon, and a graduate of the Fondation Nationale des Sciences Politiques. No doubt Jobert discussed the details with Jean-Bernard Raimond, the President's Technical Adviser from the Quai d'Orsay. Certainly Jean-René Bernard came into the affair by virtue of his key function as Secretary-General of the Inter-Ministerial Committee on Questions of European Economic Co-operation. It was with him that John Galsworthy had to deal on substantive issues of negotiation throughout. But he was also brought into the secret of the summit preparations by Michel Jobert once the talks with Christopher Soames had got going.

On the French side the preparations were confined at first to an even smaller group than on the British. The affair was 'très élyséenne, très confidentielle'. It bypassed the Quai d'Orsay, it bypassed the Hôtel Matignon – indeed it appears to have been strictly confined to two and then three people in the President's office, and while the President must presumably have been kept informed of the talks taking place in the room right next to his own on the first floor, it is by no means clear that he ever sanctioned them until a very late stage. The French partners to these talks were thus taking their careers very much in their own hands, and had things gone the other way they would indeed have been out on a limb. They chanced it in the belief that the Brussels negotiations could not be allowed to founder, that the decision had to be taken in Paris, and that it could be taken only if it was thoroughly prepared. Yet the President never seems to have done more than tolerate the preparations, could have disavowed them at any moment, and did not agree to see Heath until the very end. This was, given the nature of things, perhaps inevitable. Edward Heath also did not commit himself until the outcome of the meeting seemed secure, and indeed Christopher Soames would hardly have wished the Prime Minister to commit himself (nor could he have afforded to commit the Prime Minister) to any meeting until its success seemed virtually certain in advance.

When on 6 May the date of the summit came to be fixed, the French Foreign Minister happened to be in Moscow, and had to learn of it almost at the same time as the general public: senior Quai d'Orsay officials were told only hours before publication. Indeed, once a date had been fixed, it was announced within three days (on the afternoon of 8 May) so as to forestall any possible leak. Quai d'Orsay officials were expressly kept away from the summit meeting almost as much as they had been kept in the dark about its preparation. And in the final press conference Pompidou even gently teased Schumann and his officials for apparently enjoying the bargaining ritual over substantive trifles which he and Heath wished to appear to have transcended.

Christopher Soames and Michael Palliser, some of the French recall, were a superb team, perfectly complementing each other: Christopher Soames with all his strengths and his weaknesses, his exuberant enthusiasm, his political flair and his intense not simply political but personal commitment to the cause; Michael Palliser with his cool, business-like, Foreign Office efficiency. Their Paris partners even thought of them as politically complementary: Soames was a former Conservative cabinet Minister, while the French (whose civil service is far less traditionally apolitical in the party sense) pointed to Palliser's period at No. 10 as Harold Wilson's Private Secretary (Foreign Affairs). Having less of a tradition of marriage for purely personal reasons, they also recalled that he had married the daughter of one of the leading Socialist champions of European unity, Paul-Henri Spaak. If credit is to go anywhere for the success of the negotiations, it is frequently said in Paris, it must go to Soames, who shuttled between London and Paris, as much as to Sir Con O'Neill and his team who shuttled between London and Brussels.

So, while at Brussels the trench warfare was carried on with no mercy shown on either side, in Paris from late February onwards the secret peace talks were beginning to gel. This tiny nucleus of half a dozen people (who in the end understood each other better over these complicated questions than they understood their own fellow-countrymen) analysed the log-jam and prepared to unblock it. There was a stage when they looked at each other and asked themselves which team each really belonged to – the Elysée in which they were meeting, or the British embassy a few houses down the road. The truth of the matter was perhaps that by that point they had all become so committed personally to making sure their initiative would not fail, that, coming from either side, they were much in the same boat; and it was a boat which the French passengers, at any rate, felt had no life-rafts for them if it should founder. Their secret meetings had to write the scenario for a summit with such meticulous care that it simply could not fail.

It was the French who proposed an agenda of half a dozen points, and there was little the British wanted to add. Sterling was plainly crucial; but the basic philosophy of the Community, both in its internal organization and in its external stance, particularly *vis-à-vis* the Americans, was even more fundamental. The British knew exactly what the President wanted to hear, and the terms in which it had to be couched. The French knew just where Edward Heath could not oblige and needed concessions for his own political purposes. On the concrete issues, like sterling and New Zealand, the preparations had 'taken things to eleven o'clock'. There was no need to reach a solution on every one of them at the summit itself; indeed it was important to leave some agreements to be reached multilaterally in Brussels.

The French clearly would not risk a summit unless the atmosphere had been dramatically changed in Brussels beforehand as a pledge of good faith: the British could not afford to make concessions in Brussels unless they felt sure that the result would be a general thaw between the two sides. So for that reason also the scenario had to be widened to include a Brussels no less than a Paris performance. It was agreed between Soames and Jobert that in the second week of May each side should make a major concession – the French on sugar, the British on Community preference for farm products. In the middle of these Council meetings, Maurice Schumann was recalled from Brussels to be informed, on the morning of Wednesday 12 May, of what was expected: and later that night both sides could agree that a major breakthrough had taken place, and that at last the negotiations had begun to move.

From the British point of view it was indeed high time. The Foreign Office had, in summer 1970, envisaged a summit meeting either with the Six, or else bilaterally with France, in March, April or at the latest early May 1971. Otherwise they feared the timetable of parliamentary approval, signature, implementing legislation and ratification could not be met. The summit was already a little on the late side for the British; there was on the other hand no reason why the French should be in a hurry. To persuade them of the imperatives of the British deadlines was indeed one of the tasks of the Paris discussions. That President Pompidou was willing to see Edward Heath at this stage is proof that he was more than inclined to let Britain in. Nevertheless, though sugar had been used as a signal of goodwill, it was not at this stage an unambiguous signal in itself – as witness the difference between the English translation referring to a 'firm purpose' for a French phrase that went no further than '*aura à cœur*'. Also, the New Zealand issue, known to be sensitive for Conservative back-benchers, most of the farm finance issue, and the thorny problems of sterling all remained unresolved – issues which would allow Pompidou, if he wished, still to put up a stiff fight against enlargement.

It may, however, be taken as axiomatic that once Pompidou had agreed to meet Heath, he did not do so to become personally involved in a failure. The nationalization of French oil companies in Algeria in early 1971 had looked like a defeat for his personal diplomacy. *The Economist* in fact argued that, as a result, he might want to show that he could be a tough Gaullist by keeping the British out.[1] But in Paris, on the contrary, people maintained that it was useful that here was a different major issue on which he could score a personal success.

A great deal of comment at the time also went into showing how close on the Germans' floating of the Deutschmark on Wednesday 5 May came the announcement of the summit meeting published late on Saturday 8 May. That was a short-circuited explanation. The announcement followed far too closely for there to have been any direct causal relationship. (The dates of 20–21 May had in fact already been pencilled tentatively into some diaries on 26 April.) The general trend of German resurgence played a role in each of the two specific events, but the one in no sense triggered off the other. We need not suppose that the issue, when at last the President chose to decide it, was decided on a sudden impulse or on criteria other than its intrinsic long-term effects.

One may well ask – if the preparations were so detailed, if the President agreed finally to become involved himself (and indeed the French side suggested that a joint press conference be held at the end of the summit talks on the eve of their beginning, before the two men had actually yet met) – was the summit not bound to succeed? If the question is asked in too literal a sense, it obviously was not. Two tailors' dummies would not have done the trick. There were those in Whitehall who felt that what Pompidou wanted was a vague general *tour d'horizon*, to talk of China and America, civilization and strategy; boning up on the minutiae of New Zealand cheese and the control over capital movements was, in their view, not merely a waste of the Prime Minister's time, but likely to get in the way of the expected level of discourse. Edward Heath thought otherwise. It was a fine month of May, and in the afternoons he sat in the garden of No. 10 Downing Street with the dossiers and four or five pundits on one problem at

[1] *The Economist*, 24 April 1971.

a time – sterling, the Common Agricultural Policy, New Zealand – with a few days for reflection between topics, being given tutorials, conducting seminars on the nuts and bolts, the positions and the figures. At the weekend preceding the meeting he retired to Chequers for further study with delegation experts and with Christopher Soames. As belt as well as braces, a few days before the summit a little advance party from Whitehall had also gone over to the Elysée to check on the overtones and inflections expected of Edward Heath in Paris – and no doubt Georges Pompidou was submitting to equally careful coaching. 'We didn't want a good meeting – we needed a very, very good meeting indeed between the two men', one of the binational team later recalled.

The Paris Summit

And a very, very good meeting was what they got. On Monday 17 May, as curtain-raisers, the French President appeared on the BBC's *Panorama* programme, while the British Prime Minister the same night at the same time appeared on the ORTF – a curious little diplomatic and public relations technique of talking across each other's shoulders to each other's electorates. Edward Heath hoped the talks would lead to a clearer understanding of 'the Europe we are trying to create together': Georges Pompidou refused to rule out failure in the talks, and threw the onus of proof of her sincerity onto Britain. She had to demonstrate her sincerity both through declaring her intentions and through her daily behaviour: and Community preference implied 'a sort of disruption of the present pattern' of trade with New Zealand. Georges Pompidou comes from the Cantal, an area of green countryside where grass grows best, which is fed to cows, which produce milk, which is made into cheese, as he was to explain to Edward Heath in Paris later in the week. So he was quite frank about it on television: 'As we ourselves are producing some butter and some cheese, I think that our own reaction in this respect is not entirely sentimental.' He was also worried about the position of the French tongue – a matter on which he expanded in an interview with *Le Soir* a day or two later, saying that English was above all the language of America, so that if Europe was to distinguish herself from the United States, she should keep French as the main working language of the Community. (It was not put quite in those terms in his BBC interview, where his audience might have remembered Chaucer and Shakespeare as much as the lingua franca of computers and airline pilots.) But Pompidou also saw certain parallelisms between France and Britain: 'I would hardly imagine that the British nation, as I know and admire it, would wish suddenly to renounce its national personality.' Asked about nuclear co-operation, he did not seem to expect anything. On the French side there were no limitations to the extent of such co-operation, but he feared such limitations did exist on Britain's side.

On Wednesday afternoon, 19 May, Edward Heath flew to Orly with a small group of collaborators to be welcomed in English by the French Prime Minister, and to hold a confident press conference on the issues to be discussed. Next morning, accompanied only by Michael Palliser (acting this time as interpreter rather than negotiator) he appeared at the Elysée for the opening *tête-à-tête*. (On the French side Prince Andronikov, who had paired Michael Palliser in the Wilson–de Gaulle talks, was the only other person present.) The French government spokesman, with a fine respect for the pure French tongue that was said to be so much an issue in the talks, declared '*le blackout total*'. Round Christopher Soames' table, a few hundred yards down the road, sat the British party with nothing to do but wait in tension. The races would be won or lost all at once that very morning.

There was a very informal walk-about for the photographers in the Elysée garden after a working lunch, and later on, while Edward Heath went up the Champs Elysées to lay a wreath on the tomb of the Unknown Soldier at what used to be l'Etoile and is now (at least in theory) the Place Charles de Gaulle, President Pompidou worked carefully on a brief speech he made that evening after a resplendent state banquet at the Elysée:

Through two men who are talking to each other, two peoples are trying to find each other again. To find each other to take part in a great joint endeavour – the construction of a European group of nations determined to reconcile the safeguarding of their national identities with the constraints of acting as a community....

Our object is not to conclude a negotiation which is being pursued elsewhere and with our partners. But . . . our views are sufficiently close that we can go forward without pessimism.

Both sides were full of admiration for the performance the Prime Minister put up on the basis of his brief. Things might still have gone wrong. They could have gone wrong over sterling – the subject to which the two men devoted a great deal of their *tête-à-tête*. They might have gone wrong had their concepts of Europe and of her role in the world not been so close. They might have gone wrong above all if the two men, who had met only once or twice before, had not personally 'clicked'. They did not become chummy, or relax easily in each other's company, even when Georges Pompidou paid his return visit to Chequers in March 1972. But they evidently felt not only a certain political sympathy (which Georges Pompidou does not easily have for Socialists, any more than his predecessor did) but also – perhaps even more important – impressed each other as solid, down-to-earth, trustworthy men able to deliver the goods.

The next day, dealing with detailed questions, the two sides worked in the morning, met for lunch in the British embassy (a gracious gesture in terms of protocol, for a head of state to lunch with a mere Prime Minister), and were expected, then, to have the joint press conference announced in the early afternoon. Instead, after lunch, the talks went on, and on, and on - the press being kept waiting until finally it was evening before the journalists were called into the same room in which Georges Pompidou's predecessor had twice in the previous eight years vetoed British admission.

There was an official communiqué, but more dramatic in a way was the procedure of the press conference itself, the long handshakes, the obvious cordiality, and the President's verdict: 'It would be unreasonable now to believe that an agreement is not possible during the conference in Brussels in June.'

Edward Heath had obviously missed the race in which he had hoped to take the helm of *Morning Cloud II* that weekend – he had agreed with the President that it would be flattering if, without him, the yacht were placed second, which it was – and was driven straight back to Chequers from the airport on the Friday night to prepare for his statement to the House on Monday.

Naturally enough, in view of his past proposals for the French and British nuclear capacities to be held in trust for the rest of Europe, there was a whiff of suspicion that, at the Elysée, a secret nuclear deal had been struck – and that it was this secret deal which would be the open sesame to the EEC. The Paris communiqué had made no reference to defence, and in the House Heath disposed of the wider topic of both conventional and nuclear defence in one simple sentence: 'We had only a brief discussion of defence questions, recognizing that these were matters for the future, after enlargement.' The Leader of the Opposition returned to the point repeatedly, and so got it amplified in a manner that left no ambiguity:

I have told the House that the amount of time which we devoted to the discussion of defence was very small indeed. We both accepted that the position of
Britain, within NATO, and that of France, which is a member of the alliance
but has withdrawn from NATO, is different. If when the Community is
enlarged Europe is, in accordance with its other policies, to develop a defence
policy, these matters will have to be discussed at that time, but there could have
been no discussion last week at our meeting. As far as nuclear questions are
concerned, both France and Britain are nuclear powers, and there was no
discussion of any agreement. I was not asked for any offer; I made no offer; and
the matter was left exactly where it stands today. . . . No agreement of any kind
was reached between us on any aspect of defence. What was agreed was that if,
in the context of the enlarged Community, Europe wishes to move towards its
own defence policy, that is a matter to be settled by the European members at
the time that they consider it.[1]

There was no reason whatever to question Edward Heath's veracity on
the matter. Indeed we have already seen that the French themselves
considered, but rejected, the notion that defence provided any politically reasonable or convincing test of British intentions at this time: and
clearly no Prime Minister could commit a future successor by secret
protocol on any such issue.

Having said that, one must, however, add that that did not dispose
of the defence question either between the two countries or within the
enlarged Community for the future. Both the kind of political co-
operation envisaged and the technological and industrial policies to be
framed by the Community would in due course undoubtedly have to
lead to the consideration of joint procurement policies and some closer
mutual consultation on defence.

Moreover, the day would undoubtedly come when American
Presidents would no longer *ex officio* regard themselves as citizens of
Berlin (as Kennedy had with his exclamation in 1963, '*Ich bin ein
Berliner*'). The United States had its balance of payments worries and
might well weary of carrying world burdens in general at a time when
American society was facing considerable domestic problems jealous of
political attention no less than of financial resources. Europe would
have to fend for herself a great deal more in the future than in the past –
and that after all was one of the things that European independence of
America was all about.

So the problem would arise – but not yet. It should become less
difficult to take up once there was an enlarged Economic Community

[1] Hansard, 24 May 1971, cols 33, 36, 38.

with greater mutual understanding of political aims and attitudes. It was neither an object of secret agreements, nor a topic shelved: it was a subject deferred for constructive approaches to arise out of the Community's enlargement, rather than a precondition without which enlargement could not take place. It remained of primary ultimate importance. But it was a consequence, not a premise, in political logic and in historical sequence.

More interesting from some points of view was the question raised in the House on the same occasion by Harold Lever. The Paris communiqué of 21 May made no specific mention of sterling, but spoke only of 'economic, financial and monetary problems which could arise as a result of enlargement' and of progress towards economic and monetary union: 'The Prime Minister reaffirmed the readiness of Britain to participate fully and in a European spirit in this development. These discussions produced a useful clarification of views which will provide a firm basis for the future.'[1] Harold Lever asked two questions: 'What are our intentions on sterling? Could he also clarify whether any question of the parities and fixed parities was decided upon or discussed with the President?' But he really only obtained an answer to the second:

On the subject of sterling, there was no discussion of parities or items of that kind. It was accepted that this matter only arises in the context of co-ordination of currencies inside an enlarged Community, if we become a member, and is obviously concerned with whatever progress is made on the co-ordination of policies.[2]

We shall see that it emerged later that, on the first, a great deal had been said and the French had been substantially satisfied. The wording at this stage was allusive. A fortnight later, a three-point declaration was formally agreed on a multilateral basis in Brussels. Even this, according to some of the French officials, was to be read in the context of the good discussion that did take place, and was therefore not as jejune as it might look at first reading. It was 'the tip of the iceberg'. And we shall see that in the currency crisis three months later Britain for the first time, instead of immediately reacting in terms of United States feelings, reacted first of all – with Anthony Barber's flight to Brussels – in a spirit of European solidarity (though she then found the rest of the Europeans by no means united on the issue).

[1] The full communiqué is printed in Hansard, 24 May 1971, cols 48–9.
[2] ibid., cols 44–5.

On the wider questions, the communiqué distinguished carefully between Europe's external role, on which the President's and the Prime Minister's 'views were very close', and the internal working and development of the Community, on which 'the discussion led to a complete identity of view'. In particular, as the Prime Minister spelt out in the House,

where a country considers that an item is of major national importance to it, a decision should be taken unanimously – in other words, the member countries should not attempt to overrule a single country in something which it considers to be of vital national interest.

This was precisely the view that President de Gaulle had taken in 1965, and enshrined as France's view in the 'Luxemburg Disagreement' of 29 January 1966 that ended the great Community crisis with France resuming her participation in its institutions: 'When very important issues are at stake, the discussion must be continued until unanimous agreement is reached.'[1] It was an interpretation (or perversion) of the Rome Treaty which the other five had rejected in 1965 and 1966, basing themselves squarely on Article 148 of the Treaty which defines the rules for majority voting.

It was not a source of satisfaction among the more federally inclined Europeans, nor among the governments of the other five member states, that the new candidate had, as it were as the price of not being blackballed, agreed to support a virtual modification of one of the EEC's rules, and one originally thought vital to it (even if the course of time had weakened its apparent importance). The French might well be asked why, if their previous attitude in Brussels had always been to insist on full acceptance of the Treaty and the whole Treaty by the candidates, they had in this case (and this case only) agreed on an important departure from it. But then, as Dr Joseph Luns had said to them a long time before, '*Si vous faites l'Europe à l'anglaise, faites la au moins avec les Anglais,*' and if the French were at last prepared to have the British in, no one was eager to raise such points of Community orthodoxy to stop them.

So, in the dispute as to tactics within Britain – sticking to the other five versus talking bilaterally to the French – we may conclude (what should perhaps have been obvious from the first) that it was a question of each element being indispensable in its own way. Had the other five

[1] The full communiqué is reprinted in *The European Common Market and Community*, ed. cit., p. 128.

not kept up the pressure on France – and it seems the Italians under Colombo were at least as effective in their patient but firm influence as the Germans – the calculus of strategic options open to the French would have been very different. They knew they could not have completion without engaging in the enlargement exercise: and given the choice between either no permanent settlement of the farm finance issue or else giving the British the chance of proving they really wanted to join, it was the latter that seemed the lesser evil. But tactically to have refused to talk bilaterally to Pompidou might well have condemned the Brussels negotiations if not to failure (though this was distinctly possible) then at least to such prolonged trench warfare that the position at home would have become very difficult indeed for the government. Whether talks on Europe's political future with de Gaulle in 1969 might have led anywhere is now an idle historical speculation: that the talks which Soames and Jobert initiated two years later were essential there can be no shadow of doubt.

In 1972 John Galsworthy was appointed as British ambassador to Mexico. Michael Palliser, for his part, left Paris in the autumn of 1971 to become British ambassador to the European Communities. Christopher Soames stayed on to stage the Queen's visit in the spring of 1972. He was knighted in the New Year Honours List of 1972; but what may have given at least equal satisfaction to him was the remark which President Pompidou was reported to have made in the courtyard of the embassy after the summit luncheon there: '*Voilà la vraie affaire Soames.*'

5   The Log-Jam Resolved

Ireland and the United Kingdom shall apply from 1 July 1973 a nil duty on imports of tanning extracts of wattle (mimosa) (CCT subheading No. 31.01 A) and tanning extracts of chestnut (CCT subheading No. 32.01 C) from the Community as originally constituted

Protocol 10, Treaty of Accession

Agreement on Agricultural Transition

Even some Ministers now confess that in late March and early April 1971 they were in gloomy mood. Nothing seemed to shift in Brussels. Towards the end of April, however, the initiates saw the beginnings of a shift in Paris. And then, in early May, public events took over and made the headlines: exchange rates were once more in the news, in ways that were relevant to British entry, though it was not unequivocally obvious in which direction the balance of impact would lie.

At the very beginning of May, a heavy inflow of funds into Frankfurt led the German Bundesbank, on Wednesday 5 May, to suspend its purchases of foreign currency. In a tense all-night meeting of Finance Ministers on the following Friday night and Saturday morning, Giscard d'Estaing's attempt to prevent the Germans floating the Mark failed: the Germans were not prepared to hide their economic muscle any more in order still to appear as political dwarfs. In a neat inversion of ideological orthodoxy, the allegedly conservative or liberal French government urged exchange control, but the Social Democrats in Germany preferred the price mechanism. So, just six weeks before the first step towards monetary union – a narrowing of the permitted fluctuations in exchange rates – was to have been taken on 15 June, the Deutschmark was set free altogether.

On the one hand this development seemed to open up certain possibilities for Britain: if European monetary union had suffered such a severe setback, the sterling issue could no longer be regarded as quite such an immediate stumbling block to enlargement of the Community. And if the Germans were refusing to kowtow to the French, the French might be reminded rather brutally of Britain's 'German card' which Harold Wilson had tried to play squashed up with the General in that tiny car at Versailles. They might become more inclined to turn to Britain as a make-weight against the Germans. 'In Brussels', reported Nora Beloff, 'there was nobody who did not automatically assume a link between the Franco-German collision and the revival of the Entente Cordiale.'[1] Yet on the other hand if the Six were about to fall out with each other over exchange rates, that could make speedy agreement in Brussels all the more difficult: the French could be tempted to use the British application as an issue on which to show the Germans that they, too, had some aces up their sleeves and could stop the Germans getting their way. All this speculation, however, was cut short with the announcement, on the same Saturday afternoon, that Georges Pompidou had with pleasure agreed to Edward Heath's suggestion for a meeting.

It was not until the middle of next week, however, that the full import of the Soames–Jobert scenario was unveiled. The 'breakthrough' meetings – the sixth series – of the Ministers were held on 11–13 May. On 7 May – the day before the summit was announced – the British, who for months now had been discussing transitional measures for agriculture with the Commission on the basis of proposals made by the Commission in November, circulated a draft statement which, if it met with the Community's agreement, they were ready formally to put on record at the coming ministerial meeting on 11 May. That Tuesday morning, Jean-Pierre Brunet acknowledged that the new British draft contained undoubted progress, but there were still a few quite specific problems to be resolved. Next day, while Maurice Schumann had gone back to attend a French cabinet meeting, returning in the afternoon to Brussels, the experts were hard at work. That afternoon and evening, from 3.00 p.m. to 11.00 p.m., the Council of Ministers of the Six turned back and forth between its discussion of the transitional measures for agriculture and the problems of cane sugar. Jean-François Deniau talked to the British while the Six talked to one another, until only two difficulties remained. But then the French gave up demanding that the final abolition of customs duties on industrial goods must be on the same day as the final alignment of British farm prices to those of the Community, and allowed the one to happen six months before the other. And the Dutch, after long arguments, eventually agreed that British duties on Community tomatoes and other horticultural products need not be reduced by 10% for the nine months from 1 April 1973 until the end of the year. (They were to be reduced by 20% on 1 January 1974 in any case.)

[1] 'Week that Hit Europe For Six', *Observer*, 16 May 1971.

So, between 1.00 a.m. and 2.00 a.m. on the morning of Thursday 13 May, Geoffrey Rippon accepted the text agreed by the Six as put to him by Maurice Schumann. For the first time in the ten months since it had been set up, the Conference was making real progress on a major issue. Indeed, in that same witching hour, it also agreed on a formula for cane sugar, and just before dawn, at 4.00 a.m., the outlines of a possible financial settlement were agreed as well. Moreover, an extra meeting of the Conference was set up for June to speed up the overall settlement.

At 5.15 a.m., tired but triumphant, the two Ministers held a press conference and announced 'major breakthrough'. Two and a half of the four key issues under discussion (fish was being quite deliberately kept out of the limelight at this time) had been solved in a single night session. That this was not simply due to what had happened in Brussels but at least as much to what had happened elsewhere was patent. Clearly at last there was now a political will in Paris as well as in London to go forward and try to succeed. And the patient fretwork done quietly between the officials over many months allowed the pieces of the jigsaw puzzle to fall into place quite naturally once the political will was there.

Cane Cutters and Cane Refiners: A Test Case of Third World Policy

In 1971 Britain imported about 1·4 million tons of cane sugar from Commonwealth countries under the Commonwealth Sugar Agreement at stable prices which had as a rule proved to be well above those on the world market. For an annual crop with something like a seven-year cycle from planting to the final harvest before the canes were uprooted again the guaranteed quantities and price were worth a good deal – even if the price at times proved lower than that on the world market. Such guarantees were of particular importance for those countries whose economies – their employment, balance of payments, and hence possibly their social stability – depended in large measure on their sugar exports. Many countries also had a quota at a high price under the United States Sugar Act, and Cuba had a firm market in the Soviet Union. Further quantities were given assured outlets under the International Sugar Agreement – which the EEC had failed to join: that agreement depended on sugar-exporting countries limiting themselves to certain quotas of sales. The 'free market' was thus in fact a residual market, subject to very wide price fluctuations because it was determined by a very narrow supply and demand, of only a few per cent of total world production and consumption.

The problem arose because, under the Common Agricultural Policy, beet sugar from the Six (which meant, in particular, from the prosperous large farmers of northern France) should have been given preferential access to the British market as from 1973. Moreover, with the expected expansion of wheat production in Britain under the CAP, sugar beet production was also expected to increase within Britain: beet provides an excellent rotation crop between wheat harvests. For both reasons, therefore, Britain would have to cut back her sugar imports from the Commonwealth sugar-exporting countries: these countries would in turn not merely lose their British export markets, but be forced to try to sell their crops on the world market, driving down the price and severely threatening the future of the International Sugar Agreement. The economic, social and political consequences in the Caribbean, in Mauritius and in Fiji could have proved disastrous.

What Britain asked for, therefore, were 'bankable assurances' that present quantities and prices of imports of cane sugar from Commonwealth countries could be maintained. She was asking this for the benefit of poorish developing countries – but obviously the financial interests of British firms growing, shipping and refining cane sugar were vitally affected. Indeed the 'sugar lobby', astutely headed by Lord Campbell of Eskan, was perhaps the best organized and most active of all the British interest groups seeking to influence the negotiations. It in effect operated at two levels – that of the professional groupings of sugar exporters and refiners, and that of the generalized pressure groups on Third World policy concentrated on the sugar issue. As the *Financial Times* put it: 'It looks as if the profit-seeking UK refiners will have strong motives for allying themselves to the aid lobby. Not only under the present system do they have a greater margin of efficiency than the EEC beet refiners but they are already heavily committed in terms of capital employed (perhaps to the extent of 80% assets) to cane refining equipment.'[1] Certainly this was the professional interest group which, with the justified cry of dangers brewing to the Third World, appealed most explicitly to the public; it reckoned that it had possibly seventy MPs who would vote for or against British entry using sugar as their litmus test of the acceptability of the agreement.

The phrase 'bankable assurances' was, according to Geoffrey Rippon, coined by Robert Lightbourne, the Jamaican Minister of Industry and Trade. But it had a very literal significance, as we shall see in due course. For with a seven-year crop medium-term finance has to be

[1] *Financial Times*, 29 May 1971.

provided by someone to carry the industry from planting to final harvest: and that finance clearly had to depend on the atmosphere of confidence about the industry and its future – an atmosphere in which the banks have to share for the industry to be able to carry on.

The British sugar interests were, however, not the only pressure group in the field. Just before the subject appeared on the Ministers' agenda, the French General Confederation of Sugarbeet Growers took a full page in *Le Monde* to denounce the Commonwealth Sugar Agreement as 'the upshot of the colonial era, based on . . . the mastery of the sea': 'A hundred and sixty years after the continental blockade, will the sugar war between French farmers and British refiners break out again?' The Confederation highlighted the problem of British refiners who wanted cheap cane sugar while claiming they were defenders of the Third World. It sought allies in the French industrial sector by pointing out that this was part of the nineteenth-century British method of keeping her industry competitive by importing cheap food. It argued that one must at one and the same time help the development of the poorer countries of the Commonwealth and respect Common Market rules by paying the developing countries the Community price, not the Commonwealth price:

One only has to buy half a million tons of sugar from the developing countries of the Commonwealth and pay them at the Community price to guarantee for them their sugar earnings. Thus the EEC and Britain can prove to the Third World that Europe is opposed to the exploitation of the miserable living standards of growers in the developing countries. The colonial concept of a 'world price' would be abolished in the trade between the EEC and the Commonwealth.[1]

(The arithmetic supposed that the remaining sugar could be disposed of on the world market at a price about 20% below the average price for the last ten years.)

When the Commission made its proposals in November 1970, it pointed to a fortunate synchronism: 1974 was both the earliest date at which the United Kingdom could opt out of the Commonwealth Sugar Agreement, and also the year when the Community would have to review important aspects of its own organization of the sugar market. There was, therefore, not much point in major substantive changes in 1973–74. That far ahead agreement could soon be reached all round. It was on how one dealt with the period thereafter that there

[1] *Le Monde*, 4 May 1971, p. 26.

was a sharp divergence between the Commission and the French. The Commission felt it was impossible to fix exact tonnages and prices for future imports from Commonwealth sugar exporters in a situation on which the Community itself was not to decide for another three years. Far better to defer an exact solution and combine the two problems: to overhaul the Community's own system and at the same time conclude an international agreement that would give a reasonable place to under-developed Commonwealth sugar producers (and underdeveloped associated countries) on the Community's market. Five member states agreed with the Commission's approach on this, though there were some differences on just how to word such a present political commit-ment to a future agreement on trade.

The French on the other hand wanted the quantities of Common-wealth sugar sold on the United Kingdom market to be drastically reduced over the transition period; the sugar producers of the Six could then withdraw from the unstable 'world market', leaving it to the Commonwealth sugar exporters to fill the gap and get what prices they could; in return, the Community would guarantee, not their access to the British market, but their overall earnings – by giving them a price which might under some circumstances even be higher than the Com-munity's domestic price. It was an idea abhorrent to the Commission: and Sicco Mansholt, the Vice-President in charge of agriculture, did not mince his words on the subject at a Council meeting in March.

On sugar, then, so far it was France versus the rest. There was no give on this question until after the Heath-Pompidou summit meeting had been announced on the evening of Saturday 8 May. Immediately after, on Monday 10 May, Jean-Pierre Brunet announced to the Council of Ministers that the French government had arrived at a new conclusion on the matter. As 1974 would see simultaneously the re-negotiation of the Yaoundé Convention (which governs the association of seventeen African states and Madagascar with the Community), the review of important parts of the Community's own sugar policy, and also the earliest date on which the United Kingdom could end the Commonwealth Sugar Agreement, France now proposed that the sugar question, instead of being settled in the negotiations for entry, should be left for the institutions of the enlarged Community to solve in 1974 within the general framework of the three choices open to Commonwealth countries whose economic structure was comparable to that of the present Yaoundé associates.

The first alternative was participation in the general Convention of

Association, which would be negotiated multilaterally with the present associates. The second was a special association *sui generis* under Article 238 of the Treaty (such as was in force under the Arusha Convention with the three countries of the East African Common Market, Kenya, Tanzania and Uganda). Thirdly, they could always conclude a trade agreement. (The triple offer had been open to the independent African countries in any case since 1963, when the Community, at Dutch and German insistence, had made a Declaration of Intent to that effect a precondition of their signature of the first Yaoundé Convention.) The new element, then, was that the French were willing to offer association to sugar-producing Commonwealth countries in both the Caribbean and the Pacific as well; and they were prepared to postpone the specific question of sugar to be solved in that broader framework. There was actually no specific mention of sugar in the text now proposed by the French, but the Council adopted an addition, proposed by the Belgians, which said that the sugar problem would be solved in that context and would take account of the importance of sugar for the economies of several developing countries, notably in the Commonwealth.

To accompany a specific commitment on sugar by a general offer of association was a possibility which the Commission had in fact considered. But both the Yaoundé and the Arusha Conventions involved trade preferences both by the Community to the associates, and by the associates to the Community, and had as such been under heavy fire from the United States. The Americans objected to trade discrimination and had threatened to exclude from their Generalized Preference System to all underdeveloped countries any that discriminated against the United States by preferential arrangements such as those with the EEC. To extend this system in a quite significant way right under the Americans' noses into the Caribbean and the Pacific seemed fraught with complications at a time when the EEC's trade relations with the USA were not that cordial in any case. So the offer had remained confined to independent African Commonwealth countries and to Britain's dependent territories only. Besides, in the preparatory work in the first half of 1970 the Six had agreed that the specific problem of sugar was to be settled first, the more general relationship between the Community and these independent Commonwealth countries afterwards, and to go back on those pre-negotiation agreements might open a Pandora's box indeed. Jamaica's Trade Minister, Robert Lightbourne, came to Brussels to plead for inclusion in the offer, claiming that Washington, which he had visited, quite understood. But the Commission, at this point, had still hesitated to table any proposal.

Next morning, Tuesday 11 May, Geoffrey Rippon asked for more – for stronger guarantees that these countries could go on exporting the same amounts of sugar as at present. In the afternoon he saw the Six again to demand bankable assurances, only to be told by Maurice Schumann that he had nothing to add to the morning's declarations. On Wednesday afternoon the Council was back at work on the question, with two alternative texts in front of them, both drafted by Jean-François Deniau, of which the crucial alternative formulations were: '*aura à cœur de sauvegarder les interêts*' and '*a l'intention d'assurer une place raisonnable sur les marchés communautaires*' ('will have at heart the safeguarding of the interests of' and 'intends to ensure a reasonable share of the Community's market for'). Neither formula mentioned sugar, both spoke only of primary products. And thereby hangs a tale.

When France joined the EEC, her colonies in Africa and Madagascar benefited from preferential prices and assured outlets in metropolitan France. It was France who insisted that these colonies should be brought into a system of association – the system governed by Part IV of the Rome Treaty, the same under which the British dependencies such as the Bahamas and Bermuda, Brunei and Pitcairn, the Falkland Islands and also the associated states in the Caribbean (such as Antigua, Grenada, and St Kitts-Nevis-Anguilla) would automatically become associates from 1 January 1973. But when nineteen new independent states emerged around 1960 in the process of French and Belgian decolonization, and eighteen of them – all but Guinea – asked to remain associates, a new formula was found: that of the Yaoundé Convention associating the six states of the EEC in reciprocal rights and obligations with the eighteen African associates. France wanted the other five to give guaranteed markets for certain products, notably groundnuts, to her ex-colonies. But the other five refused, and insisted on the gradual abolition of such guaranteed access, also reducing the tariff preferences on certain products which the Community had granted to these countries.

What irked the French at this juncture was not so much the thought of giving such guarantees to sugar-exporting Commonwealth countries as seeing the Dutch and Germans falling over themselves to offer to Mauritius and Fiji what they had taken away from Senegal and Madagascar. A general formula on primary products could indeed come in useful in 1974 to renew the charge and carry off guarantees not merely for sugar, in which Madagascar was in fact interested, but for groundnuts as well.

In the end, the first of Deniau's formulae was adopted, with an addendum from the Italians which was in itself a compromise: after 'primary products', read 'and particularly of sugar'. There had in the meantime been a meeting between Geoffrey Rippon and Maurice Schumann, back hotfoot from a cabinet meeting in Paris that morning. And at 1.00 a.m. the same night Geoffrey Rippon expressed his welcome for the additional declaration the Community made on top of its 1963 Declaration of Intent, but said he must consult the independent Commonwealth countries whose interests were involved.

His delegation had in the meantime also obtained an authorized English translation of the phrase '*aura à cœur*'. Although Lord Campbell was later to say that it was what his carpenter in the south of France said when he meant that he would not in fact have time to do the job, but would feel slightly guilty about it, the official text as embodied in Protocol 22 of the Treaty of Accession translated the now classic phrase 'will have as its firm purpose'.

The sugar issue had been chosen in Paris and agreed between Christopher Soames and Michel Jobert as one with which, in return for Community preference, the pre-summit atmosphere was to be sweetened. It was one where, in any case, the French were morally on very weak ground: and the way the problem was solved even opened up for them renewed chances of obtaining something from the other five – with Britain as their chief ally.

The scene, at this point, shifts to London. This was not because the British government wanted it to happen. It hoped to have its consultation with the governments of the sugar-producing countries in the pleasanter climate of the Caribbean where press, radio and television coverage might be less intense and any untoward effects could be contained more easily, with no black faces on television and in the lobbies of the House to cause a political stir for exploitation by anti-Marketeers. But the sugar-exporting governments, advised and loosely co-ordinated by the Commonwealth Sugar Exporters' Association, had insisted on coming to London, which their Ministers love to do in any case. (It was the cricket and tennis season, and particularly in the West Indies there is a proper sense of priorities about such things.) The overseas Ministers had a long chaotic meeting in Jamaica House, so crowded the chairman could start the proceedings only after crawling under his table to the chair, and finally delegated a few of their number to help Robert Lightbourne, the Jamaican Trade Minister, with his speech during the night. Fortunately, Robert Lightbourne had already prepared himself in advance, and in Lancaster House next morning as their spokesman he appealed to the mother country not to let them down: 'You see before you a group of bewildered men. . . .' It was by all accounts a most skilful performance, hard-hitting and sentimental by turns.

However, a change was already in the process of coming about. Lord Campbell had declared himself 'appalled' and wrote to *The Times* on 11 May 'the French offer as reported makes no concession whatever to the British proposals and solves none of our problems'. But by the beginning of June he had turned the issue inside out. In tireless night sessions at the Commonwealth Ministers' and Prime Ministers' hotels, he urged them not to reject the Brussels formula, but to seize it with both hands and insist that it meant just what they had been asking for. He could of course point out that if they themselves were dissatisfied with it and proclaimed the fact to the world, how much more dissatisfied would the bankers be, and how great and possibly fatal a blow this would be to the atmosphere of confidence which sugar investments require. By dint of personality and perseverance he succeeded.

Whether he was 'selling the pass' to safeguard short-term commercial interests, as some might be tempted to suggest, or setting in motion a statesmanlike process of hoisting the EEC by its own petard, only time will prove in the end. The odds are that he was convinced by the government that nothing more could be obtained from the Community, and that he could see the parallelism of interest of France and Britain on guaranteed markets for primary products. In any case it was a decisive, if surprising, *volte-face*. 'Without Jock Campbell', someone was later to say, 'we could never have got in.' There are, as we have seen, quite a few individuals of whom that may be said – perhaps with a degree of truth in each case, for it was a task that needed many heads and hands. Certainly in Lord Campbell's case it must be remembered that he was not merely chairman of Booker McConnell, the West Indian sugar firm, but also a Labour peer, and chairman of the New Statesman and Nation Publishing Company to boot. Against his cries of conscience, quite a few Labour MPs might have found it very difficult to vote as they did, or even to abstain.

Be that as it may, on the second day of the meeting a drafting committee prepared a communiqué which was designed to interpret the Brussels formula in an entirely bankable manner. 'The British Government and the other Commonwealth Governments participating regard the offer as a firm assurance of a secure and continuing market in the enlarged Community, on fair terms, for the quantities of sugar covered by the Commonwealth Sugar Agreement in respect of all its existing developing member countries.' They gave notice to the Community: 'The developing Commonwealth countries will continue to plan their future production on this basis.'

At the 7 June meeting of the Conference in Luxemburg, Geoffrey Rippon, having first circulated the Lancaster House declaration in advance, had it distributed again round the table and then accepted the solution reached in May. Maurice Schumann, as chairman, emphasized that the document distributed was of course for information only. (Its text does not even figure in the minutes.) But then by its nature the Lancaster House declaration could not commit the Six, or anyone but the United Kingdom government. On the other hand, whatever the formal position, there is no doubt about the degree to which it highlighted the moral obligation which the Community simply by virtue of its enlargement could no longer escape in any case – as Pierre Harmel had pointed out, in the same room in Luxemburg, on the first day of the negotiations a year before.

The Virtues of Algebra: The Budget Contribution

At the crucial May meeting just before the Paris summit the British delegation had accepted a framework for progressive participation by the candidate countries in the financing of the Community's budget, in the presentation of which the French had for the first time implicitly conceded the notion that Britain might be granted more than five years before she paid her full contribution without transitional rebate. The system had been set out in algebraic terms, so as to avoid any quantitative implications at the early stage. Let A be the percentage base of the budget which Britain would be contributing had she been a member in 1970. (B served for Denmark, C for Ireland, D for Norway.) Each country's base was to be calculated by its share in the gross national product of the total Community. Thereafter it could vary by 1% until 1974 and 2% per annum until 1977. Now let N be the percentage of this theoretical contribution which the Community would actually demand from the new members in the first year of their membership, P that to be demanded in the second, and so forth, to S that in the fifth

year of membership. Then, so ran the formula, the maximum contribution to be exacted from the new members would be the agreed
percentage of the suitably adjusted base percentage.

In June it was time to assign arithmetic values to these algebraic
variables. A, B, C and D were a matter of calculation – and the
Statistical Office of the Communities had ascertained that, in 1970, the
United Kingdom would have had 19·02%, Denmark 2·24%, Ireland
0·60% and Norway 1·66% of the enlarged Community's gross
national product. (At Deniau's suggestion, the 0·02% was dropped
from the United Kingdom base figure. By the time Britain actually
came to join, no one was in any doubt, her percentage of the total
would have dropped rather further than that in any case.)

So then it came to the political exercise of how to fix N and S – the
inverse of the rebates to be granted in the first and the last year of the
transition period. Everyone was agreed that between the two values
there should be a fairly smooth progression, either linear or else para-
bolic, and since March it was also agreed that there should not be any
sudden jump between 1977 and 1978: indeed the Commission suggested
that a governing clause should still operate for two years after the
transition period, and that the corrective mechanism should ensure that
neither that jump nor the one following it be greater than the jump
between 1976 and 1977. That was a proposal which, at this stage,
Giscard d'Estaing did not wish to oppose. The Ministers were agreed
that S should lie in the region of 90%, but there were strong divergencies on the value of N: the Italians proposed 30%, the French 60%.
Since the Commission wanted to get back to about 8% or 9% of the
total budget for the first year (which some of the delegations thought
rather high), and splitting the difference between the Italian and
French proposals on N would result in just such a figure, it proposed
that N=45%. After much further discussion, this Commission
proposal was accepted by both sides.

We can thus now see a certain Gallic logic in the at first sight rather
extraordinary percentage figures to two decimal places with which
the negotiations on the issue concluded. It might most easily be set out
in the following table, in which the figures in brackets make explicit
the implied jumps from one year to the next. The clause governing
maximal increases to 1978 and 1979 would if necessary then limit the
contribution to around 21·5% in 1978 and 24·4% in 1979.

If, following the assumption behind some of the early calculations,
we suppose a Community budget of $4 billion in 1973 and $4·5

The Gross British Budget Contribution in the Transition Period

Year	Assessment base as percentage of budget	Percentage of base actually due	Percentage of budget due
1973	101% of A= 19·19% (+0·19%)	N=45% (+11%)	8·64% (+2·21%)
1974	101% of 1973 base= 19·38% (+0·39%)	P= 56% (+11·5%)	10·85% (+2·49%)
1975	102% of 1974 base= 19·77% (+0·39%)	Q=67·5% (+11·5%)	13·34% (+2·68%)
1976	102% of 1975 base= 20·16% (+0·40%)	R=79% (+13%)	16·02% (+2·90%)
1977	102% of 1976 base= 20·56%	S= 92%	18·92%

billion in 1977, that involved Britain in gross contributions of $350 million in the first and $850 million in the last year of the transition period – about £150 million in the first and £350 million in the last year. Some of that money would, of course, be coming back to Britain through the Community's spending, but not very much. Measured against the opening position of 2·6–3% on the British side and the initial French hints at over 20%, these figures seemed a fair half-way house, far removed from the rigid extreme positions at the outset. But having come off those positions and towards a compromise circuitously, by an ingeniously logical route, after a decent interval and in a very different climate round the negotiating table, this proved in fact a politically practicable way out of the impasse – and one very typical of Community procedure.

A Disappearing Act: Sterling

In another respect the discussions on 7 June took a bizarre turn. When it came to economic, financial and monetary problems, Raymond Barre went over the conclusions reached by the high-level experts of five of the six member states – proposals that fell well short of the extreme demands reiterated that very morning by the French expert before Giscard d'Estaing's arrival. The Commission wanted Britain to declare that she accepted the aims of monetary and economic union, recognized the incompatibility with such a union of maintaining a reserve currency, and would gradually wipe out sterling's reserve currency character. British discrimination in favour of the developed Commonwealth countries over capital exports must be gradually eliminated under the control of Community institutions; the British government must stabilize the sterling balances; and the Community institutions must, before April 1973, examine the problems posed by the renewal of the Basle Agreements and lay down ways for the official sterling balances to be gradually reduced, taking account of Britain's economy, of the interests of sterling holders, and of the world monetary system. In return, the Community would be assuming certain responsibilities for the solution of the problem. Its other members were in any case bound to give short-term foreign exchange assistance under Article 108 of the Treaty – even if solutions might have to be found in a larger framework than that of the EEC alone.

Several national delegations supported him, and Giscard d'Estaing – not perhaps without a wry sense of humour in view of what was to follow – was glad to note that France's partners no longer suspected her motives for going into these questions in detail. Why not ask the British what they intended to do?

Barre was asked to put these ideas in a form suitable for presentation to the British during the lunch-hour. But before he could even distribute his four-page text, in came Geoffrey Rippon, who distributed the Lancaster House communiqué on sugar, asked for the fisheries problem to be given more urgency, and was himself asked about sterling. At the Commission's suggestion he had already, at the end of the May meetings, read into the record of the Conference as a 'matter of mutual concern to us' statements he and the Chancellor of the Exchequer had made on sterling to the House of Commons. This time he could add a declaration patently tailor-made for the occasion:

Yes, Mr President, . . .

2 We are prepared to envisage an orderly and gradual run-down of official sterling balances after our accession.

3 We shall be ready to discuss after our entry into the Communities what measures might be appropriate to achieve a progressive alignment of the external characteristics and practices in relation to sterling with those of other currencies in the Community in the context of progress towards economic and monetary union in the enlarged Community, and we are confident that official sterling can be handled in a way which will enable us to take our full part in that progress.

4 In the meantime we shall manage our policies with a view to stabilizing the official sterling balances in a way which would be consistent with these longer term objectives.

5 I hope that the Community will regard this statement as disposing satisfactorily of the question of sterling and associated matters, leaving only the

arrangements for UK compliance with the Directives relating to capital movements under the Treaty of Rome to be settled in the course of the negotiations.

All fair enough, no more than the government had already repeatedly promised, and hardly very specific. The *coup de théâtre* followed as Geoffrey Rippon left the room and Maurice Schumann turned to Valéry Giscard d'Estaing. The French Finance Minister replied that he was quite satisfied with that declaration. There were gasps. Collapse of stout parties all round the table. Terrible time-bomb exhibited as maggoty old marrow. The Germans asked if they could at least have a German translation before the whole matter was regarded as settled. But if France was satisfied, the other five delegations could only in their turn accept Britain's assurances. Raymond Barre, obviously flabbergasted, said all he could do was to take note of this agreement.

Certainly people felt relief that the bilateralism they had encouraged had cleared the air. But had it not gone too far for the good of the Community's financial – and also political – future? There could not but be some resentment among the other five at having been treated in quite such an offhand manner by the French – first marched up the hill to fight the sterling battle and then contemptuously told to find their own way down again in disarray. As for the British, if they had cooked it all up bilaterally at the Paris summit anyway, then they would hardly need any more help from the 'friendly five' over things like New Zealand and fisheries – they were clearly capable of fixing their own little solutions with the French. 'We had quite a job for a time after that convincing them that we still needed their support', as one of the negotiators said later. It was a blatantly brutal demonstration of the new-found *entente amicale*: whether it was the most tactful introduction of the *entente* to the Community institutions is a rather different matter.

New Zealand and Other Issues

Compared with the mathematical complexities of the budget contribution and the verbal subtleties on cane sugar imports, New Zealand dairy products were intellectually rather plainer sailing. Britain wanted long-term guarantees of access for New Zealand butter and cheese to the British market. The French wanted Britain to buy Community butter and cheese instead, and did not want to allow any further prolongation of transition periods for one or for the other beyond 1977, certainly not beyond 1979, the latest year towards which the financial regulations had now pushed possible transitional measures. In marked contrast to the lack of any effective effort by the Australians, John Marshall, the New Zealand Deputy Prime Minister, had come to Europe in mid-May to help with his own efforts at diplomacy direct with the Six and to stiffen the stance of the British delegation. (He was even smuggled into its offices in Luxemburg by a back door at the crisis stage of the night so as to be instantly on hand.) He excited some admiration for his doggedness when, having got more than anyone could really expect him to get, he sent Geoffrey Rippon back into the conference room in the early hours of the morning with the exhortation: 'Get more!' But then he had nothing to lose,˙ only another bit extra to gain: it was the British delegation that was expending goodwill on New Zealand's behalf. Indeed, perhaps not only goodwill. Though this is denied in Community circles, the British felt, before the June session when these two main problems remained on the agenda, that the more the Six gave way to New Zealand, the less would they give on the figure for 'N'. Implicitly, at the end, the British taxpayer would thus pay the Community to let the New Zealanders sell more of their dairy products in Britain: and explicitly the New Zealand agreement was made to depend on a satisfactory budget settlement.

The New Zealanders did in fact get themselves an exceptionally favourable deal. Although they had known for ten years of Britain's intention to join the Community (and had switched some of their other exports to places like Japan), they were still heavily dependent on the British market for their butter and cheese. It followed, so Jean-Pierre Brunet argued, that only a quite definite timetable to phase them out of the British market would really get them moving towards diversification of markets or of production. The French delegation would hope that by the end of 1977 the preferences for New Zealand would have three-quarters disappeared. In no case were they prepared to see any permanent arrangement for New Zealand derogating from the Common Agricultural Policy. If they had to make any further concessions, it would be only on the side of butter. (Cheese, as we have already noted, is a commodity the French President has particularly close to his heart.)

The final outcome was again a compromise. The Commission in November 1970 had proposed – for 1977 – 50% of present imports in terms of milk equivalent (the phrase allowed some substitution if necessary between butter and cheese). In Paris Christopher Soames, now negotiating bilaterally with Maurice Schumann, was asking for 80%. By the time of the Luxemburg meeting, the Dutch had raised their figure of an offer from 56% to 61% – and one by one, with the Belgians coming along last, the other four delegations accepted that figure. Only the French were sticking at an offer that would have come to 17%.

Rather more important than the precise percentages until 1977 was the question of principle as to whether there could be a major derogation from the Common Agricultural Policy in New Zealand's favour thereafter. The Commission's November proposal had specifically included this for butter. The French said no. When it came to the crunch in June 1971, Maurice Schumann broke off the proceedings with the other five in high dudgeon at their readiness to surrender on one point after another. Jean-François Deniau was at this point in bed with fever, but Franco-Maria Malfatti presented a saving formula and then steered through not only the review clause, but also a figure of 80% for butter – much higher than anyone on the Community side had yet conceded, but which the Commission's negotiators thought, in the atmosphere of that night, they could just put through. When Geoffrey Rippon after that still wanted to improve further on the price clause, it was the Dutch Minister who firmly insisted the British must be told that enough was enough.

ϟ   What New Zealand thus obtained was an export quota to Britain of 71% milk equivalent – 80% of present butter imports, though a much lower level for cheese (20% in 1977 after 90%, 80%, 60% and 40% in the preceding years). Very important was the guaranteed price laid down for butter – a substantially higher one than New Zealand was getting only a year or two before, since a shortage of butter had raised butter prices to abnormal levels in the meantime. Moreover, there was to be a review of the butter problem by the enlarged Community in 1975. Taking into consideration progress towards an effective world agreement on milk products (towards which the Community promised to work) and New Zealand's own progress towards diversification, further exceptional measures might then be taken on butter imports beyond the end of 1977 – but not on cheese.

It was 4.00 a.m. in the morning in Luxemburg when these compromises were reached – early afternoon in New Zealand with which John Marshall was in close touch by telephone. The New Zealanders were not at all dissatisfied – where butter was concerned, they would in fact for those five years probably be better off than they would have been had Britain not decided to enter the EEC. They thought, actually, that unanimity of member states as a precondition for further exceptional measures for New Zealand beyond 1977 had been repulsed that night. They did not want to see their country's future exposed to a French veto, John Marshall had said. In fact, though missing in the White Paper, the provision turned up again like a bad penny in the Treaty of Accession (Protocol 18). But it was, after all, implicit in any case in the way the Community has worked in practice: important exceptions to normal rules require unanimity on a proposal of the Commission. (And in any case it was hardly for the British, after what had transpired at the Paris summit, to complain when a requirement of unanimity was set out in black and white.)

With New Zealand and the British contribution to the budget going so well, the tactical question must have posed itself to the British delegation how much more to try to tie up in the course of those two hectic days and nights in Luxemburg before the long summer vacation. They were later to be accused of 'slipping in a question never mentioned before' – that of hill farming. In fact hill farming had been put on the agenda in George Brown's presentation of 1967 and kept there by Anthony Barber the previous year. What may be justified is the charge that it was introduced at this meeting with relatively little preparation (a fortnight with the Commission and a few days with the member states) and resolved in only the vaguest of ways with an exchange of head-nodding courtesies set out later in the final Act of the Treaty of Accession:

Mr G. Rippon: I should be grateful for the Community's confirmation of my understanding that it is necessary for all members of the enlarged Community who face situations of this kind to deal with the problem of maintaining reasonable incomes for farmers in such areas.

Mr M. Schumann: The special conditions obtaining in certain areas of the enlarged Community may indeed require action. . . . Such action must, of course, as you have just said, be in conformity with the provisions of the treaty and the common agricultural policy.

One may leave it to the lawyers to ask what kind of international law was created by this exchange. What is beyond doubt is that it bears witness to an atmosphere of negotiation far removed from the dogged eager beaver quibbles over commas and second decimal places of earlier in the year – and even earlier in the same month.

The British delegation afterwards wondered if it should really have fish on its conscience. Might it just have been possible, in the euphoric exhaustion of that last night, to get through the Conference a solution to the problem of fishing limits before it became too tortuous, with various sub-problems involving molluscs and crustaceans, movable and immovable? In fact they tried to force the issue, unofficially proposing a *status quo* until the enlarged Community could work out a generally accepted solution; but they failed. On this point the Commission was dead opposed to the British delegation. The fisheries issue was even more important to Norway and Ireland than to Britain, and the relations between the candidates were involved no less than those of each of the candidates with the Six.

The Danes had understood that, in a Community, fishing limits could not remain a national prerogative: but the British, the Irish and the Norwegians seemed at times to imply that it was not for the Community, but for them, to decide on these matters, and their attitude thus appeared to call in question far bigger issues than those of fish. It took months – from July until October – for the Permanent Representatives of the Six even to agree amongst themselves on the framework of a solution, and the twelve-mile limit and the wording of the ten-year review clause took bitter bargaining right until Christmas – bargaining in which Geoffrey Rippon's bluntness did not always pay dividends. The bilateral channels had to be opened up again in a big way, Christopher Soames talking to Maurice Schumann in Paris in a whole series of meetings – but this time it was by no means only the French who were opposing the British viewpoint. The Commission's diagnosis that this tricky issue could only be solved last and under the pressure of impending signature had not been far wrong.

At the turn of the year, the negotiations became in fact fairly frenzied – though by now there were no further large political battles to be fought, just a great many little wrinkles to be ironed out. Points of drafting raised new substantive questions that no one had really thought through before, and of course legally valid versions had to be produced in eight equally authentic versions (including Gaelic). Hopes of signing the Treaty before Aldo Moro would cease to be Chairman of the Council had to be abandoned in November: it was little short of a miracle that the legal and linguistic experts, sitting from morning until late at night for weeks at a stretch, managed to get the whole text straight in time for the signature ceremonies in Brussels on 22 January 1972.

In the British embassy in Brussels, that day, there was a sentimental lunch-party in the pale winter sunshine. Edward Heath, fresh from Strasbourg where he had been presented for his work for European unity with the FVS Prize donated by a German industrialist, entertained Jean Monnet and presented him with the Queen's appointment as an honorary member of the Order of Companion of Honour. It was over fifty years since Jean Monnet, now eighty-four, had first worked, during the First World War, on Franco-British collaborative efforts.

In the Palais d'Egmont, meanwhile, the statesmen and elder statesmen of Western Europe were assembling for the ceremony of signature. Harold Macmillan, who had been the first British Prime Minister to feel the winds of change in Europe and had sought to reverse 'a thousand years of British history' was there. Harold Wilson, who had put in the application which was, that day, being accepted, had refused to come – he was attending a football match – but George Brown had accepted a personal invitation instead. Duncan Sandys, Jeremy Thorpe, Sir Alec Douglas-Home, Geoffrey Rippon and Sir Con O'Neill were there. Paul-Henri Spaak, Étienne Hirsch, Walter Hallstein were there – and inevitably one thought back to the ones who were there no longer, Konrad Adenauer, Alcide de Gasperi, Robert Schuman. They would have been satisfied that at last the Community was extending beyond the mere six who banded together twenty-one years before – but would they have been satisfied with the intensity of that Community, with its political cohesion, its democratic structure, its social responsibility? In so many ways the idealism of those early years had evaporated. The functional sobriety of the occasion, the uniform dark suits of the bespectacled officials, were bound to mark a slightly hollow triumph compared with the dreams of the 'forties.

For motives irrelevant to the occasion, someone threw some printers' ink at the British Prime Minister as he came to the hall, and the ceremony was delayed by an hour: lengthy speeches (including Jack Lynch's preamble in Gaelic – translated by a wit as 'you have three minutes to leave the building') and then came the procession of signatories each making their mark. The ten governments had committed themselves. But it remained for the applicants to obtain, in their own countries, the approval of parliaments or people. For the Norwegians that hurdle was to prove too high. But for the British government, also, while the battles in Paris and Brussels had been won, the battle in Westminster was by no means over.

PART TWO

6 The Government and the Conservatives

Pro bono publico, no bloody panico
Rear-Admiral Morgan Giles, MP

Whether it fully realized it or not – and the latter is probably the case – the Conservative Party took its most decisive step towards British entry into the EEC eight years before 1973. It was in July 1965 that, in the first election it had ever held for a party leader, it replaced Sir Alec Douglas-Home not by Reginald Maudling, but by Edward Heath.

Reginald Maudling was a very able politician, and might have led the party with great success. But in three particulars he is a very different man from Edward Heath. Where Heath plans his political moves (as he does his yacht-racing) with meticulous care and attention to each detail, Maudling has been known, on a number of occasions, to be prepared to make do with more approximate information and activity. Secondly, where Heath is determined at all times to win, Maudling appears a much more relaxed man, not always sure the game is worth the nervous effort. Thirdly, there is a difference in their approach to Britain's role in Europe. Maudling has no particular leaning towards the European continent, possibly even dislikes some Continental nationalities anyway, and led the negotiations in 1957–58 that sought to give Britain reciprocal free trade with Western Europe without committing her to tight Community rules or the play of Community institutions. Heath on the other hand made his maiden speech in 1950 in condemnation of Attlee's and Bevin's refusal even to negotiate for British entry into the Schuman Plan, and, while there are those in Parliament who claim that as Chief Whip in the 'fifties he 'cheerfully sat on the more ardent Europeans', he sees in British entry into the European Communities the main theme and justification of his whole political career.

Edward Heath is not a man to wear his heart on his sleeve. It is thus not entirely obvious how much of his commitment to Western Europe is reason, how much emotion. He can accuse those who see a united Western Europe as primarily a step towards a world system of ordered social change as being mere 'tactical Europeans', in contrast to his own visceral convictions. Certainly he saw something of the Continent in his early formative years:

He had first travelled as a schoolboy, and visited Germany just before the war, with his Jewish friend Madron Seligman (thirty years later he told Willy Brandt and his guests how he first came to Düsseldorf as a student, sitting and drinking on the Königsallee, and then came back in the army to find Düsseldorf destroyed).[1]

As a student he had visited Spain during the Civil War, and had then himself emerged from the Second World War with the rank of lieutenant-colonel. All these experiences were a powerful factor – if in a sense of a negative kind. Already in his maiden speech in the House, back in 1950, he had gone far beyond the line taken on the Schuman Plan by his party leaders. While Churchill argued that Britain should be represented at the negotiations to answer 'no' if anything too supranational was proposed, and Harold Macmillan said in Strasbourg: 'One thing is certain and we may as well face it. Our people will not hand over to any supranational authority the right to close down our pits and our steelworks', the newly elected Member for Bexley echoed the logic of Jean Monnet:

Anyone going to Germany today is bound to be impressed by the fact that the German dynamic has returned; that Germany is once again working hard and producing hard, and that therefore Germany will become a major factor in Europe. I suggest that there are only two ways of dealing with that situation. One is to attempt to prolong control, which the Chancellor has already dismissed as being undesirable and impractical. The only other way is to lead Germany into the one way we want her to go, and I believe that these discussions would give us a chance of leading Germany into the way we want her to go.

And he concluded squarely:

After the First World War we all thought it would be extremely easy to secure peace and prosperity in Europe. After the Second World War we all realized that it was going to be extremely difficult; and it will be extremely difficult to

[1] Anthony Sampson, *The New Anatomy of Britain*, Hodder & Stoughton, London, 1971, p. 90.

make a plan of this kind succeed. What I think worries many of us on this side of the House is that, even if the arguments put forward by the Government are correct, we do not feel that behind those arguments is really the will to succeed, and it is that will which we most want to see. It was said long ago in this House that magnanimity in politics is not seldom the truest wisdom. I appeal tonight to the Government to follow that dictum, and to go into the Schuman Plan to develop Europe and to co-ordinate it in the way suggested.[1]

He was to return to the same argument in his broadcast to the nation twenty-one years later on 8 July 1971, when the main terms for British entry had been successfully negotiated:

Many of you have fought in Europe, as I did, or have lost father, or brothers, or husbands who fell fighting in Europe. I say to you now, with that experience in my memory, that joining the Community, working together with them for our joint security and prosperity, is the best guarantee we can give ourselves of a lasting peace in Europe.

But there is also a strong positive side to his European sentiments – not simply a way of warding off evil, but one of promoting what he values. His knowledge of Continental languages is slender, and when teased after a brave attempt at the summit meeting in Paris he was to confess to the House, 'I make no claims to mastery of the French language'.[2] But he sees a great deal on the Continent that he thinks is well done, and perhaps at times done better than in Britain: concern for design and for civic amenity, a civilized style of living from food and drink to less narrow-minded social conventions – a style that, in some countries and in some places at least, avoids both the pin-headed rigidities of the British class system and the brash vulgarities of the American pursuit of the dollar. More than one of his colleagues has remarked that they sense in him a certain feeling of liberation, greater ease and more relaxed self-confidence in his dealings with Continentals than in the context of British, particularly Conservative, circles. On 14 July 1971 he was quite explicit to his party about the danger of the country 'becoming obsessed with petty internal quarrels, becoming narky, bitter and unpleasant'.

Perhaps it is his special feeling for music and the arts in general that has instilled in him a profound sense of mission, which he expressed at the Royal Academy banquet on 28 April 1971:

[1] Hansard, 26 June 1950, cols 1963, 1964.
[2] Hansard, 24 May 1971, col. 45.

'The artists, the writers, and the musicians have shown the economists and the politicians the way. We have to bring to the creation of European economic and political unity the same creative effort, the same interplay of ideas and aspiration, the same ability to share our achievements that enabled them to make a reality of European cultural unity.'

He went on to say that if we could build Europe as a city at unity in itself, that had peace within its walls and plenteousness within its palaces, then it would be a place where the arts flourished and were honoured, a place where artists could live and work, a place where men could sing the merry songs of peace to all their neighbours.

'It is no mean or selfish objective which we seek. It is a noble ideal, long established in the traditions of European thought and well worthy of the aspirations of our generation. When we achieve our ambitions then history will indeed know that the spirit of man has at last triumphed over the divisions and dissensions, the hatred and the strife that plagued our continent for a thousand years. Humanity will be grateful that our European civilization, to which it already owes so much, will be able to flower afresh in unity and concord.'[1]

It was this personal commitment to Europe on the part of the Party Leader which prevented the Conservatives from giving up in the course of the 'sixties, prevented them from opposing Harold Wilson's attempt to enter the Community, and then committed the Conservative Party to pursue that application when on all the evidence the majority of local associations and a very large section of the Parliamentary Party were distinctly cool or hostile. He had fought some lonely battles on his way up the political ladder, and come through by sheer dogged determination. At the end of 1970 and the beginning of 1971 there were some who feared that his stubbornness in this cause could split the Conservative Party and risk his being replaced as Prime Minister or destroy his government. It was one of the ironies of our story that – as in a copybook melodrama of 'virtue rewarded' – whatever other difficulties his government got into, on this issue it ended up not with

[1] *The Times*, 29 April 1971. When Edward Heath announced later that British entry would be celebrated with performances of music and drama and art exhibitions, he provoked mocking Labour laughter; the Prime Minister retorted (after promising football matches for the Leader of the Opposition) that he noted Labour's demonstration 'by its display just now that it is just a philistine party'. Actually the Conservative anti-Marketeers had the last word, Hugh Fraser suggesting entry should coincide with the Feast of the Holy Innocents and (in view of the rise in meat prices) the Minister of Food should appear dressed as a beefeater. (Hansard, 13 June 1972, cols 1256–7.)

his party, but that of his opponents deeply divided, and not his leadership, but Harold Wilson's overcast with serious doubts.

In the General Election of 18 June 1970 which put Edward Heath into No. 10 Downing Street, the EEC had been an extremely muted issue. The 8,680 words of Mr Heath's own campaign speeches that formed the subject of the Conservative Central Office handouts (and were therefore on the one hand considered most important by his own party machine, and on the other given widest coverage in the press and on television) no doubt provided the basis for the electors' impressions of the content of his message. But only 3% of those words were devoted to Conservative policy on the Common Market.[1] Admittedly 70% were about Labour's misdeeds, so that the Common Market did occupy about a tenth of the positive aspects of his message. Nevertheless, no one can claim that this was the major theme.

The Conservative election manifesto itself was careful not to go too far on the substance. Like the Labour manifesto, it did not get on to the European issue until page 28:

A Stronger Britain in the World

If we can negotiate the right terms, we believe that it would be in the long-term interest of the British people for Britain to join the European Economic Community, and that it would make a major contribution to both the prosperity and the security of our country. The opportunities are immense.

Economic growth and a higher standard of living would result from having a larger market.

But we must also recognize the obstacles. There would be short-term disadvantages in Britain going into the European Economic Community which must be weighed against the long-term benefits. Obviously there is a price we would not be prepared to pay. Only when we negotiate will it be possible to determine whether the balance is a fair one, and in the interests of Britain.

Our sole commitment is to negotiate: no more, no less. As the negotiations proceed we will report regularly through Parliament to the country.

A Conservative Government would not be prepared to recommend to Parliament, nor would Members of Parliament approve, a settlement which was unequal or unfair. In making this judgment, Ministers and Members will listen to the views of their constituents and have in mind, as is natural and legitimate, primarily the effect of entry upon the standard of living of the individual citizens whom they represent.[2]

[1] David Butler and Michael Pinto-Duschinsky, *The British General Election of 1970*, Macmillan, London, 1971, p. 444.

[2] *A Better Tomorrow: The Conservative Programme for the Next Five Years* (1970), p. 28.

The approval of the settlement was thus, according to the manifesto, to be made squarely by Ministers and Parliament – the people would only be listened to, their interests and the best ways of meeting them were to be judged not by themselves but by the politicians. (Had Edward Heath stuck to that formula, he would have avoided a great deal of pointed accusation from the anti-Marketeers later: as it was, he also used less firm language on the procedure.) On the substance, on the other hand, the party was later to regret having defined its commitment in such a minimal way. The quotation was to echo all over the country through the summer and autumn of 1971: 'Our sole commitment is to negotiate: no more, no less.'

Their opponents came to use variations of the concept of a 'mandate' to claim that the Conservatives, on the evidence of their own manifesto, were in 1971 going far beyond anything they had asked the electorate to endorse in 1970. Certainly the individual Conservative candidates in their local election addresses sent to all electors did not emphasize the picture of a party hell-bent on entry into the EEC. An analysis of 95% of all Conservative candidates' addresses showed that 62% of these made no mention of Europe at all, 15% mentioned it ambiguously, 11% were opposed to joining the EEC (7% adamantly so), 10% were pro-entry with reservations, and only 2% were strongly pro-entry.[1]

In a sense this is perhaps not surprising. For one thing, the issue hardly fitted into the conventional cleavage of 'left' versus 'right' and threatened, if it were allowed to boil up too much, to destroy the façade of unity of each of the parties. Moreover, all three party leaders were, after all, taking very much the same line – that it depended on the terms, but that if the terms were right Britain should enter: and before the opening even of the negotiations, no one had to come cleaner than that on the substance. Moreover, on the procedure, all three party leaders rejected the idea, canvassed in various quarters, of a referendum, and both Edward Heath and Harold Wilson also rejected the idea of a free vote in the House on the issue.

The Nuffield 1970 election study calls the Common Market 'the most recurrent of the issues that never really received any limelight'.[2] Only Enoch Powell and the Scottish Nationalists made it into a general campaign issue and even then it does not figure in the top ten or twelve subjects dealt with on radio, on either major television network, or in

---

[1] Butler and Pinto–Duschinsky, op. cit., p. 440.
[2] ibid., p. 159.

party broadcasts.[1] But it clearly was on some voters' minds all the same, coming after high prices but before taxes and immigration in subjects raised on the doorstep – at least where general issues, rather than private worries, were raised, which was not all that often.[2] There is, however, no evidence that any perceptible number of voters were swayed by the Common Market issue when it came to the polling day.[3]

'It is an embarrassing reflection on democracy', Anthony Sampson wrote, 'that, ten days after an election in which the Common Market was scarcely mentioned, it should emerge as the central political issue.'[4] But on 30 June 1970, just twelve days after the poll, the negotiations opened in Brussels; so in the formation of his government Edward Heath had to bear in mind that this was where his government proposed to make its major foreign policy initiative – in some senses indeed its major overall endeavour.

In certain ways this posed fewer problems than one might have expected. The press speculated about the people in the party who were thought to be lukewarm on Europe. The Foreign Secretaryship went back to Sir Alec Douglas-Home, who had occupied it (as Heath's superior) during the 1961–63 attempt to enter the Market. He proved a staunch advocate of entry. Some argued that Reginald Maudling was given the one major portfolio that would keep him, as far as departmental responsibilities went, almost entirely out of the Common Market issue: the Home Office. Yet not only was this an appointment that fell into place if Iain Macleod was to go to the Exchequer, but to see it that way was also an unnecessary imputation of motives: Reginald Maudling had made up his mind that he would do nothing to undermine party unity on the Market any more than on any other issue. Quintin Hogg, who had certainly had his misgivings in the past, reverted to the House of Lords as Lord Hailsham, and became Lord Chancellor. As for Enoch Powell, whatever services he claimed to have rendered by his speeches on immigration problems in the closing stages of the campaign, there could be no question of his serving in any government presided over by the new Prime Minister: Edward Heath was clearly revolted by the instincts to which the former professor of Classics was appealing, and which had mobilized London

[1] ibid., p. 210.
[2] ibid., p. 326.
[3] How little candidates' views on the issue affected their performance at the polls is demonstrated, ibid., pp. 405–6.
[4] *Observer*, 28 June 1970.

dockers to march in his support. Indeed Heath had publicly pledged himself to exclude Enoch Powell in any case. The Ministry of Agriculture went to James Prior, a close associate of the Prime Minister and a cheerful farming figure who was also a convinced European anxious to reorganize farming to make the most of European opportunities. And the man whom Edward Heath in June 1970 put in immediate charge of the negotiations was the same whom he had previously made his choice as chairman of the Conservative Party, and whom he was later to promote to be Chancellor of the Exchequer – Anthony Barber. He was, in other words, entrusting the negotiations in the first place to someone for whom he clearly had the highest regard and with whom he had found it congenial to work in the closest harmony.

In a list of some fifty Ministers and some further twenty Under-Secretaries of State, a certain amount of care had to be taken not to put likely anti-Marketeers into positions that would prove difficult for them to hold later – and cause embarrassment to the government if they resigned. One of those to whom the question was quite openly put as to whether he would be willing to serve in a government that took Britain into the EEC was Neil Marten, who had already held minor office as Parliamentary Secretary in the Ministry of Aviation from 1962–64. Since he replied very frankly that he would find this impossible, he was not given office. On the other hand Edward Taylor, though known to be not very favourable to entry, was thought not to require having the question put to him. This proved a minor error of judgment, for he decided in September 1971 to resign from his post as one of the Under-Secretaries of State in the Scottish Office. The only other resignation from a government appointment over the Common Market was to be that of one of the assistant whips, Jasper More. As it happened, he could be replaced by someone very doubtful on the issue, who then naturally voted with the government. ('Very neat', as one cabinet Minister agreed.) So the government – with these two very minor exceptions – remained monolithic. And what might have been feared to be a major hurdle later on – getting cabinet approval for the terms that came out of Brussels – proved to be no problem at all.

The Government and Party Leadership as Persuaders

From July 1970 until July 1971 British policy on the Common Market remained bi-partisan. On the substance, both parties were committed to attempting to join if the terms were right; on the procedure, both parties were committed to going in after a decision by Parliament, and all parties were firmly on record against any referendum. Moreover, the last vote taken by the House of Commons on the issue had been the overwhelming one of 486 against 62 on a Labour government motion in favour of the application to enter. There was, therefore, no problem for the government information services in doing what they could to explain both the issues involved and the government's policies on them. The only problem arose in not appearing to commit the government at home before it had committed itself abroad.

On the model of the broadsheets issued in the 1961–63 period by the Treasury and in 1967 by the Department of Economic Affairs, the government began in March 1971 to issue a series of eleven 'Factsheets', at a rate of something like one a week, distributed free of charge from Post Office counters, through mailing lists, and on demand from organizations and the public. A twelfth Factsheet was issued in September to cover a specific question that had arisen during the 'great debate' – that of regional policy. The Factsheets were advertised in the press and by a poster. This informational activity passed unchallenged by the Opposition at the time.

Then came the publication of the government's White Paper on 7 July. The tone of the document was very different from the tentative statistical exercise with its enormously divergent alternative estimates issued by the Labour government in February 1970 (Cmnd 4289).

Cmnd 4715 was a work of oratory:

62 The choice for Britain is clear. Either we choose to enter the Community and join in building a strong Europe on the foundations which the Six have laid; or we choose to stand aside from this great enterprise and seek to maintain our interests from the narrow – and narrowing – base we have known in recent years. As a full member of the Community we would have more opportunity and strength to influence events than we could possibly have on our own: Europe with the United Kingdom in her councils would be stronger and more influential than Europe without us.

63 A decision not to join, when at last we have the power to do so, would be a rejection of an historic opportunity and a reversal of the whole direction of British policy under successive Governments during the last decades. . . .

64 In a single generation we should have renounced an imperial past and rejected a European future. Our friends everywhere would be dismayed. They would rightly be as uncertain as ourselves about our future role and place in the world. Meanwhile the present Communities would continue to grow in strength and unity without us. Our power to influence the Communities would steadily diminish, while the Communities' power to affect our future would as steadily increase.

65 Her Majesty's Government believe that the terms which have been negotiated are fair and reasonable, and provide this country with an opportunity
which may never recur. . . . They believe that such a decision would be in the
best interests of the peace, security and prosperity, not only of the British
people, but of the peoples of Western Europe and of the world as a whole.
66 *Every historic choice involves challenge as well as opportunity. Her Majesty's
Government are convinced that the right decision for us is to accept the challenge, seize
the opportunity and join the European Communities.*[1]

What was more, hot on the heels of this typographically sober-
looking but stylistically forceful plea for the government's policy, there
came a pocket-size glossy sixteen-page brochure distributed free, gratis
and for nothing. It was illustrated with a vast tree (symbolizing the
exports of the Six to each other) as against a puny sapling (for Britain's
exports to them), and block diagrams showing the increase in the
average real income per employed person since 1958 as 39% in Britain,
76% among the Six, and demonstrating that a Community of ten would
be five times more populous than Britain on her own, and bigger in
human resources than either the USSR or the USA. It bore a message
from the Prime Minister calling for 'the widest possible discussion and
understanding of what is involved'. Both the long and the short version
laid their first emphasis on security, their second on prosperity. Both
outlined the nature of the Community, its history, British attempts to
join since 1961, and the terms secured by the end of June. Both stated
squarely that the terms were satisfactory.

It was the free short version that really riled the anti-Market Labour
MPs, who saw it as a perversion of the taxpayers' money for propaganda in favour of a course Parliament had not yet agreed. (The
government estimated the cost of the Factsheets and shortened White
Paper combined at £461,000 – including the relevant advertising and
an element of the overheads shared with other government activities.)
John Mendelson tried to raise the matter as one of major constitutional
importance deserving a motion to adjourn the House:

If it were once established that the Government . . . have a right to spend sums
estimated at between £860,000 and £2 million without any approval by the
House of Commons . . . , we are well on the road to Government deciding to
use public resources for party propaganda purposes.[2]

[1] *The United Kingdom and the European Communities*, HMSO, London, July
1971, p. 17.
[2] Hansard, 19 July 1971, cols 1057–8.

It is fair to say that, with the exception of the Factsheet on regional policy, the government issued no further persuasive documents of this kind thereafter (though probably they had never intended to, in any case). The shortened version was printed in well over six million copies: at its peak, the demand for it was running at some 100,000 copies a day – a bestseller indeed.

The government's effort then from early July to October switched its emphasis to the spoken word and to making sure that ministerial speeches were well reported in the press and on the air. The night after the publication of the White Paper Edward Heath himself went on television to broadcast to the nation. (It was a curious but under the circumstances understandable fact that the Leader of the Opposition was hesitant as to whether he should make use of his right to speak in his turn on the subject the night after.) Geoffrey Rippon alone made some 50 speeches in the country and the Foreign and Commonwealth Office circulated 80 verbatim texts of speeches on the Common Market in 1971, quite apart from those circulated by other ministries. During the July–October period about 280 ministerial speeches were made on the issue (excluding those in Parliament). In response to requests from the media for factual and technical information government departments greatly improved their facilities for providing it, and government spokesmen were tireless in keeping the press and broadcasters informed. (We shall see in the next chapter that in collaboration with the European Movement, the liaison with some leading figures in the media became in the end a very close two-way process.) All in all, it was probably one of the most massive and most expensive domestic government campaigns since the war (though it cost only a fraction of the amount spent to familiarize the public with decimalization).

The government could – and of course did – emphasize the continuity of its policy with that of the Labour government before it, and that of previous Conservative administrations going back to Harold Macmillan. But it was not able to present its arguments in too partisan a way, nor beam its campaign specifically to its own supporters. It must be remembered that on the whole in the late 'sixties Conservatives had come to be rather less enthusiastic about entry than even the Labour faithful. So towards the end of 1970 the Conservative Party launched its own campaign ahead of the government's.

The party organization set out to bring the facts as they saw them home to the various layers of Conservatives at different levels of sophistication – from the thousand or so people at the top of the party, the five thousand or so who had the chief influence in the constituencies, via the half-million regular workers to the eight million or so steady voters and beyond them to the electorate at large. It was not really a new exercise – it had already been done once ten years before. But the central leadership of the party again went out of its way to take opportunities (and create opportunities) to test the temperature in the party, get the issue debated and mobilize opinion behind the government. The fact that Edward Heath had won the election so recently – to many so surprisingly and in any case as a very personal triumph – meant that the Heath stamp on the policies (and on many of the MPs) made the task not too difficult.

Conservative Central Office through its Publicity Department, the Conservative Research Department and the Conservative Political Centre produced a flood of publications which it would be wearisome to list. They provided an Advisory Service on Common Market questions whereby MPs or their secretaries could 'phone in queries and receive speedy, authoritative replies; seventy-five or so of these replies were circulated in roneoed form. A pamphlet of questions and answers was put on sale, as was what Harold Wilson called the 'dirty little red book', *Words to Remember*. Regular publications like *Notes on Current Politics* and *Weekend Talking Point* dealt with the issue, a series of two-page highly simplified pamphlets called *Europe and You* was sold in large quantities to local associations (who asked for something simpler still) and the Research Department put out a confidential brief of over one hundred pages for the July debate in the House. There were briefing conferences for speakers, seminars in various regional centres to 'bring the Market to the people and the provinces', and steps were taken to 'stir up the constituencies', suggest they held meetings, and combat the extremely active anti-Marketeers in the country. As Jim Spicer put it for the Conservative Political Centre at the October 1971 party conference:

Many of you have taken part in our discussion groups that go on every month. This month and last month we have been discussing Europe. I can give you the facts and the figures as they are today. So far 269 groups have reported in favour of entry into Europe, don't knows 21, and 'no' to Europe 12. In terms of people voting the figures are: for, 2,698; don't knows, 206; against, 420. By the end of this month those figures will have doubled and trebled and I pledge to this Government the full support of CPC in the months ahead to tell people what it is about even more than we have done already.

The party was conscious of having to operate at two distinct levels – the ordinary audience, which did not care a fig for sovereignty but was very worried about prices, and the constituency officers, who were extremely worried about national sovereignty. No one was worried about the pound in Zurich, but they were very concerned about the pound in their pockets. What did help with some of the retired brigadiers in the shires was the security argument – the feeling that Europe and Britain separately were weak in the face of the Communist world. Beyond that, the loyalty to the party leadership and the willingness to trust it once it gave a firm lead seem to have transcended the narrower patriotic impulses of that still important strain in the party. (The importance of this group to the individual MP can hardly be overestimated, since the association officers tend to decide his renomination.) Both pro- and anti-Marketeers seem agreed that the associations were in 1970 on the whole more inclined to oppose entry, and 'had to be turned round'. In spring 1971 it was still the anti-Market MP who was the hero. Then, quite suddenly in July, the party in the country swung. Thereafter the anti-Marketeer tended to be the villain 'rocking the boat'. That was precisely the effect for which the party leadership was working. In terms of actual political mechanics it was not necessary to bring round the majority of the population. What mattered was having an opinion in the country and above all in the constituencies of MPs (Labour as well as Conservative) which made a convincing majority in the House of Commons possible. It was to the vote in the House that all the energies had in the last resort to be directed.

Problems of Parliamentary Management

So the most painstaking efforts were concentrated on the problems in Parliament, where the decision – in accordance with the party manifesto – was to be taken. For the inner group of the government which had to take thought on how best to secure parliamentary approval for British entry – Edward Heath, William Whitelaw as Leader of the House, Francis Pym as Chief Whip, Lord Carrington, not so much as Minister of Defence but simply as a key figure in the government, and the Foreign Office Ministers most concerned with the negotiations – there were many tactical problems to be solved as they went along, but there were two key strategic questions to be faced in 1971: firstly when to ask for a vote of the House, and secondly in what form to do so. In their consideration they were caught between two factors –

the timing in Brussels, and the tide of popular opinion at home. They could try to influence both these factors in their turn, but only to a limited extent: for the rest they had to operate within the margins left by those two not entirely foreseeable parameters. And at Westminster the unknowns which they had to watch and on which they could try to exert again only a limited amount of influence were the size and determination of the anti-Market rebels within Conservative ranks, and the way in which the Labour Party would act and, possibly, divide.

In their relations with the back-benchers on the Conservative side of the House the government was offered, in late summer 1970, the assistance and advice of a group of MPs who were members of the Conservative Group for Europe, one of the party-oriented parallel organizations set up by the pro-Marketeers (who were organized on a non-party basis in the European Movement). It was one of the European Movement's predecessor organizations, Britain in Europe, which had, in May 1969, set about establishing a Conservative arm under the title of 'European Forum'. Chaired originally by Alderman David Baker and administered from the Chandos House headquarters of the parent body, the Forum had, in the first year of its life, held dinner meetings at the House of Commons and a cocktail party for journalists; organized conferences with Continental parties of the Right and Centre (especially the French); formed a study group on the Common Agricultural Policy of the EEC; set about drafting guidelines for questions to be asked in the House (to encourage a wider view and to attempt to show the anti-Marketeers in a bad light); supplied speakers to Conservative meetings; and sought to organize suitable motions from the constituencies in preparation for the party conference of 1970. By early summer of that year it was strong enough to want to form three functional action groups – one for the campaign in the party and the country, one for relations with like-minded parties on the Continent, and one for parliamentary and governmental activities.

After the election, which cut across a lot of its plans, the Forum resolved at its first Annual General Meeting (attended by 40 people, of whom 14 were MPs) to change its name to the Conservative Group for Europe. Simultaneously there was a change of chairmanship to Colonel Tufton Beamish – it seemed preferable to have a parliamentarian in the post; 26 other people, of whom 10 were MPs, were elected to be the other officers and the committee. Moves were also made to enlarge the Group – by including, for example, George Gardiner, chief political correspondent of Thomson Regional Newspapers, representatives of industry, commerce and the City, and 'members with a distinctive contribution to make', such as the public relations consultant, Geoffrey Tucker. In due course the bulk of the Parliamentary Party was to join the Conservative Group. The European Movement contributed £4,524 to its funds in 1971–72, but the chairman also raised some £2,000 independently through donations to be used for purposes the Movement could not well finance, notably entertainment and some aspects of administration.

The group sent out speakers to meetings in various parts of the country, published speaker's notes and pamphlets of its own to appeal to Conservatives in general – though these were often no more than reprints of speeches – and also, together with the Federation of Conservative Students, organized the highly successful meeting at the Brighton party conference in October at which Erik Blumenfeld of the CDU, Bernard Destremau of the French Independent Republicans, and Hans Nord, Secretary-General to the European Parliament, spoke to Young Conservatives about the enlargement of the Community. The Conservative Group also provided some of the infrastructure, or at least the aegis, for the operation in Parliament run largely by Norman St John-Stevas (in much the same way as the Labour Committee for Europe on the other side of the House) to assess and to influence – not necessarily through the titular leadership – the votes of Members of Parliament on the issue. It thus provided both intelligence and support for the Conservative party managers in their diverse tasks of planning for and obtaining parliamentary approval of British entry.

The object both of the form and of the timing of their request for parliamentary approval had to be to maximize the revolt on the Labour, and minimize that on the Conservative side. But this was not a situation in which one rebel equalled another, in which one Conservative vote lost was necessarily worth one Labour vote gained. For the prestige of the government (quite apart from considerations of how to pass the implementing legislation) it was better that the votes for entry should come from Conservatives than from Labour members: a Labour vote gained was thus worth rather less than a Conservative vote lost. Over and above the general problems of putting the case for entry across to the country at large, and thereby also to MPs directly and indirectly through their constituency contacts, there was thus a special case for singling out Conservative MPs and those most likely to have influence on their views and actions. Compared with that task, embarrassing the Labour Party, making life more difficult for its Leader, and even

making it less difficult for Roy Jenkins and his friends were less important – even if an eye had to be kept cocked in their direction too.

The tactical problems in the House were not always mastered in
consummate fashion. *The Times* complained (perhaps a little unfairly):

Mr Rippon's reports to the House throughout the discussions with the Six have
been unhappy occasions. . . . His manner is brusque, bordering on the contemptuous. . . . He gives the impression of feeling that all this talk in the House is a
waste of time, that most MPs are fools anyway and that the only thing to do is
to get the unpleasant and distasteful task over as quickly as possible. To even the
most enthusiastic Europeans, Mr Rippon's approach seems almost as though he
has something to hide. . . . MPs could scarcely believe their ears when Mr
Rippon used words to Mr Roy Jenkins, one of Europe's firmest friends on the
Opposition benches, which seemed to be almost sneering at Labour's former
Chancellor for the difficulties he is experiencing within his party. . . .[1]

After what *The Times* called a 'disastrous' performance by Geoffrey
Rippon on 9 June, the Prime Minister decided with the Speaker's permission to make a statement himself next day to repair the damage, and
to explain, expand, flatter and cajole the House out of any suspicion
that there might have been a secret deal on sterling, into giving due
weight to the understanding that no country's vital interests could be
overruled by the other members, and so forth. At this stage a delegation
of Labour Marketeers went to see the Leader of the House to ask that
Rippon be told to do better. It is fair to say that thereafter Geoffrey
Rippon – perhaps also under less strain in Brussels and on his many
other trips – kept on rather better terms with the House.

Through the spring both sides within the Conservative Party were
organizing: the anti-Marketeers, meeting fortnightly, had long ago
registered themselves as the '1970 Group' with the powers that be, to
keep everything above board and escape any charges of conspiracy
against the leadership. With Sir Derek Walker-Smith very busy at the
Bar, it had fallen largely to Neil Marten to keep in touch with the
potential Market rebels, who met from time to time over a meal
(whence their nickname of 'Derek's Diner'). They shared the assignments
of covering between them all the party committees, putting down
hostile questions to Ministers, using question time as a platform for
arguments couched in the form of supplementaries, and keeping in
touch with the anti-Market groups outside the House.

The pro-Marketeers, organized in the Conservative Group for

[1] Hugh Noyes, *The Times*, 23 June 1971.

Europe, countered by equally systematic coverage of committees, planted questions to make Ministers and their case appear in a more favourable light (they put down a batch of three hundred questions at one stage) and were quick to jump in with supplementaries themselves – which proved often to be no more than promptings of the Minister to counter some 'anti' question with a stronger argument pro.[1] But these were in many ways the minor, tactical problems of managing the House. The major issues were whether to take a vote of principle before the summer recess or leave it till the autumn; and whether to put on the whips or to allow a free vote.

In June the Foreign Office Ministers and the Prime Minister – indeed the government as a whole – obviously had a major interest in getting the issue settled as soon as possible. If an equally large majority could be obtained in July as in October, the sooner the vote took place the sooner would the Treaty finally get wrapped up in Brussels and the less chance was there of anything going wrong. The fear that the rats might get at the agreement in some way had to be taken into account: unemployment or inflation, industrial relations, Northern Ireland or Rhodesia might flare up and erode support on the government benches or make it difficult for Labour Marketeers to vote with the Conservatives. The longer it was left, the more chance for the Labour Party to change its course. It would be good to have parliamentary approval in the bag as soon as possible.

On the other hand there were other Ministers, there were the whips, and there was also the party organization, who for varying reasons were unhappy at an early vote. July or early August can have its pitfalls for the whips in any case, when business is rushed after tempers get frayed at the end of a long session. In this special case the whips feared the vote would be unacceptably unfavourable: they were by no means sure yet of how many of their troops would march. At this stage, it must be remembered, it was the pro-Marketeers rather than those opposed to entry who felt that they needed time to carry their

---

[1] To take but one example of this use of the Parliamentary Question to impart rather than elicit information:

Mr Tom Boardman: Does not the result of the public opinion poll published today, showing that 45% of the electorate sounded are in favour of entry, against 42% not in favour, show that the electorate are responding to responsible leadership?

The Prime Minister: I thank my Hon. Friend for that information.

(Hansard, 29 July 1971, col. 775.)

constituents with them. Secondly, those who were undecided might well have been put off by unseemly haste in bludgeoning them into a historic decision. William Whitelaw was among those who felt that to hurry Parliament would mean that some MPs – Conservative as well as Labour – might refuse to vote in favour because they hated being rushed on such a cardinal issue of the nation's future: to give people time would at least ensure that opposition to the substance would not be swelled by those who were suspicious of the procedure. A special responsibility in all this also fell on the party organization, headed by that very experienced manager, Sir Michael Fraser. The party organization had to think beyond any particular issue, however important, and beyond any one party leader, however successful. It had to steer a path between strong action against the anti-Market Conservative MPs and tolerance of anti-Market arguments being propagated at the expense of party funds; between bringing pressure to bear on MPs through their local associations, and not damaging relationships between Conservatives at the constituency level; similarly it also had to consider how much opportunity had to be given, by not rushing things through the House, for the party stalwarts in the country to feel involved in a full process of consultation on the issue. This last consideration was, from the party organization's point of view, of very real importance. Postponing the vote to the autumn would allow MPs three months instead of three weeks to redeem their promises to talk to their constituents – and some of them held dozens of meetings to make sure their voters had the opportunity to inform themselves and could not complain of not having been consulted.

As far as the country as a whole was concerned, in June the opinion polls were still showing a very hostile popular attitude, and it was felt that time was needed to convert the country back again to the Common Market. Public opinion could hardly get any worse, and it had every chance of getting rather better, given time. To have recalled Parliament and voted before the party conferences might have looked like keeping the issue away from the party rank and file of both sides. Yet to delay beyond October would have looked bad on the Continent and might have delayed the completion of negotiations, treaty drafting and signature. So it was decided and ratified in cabinet on 16 June, on the whips' and William Whitelaw's advice and rather against the Prime Minister's and Geoffrey Rippon's original inclination, to avoid a division if the Labour Opposition did not force it, and simply ask the House to take note of the terms in a debate held on 21–26 July. In the autumn there would then be a vote of principle after the regular party conferences had been held.

On the process by which this and similar decisions were made, it would seem that, as the government was only at the end of its first year of office after six years in Opposition, there were still very good lines of communication between the more junior and the more senior members. In Opposition there had been greater equality between them, and the friendships and informal links had not yet been eroded by precedence, overwork and formal machinery. People also noted that in the whole operation – both within the government itself and in collaboration with other organizations, which will be discussed in the next chapter – there was remarkably little personal difficulty or empire-building.

Demands that a free vote be allowed in the crucial October division came from Conservative back-benchers. At a meeting of the 1922 Committee in early July 1971 in particular it came from those who intended to vote against entry, but also from some who were themselves in favour of entry, yet were anxious to protect the prestige of Parliament in taking such a unique historic decision on its own judgment, and not as the cabinet's rubber stamp. The Labour Marketeers, through their own channels, also pleaded for a free vote, hoping that there would be no Labour whip if the Conservatives were free. Figures began to be bandied about that something like a hundred Labour MPs might vote with the government on a free vote – a patent inducement to Edward Heath not to whip his own party. Some Conservative Marketeers also had the impression – on what authority, it is now perhaps not easy to say – that the Labour Marketeers promised their support on the implementing legislation if there were a free vote on the principle, but would refuse to do so if the whips were on.

Against all such pleas the Prime Minister maintained a firm public stand. On 12 July, at a 'world press conference', he was asked about a three-line whip and reiterated his stand:

It does seem to me to be a strange approach that it is accepted, in the parliamentary system, that you ask your party for support on a whole variety of issues, but when you come to a major issue such as this you say, 'Well, of course, we will withdraw all the normal means of organized government and sit back and do nothing.' We as a government are absolutely entitled to ask our supporters to support us in the lobby.[1]

[1] *The Times*, 13 July 1971.

And he also pointed to international implications: 'The leaders of the Community expect this government to use its majority in the House of Commons to carry it through. This was the only basis on which the Six were prepared to negotiate.'[1] How this fact – never before revealed in that form, and perhaps not really meant quite as strongly as it came over – squared with 'the sole commitment . . . to negotiate; no more, no less', and with the assurance at the time of the election that MPs would be left free to make up their own minds, was a question no one at the world press conference put. The Prime Minister, however, emphasized that the Six could not be expected to negotiate on the basis that at the end the government would simply say: 'We are making our position as a cabinet clear but everybody else can do as they like.'

From this and a great many other public utterances by the Prime Minister and his senior colleagues it was assumed by most people through the summer that whether or not there might be a free vote on the Labour side, the Conservative whips would be on. Nevertheless there were Conservative anti-Marketeers who believed, or stated they were sure, that if the decision had not already privately been taken to have a free vote, then it would be made once the psychological pressure on Conservative MPs had done its work through the summer, when it became clearer how many Labour Marketeers were prepared to defy a three-line whip of their own – and that was a test they could hardly be put through without the assumption of a three-line whip on the government side – and when the Labour Party had inflicted as much internal damage on itself as possible.

This was the context in which mutual games of bluff and counter-bluff were taking place in early summer: the degree of freedom allowed the Conservative anti-Marketeers was partly dependent on the resolve of Labour pro-Marketeers to save the Conservative government from Conservative defections; the degree of freedom of the Labour defectors was partly dependent on the paucity of Conservative defectors (so that the Labour Marketeers could not be accused of keeping the Conservative government in power) and partly on the absence of a Conservative whip (which might, however, increase the Conservative defections). The Conservative whip was partly dependent on the government's assessment of the resolve both of the Labour Marketeers and of their own defectors under different possible hypotheses. Unlikely people began to seek out each other's company across party and across Common Market lines, rebels in opposite parties and on opposite

[1] *Financial Times*, 13 July 1971.

sides discovered their tactical interdependence, rumour was rife and the newspapers were quick to report who had been seen hob-nobbing with whom and where. Looking back *ex post* it is difficult to recapture the sense of uncertainty – the *Financial Times* called it 'hysteria' – and the critical importance apparently assumed by intrinsically insignificant straws in the wind.

There was a variety of possible scenarios. For the Conservative party managers the happiest was that which posited a major turn-round in public opinion during the summer, as government and other propaganda dispelled popular doubts and fears. This popular swing towards a majority in favour of entry would then reinforce the constituency associations of the Conservative Party in moving towards the Market. That, in turn, would ensure an overall majority in the House made up of Conservatives alone. With the Conservatives holding 326 seats (excluding the Speaker and Chairmen) and the rest 301, the government could find its own overall majority only if it could reduce Conservative anti-Market votes to a dozen or less: but if it could do that, it was argued, there might be a sizable bonus from Labour Marketeers who could not possibly then be accused of keeping in power a Conservative government that had already secured its own overall majority – just as the remaining Conservative dissidents could not be accused of bringing the government's authority into question.

The least happy scenario from the government's point of view was one in which public opinion resolutely refused to budge through the summer, in which the constituency associations on the whole upheld the right of each parliamentarian to exercise his own judgment or reflected the anti-Market feelings of the country, and some fifty Conservatives might actually vote against entry. With under 280 Conservatives voting in favour, everything would depend on the Labour Marketeers: and if rising unemployment, the prospect of a Rhodesian settlement, a flare-up in Ulster, or some unforeseen factor whipped up party feeling to the point where getting the Tories out was not only possible but seemed the supremely urgent issue, then the 289 Labour MPs could topple the government even without the positive help of the Liberals.

Nor need this even happen on the great vote of principle: Conservative support might drain away during 1972 in the course of lengthy implementing legislation, and the parliamentary machine might grind to a halt. Under such circumstances no doubt Edward Heath would be faced by the same situation that faced Harold Wilson over the Industrial

Relations Bill: his whips would have to tell him that, though there might be a majority on the substance of the issue, procedurally they just could not get the issue through the House, and the government had better turn to other business. 'Good European though he is,' Mr Wilson is reported to have reasoned, 'Mr Heath likes being Prime Minister.'[1] How far this was an extrapolation of Mr Wilson's own experience, and how long Edward Heath himself would have been able (or even have wanted) to survive in office after such a turn of events is another matter. There were even those who suggested that in such a case Edward Heath should 'do a Mendès-France' – let the Commons decide without making it a vote of confidence. (Technically, in fact, that is what finally happened, but politically the whole prestige of the government was obviously engaged to the last.)

It was in this kind of situation that the *Financial Times*, arguing that the government had in effect to stake its political life on the issue long before it could be sure how many Conservative MPs would be willing to bring down the government rather than go into the Market, concluded that 'Mr Heath for his part could conceivably find himself shattered in morale or even deposed'.[2] Enoch Powell prophesied as late as 13 September 1971 that 'The first and most important thing to say about British entry is that it is not going to happen . . .', and while that seemed excessive certitude at so late a stage, scepticism was much more widespread in early summer. In May, with the Macclesfield by-election hanging over the party, the 1922 Committee was told by Angus Maude that, if the government took the country into the EEC, the Conservatives would meet such dire retribution at the hands of the electorate that they would be out of power for ten years – a prospect which apparently so shocked Rear-Admiral Morgan Giles as to lead him into a soothing instance of painfully homespun Latinity (not the last in this story) with the slogan, 'Pro bono publico, no bloody panico'.

Nose-counting, Arm-twisting, Weak Knees and Stiff Upper Lips

The whips of both parties, in this highly fluid situation, had their own common interests in maintaining some structure in the system to prevent the unexpected from disrupting their designs. On both sides of the House the party whips in fact thus began a period of uneasy symbiosis, each with two sets of unofficial 'cause whips' within their own parties – some for, some against entry. People began keeping

[1] *Financial Times*, 17 May 1971.
[2] *Financial Times*, 13 July 1971.

crumpled little lists in their wallets, and one was granted peeps at the constantly revised totals, or at the labels on some of the categories – 'strong', 'would like to be strong', and so forth. The successive lists from opposite sides make fascinating reading in retrospect. On the Conservative side Norman St John-Stevas, with a few others, became in effect an unofficial whip for the Marketeers within the framework of the Conservative Group for Europe. St John-Stevas had already gained considerable experience in assessing parliamentary opinion in his campaign to secure an enquiry into the working of the Abortion Act. He and his collaborators had a fairly accurate picture of the final outcome well in advance. They were fooled in a few cases (William Clark had joined their group, so they were surprised when he decided, just before the whips were off, to vote with the Opposition), but most of their errors were on the side of caution.

At the first count, made in January 1971, the Conservative Group for Europe reckoned that in addition to its own 127 members there were 90 more in favour, who, for one reason or another did not want to join the group: 33 were hostile, 75 doubtful (see table, p 188). Two junior Ministers and two whips were thought to have their doubts. Those who were hostile fell into a variety of categories. There were fifteen traditional anti-Marketeers with well-established records of opposition often dating back to 1961–63 – men such as Anthony Fell, who declared in the July debate: 'I convinced myself ten years ago, and I have not moved one jot either way since.' Sir Derek Walker-Smith, Sir Robin Turton and Neil Marten fell into that category, though the fourth member of that quartet from the early 'sixties, Peter Walker, had been converted, become the first cabinet Minister to join the Conservative Group for Europe and made a (largely unreported) speech in August explaining his change of view. There were five of the Ulster Unionists (in the event six of the eight voted against) who clearly had reservations about anything that might lead to political unity between Ulster and Eire, felt fears about Catholic influences in the EEC, and wanted to gain leverage against the government for reasons of Ulster politics anyway. There were ten new MPs. There was also a farmer worried about fishing (but he in the end voted with the government on the understanding that all would be well for the fishermen before the talks were out). Lastly there were John Biffen and Enoch Powell, who had both voted in favour of the Labour Party's application in 1967. Powell had, however, not very long after come to see the Market issue, rather like that of immigration, as one where the people needed a tribune against a political establishment too aloof from them to put their gut reactions into politically significant words. Indeed, following this train of thought, John Biffen by October expressed fears that there would be growing political violence as respect withered for institutions fastened on an unwilling public, and that determined activists would exploit a sense of alienation to destroy authority.

The doubters included men like Edward du Cann, who had been left out of a government in which, as a former Party Chairman, he might have had expectations of major office; some who were worried about public opinion, including those – like Philip Goodhart – who wanted a referendum; some on the Celtic fringe in Scotland or Wales; and some concerned by horticulture, New Zealand, boots and shoes, or other specific matters. The government whips themselves more cautiously reckoned in early February that there were 62 against, 70 doubtfuls, and only 194 in favour.

By the end of April the Conservative Group for Europe had made 41 recruits. But they all came from among the 'pros'; there had been no shift at all out of the 'doubtfuls' and 'antis' into those in favour of entry. Fishing had begun to be important, with 20 or 30 MPs' votes thought dependent on a promise of revision of the Community's policy. (Given the minute size of the inshore fishing industry, its political leverage was certainly made to look impressive.[1]) There were doubts – not unnaturally – as to whether the negotiations could succeed. People were anxious, too, to get a decision in 1971 rather than have the issue hanging over them too long. But, in the constituencies, MPs thought they noted some swing among their active party workers in favour of entry.

It was at this time that the Conservative Group stepped up its activity to a peak, concentrating on what it regarded as the persuadable doubters. Notes were made as to who 'wishes to be seen to be persuaded' or 'would trust Alec's judgment', or where one might 'speak to his wife'. A series of seminars was held in the Palace of Westminster, attended by up to 120 parliamentarians, and these seminars proved important in holding together the centre of the party at a time when there was little helpful news coming out of Brussels. On 14 May some

[1] Thus the inshore fishermen advertised Jock Bruce-Gardyne's London number in public telephone booths so that their supporters could protest personally on the fishermen's fate. Being canny Scots, however, they most frequently failed to insert the requisite coins, leaving their message to come across as a sustained series of pips.

20 doubtfuls were escorted to Paris by Norman St John-Stevas under the aegis of the Conservative Group for Europe and given lunch by Christopher Soames. (All but two of these in the event voted with the government.) There were two conferences, one at the end of April, the other in early June, with colleagues from the French and Italian sister parties, and there was a series of small dinner parties in the House, one of which was attended by the Prime Minister. Those who were susceptible to flattery were flattered, those who were likely to be impressed by the views of the eminent were given time by eminent figures in whom they had trust. The anti-Marketeers believe that one or two were seduced away from their fold by hopes of favours to come.

It was in the period of June and July that the picture suddenly became very much clearer. Abroad there was the Paris summit and the Brussels breakthrough. At home the government issued its White Paper and the Prime Minister made his broadcast and his address to the Conservative Central Council. It was also the time when Harold Wilson, though reserving the final unveiling ceremony until the end of July, was clearly seen to be fast changing his mind to oppose entry, and thereby made the issue one of party politics and party loyalties. The opinion polls noted a substantial heave – once and for all, as it later proved – in public opinion away from its very decided dislike of entry.

Thus, by the time the 'take note' debate was over, the Conservative Group for Europe had swollen to 202 members and its count of those who would vote for entry rose to 284. (All the 28 previously classified as 'doubtful-plus', 17 of the 18 'middle doubtfuls' and 15 of the 25 'doubtful-minus' characters had come round to the cause.) That left 21 die-hards, and 20 classified optimistically as 'persuadable' – of whom James Allason, Wilfred Baker, Sir Edward Brown, Hamish Gray and Fergus Montgomery indeed emerged in the end as government supporters. On the other hand there were still several nasty surprises to come for the Marketeers. Sir Donald Kaberry and Lt-Col. Colin Mitchell (whose regiment, the Argyll and Sutherland Highlanders, had obligingly been saved from extinction just before the final vote) persisted and voted against entry on 28 October, as did three others whom the Marketeers thought to have been coming round.

These mutually compensating errors apart, the prediction of the Conservative Group for Europe of a maximum of 41 defectors turned out to be extremely accurate almost three months later. On the worst interpretation, assuming that all the people they thought persuadable (plus the ones they had overlooked) had all voted against, the defectors would have been only 48 as a maximum if the vote had been taken in July. In October there were 39 Conservatives who voted against, 2 abstained, and one was genuinely ill (Charles Curran, who wanted to vote in favour). The estimate was made on the assumption of a three-line whip, and the Conservative Group felt that a free vote would not increase their estimate by more than a dozen. Norman St John-Stevas for one was at this point strongly in favour of a free vote: it would be more popular in the country, and would make life easier for the Labour Marketeers, who he understood would in that case promise support in the consequential legislation and who would more than make up for any Conservatives lost by the withdrawal of the whips; but he was also insistent that, if that decision was taken, it was to be announced only at the last possible moment.

While keeping in touch with the Marketeers, it was equally the job of the government whips to maintain contact with the dissidents, and in particular with the unofficial anti-Market whips of the back benches. Marten made periodic reports on the strength of the group to the assistant chief whip. In early August 1971, he reported a firm strength of thirty-two. (He was not including Ulster Unionists.) The figure was accepted – the whips probably felt that MPs were franker with their friends than they were with the whips' office on such occasions – but he was assured, with some pleasure of anticipation, that the figure would be down to half that by the time the House reassembled. We must, therefore, now turn to the range of instruments available to the party to secure conformity, and examine how, why and when it succeeded – and where it failed.

The influence on the wavering MP as usual came from four directions: from the party managers, in particular the whips; from his colleagues in the House; from his local party chairman, and association committee; and from his general sense of his voters' opinions. It is worth examining each in turn.

The relationship between an MP and his whip is a delicate one – and of importance to both. Whips obviously differ in their personal styles – Edward Heath from William Whitelaw, Francis Pym (the Chief Whip during this period) from both. And under any given Chief Whip, his assistant whips will each be doing the job in a slightly different way themselves, since it is such an intensely personal relationship. But if whips are named as if they were scorpions, their operation tends to be far more avuncular. 'If you insist, of course there's nothing

I can do. I wouldn't myself dream of setting the constituency on you. But you do realize that this makes me very unhappy. If other people let the side down this way, my life would become impossible. We've known each other for so long, I just can't see why you should want to be so unhelpful to me. . . .' One can see the sort of emotional appeal which would come naturally to as superb a manager of men as some whips are. There might even, on lesser issues, be discussion of degrees of awkwardness – will you be absent paired, absent unpaired, abstain unobtrusively or insist on sitting ostentatiously in the Chamber refusing to vote (perish the thought of actually voting on the other side)? Shall I tell the press, will you, or shall we not bother?

There are not in fact that many threats which a whip would state overtly – or, probably, could use without risk of becoming counter-productive. Nor would he usually dangle any very obvious carrots tied to any definite considerations. The whips do have certain rewards effectively in their gift. The hope of office is often considered one major reward for loyalty. Yet it is one the whips can use only sparingly. They cannot in any way foreclose on a Prime Minister's freedom of choice – and there are critics or potential critics of a government that can best be silenced by incorporation into it. Seats on select committees and opportunities in the Chamber can be put in the way of the good boys – but apart from the Public Accounts and the Expenditure Committees, there are often more places to be filled than people willing to fill them. Some MPs like to get abroad, and places on delegations to South Pacific Commonwealth countries, Interparliamentary Union meetings, and the European Assemblies are likely to go on the whole to men in good standing with their whips. (But even there some awkward customers can be bought off by sending them, paired, on a Caribbean goodwill mission.) But this is the small change of political life, with which habits of conformity can be cemented, but with which no one would expect to buy great votes of principle.

Unlike the situation obtaining in the United States Congress, there is really no pork-barrel system of favours for his constituency which an MP can normally hope to obtain either as a reward for loyalty or as the price of abandoning rebellion. Of course in specific instances MPs are involved in battles over the siting of an airport or the saving of a shipyard. But where works are sited with reference to local political situations – as some might claim was the announcement of a bridge over the Humber just before the 1966 Hull by-election or a fast breeder-reactor in Caithness and Sutherland – they were not favours to an MP, but attempts to secure a constituency for a party. The abrupt rise in 'winter keep' payments to hill farmers at the time of Sir Alec Douglas-Home's election in Kinross and West Perth in 1963 fell into much the same category. Only in one respect does there really seem to be a very definite bunch of carrots in the Conservative whips' larder (under Harold Wilson it was a bunch of carrots denied to the Labour whips): the honours system. An MP in good standing with the whips has a better chance of a CBE for his constituency association chairman; indeed one pro-Market Conservative was quite specific in his research advice: 'Just study the 1971 New Year Honours List'. (Even that inducement of course can go wrong unless subtly handled: one MP some decades ago was actually sent a letter saying it would be difficult to proceed with a knighthood for his constituency chairman unless . . . thus enabling him to nail the matter by threatening to publish the letter if the knighthood were not announced.)

With that, however, we have arrived at the influence of the constituency. In democratic theory, perhaps, MPs would be sensitive to the marginal voters – those who voted for him last time, but might not next; those who did not vote for him last time, but might at the next election; and the abstainers who could be won, or the hostile voters who might be induced to abstain. No doubt there are MPs who in a rough and ready way, on an issue like the Common Market, do try to make their calculations in those terms. In fact, however, one may well wonder how relevant such considerations are likely to prove in practice. The next election is a long time away – or may be presumed, on the whole, to be so. The fate of the party was likely to depend on prices and employment at least as much as on the EEC issue. And the fate of an individual MP was bound up far more with the party's fortunes than with any personal stand he might choose to take. One could, of course, never know. But the experience over past elections had been that candidates made little difference to electoral swings, and in any case his stand on the EEC would only be one small part of the personal image of the candidate in the constituency: this is likely to depend far more on his assiduity in attending local functions, answering letters, and cultivating the local press. It was thus really only to MPs in marginal constituencies that the marginal voters were of immediate electoral significance as a factor in their decision on the issue of principle.

Far more relevant to his own personal future, if he was to take the consequences of his stand into account in deciding what that stand should be, were his relations with the small group of activists in the local association – in particular his relations with his party chairman and his party agent. It was the local association that would decide if a man was to be re-nominated: and for most MPs, re-nomination was the chief factor in their re-election which they felt their attitude on this issue could affect. So it was here, in the main, that the most powerful pressures developed in the early summer of 1971. Of course there were influences on MPs from their friends and from business associates (such as chairmen of companies in which they held directorships), but the most pressing came from their constituency officers, the implied threat being that of not being re-adopted as candidates for the next election.

Different individuals in the party organization may take different views on how far they were in effect outflanking MPs and influencing the constituency associations directly, but this is more a matter of terminology than anything else. Conservative Central Office and the Conservative Political Centre, the organization at the regional and some agents at the local level all went out to convince sceptics and generate enthusiasm in the constituency associations. To some extent this campaign was directed through the constituency associations at the country at large, so as to be reflected back to Westminster in the public mood. But it also had the specific purpose of addressing MPs through their own local constituents, and in particular through those of them to whom they really owed their seats in Parliament. Central Office itself was reluctant to turn its attention too selectively to the constituencies of dissident MPs, preferring to rely on a certain division of labour. That specific job, it was understood, was best left to the Conservative Group for Europe.

The party management, in launching this campaign, faced various difficulties. In the first place they did not want to commit the party before the government had committed itself to the terms; yet they also knew that the Prime Minister might want a vote of principle before the summer recess, so that results might have to be obtained by late July, without pulling out all the stops before late June or early July – a quite impossible timetable. (We shall see how this difficulty was overcome in part by the use of the European Movement rather than the party machine.) In the second place there was at first sight an ambiguity in their task, misleadingly defined as that of setting in motion a 'great debate'. Some felt that the very call for a 'great debate' was bound to kill it. Not only was there a sense of 'I brought you here to enjoy yourself – so enjoy yourself or I'll knock your block off', but there was the additional difficulty that the debate was explicitly staged as an educational exercise rather than one of self-determination: the party was told at one and the same time that they were vigorously to debate the issue, and also that at the end of the debate their MPs were all to vote for one (and against the other) side of the argument. Thirdly, there had been for ten years a steady drip of propaganda within the party from the top down in favour of the Market; the danger – if danger it was – was thus perhaps less that the party would rise in revolt against the leadership than that they might show themselves resigned to the inevitable, bored, weary and indifferent.

The opening round in the battle for the support of local associations was fired by the Prime Minister in person at a meeting of the Conservative Central Council held on 14 July in the Central Hall, Westminster. The hall was crowded with several thousand worthies from the constituencies – local chairmen and secretaries and members of local committees. The stage was crowded with the cabinet and the national party officials. The spotlight throughout was exclusively on the Prime Minister, who arrived bronzed from his sailing in a smart dark blue suit to the cheers of the faithful. The meeting warmed to him further as it went on (the anti-Marketeers took to referring to it afterwards as the 'Nuremberg rally'). He spoke for an hour and then took two dozen questions from the floor. They tended to be read off slips of paper, dealt with sovereignty and the rights of Parliament, 'full-hearted consent' and a three-line whip: and Edward Heath's rejection of a free vote was greeted with such emphatic applause that the party managers took good note, and little more was heard of the idea of a free vote over the next three months. By the time a lady teetotaller rose to quiz the Prime Minister on lax licensing laws and public drunkenness being imported from the Continent, there was no doubt that the vast majority of constituency associations had either already come round or were well on the way to doing so.

The public opinion polls were in any case by this time showing a decisive swing away from the solid anti-Market majority of the earlier months of the year (see Diagram on pp. 362–3) and the swing was particularly marked among Conservative supporters. The timing suggests that the Central Council meeting on 14 July rode on the crest of a wave that had already gathered momentum during the preceding week or so, and had first shown itself very quickly after the great negotiating session of late June. If an illustration were required of the swing in the local associations, Macclesfield would be a clear one. In June 1971 a strongly anti-Market sales manager, Nicholas Winterton, had been selected as Conservative candidate for the by-election in preference to Douglas Hurd, the Prime Minister's political secretary, who supported the government's attempt to get the right terms to enter the EEC, but actually withdrew before the selection conference when he found that attitude to be fatal. At the end of September Nicholas Winterton was duly elected to Parliament – as a pronounced pro-Marketeer: and he had no trouble at all from his constituency association in so completely changing the tune that had originally won him the nomination.

Crucial to the whole operation were the Conservative party agents in the constituencies themselves. There are over four hundred of them, and a great many were faced with a situation that had had no precedent in their experience: wholesale cross-pressures on them from the party headquarters on the one side, and on the other from sections of their local party environment – in some cases the MP, in some the chairman, in some factions of the local committee or major contributors to local party funds, and often a combination of these. There was high praise at the centre of the party for their response under these stresses. With little to fall back on for advice on their delicate diplomatic problems in the constituency except the area organizers and the party head-quarters, agents responded as a professionally trained corps, often refusing to be the personal furniture of the local member, and falling into line with the party as a whole. As one of the national officers of the party put it, their professionalism allowed them to transcend their own private feelings on the issue where necessary, and concentrate on their function in the total organization: 'We're not paid to think. We've bloody well got to do it.' Clearly agents have to be extremely careful, since they are the paid employees of the constituency officers, who like to feel in charge. But, provided they are careful, they can – like a civil servant to a Minister, or a secretary to a committee – exercise consider-able influence. As one agent explained his position in general: 'Any agent worth his salt runs his constituency; any agent discovered to be doing so gets fired.'

A wide variety of techniques was in fact indicated, and different party regions and different constituencies had to be handled rather differently. In so far as the object was to obtain majority support from the local associations, the effort was highly successful. In early 1971 there can be little doubt that the majority of associations was rather opposed to entry. But by the later summer only a very small number of them voted their disapproval of the government's stand. In some cases a good deal of cajoling was required. In St Ives, for example, the local MP, John Nott, faced a very delicate situation. He resolved it by engaging in a lengthy and close dialogue with his constituents, touring the area of Cornwall and Devon with Peter Mills, the MP for Torring-ton, and step by step, taking care to carry at least the leading local figures with him, moved from a position of being publicly uncom-mitted to one in which his constituents felt they had been taken into his confidence and treated seriously, that their views had been given due weight, and that, together, they had chosen Europe.

In such a situation, an overkill of propaganda parachuted into the West Country from outside could well have been counter-productive. In other situations a much bolder technique could be used. The women's side of the party, for example, brought over a German Christian Democrat, Frau Marie-Elisabeth Klee, to address twenty meetings in one week – avoiding constituencies in which this would be too provocative, but (as one organizer put it in delightfully feminine im-agery) 'breathing on growth points'. It is difficult to gauge how many party meetings, and how many public meetings under Conservative auspices, were held primarily to debate this issue: reasonable estimates must certainly run into several thousand. They were coupled with – and complementary to – the distribution of literature from the party, the European Movement, the European Communities, and of course from the government itself. The party had received a bulk supply of 837,910 copies of the shortened version of the White Paper (at a cost to the government of £25,137),[1] and while there is always sub-stantial wastage in such operations the figure gives an idea of the number of people it did set out to reach.

It was of course rational that in the distribution of organizational effort, literature, speakers and publicity special attention was given to constituencies defined as marginal – that is, where a wobbling member could be helped to gravitate the right way. 'It was the grey boys who reserved their position', said the national officer already quoted, 'who brought down trouble on their heads.' The European Movement had a list of 68 Conservative and 28 Labour constituencies regarded rightly or wrongly as marginal. It included Aberdeenshire East (Patrick Wolrige-Gordon, Secretary of the Conservative Parliamentary Fisheries Committee, who abstained on 28 October), Brierley Hill and also Cannock (of which two constituencies more anon), Gillingham

[1] Hansard, 23 July 1971, cols 1899–1902.

(Frederick Durden, a Safeguards Campaign patron who in the end voted for entry), Hemel Hempstead (James Allason, an anti-Marketeer who finally came to heel), Maidstone (John Wells, who became a patron of the Safeguards Campaign in early 1971, heavily stressed his fears in the July debate, but then voted for), Oxford (where Monty Woodhouse, whom many had thought to be rather sceptical, came out very late in the day after polling a thousand of his constituents to vote in favour without enthusiasm), Sudbury and Woodbridge (Keith Stainton, another patron of the Safeguards Campaign whose election address had proclaimed: 'Keith Stainton says "No" – unless there is clear public support', but who then voted with the government) and Taunton (Edward du Cann, who voiced 'deep anxieties' in the July debate, and in October duly abstained). In fact from their list of marginal constituencies only Angus Maude, Lt-Col. Colin Mitchell and Harold Soref voted against entry – but this may be a tribute to the Movement's realism as to where it could still hope to affect the outcome as much as to its actual effectiveness in doing so.

The anti-Marketeers themselves saw a pattern in what happened in different places, and concluded that there must be a common origin to these events. In Banbury, Neil Marten's own constituency, the agent, the constituency chairman, and one or two other officers saw the national Party Chairman, Peter Thomas, on the morning of the Central Hall meeting of 14 July. A few days later, the constituency association sent out a letter to all members of its executive giving the requisite twenty-eight days' notice of a meeting to be held on 12 August, right in the middle of the holidays, to discuss Neil Marten's meetings on the Common Market, and adding – oddly in view of the apparently anodyne subject on the agenda – that because of the vital importance of the meeting everyone was urgently requested to attend. On the day before this meeting Neil Marten was presented with an emergency resolution (which needs seven days' notice, notice that had indeed been given, but not to the MP) expressing the association's confidence in the government and its support for a three-line whip over the Common Market. Next evening in Woodstock town hall Neil Marten argued that Edward Heath had himself at the Central Hall declared the issue as being 'above party politics', and that, since his own election address had declared in black and white, 'I am opposed to Britain's entry into the Common Market. . . . I simply do not believe (for political and economic reasons) that it is in the best interest of the British people to join', he could hardly rat on his own election pledge. The meeting, however, passed the resolution by 49 votes to 10, and hard feelings not surprisingly subsisted in the constituency for some time thereafter.

This was the kind of pressure which new members in particular found it most difficult to resist: they still felt in debt to their committees for selecting them as candidates, had not yet been able to bank any credit for their constituency work, and had not yet the self-confidence and experience for dealing with such local party pressure. It became one of the functions of the more seasoned leading anti-Marketeers to advise them on their constituency tactics and try to stiffen their morale. In the case of some new members – like Toby Jessel and Carol Mather, who came under tremendous pressure from their commuters' constituencies of Twickenham and Esher – they were successful; both had ample majorities, though these were no guarantee against not being re-adopted. Where the majority was small – as in the case of Derek Coombs, who had entered Parliament for the first time in 1970 by a margin of just 120 votes in Yardley and become a patron of the Safeguards Campaign in early 1971 – revolt against the party line (even in agreement with the popular opinion polls) was not in the end carried into the division lobby. He gave unusual grounds for his change of view in the July debate:

What has changed, however, is what I regard as one crucial factor in the balance of my personal judgment. It is simply that, whereas until recently I believed that Britain's refusal to join would, in effect, block the political development of the Community, I am now convinced that, whether we are inside or outside, we shall ultimately see the gradual unfolding of what will amount to a new super-power. In those circumstances, Britain herself could well become an offshore island, and this would plainly be unacceptable.

Specially acute problems were posed where constituencies were being re-distributed, so that the sitting member had to be adopted *ab initio* by a new constituency organization. Thus both Patrick Cormack, a new member sitting for Cannock, and Fergus Montgomery, sitting for Brierley Hill, had signed the 1970 motion of the anti-Marketeers; redistribution implied that only one of the two could hope to sit for the new constituency of South-West Staffordshire. Patrick Cormack had said in his election address, 'I cannot promise that I will always toe the party line – I am opposed, for instance, to entry into the Common Market', and he told his story in the July 1971 debate: 'When I was elected I made it plain that I was opposed to entry. . . . I am prepared to admit that I was wrong.'

That very evening he would begin a campaign in his constituency to tell them so. He had seen the light in fact only just before the debate, in almost poetic circumstances:

Two things have preyed on my mind more than anything else, the thought of the town of Cannock and the future of my small son. . . . I searched my soul last Sunday when I had the privilege of attending evensong at King's College Chapel, Cambridge. This glorious monument to the best in our civilization was packed, mainly with young people from all over the world, particularly from Europe. I stood next to a German, and I did search my soul. I thought that I could, perhaps, write a footnote to what might be the most glorious chapter of all in the history of our civilization, the chapter that I would call 'Pax Europa'.[1]

This conversion obviously made it very much more difficult for Fergus Montgomery to avoid a Damascus of his own. On 1 August – just after the debate – the Conservative Group for Europe checklist classified him as persuadable, and very sensitive to constituency reactions. On 28 October he joined Patrick Cormack in the government lobby. (In June 1972 he appealed against Patrick Cormack's adoption for the new constituency of South-West Staffordshire, and a bitter public feud ensued, in which Cormack carried the day.)

The anti-Marketeers were not sparing of allegations that people had been leant on to fall in line – indeed they saw it as the culmination of a process that had been deliberately begun in 1964. At their Brighton rally in October 1971 Timothy Keigwin declared that winnable seats had over the past seven years gone to pro-Market aspirants. He himself had fought North Devon against Jeremy Thorpe on a Conservative anti-Market ticket in 1966 and again in 1970 and come within 369 votes of winning the seat the second time; but then he was excluded from the list of potential prospective candidates because of his anti-Market views. He did not expand on 'the kind of pressures I've been subjected to' – from the response of the audience they appeared to understand anyway – before he was finally put back on the list of possible candidates. At the same meeting Sir Gerald Nabarro (who had a majority of 17,000), was blunt about some of his colleagues: 'Quite a few marginal seats were won on a Tory anti-Market ticket, but very few of them are still anti-Marketeers now. I cannot describe the contempt in which I hold them.' (One should perhaps in fairness add that three of those who voted against the government, David Mudd, Sally Oppenheim and

[1] Hansard, 23 July 1971, col. 1902.

John Sutcliffe, had majorities of under 2,000 votes, in the last case indeed of only 388.)

None of these various generalized correlations of fact need force us into any particular causal inferences. Certainly they do not in any individual case impugn the sincerity of the vote of anyone who decided late, or changed his mind, on the Market issue. Consistency being the hobgoblin of little minds, it is equally logical to cast suspicion on the sincerity of those who were so deeply committed in advance of the final package that they would have discredited themselves if they had let it be known that on further evidence or further reflection they had in fact begun to have their doubts concerning long-advertised convictions. And this was a highly complex issue, in the context of a changing world (the monetary issue, for one thing, looked rather different in October from July) so that it was not illogical to suspend judgment at least until July, or to change one's mind in the light of events and constituency contacts and further reflection during the summer recess, or even later as the tactical position in the House crystallized in October.

Moreover, it is all too easy in any study of an isolated issue to lose sight of the total context in which a man or woman has to take his or her stand. As we saw over the Soames affair, even important decisions in foreign policy are at times passed over in silence in favour of the farm price review, or made hastily between Stephen Swingler's funeral and rushing off to Ipswich. They are paralleled on the home front and at humbler levels by the competing claims on the total aggregate of an MP's political influence, his constituency's manifold interests, and the survival of the government to support which he campaigned and was elected. Indeed in one sense there was here a serious political dilemma for those who were hostile to entry on balance rather than on principle. If entry was threatened by the possibility of government defeat in the House, one could hardly rock the boat and let the Socialists back into power. If on the other hand approval of entry was guaranteed by the Labour Marketeers anyway, why vote against the inevitable – in fact how much better that it should take place under a strong government, seen to command a proper control over its own members.

We should also not underestimate the advantages of being uncommitted or open to persuasion. No doubt there are deep psychological satisfactions at the bar or in the tea-room from being a stalwart, trusted and counted on, or a last-ditcher, taking his political life in his hands for one principle as against all others. But the leverage of one who has to be courted, the margin of influence of one who hawks his conscience round both sides, is also – at least in the short run – considerable. For many who did not regard their vote as being decisive to the issue there must have been a fine tactical calculation as to whether the likely carrots outweighed the possible arm-twisting that might form their complement, whether labels like 'a charming wobbler', 'no longer just corruptible, just corrupt' and others one could hear in the Palace of Westminster on both sides were worth it in the long run. (For some, of course, the long run may not have been as important as the immediate need to avoid what they feared would be political suicide.)

Nor can we isolate political from personal life. We shall see in the case of the Labour Party in particular that in the psychology of rebellion personal friendships can play a peculiarly sustaining role: of one Left-wing Labour MP it was said again and again that he found it in the end intolerable to fight his own best friends in the party, and personal loyalties – such as those between former Parliamentary Private Secretaries and their Ministers – undoubtedly played their part. Asked what mistakes were made in organizing the Conservative rebels, one of them sadly reflected: 'We neglected the social side' – a mistake the Labour rebels, if they made it, made in rather a different way. Professional alternatives also made their impact. A barrister who earns at the Bar a multiple of his parliamentary salary or a financier with ample private means is clearly in a very different position to risk his political future from, say, an ageing clerk whose financial and personal future outside the House would be bleak indeed. Thirdly we must not – in judging an MP's stomach for a fight with his own party – underestimate even more private factors. An optimist supported by a united family who share his convictions may find rebellion almost a challenge. But several of the people involved in this and the Labour story of rebellion or non-rebellion were at the time seriously ill; and at least four of them were, during this period, facing marital breakdown. These are the kind of personal factors which no computer printout – and few theories of decision-making – can fully discount, and are often known only to a man's most intimate friends (and in illness sometimes not even to himself) yet without which our political judgments can go unfairly awry.

The Conference and the Free Vote

By the time the Conservatives met at Brighton for their annual party conference from 13 to 16 October, it was, as far as the party in the country was concerned, all over bar the shouting. To lance the boil immediately and not let it infect debates on other subjects the debate on the Common Market was set for the first afternoon of the conference – a piece of timing that completely stymied the anti-Marketeers, who had booked a hall for that evening to rally their forces. On the order paper were 69 motions of unqualified support – 12 'supporting', 14 'welcoming', several 'applauding' and 22 'congratulating' the government. There were also 25 motions from 24 constituencies whose support was qualified in some way, or, in 4 cases, which expressed outright opposition.

The one amendment (from the West Midlands Area) which it was originally proposed to debate sought to add 'and respectively remembers the Prime Minister's pledge that he would not consider entry without the whole-hearted support of the British people' (whether it meant respectably, regretfully, respectfully, retrospectively or what was a question the pre-conference press briefing was never able to resolve); but in the event even that amendment was never called, and the debate and vote took place simply on the motion of the Young Conservatives' National Advisory Committee: 'This Conference welcomes the successful outcome of the negotiations to join the European Economic Community and urges full support for British entry.'

The 'great debate' was all over in three hours. In contrast to the Labour conference's emphasis on bread-and-butter issues, the Conservatives were worried about abstract issues like sovereignty, and sought to grasp opportunities primarily of a political kind. The Young Conservative opener, Peter Price, dealt neatly – perhaps too neatly – with the mandate problem: 'The Leader of the Opposition is a well-known follower of public opinion polls. That is why he is Leader of the Opposition.' Sir Tufton Beamish, the CGE Chairman, read a Churchillian oration claiming entry was 'natural and right. It is dictated by yesterday's tragic mistakes, demanded by today's grim problems, and supported by the hopes for tomorrow of all who love freedom and prize peace.'

Geoffrey Rippon breezily reviewed the terms and quoted Arnold Smith, the Secretary-General of the Commonwealth: 'I believe that British EEC entry will make the Commonwealth more important, not less so, to all the thirty-two members.' He asked the conference to remember that if some feared our entry would be a national defeat, 'they are equally frightened by us . . . that the armoured brigade of our language, our technology and our way of life would be thrusting

THE GOVERNMENT AND THE CONSERVATIVES

across Europe once Britain joined'. He reiterated the Labour government's pledge that pensions would be raised to meet rising prices, and for the benefit of the inshore fishermen who had come in two dozen boats off the Brighton promenade with anti-EEC slogans and Very pistols he promised (what was already accepted in Brussels) that the fisheries policy would have to be changed before Britain would join.

Norman St John-Stevas envisaged the Queen as a potential Empress of Europe and was greeted enthusiastically by the block of Young Conservatives. A Conservative student breathlessly wanted 'to share with you a little of my excitement at the prospects' (to be stopped by shouts of 'Whack-ho') and went on to list three preoccupations that excited young people: pollution, 'a viable deterrent which we shall hold on trust for Europe' and aid to the Third World. Winding up the debate Sir Alec Douglas-Home, long a great favourite of the conference, confessed: 'I would not like to urge a young man to contemplate his future in a Britain which has rejected the opportunity to join a European partnership.'

The speeches from the 'antis' were perhaps the more interesting. Sir Derek Walker-Smith made a sombre barrister's presentation (greeted by Young Conservatives with cries of 'Cheer up!'): 'I have sat on no fences and jumped on no bandwagon – I've studied the evidence as I've been trained to do.' He drew a clear distinction between the costs, which were certain, and the benefits, which were not proven. Enoch Powell, quaking with emotion, emphatically read a prepared statement. He recalled Mr Heath's words in June 1970 that MPs 'would be absolutely free to vote in the way they so decided'; stressed that what mattered were the long-run political consequences; and ended, reminiscent of Martin Luther:

I do not believe this nation, which has maintained and defended its independence for a thousand years, will now submit to see it merged or lost; nor did I become a member of our sovereign parliament in order to consent to that sovereignty being abated or transferred. Come what may, I cannot and I will not.

In the conference hall there was some applause, but also some shouting against him. (That night at a crowded Safeguards rally he seemed less solitary, martyred and on edge. Indeed the fervour he could still inspire came through clearly from one of the lady stewards after the meeting. 'There's only God above Enoch – and only just. I could die for that man.')

A fruit-grower from Dover and Deal came nearer to raising an authentic *vox populi*:

How the hell I am going to take a lower price for my fruit and vegetables I'm damned if I know. . . . If we join Europe and throw away half our trade with the southern hemisphere, we'll be handing it over to the little yellow Nips – and I'm no brother of them. Some of you are brothers to all, but I'm not. I'm not pro-European. I'm not pro-Commonwealth. I'm pro-English, and I think it's about time we all were.

(He ended with the touching peroration: 'Surely it's better to be out of Europe and have a Conservative government than be in Europe and then be lumbered with Wilson? Mr Prime Minister, I'm sorry if I've been disrespectful.')

When the Chairman called for a show of hands, very few indeed went up publicly to oppose the motion. But the Prime Minister himself, it appears, had insisted on a card vote – it set a unique precedent in a Conservative conference that such a vote should be demanded in advance (it is very seldom demanded at all). When the ballots had been collected in bread baskets and plastic liquid containers, the vote came out at 2,474 for the motion, 324 against – a ratio of eight to one. (In theory just over 4,000 people had a vote, but some had mislaid their ballot papers, some were out at tea, and some just could not get into the overcrowded hall and overflow hall to vote. Some, of course, may also have abstained.) The show of hands, however, was enough for the victors. Blue balloons were let off by a block of Young Conservatives who wore badges declaring 'I'm for Europe', half a dozen 'Euro-dollies' in peasant dress hired from a local theatrical costumier advanced on the rostrum with the star-spangled blue flag of European unity, and the Chairman had to call for order.

At the time of the party conference in Brighton, the anti-Marketeers had not met again since Parliament adjourned, but Sir Derek Walker-Smith and Neil Marten believed that they still had over thirty firmly committed to vote against entry in the face of a three-line whip. Admittedly, by that time it had become very clear that their numbers would be more than offset by Labour Marketeers willing to defy a three-line whip on their side to vote in favour. The 1970 Group met again the week after; on the morning of 18 October Neil Marten told the government whips that his figure was still thirty-two; and that evening – to the anti-Marketeers' minds, *post hoc, propter hoc* – in a special statement issued from 10 Downing Street, the Conservative

Party, the Labour Opposition and the public learnt that the whips would be off on October 28. The anti-Marketeers were almost sorry that, at this late stage, they should be deprived of the martyr's crown, and it is very doubtful if their number was swelled by more than two or three at that very late stage thanks to the official freedom of the vote. (Had it been declared a free vote in early summer, some of them believe their score would have been double.) As it was, in the final division there were 33 Conservatives and 6 Ulster Unionists who voted against, and 2 Conservative abstentions.

We thus have, in fact, two contradictory theories by the rebels of how the decision to call off the whips was handled. One theory maintains that this had always been the intention, but that the rebels had been cynically forced to wrestle with their consciences and the consequences to themselves of defying a three-line whip by being led up the garden path. The other maintains that it was only by standing firm and being seen to do so that, at the very last moment, the rebels changed the government's mind and obtained a free vote. The second is in fact much closer to the truth than the first theory, though it, too, is an overstatement in black and white terms of a truth that was a little greyer, and of a calculation in which the Labour rebels entered just as much into the simultaneous equation.

Whether or not the possibility of a free vote had been left deliberately open in the phrasing of Edward Heath's and Anthony Barber's pronouncements, in the course of the party conference in October Francis Pym came to the conclusion, after re-checking all his lists, that a free vote would lose only two or three votes on the Conservative side by then, but that there was – and the information coming from the Labour side gave them some encouragement for that view – a substantial potential gain in Labour abstentions or even votes in favour outweighing any such loss on the Conservative side. It was not really thought that Harold Wilson might seize the initiative and be the first to declare the vote free on the Labour side: but some Conservative Ministers did not imagine in their wildest dreams that he would not follow suit, once the government took off its whips. (They had a somewhat anxious ten days wondering if they had left the move too late.) Others regarded the calculation as valid whatever the Labour Party decided about whipping: in terms of the party battle in the country, 'dishing the Whigs' by reversing what might be thought the more proper constitutional course – a whipped government and a free Opposition vote – could only do good anyhow. What is more, before

Estimates of Conservative Rebellion

	CGE estimate 1 Feb. 1971	Whips' estimate 3 Feb. 1971	CGE estimate 1 May 1971	CGE estimate 1 Aug. 1971	Vote 28 Oct. 1971
Members of the CGE	127 ⎫ 217	⎫ 194	168 ⎫ 217	202 ⎫ 284	For: 282
Others in favour	90 ⎭	⎭	49 ⎭	82 ⎭	Absent: 1
Doubtful ⎧ +	27 ⎫ 75	⎫ 70	28 ⎫ 71	'Persuadable' 20 ⎫ (41)	Abstained: 2 ⎫ (41)
⎨	19 ⎬	⎬	18 ⎬		
⎩ –	29 ⎭ (62)	⎭	25 ⎭		
Against	33 ⎭	62	37	21 ⎭	Against: 39 ⎭

public opinion on the Continent a free vote would appear far more convincing.

The issue was discussed among a widening circle of senior Ministers while the Brighton conference was still on, and one by one Francis Pym brought various Ministers round to open their minds to a possibility which some of them had mentally discarded months before. But in the hurly-burly of such a conference, really concentrated and efficient discussion with everyone there at once is difficult to organize: so after rather tiring discussions the matter was left in suspense. In any case there did not seem to be any immediate hurry, for though the possibility of announcing a free vote in the course of the Prime Minister's winding-up speech on the Saturday was considered, it was rejected as a somewhat incongruous juxtaposition with his main clarion call for entry – and not a measure in any case that would be very popular with the assembled constituency stalwarts. So the decision was not actually taken until Ministers were back in London, on the Monday afternoon; but it was announced immediately thereafter. Three days later Sir Alec Douglas-Home opened the great parliamentary debate.

7　The Campaign in the Country

Gut tuggit in tuggit awn
　　The Unity

Converging Elements in the European Movement

In the previous chapter we have already looked at the propaganda deployed both by the government itself and by the Conservative Party. Important as this was, however, some of it began rather late in the day. In any case, these were by no means the only persuaders in the field. The government had more than one ally on this issue, and some of these allies went ahead long before the government's own campaign began. One of the most important will be described in this chapter; several others will be discussed further on in the book.

In its public information effort the government was able to work with a wide variety of bodies and groupings. One or two of these were in themselves in some respects innovations: what certainly was breaking new ground was the care with which these very different bodies and their activities were co-ordinated. The co-ordination was by no means always successful. But this degree of mutual harmonization between the various information services of the government, the Trade Union Committee for Europe, the Conservative Political Centre, the Labour Committee for Europe, the Confederation of British Industry and individuals with positions of influence in normally contrasting and indeed competing media of communication – to mention only some which would, at first sight, seem unlikely bedfellows – was possible only in a cause that transcended the traditional barriers of British public life, where men and women were concerned about the country's future and prepared to sink their more usual sectarian habits of co-operation to serve that overriding national concern. And it would hardly have been feasible had there not existed for years – indeed for two decades – a cluster of inter-party organizations in Britain dedicated to the European cause.

The British Council of the European Movement was not formed until 1969, but it resulted from the amalgamation of two earlier bodies – the United Kingdom Council of the European Movement and

Britain in Europe. The UK Council was an eminently respectable body. Its patrons were the five heads of the chief religious denominations – the Archbishops of Canterbury and Westminster, the Moderators of the Church of Scotland and of the Free Church Federal Council, and the Chief Rabbi. It had been presided over for many years by Harold Macmillan's friend, Sir Edward Beddington-Behrens (the knighthood conferred in 1957 was no doubt earned at least in part for services to and through the organization). Sir Edward was a financier, and had used his influence in the City to raise funds for the UK Council, which spent some £16,000 in 1960, ran conferences and published a glossy magazine well supported by prestige advertising.

As an organization it had never clearly opted between the larger free trade area concept of the Maudling negotiations, EFTA, North Atlantic free trade proposals, and accession to the Treaty of Rome. It tended, in fact, to follow rather than lead government policy even in 1961. When Sir Edward died late in 1968, the UK Council did not as it happened sit on any particular financial treasure. But it had on its notepaper a wide variety of politicians, businessmen and academics (some of whom proved active opponents of entry in 1970–71), and it enjoyed a great deal of goodwill with the British Establishment. As the issue was focusing again on EEC entry and there was no reason to have two competing organizations working for the same basic policy direction, it thus became a natural and attractive partner for Britain in Europe.

Britain in Europe was a more active, intellectually more committed and politically tougher body. It was set up by a group of people a generation younger than the typical UK Council supporter. Some of them had served in the war, some had been conscientious objectors, some had been too young to be either and perhaps for that reason felt all the more keenly a personal responsibility to contribute to making any recurrence of war in the future impossible. It was this generation that had been catapulted into political adulthood by Hiroshima, to whom – if any such concept could have validity – collective war guilt seemed universal, and who felt a corresponding commitment to peace aims and the construction of a new system of international order. Many of them were federalists in the late 1940s, and some of these regarded European federalism as a first step, both pilot project and pace-maker, for a new world system. Some had met through the Council for Education in World Citizenship, Youth Parliaments and such like before they left school, some at the universities, particularly

Oxford, Cambridge and Glasgow, some through the various proliferating youth and international conferences of the period, like those of Federal Union and the Crusade for World Government. Though not all would have described themselves as federalists, many were associated with the Federal Trust for Education and Research, established in 1945, which in practice came to concentrate on research, study and the propagation of ideas on European unity.

One way or another there were up to twenty-five years of study groups, conferences and common travel, memoranda, pamphlets and manifestos, personal friendships (and sometimes rivalries) behind them by the time events – not through their doing – turned more in their favour.[1] They came from a wide variety of backgrounds: one the son of a peer, another who left school at fourteen, one the son of a small tailor, another the son of a bank clerk, several with family origins on the Continent, some candidates or local councillors of the Labour, some of the Liberal and some of the Conservative Party, some fulltime trade unionists, some lawyers, some in public relations, one who worked for the British Council of Churches, another for *The Economist*, several at universities or various research institutions.

Come 1971 a few of them with the requisite professional experience were in the forefront of the propaganda battle; others were exerting

[1] One could trace the continuity of personnel of one of the strains in the European Movement through various *groupuscules* forming and re-forming in the 'forties, 'fifties and 'sixties. To pick out only a handful of names which recurred in the minutes of Federal Union in the late 1940s (most of them were then in their late teens or early twenties): Ota Adler, David Barton, Norman Hart, Martin Maddan, John Pinder, Noel Salter, E. G. Thompson, Sheila Webster (now Kitzinger). In the early 'fifties Noel Salter (from 1950), Uwe Kitzinger (from 1951), François Duchêne (from 1952) and Richard Mayne had become European civil servants in Strasbourg or Luxemburg, and David Webster was secretary of World Student Federalists in Amsterdam.

The British delegation to the Wiesbaden Conference in January 1959 included (together with Roy Jenkins and Geoffrey Rippon) Ota Adler, David Barton, Norman Hart, Martin Maddan, John Pinder, E. G. Thompson and David Webster. In the late 'sixties the Council of Management of Britain in Europe and the Campaign for Europe included Ota Adler, David Barton, Norman Hart, Uwe Kitzinger, Martin Maddan, John Pinder and Noel Salter. On the night of 28 October 1971 there was a party in Ota Adler's house, attended not only by Sir Alec Douglas-Home and Geoffrey Rippon, but also by many of the 'old guard' who had met so often in the same house twenty-odd years before. And at the general purposes committee meeting of the European Movement in June 1972, of the fifteen members present, five were accounted for by the faithful Ota Adler, David Barton, Norman Hart, Martin Maddan and John Pinder.

influence within their administrations; others stood on the touchline supplying briefs, intervening in public only for specific limited purposes, maintaining contacts abroad, or proffering more (or less) useful advice.

It is easy enough to make out a conspiratorial theory of history about them – a theory that both flatters their vanity and serves the interests of their political opponents.[1] But this would be grossly to overrate their influence, for that influence would have remained minor had not national fortunes and demands, and therefore national policies, evolved in directions they had more or less anticipated and advocated. Nor was there ever any clear leadership. What mattered was that most of them, while pursuing their own chosen careers in different fields in which they could remain useful to the cause, had remained in close touch with several others of the larger inter-connected 'mafia', that their political thinking had remained along broadly parallel lines, and that underlying often sharp tactical disagreements there were common reflexes as to aims and strategy – very much indeed as had been the case with the older 'Establishment generation' against whose national patriotism and mismanagement of international affairs they were (albeit in what today might be thought of as a rather genteel fashion) in clear revolt.

Britain in Europe was the by-product of a detailed study made by the Economist Intelligence Unit in 1957 under that title. The study had made money because, faced with the (to them unexpected) crystallization of a trading bloc on the Continent, British industry and finance suddenly had to turn to this younger generation (who had learnt languages, travelled, done their homework, and knew their opposite numbers on the Continent) for information and advice on how to safeguard their own business interests. After the 1963 veto the same group round the Federal Trust continued its activities at conferences (frequently in Sussex) and working dinners (hence the title 'Eurodiners' or 'Criterion Group') out of which came first joint publications (like the July 1965 issue of the *Journal of Common Market Studies*) and later another organization housed in the same offices as Britain in Europe, the Campaign for a Political Community. Under a variety of labels with

[1] Compare for example 'The Federalist Pressures in Britain', by R. Hugh Corbet in *Britain, Not Europe*, Anti-Common Market League, London, 1962, pp. 20–4. The theme is taken up again in similar vein in the pseudonymous pamphlet by 'Cato', *Pride, Prejudice and Persuasion: How the Establishment Got Hooked on Europe*, David Rendel, London, 1971.

interlocking committees and groups of officers they ran a wide range of study groups, seminars, training courses and public lectures, those of direct benefit to business being priced at what the market would bear to help finance the political side of their activities.

They were very much a small though expanding group of 'Euro-fanatics' at the time the second British application was being planned by the Labour government, though they felt the time was coming when they should be able to appeal to a much wider section of the community. In 1967 Ernest Wistrich (who had just sold up his timber company to go into Labour politics on the national level, but narrowly missed winning Hendon North in the 1966 election) took over as Director of Britain in Europe. It had then an income of some £7,000 a year, derived largely from corporate subscribers, though the sum also included a yearly travel grant of £2,500 from the Foreign Office which Lord Chalfont tripled in 1968. That year it also raised £25,000, mainly at a dinner presided over by Lord Gladwyn with Giscard d'Estaing as guest of honour, thus making it possible to employ the services of a professional fund-raiser – Arrow Services, as it happened, run by Jeffrey Archer (later MP for Louth), which normally charged 10% commission but was prepared on this occasion to act for a flat fee. The group organized a dinner in July 1969, held in the Guildhall and attended by Harold Wilson and Edward Heath, where £450,000 was pledged, chiefly in the form of seven-year covenants exempted from tax, to a European Educational Research Trust. This was to promote the exchange of young leaders with Continental Europe and engage in similar educational and research activities, many of which were to have a longer-term effect parallel to that of the Movement's campaign.

It was this group of people also which organized George Brown's trip round the capitals of the Six in 1968–69 calling for a 'second Messina Conference' to launch a political community including Britain. This plan was meant as a way of by-passing the French veto at the same time as heading directly towards foreign policy discussions and thus also by-passing the problems of economic harmonization. Some of the group believe that it was George Brown's visit to Michel Debré on that tour which triggered off the Soames affair. The same group through their federalist connections (Altiero Spinelli in particular) organized the initiative out of which was to come the Anglo-Italian declaration of 28 April 1969 pledging the two governments to the direct election of the European Parliament. The declaration stood out, rather oddly, as an isolated gesture; but as the whole initiative depended on the assumption that President de Gaulle would continue to prevent British accession to the EEC, his departure from the Elysée changed the rules of the game back again to a negotiation on the basis of the Rome Treaty.

The formal merger of Britain in Europe with the United Kingdom Council also came in summer 1969. The physical merger was completed by the end of the year, and when the former Director-General of the UK Council resigned in February 1970, what began as a merger became in effect a take-over by the newer and politically more vigorous organization.

The idea of a massive public relations campaign by the European Movement in support of the re-activated attempt by the government to enter the EEC was thus an obvious one, discussed with one or two Labour Ministers not long after the Hague summit, and before the election in which the government was generally expected to be returned for another term of office. When Edward Heath, instead of Harold Wilson, turned out to have won the battle, that did not fundamentally affect this issue: just as Conservatives in the European Movement had been preparing to help though the attempt was being conducted by a Labour government, so now Labour men in the Movement saw no reason not to proceed with the same crusade. Ernest Wistrich brought in two former Labour MPs (Alan Lee Williams and Stanley Henig, both conveniently available after their election defeats) and a number of other Labour people as organizers in the Movement and maintained a strict political balance between Conservatives and Labour people in the Campaign Group and in the Movement as a whole. Alan Lee Williams in particular worked closely with the Labour Marketeers in the House while also building up the Movement's regional organization.

Much later on, at the end of 1971 and in early 1972, there were accusations to be heard that here were Labour people co-operating with a detestable Conservative government. On the other hand Labour Marketeers felt it would have been grotesque and almost unthinkable for them to have abandoned the cause for which they had in some cases worked for ten or twenty years simply because the balance of view among their party friends on this issue was beginning to shift. Indeed it would hardly be necessary to write all this if there had not arisen, after the event, doubts as to how much of their work for the European cause should be recorded, how much discreetly suppressed from this story.

The doubts (which themselves took on a certain historical significance in their turn) only arose out of fear of a future misunderstanding of the course of past events – combined with a feeling that while those on the extremes of the political spectrum could have every freedom to work for their views against an agreed party line, those who shared common ground with other parties might not even work for their own party to stick to its previously agreed position. The fear was that – looking back on the first nine months of 1971 from the vantage point of a later period, in which the Labour party conference had effectively reversed its stand (from being on principle in favour of entry to being against, at least on the terms secured) – their enemies in the constituencies and the House might be tempted to draw the conclusion that Labour Europeans must, at this time, have been in a dilemma of conscience.

Any such view would constitute a fallacy, rewriting history by foreshortening events. Until the end of July even the Party Leader was suspending judgment on the substance of the issue. Until October the party leadership had made it perfectly clear that every wing of the party was free to campaign for its view on the issue – those who wanted Conference to continue its pro-entry line, and those who wanted it to reverse its position at least as far as entry on the available terms was concerned. For any Labour Marketeer to have anticipated a reversal in party policy that went against the grain of his convictions and to have ceased to campaign for the cause in which he believed would have been alien to the whole tradition of conscience and courage in the Labour Movement. It was some of the Labour anti-Marketeers in the party, at this stage, who were planning together in the Safeguards Campaign and in the Palace of Westminster, sharing platforms in the country and marching literally shoulder to shoulder in the streets of London with Right-wing Conservatives to campaign against the policy laid down by Conference – and whose right to do so remained, quite properly, unchallenged.

As it happened, the issue of where Labour Marketeers should see their duty in the August-September period (when the National Executive had taken a stand on which Conference had only a fortnight before refrained from taking a decision) was raised quite explicitly by a young full-time official of the Labour Committee, Bruce Reed, who wrote to members of the Committee off his own bat that they could no longer speak publicly in favour of entry: 'It is essential we do not lay ourselves open to the charge of publicly splitting the party.'[1]

[1] 'Bent Reed', The Times, 2 August 1971.

His letter was immediately repudiated in full accord with his leading colleagues by Geoffrey de Freitas as Chairman of the Labour Committee for Europe: 'This letter was unauthorized and inaccurate. As the General Secretary of the Labour Party has explained, those members of the party who are in favour of British membership are, of course, free to argue their case. Our members are resolved to pursue this debate with vigour.'[1] Indeed so categorical was the Labour Committee's reaction that Bruce Reed was immediately sent on leave and thereafter employed on research work at home. It was on the rebound from Reed's attitude that Roy Jenkins initiated the organization of a series of meetings in September in direct contradiction of the anti-Market meetings organized by the National Executive; and Harold Wilson restated the position squarely later, when he wrote to Roy Jenkins on the latter's resignation of his hope of 'continuing the great debate of last year where absolute freedom was enjoyed, and I think the party benefited therefrom'.

Problems of the Harmonization of Effort

With Whitehall, the European Movement, and people on both the Labour and Conservative sides all eager to contribute to the cause of a wider West European integration, the first need was clearly for the integration of the efforts of such very disparate allies themselves. The European Movement's own Campaign Group came as close to providing an inter-party body as any; but its function was in the main an executive one, managing the Movement's own campaign and that of its different political wings and functional sub-sections. Its efforts had to be planned in the wider context of the overall national campaign of information and persuasion; and to keep the Movement's campaign in tune with the government and the press, and the government and press in tune with the Movement, two other gatherings established themselves alongside the Campaign Group: the government's co-ordination group, which eased collaboration between the government, the Movement, and some of its other allies on the issue, and the so-called 'media breakfasts' which aided closer contact between the European Movement, industry, the press, radio and television, and the government.

    With an overlapping membership of people, most of whom held influential positions in other bodies and organizations, these three groupings also had overlapping functions. They attempted to crystallize

[1] Letter to *The Times*, 5 August 1971.

a grid of links between like-minded people, none of them directed in any sense from above (civil servants, of course, excepted). It was the kind of network without which no democracy can really work, but made more explicit on this issue because time was short and the issue sharp.

The technique of co-operation thus evolved, some of its architects now argue, should be used more deliberately in future on other issues that transcend party – be it inflation or environmental pollution, venereal disease or the problems of the aged. While the issue was under topical party and intra-party dispute, there was some reticence on the extent to which the co-operation was consciously fostered. Some of the participants did not even mark the meetings in their diaries, and when on one occasion the presence of a civil servant who regularly attended the meetings of the Campaign Group of the European Movement was minuted by mistake, an erratum slip was circulated to delete his name. As key a figure as William Rodgers was simply not aware of either the co-ordinating meetings or the breakfasts while they were going on. Now that the battle is over, however, the story cannot be told without reference to these experiments; indeed they must be described, in so far as they have long-term relevance to the political process, so as to allow an assessment of their value and disadvantages. Moreover, neither their originality nor the problems they raise are a matter of party politics. There is evidence that had Labour been in power it might well have wished to foster much the same kind of co-operative effort on the issue.

The attempt deliberately to evolve a broad consensus on information policy arose out of a set of common problems that had to be faced by all those, whether in government or out of it, who were seeking to win the assent of the nation to British entry into the EEC. The first of these difficulties was the nature of the issue itself. It was so complex as to be virtually beyond the grasp of anyone in its entirety (one would have had to be a constitutional lawyer and an agricultural economist, a diplomat and an international monetary expert, a lobby correspondent and a social security specialist to understand it all); yet at the same time the question had been with the long-suffering public for too long – through two attempts full of hope, to be dashed by two vetoes from the Continent – so that it had also become a crashing bore. On the one hand there was ignorance and apathy combined with a conscious or unconscious mistrust of change and of anything alien. On the other hand the desire simply for something to happen – some panacea to lift the country miraculously out of its rut of slow growth, rising prices, difficult labour relations and declining influence in the world – did not meet the bill either. It was essential not only to explain the issues as clearly as possible but also to generate public acceptance for a leap into many as yet dimly perceived changes, and then to prepare the country to adapt to the new context in which it would have to live and earn its living.

The second set of difficulties was political and constitutional. While a very massive public relations exercise was required, it could not be undertaken on the requisite scale at the requisite time by the government alone. Indeed the government on its own could probably not have done it in any case, however much time and money it might have spent: there is enough built-in resistance to government in British society, enough of a tradition of voluntary action and pluralist inter-action, for purely governmental information and persuasion to have been discounted simply as 'propaganda'. (In the event, much of it was still thus dismissed, even in the way it finally came to be handled.) But, in any case, the time-scale imposed crippling limitations. On pain of looking as silly as the Labour government had in some ways looked after the 1967 attempt, the government could not pull out all the stops on its European enthusiasm until it knew that it really could this time gain entry. Nor could it advocate going in at a specific juncture on specific terms until, in order to improve them, it had finished arguing in Brussels and Paris how thoroughly inadequate the proposed terms were: only after that could it start arguing at home just how satis-factory the terms agreed had turned out to be. It therefore had to hold much of its fire at home until the main battle was over abroad. Thirdly there were constitutional limitations – on the extent to which official government resources of man-power and money could be deployed in the advocacy of entry; for that cause increasingly threatened to become one side in a highly divisive political battle, and had in any case not been approved by Parliament – at least not since 1967.

On the other hand, in partial mitigation of these three difficulties, the cause espoused by the government also disposed of a major potential asset: the goodwill – indeed the enthusiasm – of a large number of highly qualified people outside the official machine and often out of sympathy with the rest of the government's aims. There were trade unionists and representatives of industry, there were Labour politicians and there were wealthy individuals, there were highly professional journalists and there were knowledgeable 'Europeans', all of them eager to help, in what ways they could, to inform the public and to persuade it. It was clear that, just as the country needed a lead, so all these potential allies needed a lead or at least a forum in which they could concert their activities. It was not unnatural that that lead or forum was provided among others by those who were professionally most involved in the unfolding story, who were the best informed on progress in Brussels, the likely timing and political exigencies in Westminster, and who also controlled the largest information service in the country – the government.

The Minister responsible for the government's information programme was William Whitelaw, as it happened also the Leader of the House. This was a politically useful combination of functions: it was, after all, not least because of its effect on the decision in the House of Commons that the state of public opinion on this issue was important. William Whitelaw's blunt honesty, sane humanity and unassuming warmth made him, though at the time little known outside Westminster, perhaps the least divisive member of the government, and more acceptable beyond Conservative ranks than any other leading Conservative. It was thus in William Whitelaw's office that some of the first formal meetings took place late in 1970 to discuss how the government, the European Movement and their various allies could best cooperate in their efforts. Some six months later the regular meetings of the coordinating group were normally held at the Foreign Office and presided over for the government by Anthony Royle, the Under-Secretary of State who worked particularly with Geoffrey Rippon. The group met, generally in Anthony Royle's office, up to twice a week, continuing its work through the usually dead month of August. The meetings started with only a handful of people, attending very much *ad hoc* and partly in a personal capacity, but grew by Parkinson's Law. The Prime Minister's office was represented, later civil servants were drawn in and then appeared flanked with aides or deputies – until the group finished up as a rather unwieldy body ringed with silent observers and note-takers. A co-ordinator with his staff ensured the follow-up to these meetings. In early November Anthony Royle disbanded the little group with a letter of thanks for their work from the Prime Minister, who saw in this kind of co-operation a very useful lesson for the future.

The effort of which these meetings formed a part aimed of course not at monolithic unity but at voluntary co-ordination of effort by 'indicative planning'. Indeed in some ways it remained a rather uneasy operation: it was one to which civil servants were not accustomed, and occasionally they seemed too timid or even naïve to the seasoned publicists or those concerned with immediate politics. In turn, of course, the publicists may have seemed brash to the civil servants, who were very conscious of long-term problems of constitutional propriety, and those with their finger on the pulse of party politics may even have seemed to the rest unduly preoccupied with problems of personality and coterie rather than with the primary job in hand. But it was precisely in this interchange of experience in different walks of life, sharing of topical information, clash of attitudes and pooling of ideas that the value of the exercise lay.

We have seen that the common cause was such as to transcend some normally rather high conventional barriers. In the overriding national interest as they saw it men with little else in common than their belief in the European cause – indeed some of them more normally fighting on opposite sides of the political fence – at these different types of meetings exchanged detailed information on the situation in different cities and parts of the country, discussed how best to get the greatest visible consensus in favour of entry or helped one another to place letters and other relevant matter in the national newspapers. We shall see that William Whitelaw and other Ministers in any case had frequent communication through 'unusual channels' with some of the senior Marketeers on the Labour side; the interpretations and forecasts of the evolution in the Parliamentary Labour Party available to the European Movement provided a second – and usually similar – opinion. In much the same way the Conservative wing of the Movement supplemented and amplified – possibly even on occasion qualified – the information the government was getting from its own whips, and these reports greatly helped the Labour Marketeers, to whom it was useful not only to know more of the government's thinking and intentions, but also to have some awareness of the state of mind and likely voting intentions of the Conservative Party in the House. Moreover, the fact that these meetings included people normally engaged on the sides of industry or the trade unions provided information about what was happening in these quarters also. In addition, everyone concerned could benefit from reports on the opinion polls commissioned by the European Movement and from the lessons to be drawn from them. (The government did not have any polls of its own in the field.)

Such information, and the comparison of impressions of the overall situation in which each separate element was trying to conduct its own operation, was thus the first function of the co-ordinating group. The second was to keep each other informed of what each was doing and intended to do in the common cause. But of course things did not and were not meant to stop at a purely cognitive exercise. There were all sorts of ways in which Whitehall and the publicists, politicians and the organizers of voluntary bodies could be actively useful to each other. An experienced journalist could help the civil servants in the drafting of a popular document for government distribution. Representatives of industry could be asked to provide, for use in the debate, examples of Continental investment planned in Britain if Britain joined. The government could keep voluntary bodies in touch with visits from foreigners who should be entertained or might prove useful, the European Movement could offer platforms for Ministers and the group could pool lists of government, Opposition and non-party speakers for joint meetings in various parts of the country.

Many of these were little things that could in theory have been done bilaterally over the telephone, or through regular written memos or circulars. Few would have thought that any of this collaboration raised any constitutional issue if it had been done that way. But that way it could all too easily not have got done, or have been done only partially with someone left out; so for greater efficiency people sat down round a table together at a specified time each week, pooled what they knew, sparked bright ideas off each other and bounced them around; and it is only really in meetings for 'group-think' of this kind that new syntheses of plans can be worked out. This was no forum for decision-making. But it could help to air and test in discussion advice which it might have been more difficult to weigh if received bilaterally from each source in isolation. The emphasis was on function rather than role, on getting the common job done most efficiently rather than on who was paid by whom. Whether or not this co-operation was finally effective in per-suading the country, it certainly helped to sustain and reinforce enthusiasm and got people – on the whole – thinking and working together along more or less parallel lines.

One of the first things for these meetings to decide was the emphasis of the public relations effort in any given week or month. Concentra-tion, as we shall see, had to shift from one set of issues to another in response to events, to arguments brought up on the other side of the debate, and to shifts in public mood. It was clearly important that with something like eighty Ministers of various grades of seniority speaking at different types of function up and down the country, they should not contradict each other. Thus particularly the Labour element in the European Movement was arguing that British wages would be on average £7 a week higher if they had grown as fast as those of the Six since the EEC was formed. Simultaneously a Minister replied in the House that exact international wage-rate comparisons were statistically dubious exercises. Both statements were, no doubt, true at their own level – indeed the first was little more than a pleonasm – but the conjunction of the two could only cause hilarity at anti-Market meetings, so that the emphasis here had to be co-ordinated a little.

Nor was it sufficient to avoid this kind of needless apparent self-contradiction. While there were clearly special occasions or special Ministers for plugging away at special topics, by and large it was desirable that Ministers and others should mutually reinforce each other by speaking to much the same themes. This was not to gag anyone, but it did imply first suggesting passages for insertion in speeches, or writing parts of speeches for busy Ministers with many other responsibilities, and then putting the useful parts of these speeches into the press releases issued by party headquarters or by the European Movement. Naturally, leading Labour pro-Marketeers chimed in with their own variations on similar themes, and on occasion the co-ordinating group could be the channel through which it was made known that such and such a Minister would do most service to the European cause at some moment at which he was, perhaps, particularly unpopular, by not adding his voice to the pro-Market chorus just then. As usual, not all the speeches that were reported were actually physically delivered to any audience. In any case the links with the media – not least through the 'media breakfasts' – could also influence the emphasis of press and television coverage and argument, and reciprocally the media experts could advise on where they thought the government and the various parallel organizations advocating entry should at any time place their stress.

Far from confining itself to mere reviews of parliamentary opinion, the co-ordinating group could discuss parliamentary tactics such as, for example, the placing of parliamentary questions by pro-Marketeers on both sides of the House. The same kind of question-placing was of course being organized simultaneously by the anti-Marketeers, though the pro-Marketeers were perhaps rather more successful at getting their questions called – they were more numerous, knew their way around better as to how a question should be phrased and how best to insert it into the parliamentary sausage machine. (It was a practice that ran into trouble a little later, when it became public knowledge that on quite a different issue civil servants had taken an all too obvious part in building up a bank of questions designed to filibuster and avoid awkward tests for Peter Walker, the Secretary for the Environment; but the Marketeers did not use the same mechanism, and the effects of their question-placing were quite different.)

Both at the meetings of the co-ordinating group and at the media breakfasts it became one of the most important functions to be performed to stop the battle on the issue from turning into one between the parties. When the issue went sour on the Labour Party late in the day it became an 'objective function' from the government's point of view (though it had not really been a primary purpose originally) that these different types of meeting also made some Labour people – journalists in particular – feel directly or indirectly part of the show. There was a luscious political temptation for Conservative Ministers and for the press to lay into Harold Wilson, confront him with his European record and damn him out of court. But the Labour participants in these meetings again and again urged understanding for Wilson's position of attempting to keep a coalition of Marketeers and anti-Marketeers together, and pressed the Conservatives to consider the consequences if the government, instead of simply fighting for the European cause, counter-attacked and exacerbated the Labour split. They influenced the phraseology of the debate to keep it from becoming too divisive in party-political terms. They insisted on the vital necessity for the Conservatives not to embarrass Roy Jenkins and his friends with praise, and to avoid anything that might make their life within the Labour Party more difficult. They came, indeed, to feel some respect for the self-discipline which (with very few exceptions) the Conservative Party managed to impose on itself to resist these openings for the scoring of party-political points.

The Labour participants also managed to stop one or two newspapers from doing any really vicious 'carve-up job' on their Party Leader. For weeks in the early summer they helped to hold several different quality papers to a remarkably uniform line: pained incredulity and urgent appeal to Harold Wilson that surely he could not, surely he would not, rat on his European past. If one had to point to any one achievement of these various kinds of meeting, perhaps one should mention the degree of concerted self-restraint with which both the Conservative Party and the press refrained from going to town against Labour on the issue as much as they could have done in purely partisan terms.

The European Movement's media breakfasts were one of the responses of the pro-Market forces to demands from some of the media (notably television) for easier access to the vast body of disparate data they required to do their job of information properly, and for better communication with those who could help them gain some overall sense of perspective of the complex issues and tortuous processes of the Brussels negotiations. Some of the men in the media were at the same time long-standing Marketeers anxious to awaken both the government and the private pro-Market organizations to the importance of more skilful public relations. To paint the result – as some will no doubt try to do – as an insidious attempt by the government to rape the media would be inexact. It was, if one wanted to put it in such terms, almost as much an attempt by the media to seduce the government into much greater efforts to bridge the gap between 'them' and 'us'.

As a crystallization of the government's and the European Movement's will to inform and use the media, the breakfasts appear to have been largely the brainchild of Geoffrey Tucker, the public relations consultant who, after being the Conservative Party's publicity director until the day after the successful 1970 election campaign, later set up on his own. In America he would no doubt be described as a lobbyist – or rather perhaps as a lobbyist in reverse, since he lobbied not so much the government on other people's as other people on the government's behalf. On the television side, Jim Garrett proved an equally useful contact; he had been largely responsible for the Conservatives' party-political television programmes in the 1970 election. But of course Whitehall itself had at its disposal its own information officers with excellent relations, particularly with the press, and these civil servants were obviously deployed by their Ministers on an issue that was so crucial to the government simultaneously in home and in foreign affairs.

What any public relations campaign of this kind requires is people with a mastery of the art of 'listmanship' – of knowing, or of knowing how to find out quickly, not only what eminent bureaucrat lays down the policy on television news bulletins, but also which shirt-sleeved script editor actually decides what goes in, and in what form, just before the bulletin goes out over the air. It needs understanding of cascades of opinion – which journalist is read by which other journalists who will reflect his attitudes or at least not lightly contradict them. It needs also awareness that on one newspaper it is the lobby correspondent who really matters, while on another, if one wants to place something in the gossip columns, tensions on the staff are such that to go through the editor could be counter-productive. It requires people who understand the logistics of editorial policy: that personnel has to be planned for well in advance if there is to be good coverage from Brussels, that budgets have to be rejigged to allow for foreign travel, and other mundane but all too often determinant nuts and bolts of the profession.

It was Geoffrey Tucker who largely organized and acted as chairman of the 'media breakfasts'. We have already seen that Tucker was a member of the Conservative Group for Europe, as were leading Ministers of the Crown. Ministers and some of their civil servants regularly attended the more or less weekly early-morning breakfasts organized by the European Movement at the Connaught Hotel, at which a dozen or more people – politicians, representatives of industry, organizers of voluntary groups and television and newspaper journalists – came together. Unlike the members of the co-ordinating group that usually met in the Foreign Office, and of the Campaign Group meeting in Chandos House, the participants at the Connaught Hotel breakfasts varied from one week to the next, according to what might be a topical theme or a perceived need. (Thus at one stage financial and City editors were drawn in to supplement the briefings the journalists were getting from the Treasury – thought by some to be lukewarm – and to let them meet some representatives of industry who were really keen on entry.) The breakfasts saw hard-nosed exchanges of view between different people each involved in their own way in the handling of the issue. The journalists were able to tell the European Movement and Whitehall frankly what they thought of their public relations efforts and how they could be improved – that such and such a line of argument was too airy-fairy, or that it needed quite a different speaker to put it over if it was to get across. Party politicians and industrial representatives could suggest lines of argument for the press to explore.

What the breakfasts tried to do – and to some extent they succeeded – was to act like a telephone exchange 'plugging people into each other', and help lay down a system in which a stimulus occurring at one point could provoke a swift response at quite another. Pro-Market politicians could be detailed to shadow anti-Marketeers, being warned of any declarations likely to hit the headlines – and of the deadlines by which they had to make a counter-statement to appear in parallel on the media. A powerful pamphlet or article from the anti-Market side could be given a quick reply by an article written for or placed in a friendly daily or weekly. In this exchange and mart of news and views the volume of transactions at the breakfasts and arising out of them bilaterally was said by one of those involved to have been 'fantastic'.

Underlying much of this exercise was the feeling that time was short – the campaign had to peak in July in case of a vote before the recess – and that the printed word takes longer to make its impact than the spoken or the visual image. The weeklies could not be neglected, for they set the intellectually respectable tone from which popular journalists did not like needlessly to depart. The quality dailies mattered in themselves and for much the same indirect reason. But the cutting edge of much of the public relations exercise lay in papers like the *Mirror*, popularizing to a readership of perhaps 12 million, in the ITN news in the evening with a 10–15 million audience, and in the BBC's *Today* programme with 8 million listeners in the early morning when they are fresh to take in news and opinions.

On the *Mirror*'s attitude there was never any doubt – though it could have wavered. Nigel Ryan, editor of the ITN news, felt it his duty as a public service to put on, for most of July, a five-minute item giving information on the Common Market every weekday evening just after the main bulletin – television time which would have cost advertisers something like £1¼ million in that one month. In one or two cases some people even claimed – perhaps quite wrongly – to have detected a certain change in tone. The *Today* programme on BBC radio had for some time been felt to be unhelpful. It was for the campaign a perhaps fortuitous but not unwelcome by-product of the departure for other reasons of Jack de Manio, and his replacement by Robert Robinson, that with John Timpson's excellent detailed reporting from Brussels the programme started the nation's day with a certain amount of interest in and even at times apparent enthusiasm for the cause.

There is always the temptation – and for good bread-and-butter reasons, no less than personal satisfaction in a job well done – to over-estimate the impact of any particular public relations exercise. In a sphere as subtle and intangible, as polycentric and as ornery as the communications industry, cause and effect are in any case almost impossible to measure. But if, one way or another, the Market cause had quite a few lucky breaks in 1971, no doubt Stephen Leacock's adage would seem to some of its organizers to be relevant: 'The harder I work, the luckier I become.'

The Organization of the Movement's Campaign

The third in the cluster of gatherings that loosely co-ordinated the total effort was the European Movement's own Campaign Group. It was this small group of youngish people who, under Ernest Wistrich's direction and in close consultation with the government, conducted the main unofficial public relations exercise. To ensure close liaison with the government's efforts, it was attended regularly by a member of the Foreign Office staff. It met practically every week, usually on Tuesdays, for exactly one year, starting on 3 November 1970 with an agreement to maintain strict security about its activities, and concluding on 3 November 1971 that it had attained its general objectives. These it defined retrospectively as being: 'to build up and sustain support for entry among opinion-formers in all sections of society to enable MPs of all parties who supported entry to vote for it.' In other words it neither concentrated on persuading MPs directly (a job best left to fellow MPs or individual initiatives) nor tried to appeal directly to the public at large – too big and in many ways, given the time factor, an unnecessarily ambitious task on which to embark immediately: better to leave that task to the government later and to the opinion-formers on whom the campaign sought to concentrate. (We shall see that in fact, however, there were times when the campaign also worked the other way round, seeking to influence the opinion-formers by activities directed past them at the general public.)

The Movement's campaign was managed from its somewhat ramshackle suite of offices in Chandos House, Victoria, where the various parallel organizations grouped under its umbrella had their headquarters, served very largely by the identical administrative staff. The plethora of names on the door-plate was reminiscent of those on a tax-haven solicitor's office: the United Europe Association and the Campaign for Europe, the Trade Union Committee for Europe and the Conservative Group for Europe, the European Educational and Research Trust and the European Luncheon Club, the Young European Left, the British Section of the Council of European Municipalities, the Young European Management Association, the Labour Committee for Europe and the Committee of Student European Associations. All these were serviced essentially by a dozen administrators with another dozen secretaries and a good deal of voluntary help, plus as the campaign went on some dozen regional organizers, until at the climax – opposing as it were the handful or so of anti-Market professionals –

there were fifty-three people full-time or part-time on the payroll, including Philip Zec, the former *Daily Mirror* director and cartoonist, retained as a consultant.

In addition the campaign retained the PR firm Collett, Dickenson, Pearce and Partners for a fee of £1,500 per month, with John Pearce acting as advertising consultant. A long-standing federalist and former Labour candidate, Norman Hart of Gwynne Hart and Associates, was in charge of public relations for the Labour Movement. Another professional, Roland Freeman of Freeman and Garlick, was on the Campaign Group and on the Conservative Group for Europe Committee, whose PR he handled. The regional organizer for Northern England and former Conservative candidate Brian Baird was assisted by the firm of Ramsey Baird and Associates, the Scottish organizer and the Yorkshire organizer each had a professional PR firm at their elbow, while the organization at various times boasted Mrs Spicer assisted by Major Spicer (Chairman of the Conservative Political Centre) and the former Labour MP Stanley Henig assisted by Mrs Henig. The paper and colour printing of its tabloid was largely done by a firm controlled by the former Labour MP Woodrow Wyatt. It was, in other words, a cross between a group of old friends interlocking with both the political parties and a cluster of professionally retained PR enterprises.

Such campaigns obviously cost money. The original budget was for a two-year campaign of £250,000 per annum: £85,000 for advertising and publications, £7,000 for exhibitions, audio-visual aids, speakers' training, etc., £20,000 to be transferred to associated bodies in cash, £15,000 for opinion surveys, £10,000 for public relations at the centre, and £50,000 for administration – half at the centre, half in the regions. The way things developed, however, total spending for the single financial year ending 31 March 1972 ran at nearer £550,000 – some £450,000 above what the Movement thought of as its 'normal' level of activity, or at least what it had spent the previous financial year. The degree to which the European Movement geared itself up for its effort in the summer of 1971 is illustrated by nothing as vividly as by its accounts for the three years ending on 31 March of each year (see p. 210).

On the expenditure side, the opinion research was, naturally, carried out largely before the main battle began: but the continuous monitoring of public opinion (on which we shall draw in a later chapter) continued through the financial year. The 1971–72 grants to allied or subsidiary bodies in Britain went chiefly to the Conservative Group for Europe, the Labour Committee for Europe, the Liberal European Action Group, the Trades Union Committee for Europe, women's European groups and a few other bodies – in varying amounts down to £16 for the European Association of Teachers. The other figures are a faithful reflection of the sheer volume of activity deployed by and through the Movement – almost as if what had been a well-connected shell company in 1969 had been injected with new management and finance and become a go-go operation.

Rather over half a million pounds spent on public relations in the widest sense is in one way a fair sum of money. It was perhaps eight or ten times what the various anti-Common Market campaigns could deploy between them. Yet when measured against the total exposure of the broad public and the opinion-formers to arguments about the Common Market, the Campaign was only a small, if striking, component injected into the debate. Measured against other campaigns of persuasion it was also hardly very impressive. An article in the *New Statesman* (as hostile a journal to the Marketeers as one could wish – though it still underestimated the true cost of the Movement's campaign) put it in perspective: 'A total advertising budget of £150,000–£200,000 may sound a lot, but it is pathetically little with which to sell a complex package deal like the Market. . . . Out of the whole Birdseye range, the appropriation for pies alone would match the European Movement's total budget.'[1]

'Where', asked the Safeguards Campaign, 'does the money come from? . . . Some of it is secret, hidden or foreign. But some of it is quite open – taxpayers' money, yours and mine.'[2] Taxpayers' money, of course, paid for all the government's public relations on this as on everything else. But as far as the European Movement was concerned, the £7,500 travel grant it received from the government had to be accounted for as being used solely for travel to international conferences (with not more than 20% administrative costs), and the details filed in the House of Commons Library. Compared to subscriptions and donations, which amounted to nearly £900,000 in 1971–72, this was a marginal bonus.

Both the European Movement and the government categorically denied that any of these donations came from the government, and the Director of the European Movement also repeatedly stated that it

[1] Michael Jackson, 'Marketing the Market', *New Statesman*, 6 November 1971.
[2] *Bulletin*, No. 5 (August 1971), p. 1.

Summary of Accounts of the European Movement

	1969/70	1970/71	1971/72
Income	£	£	£
Subscriptions and donations	4,897	9,149	895,766
Foreign Office grant	7,500	7,500	7,500
Contribution to administrative expenses from European Educational Research Trust	6,000	8,773	6,000
Other contributions (from allied organizations)	3,849	4,187	1,000
Fund raising appeal	6,694	3,223	—
Publications and pamphlets	926	722	1,737
Miscellaneous (net of corporation tax)	765	3,540	4,901
Total	30,631	37,094	915,904
Expenditure			
Fund-raising appeal expenses	3,000	—	3,890
Life assurance premiums	—	—	94,824
Rent, postage, depreciation, etc.	8,286	12,023	27,383
Salaries	10,308	17,572	40,734
Regional organizers' fees and expenses	—	13,844	66,658
Opinion research and polls	—	12,982	5,320
Advertising and public relations	1,600	18,356	270,070
Cost of publications and pamphlets	1,884	9,790	69,970
Speakers' seminars and conferences, training and expenses	6,221	4,324	10,953
Visits to and from Continent	5,622	8,456	18,727
Grants and subscriptions to: European Educational Research Trust	—	—	4,500
Allied bodies in Britain	466	2,250	28,941
Other expenditure	3,619	6,061	2,764
Total expenditure	41,006	105,658	644,734
Surplus or deficit	− 10,375	− 68,564	+ 271,170
Net balance carried over at end of year (adjusted for market fluctuations)	− 4,052	− 66,078	205,432

received no subsidies, subventions, grants, etc. from the European Communities or other foreign sources, nor from British political parties. All literature produced by the Fabian Society, Conservative Political Centre or other outside bodies distributed by the Movement was purchased from these organizations. Moreover, as far as donations and subscriptions were concerned, he stated that 'both in amount and number of donations and subscriptions to the Movement, individuals outnumber companies considerably'.

The Movement published the names of the companies that subscribed to it, usually £100 per annum, and an article in the *New Statesman* enjoyed itself with this list:

Some of these companies were those influenced by leaders of the Movement – thus while Lord Gladwyn was on the Board of Warburg's they contributed, but ceased as soon as he left. Others were companies suggested by MP activists as likely to profit by Market entry. Analysis of the Movement's corporate supporters shows up some oddities. Most of the big banks are there: Barclays, Lloyds, Midland and National Westminster. But the merchant banks are more unevenly represented: Lazard, Rothschild and Sassoon are there, but Warburg and Hill Samuel have dropped out, and others have never favoured the Movement. There are a good number of big British firms – BAT, BEA, BET, BP, British Ropes (Barber's old firm), Courtaulds, Distillers (Patrick Jenkin's old firm), Dunlop, Imperial Tobacco, ICL, Laporte Industries, J. Lyons, Marks and Spencer, Metal Box (Carr's old firm), Morgan Crucible, Reckitt and Colman, Shell, W. H. Smith, Watney Mann. But a great many obvious ones are not there – including British Leyland. In fact the big American firms seem better represented: Caterpillar Tractor, Esso, Heinz, Honeywell, IBM, Kelloggs, Kodak, Singer and Woolworth. . . . In many firms there are enthusiasts on both sides of the argument. Indeed, until last year Lord Kearton, who is pro-Market, could refresh himself with the single-minded enthusiasm of Lord George-Brown, Courtaulds consultant, or depress himself with anti-Market propaganda of Douglas Jay, Courtaulds director.[1]

When all is said and done, however, some sixty companies subscribing £100 each bring in only £6,000. A thousand individuals subscribing £3·15 each adds another £3,000 – and that brings the total up to the £9,000 of 1970–71. Clearly there was a sudden, quite enormous inflow of donations in the campaign year 1971–72 – the total sum must have been well over £850,000. If it might seem *a priori* unlikely

[1] Andrew Roth, 'Market Propaganda: Who Pays?', *New Statesman*, 6 August 1971.

that the bulk of this could be raised from private individuals rather than companies, the Movement's claim is, however, supported heavily by what at first sight looks like a very peculiar item in its accounts for 1971–72 – the nearly £100,000 spent on life assurance premiums. These were taken out to cover the Movement in case one of the donors died before the five year period after which gifts *inter vivos* become free of estate duty.[1] Unless one knows the ages of the lives insured and the sizes of the estates involved, it is difficult to work back from the total of premiums to the size of the total sums donated: but it is a fair guess that the sums involved in very big donations from private individuals and requiring life assurance were in the region of £800,000.

An article in the *Spectator* named Sir Michael Sobell as a donor, with £500,000 as the figure for his donation.[2] The name was correct, unfortunately the sum was not – but the European Movement could hardly be so churlish as to come out with a statement minimizing the extent of his generosity. He was in point of fact the second largest individual donor. The article in the *Spectator* suggested that Sir Michael's knighthood in the New Year Honours List of 1972 was due to this contribution to the European Movement rather than to his many charitable donations – an imputation deplored by the Prime Minister in the House of Commons when the matter was raised as one of privilege shortly afterwards.

Given this enormous generosity to the Movement by two or three individuals, its inflow of funds in 1971–72 was substantially larger than its expenditure, leaving it with a surplus on the year of a quarter of a million pounds. Thanks to this surplus, the Movement could go into its financial year 1972–73 with net assets of £200,000. It also had the assurance that the government was increasing its annual grant from £7,500 to £20,000 – though on the other hand it could, obviously, not hope to maintain the sudden flow of private donations that had allowed its work to peak so dramatically in 1971.

It is also clear from the balance sheets that, with gross current liabilities on 31 March 1971 of over £70,000 as against gross total assets worth less than a tenth of that debt, the Movement must have had financially powerful backing to tide it over until the big money came

---

[1] British fiscal legislation makes the beneficiary of a gift liable to estate duty at a graduated rate if the donor dies within five years.

[2] Hugh MacPherson, 'Faith, Hope and Charity', *Spectator*, 4 March 1972. The fact that Sir Michael was then aged 78 would account for the high rate of premium on at least part of these donations.

in during 1971. Its bankers, Coutts, required no guarantee for its over-draft from anyone.

All this is inherently rather dull stuff, but since during the campaign it became highly controversial we should also briefly examine the finances of the Movement's companion organization, the European Educational and Research Trust. The Trust had charitable status so that the covenanted subscriptions to it were free of income and corporation tax; but it shared premises and staff with the European Movement, and three of its Council of Management of six were simultaneously officers of the European Movement, while a fourth was on the Movement Committee.[1] Its accounts are set out on p. 214. It is by no means abnormal these days for charities to be paying out close on ten per cent of donations to a professional fund-raiser on that part of their income which would not accrue but for the fund-raiser's efforts. The service charge by the European Movement obviously has to be slightly arbitrary: but it does not seem to contain any concealed subsidy to the Movement. If it did, the Trust would be in danger of losing its charitable status, so that the full-time chartered accountant the Trust shares with the Movement would be running grave risks if he allowed any such subsidy (as would the auditors, who include David Barton among their partners). The Trust has repeatedly sought Counsel's advice to be certain that they were not perverting charitable funds to political purposes. (Professional charges came to over £1,000 in the two financial years 1970–72.) The fast accumulating credit balances in fact represent not money with Lloyds and Hill Samuel, their bankers, but mainly tax credits not yet recovered from the Inland Revenue.

The Trust's own research was on matters such as youth exchanges, but their main operational expenditure was on seminars and travel grants. The beneficiaries included the British Council of Churches (Youth Department), the Lambeth Borough Council for young guests to its youth week, the Universities of Keele, Manchester, Reading and Sussex and the London School of Economics for conferences and study visits, the YMCA and YWCA for participants in a workshop for youth leaders, the Young Fabian Group for a party of largely anti-Market young Fabians to visit Brussels, the Young Conservatives, the Scottish Association of Young Farmers' Clubs and various European and federalist bodies. In the year 1970–71 70% of the money went to schemes specifically covering people in the 18–35 age-group.

In one sense, of course, one can describe this as the highbrow educa-

[1] Lords Gladwyn and Harlech, Martin Maddan and Norman Hart.

Summary of Accounts of the European Educational and Research Trust

	15 months to 31 March 1970	1970/71	1971/72
Income	£	£	£
Donations and grants	33,545	26,782	26,917
Donations under covenant and recoverable tax	40,601	34,084	41,283
Miscellaneous income	1,079	1,062	413
Total income	75,225	61,928	68,568
Expenditure			
Fund-raisers' fee	36,500	3,900	4,800
Service charge by European Movement	6,000	8,733	5,000
Other administration etc.	2,283	6,937	8,366
Own research	784	2,553	1,201
Grants mainly for travel and expenses	13,764	31,700	38,477
Total expenditure	59,331	53,863	57,844
Surplus or deficit	+ 15,894	+ 8,065	+ 10,724
Net balance carried over at end of year (after tax and other adjustments)	+ 15,946	+ 20,267	+ 31,631

tional arm of a Movement that wanted to get people thinking about Europe: in the same sense in which any discussion of Europe is regarded as already a prejudging of the issue – and in which any discussion of the Commonwealth or the United Nations or NATO is a prejudgment that here is something important that cannot be neglected. On the other hand, as its pattern of expenditure no less than its beneficiaries show, it remained and had to remain a purely research and educational body, so that its relation to the political cause of the European Movement was an indirect and long-term, rather than an immediate one.

Only its grants towards the exploratory study of attitudes in the United Kingdom to the idea of the European Community and to Stephenson Research Associates on attitudes in industry might have been of immediate direct benefit. That having been said, clearly there are all sorts of interlacing advantages in running long-term educational and conference programmes for any political cause and any political organization. In that sense it may be that the anti-Marketeers not only did not have anything like as much money as the cluster of 'European' bodies, but that they also left unexplored some ways of raising more and of administering more efficiently what they had.

Strategy and Tactics

Almost the first essential step in such a professional campaign was to prospect the market before styling the product. Of obvious interest was the use the Movement made of modern survey methods – on the one hand to discover for its own use popular interests, knowledge, and attitudes, and on the other hand also to forward its cause by the publication of selected polling results. It used mainly for the first purpose the firm of Social and Community Planning Research with a small-scale exploratory study late in 1970, and then with a much bigger survey in early 1971.[1] Thereafter it commissioned regular surveys from the Opinion Research Centre (and also used National Opinion Polls).

The type of question commissioned for public relations purposes was, for example, 'Do you think that the present negotiations will be successful?', followed by 'If these negotiations are successful, would you accept the terms negotiated by the government?' and 'How much are you in favour of or against Britain joining the Common Market?' Other questions dealt with issues where the Movement felt on strong ground, such as the effects of entry on future generations (which the Movement wanted to stress as against short-term costs), and whether it was in the national interest for Britain to join. In October there was a last-minute question on whether Labour MPs should be free to vote according to their own views. These and such other survey results as argued against referenda or showed the better-informed to be more favourable to entry came in handy and cast an interesting searchlight

[1] Jean Norton-Williams, *Attitudes towards the European Common Market – Report of an Exploratory Study*, Social and Community Planning Research, January 1971, and Barry Hedges and Roger Jewell, *Britain and the EEC: Report on a Survey of Attitudes towards the European Economic Community*, Social and Community Planning Research, July 1971.

on the straight for-or-against results widely canvassed in the press, on the radio and elsewhere.

Already in January 1971 the SCPR pilot survey had concluded: 'The campaign must both satisfy personal needs and appeal to the more abstract ideals. . . . One feature of the campaign will be the need to demonstrate that the two are not in conflict. Wherever possible the publicity will need to allow members of the public to portray the "policy image" that each person wishes to project in the various roles he plays. . . . Even the convincing rebuttal of their objections could distract energy and attention away from the issues which have real importance to people. . . . They were bored with the way in which the issue was dealt with in the media . . . these were felt to present arguments at the abstract level but never to give the basic *facts* as to what was proposed and what the outcome for *them* was likely to be.'

Partly basing itself on intuition, partly on this first SCPR and other survey results, the campaign then set itself five themes at the outset: higher standards of living, better social welfare, strength through unity, protection of national interests through participation in European decisions, and Britain's world role. In April when the second SCPR report became available, the emphasis was slightly modified, stress being laid on social security, the strengthening of trade union links, and the peace and security arguments. Above all, however, entry into the EEC was to be linked with the solution of British economic problems and the re-establishment of British influence in world affairs. Further consideration of the report led, in May, to concentration on the material benefits to the ordinary person, and on comparisons of spending money rather than of simple prices.

In mid-August there came the dollar crisis. The campaign reacted quickly with press statements emphasizing that this was of significance in two respects: it stressed the dangers of Britain remaining isolated, out in the cold in a world that might disintegrate into trade blocks, and secondly it proved that influence was shifting back across the Atlantic towards Europe, and that Britain must be sure, therefore, of playing her full role there. More and more thereafter, as the unemployment figures came to cause concern, the campaign concentrated on the problem of industrial expansion, and in late September it was decided to have large stickers placed across the national poster of flag-waving children – to symbolize the future – which had been launched in August and designed with such last-minute flexibility in mind. The stickers proclaimed, 'For more jobs in Scotland/Wales/The North' as appropriate, or elsewhere 'For more jobs in Britain', to motivate the original message of 'Say Yes to Europe'.

In the spring of 1971 the advertising campaign had originally been planned to take place in three successive phases. The first, up to July, was to concentrate on the dissemination of facts ('By now you must be tired of waffle . . .', began the first full-page display in *The Times*). The second phase, from agreement of the terms in Brussels until the end of the party conferences, was to see a national poster campaign; while in the final stages before the substantive vote (which the Campaign Group then expected at the end of 1971 or the beginning of 1972) the effort was to concentrate on the constituencies of 'marginal' MPs – those whose vote could, one way or another, still be influenced, whether they were supporters who needed help to make life less difficult with their constituencies, or whether they were sympathetic but uncommitted, or quite undecided MPs of whatever party. And of course some funds were held in reserve to pay for any advertising that might be needed though not yet foreseen.

But by 27 April it was decided to bring that third phase forward and put it into action as soon as possible to run alongside the national publicity campaigns. Public meetings of all kinds had of course been taking place for quite a long time with the European Movement either merely supplying a speaker or else organizing things from scratch. On the whole it was better to use an existing organization to convey one's message under their already respected and familiar cover format than to hold meetings *ad hoc*. The Movement's published diary of events may give an idea of the kinds of meeting on the subject of 'Britain and Europe' in which the Movement was involved on just one day – 28 January 1971 – before it had really got into its stride and become too busy to maintain a published diary: Rotary Club of Crewe, Pinner Grammar School, the Association of Light Alloy Refiners and Smelters in London, and the Seaford Afternoon Townswomen's Guild. On the 27th it had been the Lawford Wives Group of Chelmsford, on the 29th it was the turn of the Ross-on-Wye Round Table. In July there were over 700 meetings and altogether the Campaign Group reckons it serviced 3,000 to 4,000 meetings attended by perhaps 100,000 people. But it was not merely meetings, it was also the letter-writing campaign that was to be stepped up, and special advertising and articles of local interest placed in some 160 local papers at a cost of up to £35,000, while special literature distribution from door to door and even local cinema slides were also considered.

Yet the Movement was not really equipped for mass grass-roots action. It was quite a disadvantage, for example, that in some areas the regional organizer had previously been a Conservative, in some a Labour candidate, who might now have to act along lines meant to influence opinion within the constituency associations of the opposite party. There may in fact be one measure of the moderate success of some of the mass activities at constituency level. The Movement sent out some 290,000 pre-paid postcards expressing support for entry to be returned signed to Chandos House for forwarding to the constituent's MP. In August it was decided to make distributing these the main activity of the Movement's supporters for September and October, but they then bungled the operation. In contrast to the Safeguards Petition's 600,000 signatures at the time, by mid-October only just over 6,000 of these postcards had been returned. Though they could form the basis of a card-index of known supporters, they could be forwarded with any great impressiveness only to a selected number of MPs for those constituencies where there had been a response well above the average. (Another 4,000 or so came in after the October issue of the Campaign's tabloid had carried a foldable version.)

Such figures emphasize the dilemma in which the Movement found itself over the various unofficial referenda. Clearly it was against the principle of a national referendum. Few pro-Marketeers were in favour of it. *Ad hominem* the Movement argued that anti-Marketeers could not logically champion both a referendum and the sovereignty of Parliament. More substantively, though in terms that might be open to the charge of élitist overtones, it highlighted popular ignorance. Under the title 'Referendum Madness' its tabloid exclaimed: 'It is incredible how many people . . . do not know how many or what countries are in the Common Market, yet these are the people that so many anti-Marketeers want to use as the referendum. How stupid can you get?'[1] Perhaps it was on safer ground when it pointed to the result of its own opinion surveys, which showed that 80% of people thought they were not well enough informed to vote in a referendum and that, of people who felt very strongly on the Common Market issue, more were strongly against than strongly in favour of entry. Unofficial referenda with low turn-outs, the Movement could plausibly argue, would therefore falsify 'real' opinion with a bias against entry. The Movement could scarcely hope to whip up so much enthusiasm as to obtain a really representative turn-out. On the other hand it could hardly leave the

[1] *British European*, No. 3 (April 1971), p. 3.

field to its bitterest opponents. So it decided to debunk referenda in general, to advise its supporters to boycott them as open to fraud and deception, claim that they were bound in any case to be pretty meaningless, but enter the battle itself at any rate in Beckenham, where it had the sociological composition of the electorate heavily in its favour compared with most other constituencies in the country. Though there was concern about lack of canvassers and of specifically European Movement meetings, one of the Movement's full-time organizers did become very active in the referendum (and its result turned out marginally in favour of entry, as can be seen on p. 249).

By early summer the Movement also had to consider yet another aspect of timing: once the government had declared the terms acceptable in its White Paper, the particular gap which the Movement had sought to fill while the government was condemned to inactivity would be over. With the government going beyond its apparently anodyne Post Office Factsheets into a stirringly political White Paper, and the Conservative Party machine pulling out all the stops, the Movement really had to redefine its role. It could simply work alongside the government; but it could also pursue lines of argument that the government would not wish to use itself – such as the dangers of staying out – and it could adopt a slightly more broad-brush line. However, to avoid dissensions, it could also delegate more controversial activities to separate, more activist bodies, such as the Liberal European Action Group or the Militants' Group, and concentrate on the special targets on which its parallel organizations were aimed. With the Labour Party clearly about to come out officially against entry, the function and the operating methods of the Labour wing might have to part company sharply with those of the Conservative wing. Not everyone, for example, would have been delighted that the Movement took steps to invite Young Conservatives to go to the Labour Party's Central Hall rally on 18 October. There were times when, as one organizer afterwards wryly observed, 'our brilliant brainwaves at Tuesday's Campaign Group looked appalling at Wednesday's Labour Committee for Europe'. It was, therefore, essential to find solutions as one went along to the problems of conflict between policies acceptable to the different elements within it, and policies acceptable to the Movement as a whole. That was not always easy.

Particularly in the summer and autumn the Movement felt that it must address itself over (or under) the heads of the opinion-formers who were meant to be its primary target straight to the general public.

It was no use convincing MPs of the preponderance of their arguments if the MPs thus persuaded were left without any sense of support in the public opinion of their constituents and of the country at large. Advertisements in the *Daily Express* and the *Sunday Pictorial*, the *People* and the *News of the World* (not to mention *Private Eye* and *Oz*), a specially designed tea towel, carrier bags, lapel buttons and blue balloons saying 'Yes to Europe', European Evenings for Housewives, a flashing light panel quiz at the *Daily Mail* Ideal Home Exhibition (which was specially insured in case of attacks by 'right-wing extremist elements'), and a student demonstration five days before the Commons vote complete with jazz band and flaming torches – these were hardly designed to persuade opinion-formers of the merits of the case so much as to highlight the fact that whatever popular feelings as reported in the opinion polls might be, the pro-Marketeers were quite prepared to be active, to appeal in popular ways and to dramatize their convictions beyond the pages of the élite dailies. They even issued a Decca record of the campaign song (on the theme of the slogan the Movement had asked its supporters to introduce into their conversations) set to a rather frightful piece of noise which, though they feared a boycott because of its political nature, was in fact played by the BBC a few times in spite of its musical qualities.[1] But then it is no use being snobbish or prissy on such counts. The Campaign Group was not simply enjoying itself, it was also trying to escape from the charge of highbrow theoretical

---

[1] The sentiments on the other hand, in so far as the incongruously mid-Atlantic accent of The Unity yielded them up, seemed admirable, if a trifle optimistic:

> Gut tuggit in tuggit awn,
> We must move ahead or we fa-hall behind,
> Nothing in life stays the same,
> We've got tuggit in tuggit on.

> Once into the new world, come out of the pest,
> Your doubts and your worries will disappear fest,
> Take a big step and move into tamarraw taday:
> Gut tuggit in tuggit awn. . . .

> The light is so bright while it's beckoning you
> The hopes that you cherish at last will come true,
> Give in to the future where everything's su-hure to be right;
> Gut tuggit in . . . .

> Don't be afraid, there's nothing to fear,
> The road up ahead is certainly clear
> Take up this task 'cause the good life is waiting for you-hou:
> Gut tuggit in . . . .

élitism. No one ever marched pro-entry, an anti-Marketeer had claimed in 1963. This time the Movement set out colourfully and emphatically to refute that kind of accusation.

As the summer silly season came and then the battle reached its height before the parliamentary vote of principle, the Movement became if anything even more conscious of the need for 'managed news events' and such like to stay in the limelight. As part of its women's activities, it sent six semi-finalists of its European Woman of the Year competition, each accompanied by a local journalist, one to each of the EEC countries, and the winners got a fair amount of broadcasting and newspaper publicity in December. In addition to organizing beacons on the cliffs of Dover to be lit on the night of 28 October with answering beacons in Calais, it planned (but was forced to abandon) a passport-burning demonstration in Parliament Square and a crossing to Ostend by a group of students minus passports the weekend after (whom the Belgian police threatened to turn back). Other enterprising ventures considered but dropped at various stages had included a weekly European Forum at eight Butlin holiday camps including the preparation of a Continental dish, a week-long outdoor marathon debate, the distribution of 'Yes To Europe' car stickers through oil companies and garages, and the giving away of beer mats and paper hats. But there were people who felt that some of these brainwaves were too fanciful or vulgar – that Europe could not, or should not, be sold like a new brand of toilet soap; and for that matter time, man- and woman-power, and money were also limiting factors.

Still, the campaign distributed some six and a half million items of literature – quite apart from those which went into the substantial pulping operation after 28 October. There were serious pamphlets and snappy hand-outs, roneoed booklets of guidance for local letter-writers and a forty-page booklet in question-and-answer form sent to over twenty thousand Borough and County Councillors. The Movement also produced an extremely intelligent and well-done 'Common Market Information Kit' with briefings on 'Political Structure', 'Money', 'Association and Aid' and other subjects – of which, for example, ten thousand copies were sent to the Women's Institutes as part of the Movement's very vigorous women's activities: judging by the fact that, at one meeting of over 1,000 women, 700 of whom entered a competition to answer five simple questions about EEC, only 11 got the answers right, this was just what was needed (unless perhaps even this was not elementary enough).

But the most substantial effort was put into the *British European*. This was a monthly tabloid with an edition that rose from 20,000 copies in January (costing £365 to print) to a record 1,500,000 copies for the holiday issue of July–August: it was given away by supporters, distributed by mini-skirted students on Dormobile minibuses at holiday resorts, handed out by volunteers at railway stations, football matches and party conferences, and sent in duplicate to all general practitioners, dentists, opticians and hairdressers.

The *British European* was not exactly aimed at the élite and not concerned to pull its punches. 'Holidays are sunnier and much longer' claimed the January issue, without substantiating the climatic changes signature of the Rome Treaty was bound automatically to produce. Marjorie Proops of the *Daily Mirror* had a double-page spread in No. 3 answering such transparently bogus letters as:

Dear Marje, . . .   Will joining mean duty-free scent? Jennifer G.
Dear Jennifer,   You'll be able to waft around extravagantly in your favourite
   perfume.
Dear Marje, . . . I do love wine with my dinner. Will it be cheaper when we
   join? Peggy B.
Dear Peggy,   Yes. Cheers!

No. 4 featured the Union Jack with the headline 'It's time we carried our flag into Europe!' and in bold type declared on the front page: 'It's time Britain woke up, stopped being a looker-on and grabbed a share of the European gravy.' The cover of the July–August holiday issue featured a well-built blonde model barely held in by a bikini made of Union Jack remnants with the slogan 'Europe is fun!' and promising with further exclamation marks 'More work, but more play too! . . . No passports to pleasure!' The issue was returned in bales by one highly committed MP as embarrassing to him in his constituency, was widely thought provocative only of puritan back-lash and – ultimate humiliation – 'unanimously condemned . . . as being totally unsuitable for Beckenham'.

In the September issue a quiz cited in favour of entry such experts on the complex problems involved as Petula Clark, Bobby Moore, Kenneth More and Mary Quant. (In *The Times* on 22 July the Movement had proclaimed in bold type the support of Henry Cooper the boxer and Jilly Cooper the columnist, Len Deighton and Polly Elwes, Jimmy Greaves and Hayley Mills, Yehudi Menuhin, Sir Alec Rose and Jack Solomons.) The *British European* also maintained, incomprehensibly, that the answer to the question: 'In the fifth year after our entry to the Common Market, what will be Britain's share of the Community budget?' was '$\frac{1}{2}$np in the £, which is 1/200th of our national income!' The October issue showed a cartoon with Roy Jenkins and George Brown (or was it Harold Lever?) cheering on Rippon and Heath, which was thought embarrassing by Roy Jenkins and was after some discussion delayed but finally not withdrawn. Emmwood also produced a cartoon of a sinking British ship of fools which in its depiction of Japanese competition, at any rate, looked suspiciously racialist, but which the Movement decided all the same to use for a pamphlet.

The European Movement made it its business to keep itself well informed of what the opposition was up to. When the Safeguards Campaign on 7 June 1971 exceptionally bought three columns of *The Times* for its advertisement 'Let the People Decide', they found a European Movement front organization, the 'Liberal European Action Group', had shadowed it with a knocking advertisement: '*Also* against the Common Market: Communist Party of Great Britain, the League of Empire Loyalists, the National Front, the IRA, the Right Honourable Enoch Powell MP, Union of Soviet Socialist Republics.' (The Safeguards Campaign suspected *The Times* of a leak, but the European Movement insisted that the circular preparing the Safeguards advertisement had been sent to one of their supporters, who passed it on to Chandos House; and then the counter-advertisement was booked for whatever date the Safeguards advertisement might appear.) When Women Against the Common Market held a Trafalgar Square rally in March 1971, female Marketeers picketed the occasion (one of them with the European flag stitched to the seat of her hot pants) and claim not only to have hogged more publicity than the rally itself but also to have formed the larger part of the audience. In June 1971 Alan Lee Williams used his Thames lighterman's licence to steer an 180-seat catamaran loaded with supporters paying £2·50 a head for trip and picnic lunch to meet protesting fishermen who then failed to appear. Contingency planning was put in hand in case there should be referenda in various constituencies. The aim always was to anticipate, cover and neutralize whatever initiative the anti-Marketeers might take in any conceivable field. Indeed it is also remarkable that, while the full report from their opinion pollsters showed that 'the feeling that our sovereignty would be threatened was one of the main arguments against going in', in their accounts of the survey to the press the campaign managers laid the stress on their economic findings. They were no doubt hoping to mislead the anti-Marketeers and steer them towards the economic arguments, on which the European Movement felt on safer ground with popular opinion. (The European Movement was heartened when, after a debate, one of the anti-Marketeers jokingly thanked them for 'doing our research for us'. They appeared to have swallowed the bait.)

There was certainly no lack of tactical ideas in the European Movement. The Liberal European Action Group had planned an advertisement for 18 June entitled 'Jim Callaghan speaks on Europe', quoting some of the former Chancellor's more commitedly pro-entry pronouncements: but at the urgent insistence of Roy Jenkins, whose target was Harold Wilson and who did not want to pick fights with Jim Callaghan, the advertisement was first postponed and then withdrawn. (Rumour had it that the gesture was appreciated, and that Jim Callaghan did not from that point proceed with any plans he might or might not have had for contesting the Deputy Leadership. Unconfirmed though the story may be, the mere fact of its circulation was another indication of the intra-party consequences of its actions which the all-party Movement had constantly to bear in mind.)

The Labour Committee for Europe

We have looked at the Conservative wing of the European Movement in the previous chapter and mentioned its Liberal Action Group in this one. Far older than either of these, however, was the distinctively Labour-oriented group of the Movement. In the stage army of the moderate good the Labour Committee for Europe can claim a pretty impressive pedigree: by Federal Union out of the Campaign for Democratic Socialism. Its predecessor, the Labour Common Market Committee, was founded in September 1961 as part of the deliberate federalist strategy of setting up parallel organizations working for the same ends in different sectors of the polity. Its first chairman was Roy Jenkins, its first treasurer Jack Diamond (who as a professional accountant was simultaneously treasurer of the Fabian Society and of *Socialist Commentary*), its first secretary Colin Beever. Among its most active early members were Norman Hart, Labour candidate for Bridgwater in 1964, and in Parliament S. Scholefield Allen and Harry Hynd – all three active federalists. But it would here, as elsewhere, be absurd to carry the conspiratorial theory of politics too far. Bob Edwards was not of the Right wing of the party, Norman Hart had been opposed to the

CDS, while most of the Labour parliamentarians involved had had no part in Federal Union, and some of the leading Labour Marketeers of the epoch were not to be found on the notepaper of the Labour Committee for Europe in any case: Alf Robens, George Brown and Anthony Crosland had no formal connections with it at that time.

To trace the beginnings of the 'pro-Europeans' in the Labour Party one must in fact go back well beyond the formation of the Committee, starting with R. W. G. Mackay, an Australian by birth and a lawyer conversant with the Australian federal system, who was from 1945 to 1950 MP for North-West Hull and then Reading. His book *Britain in Wonderland* (Gollancz, London, 1948) called for a Socialist United States of Europe with Britain as an integral member. Kim Mackay was derided in his time as an eccentric prophet, though at the Hague Congress and in the first session of the Council of Europe at Strasbourg in 1949 he was one of the very few Labour politicians in step with his Continental Socialist comrades, such as Spaak and Mollet. Though Clem Attlee certainly backed Bevin's negative attitude to the European federalists, he did have the foresight to send a group of promising young people in their thirties to Strasbourg as Labour representatives, saying to one of them at the time: 'I don't understand Europe, but in twenty years' time the party ought to have some people who do.'

Among these Labour representatives in the 'fifties were Alf Robens (leader of the delegation 1952–54), Arthur Bottomley, Geoffrey de Freitas (delegation leader 1965, President of the Assembly 1966–69), Roy Jenkins, Fred Mulley, George Thomson and John Edwards (delegation leader 1955–59, President 1959–60). John Edwards had in fact, before his untimely death in Strasbourg in 1960, made Political and Economic Planning into one of the main research and information centres on European Community affairs in Britain. One may say that Attlee's older men were in government and therefore unable to go: but on the whole he did not use the Strasbourg delegation as a consolation prize for the older generations left out of office, and in fact laid the foundations for Labour's pro-European leaders of the 'seventies by giving them the opportunity to gain insight into what the Europeans on the Continent were aiming at and how their minds worked in the formative years of Community-making. With the odd Early Day motion,[1] Parliamentary Question and foreign policy speech in the

---

[1] One method for British parliamentarians to declare their views jointly is to put down a motion for debate at an 'early day' – a euphemism for the Greek kalends.

House, this group, if it did not bring the issue to life in British politics during the 'fifties, at least from time to time pointed to its existence and the possibility that it could come actively on to the agenda some time in the future.

These Strasbourg delegates were to prove – with some surprising additions – the Labour Marketeers of 1962: George Brown, to whom Gaitskell refused to show his Brighton speech before delivery, Roy Jenkins and Anthony Crosland, who pleaded with him the night before he made it, and Fred Mulley and George Thomson, the men later charged with negotiations for entry, the one at the outset in 1966–67, and the other at the very end of the Labour government's period of office. Other Marketeers in 1961–63 came from the Left: Walter Padley, Fenner Brockway, Eric Heffer, for a time Frank Cousins. But the Strasbourg delegation remained the backbone within their age-group, the Council of Europe's adult education function having, in fact, not been in vain.

They were joined, especially after 1964, by the younger generation of MPs, many of whom came down from the Oxford University Labour Club of the late 'forties and early 'fifties, where Shirley Williams, William Rodgers, Dick Taverne, Michael Shanks and Shirley Summer-skill had sat on the same or overlapping successive committees as contemporaries of Jeremy Thorpe, Peter Kirk, Geoffrey Johnson Smith and the editor of The Times, William Rees-Mogg; perhaps none of them were 'Europeans' at the time – though some of them joined the Oxford University Strasbourg Club founded by Noel Salter in the late 'forties – but they were a group of post-war students very much open to rethinking Britain's place in the world.

After the collapse of the negotiations in January 1963 the Labour Common Market Committee was re-formed as the Labour Committee for Europe, with the same officers, and it continued its existence without major incident after the Labour victory of 1964, when Roy Jenkins became Minister of Civil Aviation and Shirley Williams took over the chairmanship; she was followed briefly by Austen Albu and then by Geoffrey de Freitas, who had left Parliament to become High Commissioner in Ghana and thus – in the same way as Alf Robens – had effectively excluded himself from the band of those who had gone through the 'thirteen wasted years' together and in 1964 together formed the government. The Committee's main activities over this period were seminars and briefings, the provision of speakers, contact with Continental Socialists, and the publication of a small broadsheet,

Europe Left. Until 1970 the Committee did a quiet job on a budget of £2,000–£3,000 a year financed by donations and the nominal subscriptions of its membership, which even in early 1971 still stood at under 200 – some 90 MPs, 20 Lords and about 80 non-MPs.

In one sense, perhaps, such a membership was really much too large. It made a good letterhead, but at the cost of dilution: it included for a time Eric Heffer, who later changed his mind, and up to July 1971 Brian Walden, who became a speaker for the Safeguards Campaign in the autumn. Anthony Crosland, who had been reported as announcing that he would vote with the Executive in summer 1971 (but then abstained), remained a vice-president throughout. There was a core group that met to inform itself, debate long-term political strategy for Europe, and try to formulate a policy for the Committee, but it remained a heterogeneous group of fundamentalist Community-builders on political grounds together with others who wanted to seize economic opportunities and yet others who sought a substitute for Britain's past international leverage (with, of course, some overlap between them).

As there was an inevitable mixture of motivations so there was lack of clarity as to the Committee's own tactical role. While Labour was in government, public relations in general had to be handled with care, lest they pinpoint too many of the things that were going wrong with Britain; yet private influence on Ministers was pre-empted, naturally enough, by the civil service, and when the government was in fact converted it was as a result of external circumstance, not LCE arguments. In 1966–67, while the government was committed first to its probe and then to its application for entry, the Committee, instead of taking the case to the rank-and-file of the party, decided to wait on Transport House and the government: it felt that its cause was now winning, with all three parties committed to it, and that divisiveness had never paid off inside the party. (Several of its previous activists, in any case, were preoccupied with their governmental problems, so there was a certain vacuum in its leadership.) Then from 1967 until 1969 the road was blocked for Britain so that only long-range thinking and persuasion were open to the Committee – and these were tasks not always best performed by collective letterheads. Then, as soon as Labour had lost office, the Committee had to be careful not to get too much in the way of the Opposition's attack on the government, and in any case did not really react fast enough to define its new role before the issue boiled up again.

The Committee had not thought through with any rigour what its function was to be in relation to the party leadership, to the Parliamentary Party, to the constituencies and to the unions. It had never seriously contemplated the possibility that there might be a change of government before entry, and therefore felt that it could rely on the government to use its influence and machinery to jolly the party along into Europe without the Labour Committee for Europe having to engage in divisive (and thus perhaps counter-productive) activities within the Labour Movement. During that period a more lightweight and 'irresponsible' leadership would have attempted greater activism even at the risk of being counter-productive. After the change of government, while Roy Jenkins was (with George Brown and Michael Stewart) joint president, he did not take much overt part in the Committee's activities – whether due to political strategy, a matter of political style or personal factors. Certainly, whatever other reasons there might be, Roy Jenkins had to avoid the appearance of organizing a party within a party for as long as the issue could possibly be kept open.

There were others who made themselves the interpreters of Roy Jenkins' wishes, but that did not prevent occasional mutual embarrassments being caused to the parliamentary leadership and the Committee by misunderstandings between them. The Committee was useful in organizing fringe activities at both the July and October 1971 party conferences and in securing publicity for the European cause. It also organized a series of 10 rallies in the country in September 1971 to signal a counterpoint to the 17 organized by the National Executive on the other side. (Attendance varied from 45 to 500, but of course local and national media magnified the impact to some extent.) It provided the main platform for Roy Jenkins at Brighton in October, when he was precluded from speaking in Conference itself. For the rest the two worlds of effective parliamentary leadership and the mechanisms of the Labour Committee did not really interact, and as we shall see in a later chapter the rank-and-file pro-Market MPs' organization led by William Rodgers also had reason to tread warily, though operating mainly within the membership of the LCE itself.

At the same time the LCE was really far too small to perform a useful function in converting the rank-and-file. It never really set out to have a mass membership in the constituencies in the way that the Campaign for Democratic Socialism had done. Perhaps it would not have been very productive for it to do so. Certainly if there was a fair showing of constituency votes at Brighton against the Executive's resolution rejecting entry on the Tory terms, this was to some extent helped by the very extensive speaking programme arranged by the LCE in 1971, but better results might well have been obtained by a much earlier systematic cultivation of the local party notables. The non-parliamentarian members were mainly ex-MPs such as Jeremy Bray or Evan Luard, recently lost to the House, or parliamentary candidates with the odd academic thrown in. Apart from a very few like Sir Mark Henig in Leicester and Frank Pickstock in Oxford, autochthonous constituency figures were conspicuous by their absence. Membership was by invitation, and it is perhaps significant that when one of its subsequent officers asked to join the Committee in 1967 he was told a little coldly that 'of course there are an awful lot of people wanting to join just now'.

A certain effort was made towards the trade unions, and Lord Cooper of the General and Municipal Workers, Roy Grantham of the Clerical Workers and Tom Bradley of the Transport Salaried Staffs Association figured among the LCE's vice-presidents. In addition a special Trades Union Committee for Europe was set up in 1970 with Tom Bradley as chairman and the former Labour MP Alan Lee Williams as secretary. Tony Carter of the Post Office Workers, Geoffrey Drain (assistant general secretary of NALGO) and Roy Grantham of the Clerical Workers were active in promoting its aims. But TUCFE, too, found that without a good contact list at the grass-roots level it could not really make much headway. It held fringe meetings at trade union conferences and distributed literature, but did not in any effective sense get off the ground. Perhaps there was nothing much any body of that type could have done at any time to change the vote at the party conference or to prevent the National Executive of the party rejecting entry on the terms negotiated. Perhaps by the time it started it was already too late. But whatever the reason, the Committee had little effect on events in the branches, the lodges and the chapels, or higher up the union structure.

It was in a sense this early neglect of a mass membership in the unions and the constituency parties which drove the Labour Committee for Europe in the last few months and weeks into trying to reach someone, somehow, by an advertising campaign with whole-page advertisements which reprinted pro-Market articles in *Tribune* and the *New Statesman* to counter the very hostile editorial policies of those papers. Clearly it could not meet such expense out of its own resources, and it was thus accused, in particular by Clive Jenkins, of being

financed out of the same source as the Conservative Party in an attempt
to split Labour. There is no reason to believe that the campaign made
very many converts but it may have helped to hold supporters; and
one constituency party was, it seems, swung by one of these articles.

Certainly the dependence of the Labour Committee for Europe on
the European Movement during this period of extreme activism is
illustrated by its accounts for the years ending 30 September 1970 and
30 September 1971. In spite of the multiplication of its activities
between the two years administrative expenses were nearly halved –
falling from £811 to £445: clearly a good deal of the overheads were
simply shifted during this period on to the European Movement's
general budget. Conferences and meetings, on the other hand, nearly
quintupled in cost – £1,261 in 1969–70, £5,837 in 1970–71. The cost of
publications quadrupled – from £418 to £1,830. But almost three-
quarters of the budget went in advertising and publicity, on which
nothing had been spent in 1969–70, while £15,462 went on it in 1970–
71. (Further advertising expenses were incurred during October 1971.)
Total expenditure thus came to £23,574 in the year ending September
1971, as against £2,528 in the previous year.

On the income side of the account, on the other hand, subscriptions
and donations (pretty well exclusively subscriptions in 1969–70) rose
from £277 to £5,563 in the year ending September 1971: the generosity of a few of the Committee's wealthier members, in particular its
chairman, took care of the increased conference activities. But the
additional bills for publications, advertising and publicity (£16,874)
were picked up almost entirely by the European Movement. It
increased its grants to the Committee, under various heads of
the Movement's budget, from £1,869 to £18,000. The imprint of the
Labour Committee for Europe, in other words, was evidence of the
editorial responsibility of the Committee, but financially it is perfectly
true that the Committee's publications were simply one channel of the
European Movement's campaign.

It can well be argued that if you want the Labour Movement to
take notice you cyclostyle boring prose on grey paper and you do not
print glossy photographs of yourself in your own monthly or buy
two-page spreads in the *Statesman*. 'It's not in the tradition of the Movement', it was said, with some shaking of heads. The May 1971 edition
of *Europe Left* with the banner headline 'On Being Raped – by Norman
Hart' may have been some kind of in-joke, but it was not a whimsy
appreciated by the earnest Europeans of the Left in the provinces. There

were times when some of the Labour MPs in the firing line longed for more sensitivity on the part of the organizers to their particular problems, and the thought of somehow disaffiliating the Committee from the European Movement, as being too identified with an Edward Heath conception of Europe in its ends, and with slick brand-promotion in its means, seems to have crossed more than one mind in the summer. On the other side there were those who felt that the LCE people knew their public relations business and the parliamentarians should stick to their own lasts rather than send emissaries to see what the boys from the European Movement were up to and tell them to stop it.

The final verdict thus really depends on our definitions. The Labour Committee continued as it had begun, with a dual character: at once a special branch of the European Movement and an organ of the pro-Market Labour MPs in the House. If we regard William Rodgers' operation for mutual encouragement between Labour pro-Marketeers in the House (discussed below), in which the formal leadership of the LCE did not fully participate as a body, as something that could have been done without the formal organization of the Committee, then one must praise the Committee for having done a fair job, though without excessive distinction. It did more good than harm to its cause, but had no major influence either on the Labour government in office, or on the Labour leadership and party conference in Opposition. Real power throughout remained with the main-line general-purpose leadership of the unions and the party, and their freedom of action was never really restricted by anything the formally organized antis or pro-Marketeers outside that magic circle could do. But in so far as the LCE was one hat worn by a determined group of parliamentarians in support of a cause championed by one of the two top men in the party, then its role was crucial and historic. Without it, it is difficult to see how Britain could have become a member of the Community. It is ironic that its role was precisely the opposite of that which, in his last Conference speech, Hugh Gaitskell would have wanted to see that group play: putting an end, in his words, to a thousand years of British history. But then the LCE would have put it the other way round: opening up, after years of chiefly national attempts at building Socialism, a future for Social Democracy on a European scale.

8 The Anti-Market Campaigns

They have the money, but we have the people
CSMC *Bulletin*, March 1971

Over against the public relations organizations of the government and the European Movement there stood a cluster of very much smaller and poorer bodies dedicated to presenting the case against entry. Like the European Movement, they had their antecedents in committees formed in earlier years. Like the European Movement, they displayed frenzied activity in the summer and early autumn of 1971, and continued a high level of activity into 1972. As was inherent in the nature of such organizations, they often faced similar problems on both sides of the fence. Yet they conducted fascinatingly different operations according to their different characters.

ACML and the Labour Safeguards Committee

In one way the body to cast its net most widely was the Common Market Safeguards Campaign. This was not set up as such until late 1969. Its task was to act as an umbrella for various older organizations that had been active in the early 'sixties (and had in some cases remained active more or less ever since). It coexisted and collaborated by interlocking committee membership with various other bodies, chief of them the Anti-Common Market League and the Keep Britain Out Campaign. Other bodies closely involved were the National Common Market Petition Council and the Conservative Anti-Common Market Information Service. (Both these had the same address in Park Lane as the Safeguards Campaign, an office block which had also been the address of John Paul's Political Intelligence Publications. The premises were in fact provided by Sir Ian Mactaggart, Vice-Chairman of Keep Britain Out.)

The Anti-Common Market League had been set up in August–September 1961 to oppose Harold Macmillan's first bid for membership. It was originally a purely Conservative body whose members had to certify that they were members of the Conservative Party. Though it attempted later on to shed that Conservative image and become a non-partisan organization, publishing Douglas Jay's speeches as well as pamphlets by Enoch Powell, it never really made much headway beyond the Conservative political landscape.

The ACML was led by a former Conservative candidate, John Paul, who subsequently lost his job as director in an American oil company as he became more and more preoccupied with his campaign of meetings and pamphlets and fell foul of the personnel (and perhaps political) policies of his employers. Though men like Sir Derek Walker-Smith spoke at its meetings, it saw itself as essentially a grass-roots reaction to fashionable pro-entry trends: 'The League feels justly proud of its humble beginnings, and more, of its growing support amongst ordinary private individuals widespread throughout the British Isles.'

Michael Shay, the ACML's Honorary Secretary, described Edward Heath in its main 74-page pamphlet *Britain, Not Europe* (whose contributors included Peter Walker) as 'a middle-aged bachelor and occasional choirmaster . . . his brief experience of business with a firm of merchant bankers may well have helped to confirm this slant. The ranks of the merchant banking fraternity include many ardent "Europeans", many have but recently come from the Continent.' A pronouncement by Peter Thorneycroft he qualified as *Mein Kampf*-like, of Sir Edward Boyle he wrote 'he must be embarrassed by over-enthusiastic friends describing his "double-first" at Oxford', while both Harold Macmillan and Edward Heath were reproached for their campaign at the 1938 Oxford by-election 'on behalf of the Left-wing Independent candidate Mr A. D. Lindsay, against the official Conservative candidate, Mr Quintin Hogg (now Lord Hailsham)'.

It was thus hardly surprising if the Anti-Common Market League did not attract Labour support at this stage. But then in the same summer of 1961 the General Secretary of the National Society of Operative Printers (NATSOPA), Richard Briginshaw, had set up another body with greater appeal to Labour, the 'Forward Britain Movement'. (If the title of the Conservative ACML was no doubt deliberately and quite fairly reminiscent of the Anti-Corn Law League, its parallel on the Labour side made itself sound rather on the nationalist wing.) FBM could claim to have been on the winning side a year later, in 1962, since the Labour Party came out against joining the EEC except on five conditions. But this made even greater the sense of betrayal with which some quarters within the Party watched Harold Wilson, one of the most effective critics of EEC entry in 1962, try to join it 'at one hell of a pace' five years later. Within the Parliamentary Party in 1962 there had been a group called the 'Britain and the Common Market Group of Labour MPs and Peers' led by John Stonehouse and William Blyton, with which Emanuel Shinwell, Richard Marsh, Douglas Jay and Barbara Castle were associated. Though some of these MPs were now in the government, seventy-four others signed a statement published in *Tribune* on 5 May 1967 stating the political and economic case against entry under any likely conditions.

Outside the House of Commons at this time Ron Leighton, a NATSOPA member whom Richard Briginshaw had asked to become secretary of the Forward Britain Movement, felt that with all three party leaderships committed to entry the ordinary man in the street was helplessly disfranchised unless someone spoke up. He persuaded a fellow printer to print on credit five thousand copies of a pamphlet which, in scissors and paste style, reminded the party of its previous stance. He distributed it widely, formed a committee, the Labour Committee for the Five Safeguards on the Common Market, and proceeded to organize meetings. One of these, held on the eve of the Labour party conference in 1967, was called jointly with the parliamentary group and addressed, amongst others, by Alf Morris and by Douglas Jay, who had then recently ceased to be a Minister.

The last few months of 1967 saw the formation of a Labour Committee for Safeguards on the Common Market (the explicit reference to the five conditions of 1962 was dropped from the title as the Committee became a more substantial reality). It was a conjunction of the parliamentary group 'Britain and the Common Market' with the outside Labour anti-Marketeers. Douglas Jay became its Chairman, Ron Leighton its Secretary. The Committee continued its activities in 1968 and 1969, organizing fringe meetings at Labour party conferences. But it remained a purely Labour affair, with Emanuel Shinwell and Michael Foot in particular resisting any attempt at joining forces with the Right – and while the question was in abeyance after the second veto there was, after all, no particular urgency for such potentially compromising collaboration.

The Safeguards Campaign

All that changed when, in autumn 1969, it looked as if negotiations might actually be opened in Brussels. With all-party groupings in operation to campaign on the other side of the Common Market fence, it made sense to form a broader inter-party organization. Party meetings, after all, are not the only or even the best vehicle for the spread of ideas: and meetings of professional bodies, Round Tables, women's organizations and the like did not particularly want speakers with party-political labels that were only distractions from the Common Market argument. So the Common Market Safeguards Campaign was formed late in 1969 and publicly launched at a press conference in February 1970. Its Chairman and Director, Douglas Jay and Ron Leighton, were drawn from the Labour Safeguards Committee. Its President was Sir Arthur Bryant, a venerable literary figure of the conservative Right; one of its Vice-Chairmen, Sir Robin Williams, Bt, its Hon. Secretary, Tom Neate, and its Hon. Treasurer, Richard Kitzinger, came from the Anti-Common Market League.

The Campaign's list of patrons included 22 Conservative MPs (18 of whom voted against entry on 28 October) and 38 Labour MPs (including one, Maurice Orbach, who was simultaneously on the note-paper of the Labour Committee for Europe): Ian Mikardo, the 1970–71 Chairman of the Labour Party, Barbara Castle, Peter Shore and John Mendelson were among the patrons. The unions were represented by, among others, Jack Jones, Clive Jenkins and Dan McGarvey. Business and finance were represented among the patrons in the persons of two shipbuilders, Sir John Hunter, Chairman and Managing Director of Swan Hunter, and for a time M. A. Sinclair-Scott of Scott Lithgow, Sir George Dowty of the aircraft and aero-space industry, Sir George Bolton of the Bank of London and South America, and Lord Campbell of Eskan, chairman of the Commonwealth Sugar Exporters; Sir Ian Bowater, the industrialist whose interests were largely in paper, shared the vice-presidency with Lord Shinwell and Sir Robin Turton. Among academics, Nicholas Kaldor, Sir Roy Harrod, Richard Titmuss, William Pickles and Peter Oppenheimer figured as patrons, as did Fred Hoyle the astronomer, and John Osborne the novelist. Other patrons were John Paul's widow and Victor Montagu (previously Viscount Hinchinbrooke), the Chairman of ACML.

The Safeguards Campaign had difficulty in raising much money, in spite of its manifold connections. If there were many other businesses beyond paper, sugar and shipbuilding who felt themselves threatened by entry into the EEC, they seem not to have known it – brainwashed, no doubt, by propaganda, as the Safeguards Campaign saw it – or else if they did know they must have been unwilling to support the Campaign. The Safeguards Campaign in fact argued that those who did want to make corporate subscriptions feared that their boards of directors were not prepared to spend shareholders' money to subsidize

opposition to government policy – and thus possibly to risk government disapproval (which might express itself, they said, in the withholding of licences, grants, contracts or honours). One prominent
industrialist, whose name figured on the early list of the Campaign
patrons, asked for it to be deleted without in any other way withdrawing his support; his industry was one particularly dependent on
government aid. Indeed it was especially the industries in trouble that
felt themselves most threatened by entry; and they were the ones with
least (or no) profits to donate, and the greatest dependence on government good will. Trade unions, for their part, were not prepared to give
much financial help either: they mostly had no political funds to spare
for the CMSC and, where they had political funds available, preferred
to run their own campaigns. It might be thought surprising that a
hundred-odd patrons publicly committed to the cause, not all of them
poor or uninfluential, did not club together to prime the pump for a
professional fund-raising operation. The Campaign's answer was that
little could be expected from such fund-raising among the rich. Since
entry would mean less direct and more indirect taxation, the rich stood
to gain, the poor to lose; and the poor cannot give large donations.

On launching the Campaign, its organizers received some ten thousand individual subscriptions. Their literature insisted throughout on
the efforts to be made by the membership. 'We ask you to assist us by
approaching at least three people whom you feel would agree with our
stated aims and ask them to join our Campaign and signify their support by sending us a minimum of ten shillings.'[1] And 'We must oppose
their funds with our fire and conviction. . . . Go out and knock on
doors – win over your fellow citizens one by one, and where possible
recruit them to membership and collect a subscription.' Another appeal
in summer 1971 raised a further £3,000 in amounts of up to £200.

Altogether the Campaign spent a little over £15,000 in 1971, a
quarter of that sum going on salaries and office expenses, a tenth on
public meetings, and the rest on printing, postage and advertising. As
one of the papers put it, 'Its offices in Park Lane are small and manage on
a slender staff. Blonde actually.'[2] For most of the 1971 campaign, its
sole full-time employees were Ron Leighton with at first one and then
two secretaries.

Yet the Campaign was not really all that concerned at its lack of

[1] Quotations in this section not otherwise identified come from the CMSC
Bulletin.
[2] Michael Lake, *Guardian*, 2 February 1971.

funds. It was of course helped by numerous voluntary workers, and in a way it rather prided itself on being the ordinary man's come-back – the authentic voice of the people against the massive public relations operations of the élitist conspirators. It used a PR adviser for its initial press conference but got little joy out of employing him. Thereafter, as Ron Leighton put it, 'it never occurred to us to tell the press what we were doing'. As another paper reported:

The Safeguards Campaign is a most decorous group. Mr Leighton tends to wince at suggestions of mass rallies in Trafalgar Square and processions of tractors down Whitehall, and is half pained and half amused when he mentions that a member of Keep Britain Out plans to climb Nelson's column on June 5th and wave a British flag.[1]

They both resented their lack of publicity a little and made quite a point of it at the same time, as lending credence to their argument. They felt that the Trade Union Committee for Europe was counter-productive, accosting union officials in hotel bars in what some of them thought of as Moral Rearmament style with invitations to Brussels (where everyone was nice and the food was good and one would not want to be rude about it all in later life). No one on the other hand could feel got at by their penurious and on the whole stuntless campaign. When they had a meeting in the Central Hall in June, the fishing fleet from Brixham, which was to have come up the Thames to dramatize one of the arguments, was held back by bad weather – leaving the European Movement with a large catamaran decked in counter-slogans in occupation of the river. Only at the time of the Conservative party conference in 1971, when the smacks from Brixham bobbed off the Brighton promenade, did the Campaign really get much pictorial coverage from the press.

The Campaign had a private meeting on 14 December 1970 with Geoffrey Rippon, who blandly told them that he was really the Minister for negotiating the safeguards, so he was glad they were working for safeguards too. Their name was ostensibly minimalist, designed to catch as many members as possible by concentrating on the lowest common denominator of agreement. It was in any case difficult to oppose people who were committed only to negotiate to find out the terms – 'no more, no less'. But of course the Campaign realized from the start that the sort of safeguards they wanted would simply not be

[1] *Financial Times*, 15 May 1971.

available from the EEC as it stood or was likely ever to stand. So their
title was in fact a commitment to outright opposition.

If they concentrated in much of their written argument on the theme
'No entry without consent', this was another politically perfectly fair
method of broadening the basis of agreement to cover as much of the
political spectrum as possible: it was a position that could be taken quite
sincerely by those who actually also wanted to see Britain inside – but
only if she was wholeheartedly committed to the EEC. The Safeguards
Campaign – unlike Keep Britain Out under Christopher Frere-Smith –
never got itself explicitly committed to a referendum. To its Chairman

the substance is more important than the form . . . in both 1831 and 1910 the
two main parties were in clear disagreement about the major issue at stake; and
a general election was, therefore, clearly the right way to decide. So it would be
now, in my view, if the main parties were so divided. If, however, they were
not so divided, it would certainly be better, in my judgment, to give the electorate the chance of a direct vote on this issue. . . .

In the House of Commons the Safeguards Campaign produced its
analogous all-party group with Sir Robin Turton as Chairman and
the secretary of a Liberal MP, Peter Bessel, as Secretary. They met
fairly regularly, inviting outsiders to address them, decided on tactical
lines to be taken at Question Time, and invited other MPs to attend
meetings (including two Teach-Ins in the Grand Committee Room)
organized by the Safeguards Campaign. A good deal of this work
seems to have fallen on Douglas Jay. But as usual with such groups in
Parliament, attendance was normally low – six to ten people might be
typical: MPs have many other equally pressing commitments, and
worry about a great many problems other than entry into the EEC. In
any case the main parliamentary activity was carried out within the
two separate Parliamentary Parties.

Of the possible targets for the Safeguards Campaign – the government (actually to extract safeguards), the Opposition (to ensure their
swing against entry), the back-benchers of both parties (to secure their
votes), the press and broadcasting (to influence opinion indirectly
through them), selected constituencies (to put pressure on MPs from
behind), and the mass public at large – the Campaign modestly but no
doubt realistically wrote off pretty well all but the straight undifferen-
tiated appeal to the broad public. Clearly it could not influence either
party leadership. Its friends in the Conservative Party, notably Neil
Marten and Sir Robin Turton, were better placed than Ron Leighton

and Douglas Jay to encourage MPs to defy their own government. Labour MPs could well be left to the Labour whips.

The indignant fervour of much of its activity no doubt sprang from the sense of the people having its will, its institutions and its nature violated by its leaders' betrayal. This theme ran right through its campaign pronouncements. Before the election it warned:

It would be monstrous for the next Parliament to claim the right to decide such an irrevocable constitutional change without any mandate whatever from the electorate. Or for aspiring members of Parliament to intend to vote away our liberties and livelihoods, yet conceal this from the electors.

FRAUD

To play down the Common Market in the election, but prepare to rush us in as soon as possible afterwards, would be to practise a gigantic fraud on the British people.

In September 1970 it returned to the point:

OUTRAGE

To force this alien idea through Parliament by a 9-line Whip of all three parties in defiance of the wishes of the electorate would be an outrage which would grievously damage Parliamentary democracy.

And after the House of Commons had voted in principle, it insisted that that vote

settles nothing . . . the approval of Parliament alone is not enough. . . . It is therefore now the duty of every patriotic citizen – everyone who wants to save this country from the national decline inevitable if we are driven into the EEC – to resist the Government's proposed legislation by all means in our power. A mere vote by the House of Commons on a vague motion, or even the signing of the Treaty of Accession by the Government, cannot take Britain legally into the Common Market, until the legislation suppressing the rights of the British electorate has been passed.

The Government has not yet introduced, or even drafted, this legislation. When it does, it will be resisted to the last by the patriotic section of the House of Commons in both main parties. With the powerful support of public opinion in the country, this resistance can and will be carried on until Mr Heath is compelled to ask the views of the electorate.

For the rest the bulk of the argument was on neither the safeguards nor the consent grounds, but on the economic arguments on the one hand and the loss of sovereignty on the other. A 5p booklet, *The Truth About The Common Market 1971–72* (originally published by Political Intelligence Publications in 1967), dealt at length with the economic but also with the political case for staying out and advocated 'a larger but looser association' based on fostering and widening 'the group already practising the democratic and free trade principles of EFTA and the Commonwealth'.

The Safeguards Campaign's only more or less regular, or at least serial, publication was an occasional one-sheet (originally litho-offset) *Bulletin*. It was edited by Ron Leighton, and carried almost no advertising – except once for a bedsitter for Ron Leighton's secretary. The November 1971 issue devoted about half its contents to the cry of 'No entry without consent'. The other half highlighted some of the main substantive themes: the headlines were, on the political side, 'Britain "must give France atom secrets"', and on the economic, 'Danger – Good Harvest', 'Common Market Recession', 'Alien Control over Regional Policy' and 'Mass Unemployment – the Cost of Market Entry'. Earlier issues of the *Bulletin* reported on a 'Belgian invasion' of 1,700 Belgians arriving in Folkestone on a special ferry from Ostend for a shopping expedition (notably to Marks and Spencer's). The *Bulletin* cited *The Times* on 'Child Labour in Italy' involving half a million boys between the ages of eight and fifteen, and explained the 'Threat to British Food and Drink' arising from draft Community rules:

We could not have our usual kippers because of their brown colouring, likewise our jelly marmalade falls foul of the draft directive on conserves, and worst of all, the draft brewing rules according to the Brewers' Society 'would mean the end of British beer as we know it'.

The *Bulletin*'s edition eventually rose to 100,000 copies.

Any propaganda exercise can be caricatured by citing its more marginal pronouncements. *Talking Points* edited by Neil Marten highlighted a 'Midwife Shortage' on the front page of the first number. *Why Join The Common Market – Your Questions Answered* argued that 'the atmosphere of tax fraud, which corrupts so much of Italian and French society and is a major cause of political extremism, would tend to infect Britain'. In its leaflet *The Price of the Common Market in Your Shopping Basket* (reprinted by courtesy of the *Daily Express*) the Safeguards Campaign argued 'British membership of the Common Market would mean savage rises in the price of food as these comparisons show' and committed about every statistical fallacy in the book by constructing a notional total for a single basket of British-taste goods as assembled from shops in five different countries including

¼lb tea	Paris	9s 0d	London	1s 11d
5oz packet jelly	Rome	4s 0d	London	11d
11 oz tin custard powder	Brussels	3s 6d	London	1s 8d
16 oz packet cornflakes	The Hague	5s 2d	London	2s 3d
1 oz tin pepper	Rome	6s 0d	London	9d
. . .		. . .		. . .
		£5 11s 9d		£2 12s 8d

In the 1961–63 debate, some anti-Marketeers had at times displayed overtones of xenophobia or appealed to racial or religious prejudice. In 1962 Victor Montagu had explained just before becoming President of the Anti-Common Market League that 'those of us in Britain who oppose the Common Market don't want to subject ourselves to a lot of frogs and huns',[1] and speaking at the Albert Hall countered the arguments of merchant bankers by arguing that their origins were 'in Hamburg and Frankfurt' anyway,[2] and in 1962 a former High Sheriff of Oxfordshire could deliver a speech embodying a series of national stereotypes such as France being 'the whore-house of the world', the Germans 'good soldiers but follow bad leaders', the Italians as 'pretty women, rather greasy little men terribly anxious not to be hit or kicked . . . the scum of the earth' and dismiss the lot as 'that gang of scarecrows'.[3]

In 1970–71 this line of argument had very largely disappeared in public, though there were sediments of it to be heard and read in private. The difference is significant perhaps not only of the passage of time and the realization of changes in Britain's relative position in Europe and the world beyond, but more interestingly perhaps also of changes at home. The self-confidence of effortless superiority and also the social stereotypes of British society had waned during the 'sixties.

Nevertheless it would have been surprising had such sentiments not surfaced at all. Thus the *Financial Times* published two letters on the same day (3 November 1970) of which one – by a member of and

[1] Lieber, op. cit., p. 210.
[2] ibid., p. 213.
[3] Kitzinger, *The European Common Market and Community*, ed. cit., pp. 180–2.

speaker for the Anti-Common Market League – reiterated an earlier argument warning against an 'Afro-Euro-Turk amalgam' on the grounds that 'the present EEC contains 4 to 5 million Asiatics and Negroes and would soon contain Turkey, so that the resulting Eurasian melting pot would not be Western European nor probably have much culture or standards' (G. J. A. Stern); the other, based also on a decision of the Human Rights Commission, added: 'this foretaste of the destruction of our sovereignty may mean flooding our country with unknown millions of Asiatics . . . the logical result of this policy will be the destruction of Great Britain and, for that matter, of the white race in Europe' (K. T. Moore).

We shall see in the next chapter that, in addition to race, creed also entered into the emotions on this issue. But then over the Common Market issue both sides found themselves with very strange and unwelcome bedfellows. As Richard Briginshaw said of those who actually organized themselves (rather than merely wrote letters over which the Campaign and its affiliates could have no control): 'People come together who would not want to be seen dead in the same coffin.'

Parallel Bodies

Some of CSMC's work was done through the pre-existing organizations which the Campaign sought to consolidate, some through subsidiary bodies of a more or less shadowy or substantial kind which its members created for specific purposes. Thus the Safeguards Campaign set up a National Anti-Common Market Demonstration Committee to organize a march from Marble Arch to a meeting in Trafalgar Square on the Sunday before the House of Commons vote, 24 October 1971. It was addressed by among others Judith Hart and Michael Foot, Lord Woolley and Edward Taylor (the former Under-Secretary at the Scottish Office who had resigned in early September 1971 over the Market issue). Feeling was running high, and Ron Leighton by this time thought it wise to admonish supporters before the rally: 'to maintain unity and avoid friction. I urge marchers not to bring party banners but to bring anti-Common Market banners.'

A National Common Market Petition Council organized a petition to be presented to the Queen. Beginning in ornate gothic lettering, it read as follows:

A PETITION concerning the proposal that Britain should join the European Common Market (EEC) under the terms of the Treaty of Rome.

TO THE QUEEN'S MOST EXCELLENT MAJESTY:
The Petition of Your Majesty's loyal subjects whose names are appended hereto showeth:

WHEREAS joining EEC by acceding to the Treaty of Rome would have many adverse effects for our country, such as:
1. increasing the cost of food to the British public;
2. worsening Britain's balance of payments;
3. injuring Britain's trade with Commonwealth countries;
4. limiting Parliament's rights to legislate on many matters; and
5. subjecting us, without protection from British courts of law, to regulations and directives issued by EEC authorities.

NOW THEREFORE, being convinced that this proposal to join EEC is without precedent in the history of this realm (and that it puts in danger the rights of Your subjects freely to enjoy those full political and economic liberties which they have inherited from the past), WE humbly pray Your Majesty, in the exercise of Your Royal Prerogative, to call upon Your Government to explain the full implications of this policy and to allow Your subjects the opportunity to express their wishes before any irrevocable step is taken.

The Petition was launched before the 1970 election, and in the election campaign 'our members, often after collecting signatures to the Petition to take with them as evidence of local feeling, have arranged interviews with their election candidates.'[1] Supporters were advised always to carry a Petition form in their pocket, so that they could whip it out when a potential signatory swam into their ken. In summer 1970 the International Federation of Meat Traders' Associations sent a copy of the Petition to each of their twelve thousand members for display in butchers' shops throughout the country. 'Large numbers of house-wives, realizing the vastly increased prices for meat which Market entry would mean, have hastened to sign the Petition.'[2] A year and a half later, after the vote of 28 October 1971 had been taken, the Petition had still not been presented. The Council could claim 600,000 signatures, but – presumably regarding this as an inadequate total – 'thought it right to continue with the Petition for some months more with a view to presenting it during 1972. . . . It is, therefore, of the utmost importance that we should all redouble our efforts to collect signatures. . . .'[3] When it was presented on 2 May 1972 it bore 764,107

[1] *Bulletin*, No. 2 (June 1970), p. 1.
[2] loc. cit., No. 3 (September 1970), p. 8.
[3] loc. cit., No. 6 (November 1971), p. 2.

signatures – an impressive total. But the collection of further signatures continued.

The Safeguards Campaign appears in fact to have become more publicity-conscious in early 1972. On the day the Treaty was signed, while Keep Britain Out was demonstrating in Brussels, the Safeguards Campaign presented a letter to the EEC Permanent Representation in Kensington Palace Gardens. Ron Leighton wrote to his supporters:

We are asking for several thousand of our members to accompany the deputation with banners and posters. . . . The success of the operation will depend on members converging on the entrance to 'Millionaires Row' exactly at 12 noon. Do not arrive before or the police may move you on. Wait in side streets or in Kensington Gardens and move to the entrance precisely on the hour.

We may all be able to proceed up Kensington Palace Gardens to number 20, or, if prevented, we can congregate around the entrance to this private road until the deputation returns.

The news cameras should be waiting to report the event which we hope will demonstrate the fact that public opinion repudiates the signing of the Treaty of Accession. I do most strongly urge you to assist in this and to disperse peacefully afterwards.

In all this the Safeguards Campaign was working closely, through its interlocking management, with both the Anti-Common Market League and the Labour Safeguards Committee. The League in fact spent much the same amount as the Safeguards Committee in 1971, though its spending on meetings was negligible, and all but the tenth of its expenditure that went on office expenses went on printing, advertising and postage (83%), or on donations to other organizations such as the Petition Council and the Trafalgar Square rally organized under Campaign auspices (7%). After distributing some half a million items of literature in 1970, it stepped up its campaign to 1·2 million items in 1971, and like the Safeguards Committee it regarded 1971 only as a single battle in a longer war – with fiercer conflicts to come in 1972, 1973 and thereafter, until Britain had regained her self-government.

The Labour Safeguards Committee, also, carried on under its own steam through this period, publishing more pamphlets in editions of several tens of thousands for despatch to local Labour parties and branches and chapels of unions, sending speakers to half the constituency parties in the country, organizing delegate conferences in provincial centres, and submitting articles for insertion in trade union journals. Their style remained rather different from that of the Labour Marketeers, and they felt they were being more effective. The Marketeers might talk to Nora Beloff and get themselves written up in the posh Sunday papers; but this, the Labour Safeguards Committee felt very strongly, was not where real politics happen. What mattered to them were the grass-roots activists of the party in their smoky ward meetings and at the bars of local trades council halls, and that is where they took their message. By making a profit on some of their pamphlets and taking coin collections at their meetings, they managed to run their activities for five years on less than a thousand pounds of donated finance.

Keep Britain Out

We have already repeatedly had to make reference to the body that called itself quite unequivocally Keep Britain Out. KBO had been founded in the early 'sixties by a journalist, S. W. Alexander (who had been at various times secretary to Lord Beaverbrook and City editor of the *Daily Express*), and had been led by a vice-president of the Liberal Party, Oliver Smedley. KBO's adherents were basically free traders who saw entry into the Common Market as a total reversal of the repeal of the Corn Laws. Their lunch and dinner meetings appealed to a somewhat different audience from the ACML and the Forward Britain Movement, but brought together a wide range of people hostile to entry. The organization rather went to sleep after 1963, but it was given a new lease of life in 1966 by a former Liberal, free-trading solicitor educated partly in Holland as well as Cambridge, Christopher Frere-Smith, who became its Chairman. Christopher Frere-Smith had stood for Marylebone as an anti-Market candidate in the 1966 election campaign but now felt that to play the game the way the parties wanted it was self-defeating, and badly understated the opposition to entry: in 1970 he spoke for anti-Market candidates whether Labour, Liberal or Conservative in all sorts of constituencies. Very closely associated with Christopher Frere-Smith were the two Vice-Chairmen, W. A. Newton Jones and from 1970 on Sir Ian Mactaggart. Sir Ian had contested Glasgow (Gorbals) in the Conservative interest as a very young man in 1945, and then, in 1970, came within 3,500 votes of beating Michael Stewart as his Conservative opponent in Fulham. Their committee included Donald Stewart, sales director of a Harris tweed firm and Scottish Nationalist MP for the Western Isles, John White of NATSOPA, Oliver Smedley and Richard Body, Conservative MP for Holland with Boston. Anne Kerr, the former actress, former Left-wing MP and then Chairman of Women Against the Common Market, joined the Committee after that body (euphoniously known as WACM) had been formed with a gift of £100 from KBO.

The KBO Campaign did not believe in getting itself bogged down with card indices of membership and correspondence: it invited people to send in £1 each, but then left it to autonomous local action groups – and there were several dozen of them, at first mainly in Greater London and East Anglia – to organize themselves with the help of car stickers, posters and leaflets generally supplied free from headquarters. Depending on local conditions, some of these groups consisted of Conservative die-hards, some of Leftish Labour people, so too much attempted co-ordination would have been a waste of time anyhow.

KBO had no one on its payroll until well into 1971, but several people devoted themselves almost full-time to running its campaign. The largest single donation they ever received was of £10,000, and in the twelve months from June 1971 they were able to raise £25,000; by the end of 1971 they were able to employ a research assistant who could help both the 1970 Group of Conservative MPs and the Campaign's friends on the other side of the House like Michael Foot and Peter Shore. They were not happy with what the Anti-Common Market League was doing, regarding it as too parochially Conservative, and felt that the Safeguards Campaign were always looking over their shoulders, worried about playing a straight bat and the future of their political careers. Where the Safeguards Campaign scored with opinion-formers, KBO sought to dramatize the issue for the wider public.

They paid for posters on the railways (though the London Underground refused to advertise the Trafalgar Square rally on the grounds that it was 'political') and they also did a fair amount of fly-posting; they advertised occasionally in the national press and a great deal in the local press – particularly in the constituencies of MPs who had pledged their fight against entry but seemed to be flagging in the good fight in early 1972 – such as Sir Eric Bullus and Sir Gerald Nabarro (both of whom voted against Clause 2 in June 1972). Their 1971 advertisements read, for example:

HM Government Ltd. auctioneers and valuers FOR SALE BY ROME TREATY the Freehold of England and Scotland, Wales and the Northern Part of Ireland, together with the undisputed right to frame and impose laws upon the land and upon all of Her Majesty's subjects. Negotiations proceeding.

Stop the greatest sell-out ever. Keep us out of The Six. Britain must not become No. 7.

or

Common Market entry would cause – 1. Food prices up 50p per person per week. 2. Immigrants from the Continent admitted without restriction. . . . 6. Burden of £1,000 million each year on our balance of payments. 7. Independent Britain reduced to a province of Europe. . . .

Compared with the European Movement's expensive operation with its glossy handouts and cocktail parties for journalists, the KBO Campaign displayed a fine flair for getting themselves into the news on a shoe-string. Indeed the European Movement regarded KBO rather than the ACML or the Safeguards Campaign as their most effective opponents – no doubt because KBO thought very much in publicity terms.

In 1967 KBO got good photographic exposure both with a top-hatted procession of mourners in Whitehall round a coffin marked 'Common Market – Death to British Democracy', and also when their young secretary was arrested and stripped by the Rome police and she was pictured full length in much of the press (fully clothed). They picketed Chequers repeatedly, wrote to Sir Alec Douglas-Home to ask for £7,500 like the European Movement, but above all specialized in two activities – letting the Continent know how little support there was for entry among the British people, and holding mini-referenda in ten British constituencies to prove the point all round.

In 1970–72 the KBO Campaign took several groups of housewives and others to Brussels and the wife of one of the committee members came back 'aghast' at having had to pay £1 for three cups of tea and 9/6d a pound for English cheddar cheese, but found there was plenty of horsemeat around. But their trips abroad were usually meant more for Continental consumption. In 1970–72 Christopher Frere-Smith and Sir Ian Mactaggart (sometimes joined by other members) made various trips to the Continent to demonstrate and hold press conferences explaining the opposition of the British people (Christopher Frere-Smith was arrested on three occasions on the Continent, one of them the day of the signature of the Treaty in Brussels.) They even turned up, curiously enough by invitation, at one of the British delegation's press conferences in Brussels, but were given a drink and asked to leave like good boys.

In April 1972 they organized a joint demonstration with the *Confédération Générale du Travail* in Calais, during the referendum campaign, in which the French police, as so often happens, over-reacted. They boarded the *Invicta*, there were scuffles, and the KBO group of 230 people were in fact never allowed to land. But the incident received excellent publicity in Britain and became a topic in the French referendum campaign taken up particularly by *L'Humanité*. The spectacle of some rather Right-wing English gentlemen with their umbrellas demonstrating with the CGT in the streets of Calais might have been even more impressive, but the photographs of the fighting with the French police were spectacular enough. The heterogeneity of KBO emerges clearly from the *Guardian*'s account of the fracas:

The punches began, directed at the police from trade unionists and grey-haired middle-class Englishmen and women. . . . At one stage the Left-wing section of the group were shouting 'Gestapo swine' and 'Fascist pigs', while the nationalist element were singing 'Rule Britannia'.[1]

At home, once the KBO had a sufficient sum of money assured, it embarked on its unofficial referenda, with three held at the end of July 1971 and another seven in October. In June they invited the European Movement to participate in the selection of constituencies: Lord Harlech replied in the negative, with the (for a European Movement slightly insular) reasoning that 'a referendum, which is not a British method of sounding public opinion, would be a misleading mechanism'.[2]

Lowestoft was the first constituency to be polled: Jim Prior had, during the election the year before, promised not to support entry without the backing of his constituents. Prior now pointed out that he did not then know he would become a Minister and would have to make up his mind so soon: but he would have a series of meetings to consult his constituents. (He afterwards complained they were very poorly attended, so that there could hardly be much feeling on the subject.) With strong local links in the area, the KBO Campaign managed to get over a third of the electorate to vote – and obtained more than a 2:1 majority against entry.

This 2:1 ratio remained the typical result whether in Brentford and Chiswick (the constituency of one of the most dedicated Labour Marketeers, Michael Barnes), in Macclesfield (where there was a by-

[1] *Guardian*, 17 April 1972.
[2] *The Times*, 28 June 1971.

Constituency Referenda Results

Date	Constituency	Against	For	Don't Know	Poll	Percentage of Electorate
25 July	Lowestoft	17,537	7,123	154	24,814	35
26 July	Brentford & Chiswick	5,459	2,613	257	8,329	22
31 July	Macclesfield	13,865	7,435	1,660	22,960	32
11 October	Middlesbrough	19,256	8,438	141	27,880	47
12 October	Wellingborough	27,443	11,757	1,187	40,387	48
		83,560	37,411	3,399	124,370	39

Sample Constituency Referenda Results (every tenth household on electoral roll)

Date	Constituency	Against	For	Don't Know	Poll	Total votes circulated	Percentages of total votes circulated
15 Oct.	Eye	4,580	2,195	53	6,828	10,469	65
15 Oct.	Bury St Edmunds	6,250	3,703	55	10,008	13,979	72
15 Oct.	Sudbury & Woodbridge	6,436	3,517	74	10,027	13,568	74
19 Oct.	Banbury	3,956	1,965	87	6,008	9,720	61
19 Oct.	Maidstone	2,832	1,685	36	4,553	8,294	52
		24,054	13,065	305	37,424	56,030	67

Results of other referenda (not conducted by KBO)

Date	Constituency	Against	For	Size of Electorate	Percentage Voting
July 1971	Hexham (Town)	2,826	1,034	7,374	52
Oct. 1971	Bexley	4,889	1,983	19,555	36
Oct. 1971	Beckenham	3,587	3,757	60,874	12
Oct. 1971	Gloucester	17,406	13,120	61,229	50
Oct. 1971	South Bucks (part)	13,645	10,309	51,650 (part)	47
Oct. 1971	Hastings	11,592	3,472	55,297	27

The polls at Hexham and Bexley were conducted by the Political Freedom Movement, those at Beckenham, Gloucester and South Bucks by their respective MPs, and that at Hastings by local people. All were conducted by post, except Beckenham (4 polling stations) and Hastings (17 polling stations).

election pending), or in October in Middlesborough and Welling-borough (where two Conservative MPs who were to vote against entry on the 28th encouraged the referenda to take place). The results declared by the KBO Campaign are set out on p. 249. They are rather different from the narrow majority in favour in Beckenham's unofficial referendum, organized by the sitting MP Philip Goodhart: this is no doubt a matter of the KBO Campaign's choice of constituen-cies as against the rather special situation in Beckenham (with its middle-class southern Conservative electorate with an unusually high ratio of employment in the tertiary sector, particularly in financial services). The difference from the public opinion polls would also be accounted for in part by the depth of feeling and motivation needed actively to take part in a private referendum as against the lesser effort of just answering a question put to one orally. It was certainly remark-able that in the two October constituency referenda the response was in the region of half the electorate.

ACML, the Safeguards Campaign and KBO were highly specific cause groups concentrating entirely on this one issue of EEC entry, and could therefore on the whole disregard other aspects of public policy. They were joined in their battle by a number of other groupings which existed for much broader purposes, and therefore had many other functions and criteria of membership. The Labour Party and some of the trade unions came out on the same side of this particular barricade, and of course made an impact on the battle by comparison with which these specific anti-Market groups were little more than snipers; but there were also minute groupings such as Wing-Commander Don Bennett's Political Freedom Movement run from Blackbushe Airport in Sussex which wanted referenda used much more generally, and newsletters such as *On Target* edited by Don Martin (who may not have been generally known but felt that to sit down and enumerate the activities of his organization in opposing entry would in itself almost entail a book). The study of such *groupuscules* is full of fascination in itself, but not really justified within the confines of this book.

There are, however, two things to be said. First, if the anti-Market campaigns had not existed, the government and European Movement ought to have invented them. The balance of campaigns was unequal, and to have had the balance any more unequal would have thrown grave doubt on the vitality of British democracy. It is on the individual initiative of men concerned with the public good and prepared to sacrifice energy, time and money for their convictions that creative democratic tensions within society depend. (The anti-Marketeers in 1971 were still much less Heath-Robinson, less penurious, more professional and vastly more respectable than the federalists and proto-Marketeers of the 1950s.) And secondly, in the struggle for public opinion it was they, not the government, who were in the ascendant and remained in the ascendant for most of the battle in 1971 - and the 'war' was by no means over as this book went to press.

9   Churches, Employers and Trade Unions

It is a disgusting capitalist-oriented society
Neil Hutchison

The Churches and their Congregations

There is no evidence that churchgoers in their pews held any very
different attitudes to the Common Market than non-churchgoers of
similar age, sex and class – which, given the social composition of most
congregations, probably meant they were on balance inclined to be
against. Church leadership, on the other hand, was on balance very
much more in favour of entry. It was perhaps not surprising that the
unofficial though influential Roman Catholic Institute of International
Relations should feel that

Christians who, by definition, believe in the breaking down of barriers between
races cannot but welcome the opportunities for contact with the European
peoples which the Common Market offers. . . . Secondly, closer contact and
stronger political and cultural links with Europe should help people in Britain
to work more effectively with other Europeans for a more just and equitable
society within Europe. . . . Thirdly, and perhaps most important of all, is that
a realization that national interests and national boundaries are not the ultimate
consideration will enable us to progress towards that universal outlook which is
the fully Christian, as well as the fully human, ideal. . . . Membership of the
EEC . . . must be seen as valuable precisely because it points beyond itself.[1]

Indeed the Commission for International Justice and Peace of the
Roman Catholic Episcopal Conference of England and Wales in
October 1971 unanimously adopted a lengthy statement on the entry
of Britain, which stressed the duties of Christian citizens in the event of
Britain becoming a member 'to ensure that the enlarged Community
adds to the achievement of Western European peace and reconciliation, the establishment of a new dimension of planetary justice' and
emphasized the need for Britain to take a lead in the development and
expansion of the EEC's 'already considerable effort to help the developing countries'.
   More surprising perhaps was the near unanimity of the Anglican

[1] Catholic Institute for International Relations, *Comment* 1, pp. 5–6.

bishops, eleven of whom (led by the Primate of All England) filed out with the 'Contents' in the House of Lords division of 28 October 1971, rather giving the impression that even 'God was on the side of the Market'.[1] The Archbishop of Canterbury, in his Diocesan News Letter for September 1971 (according to a press release from the Church Information Service evidently designed to give it wider publicity), wrote:

The decision to be made by Parliament about the entry of this country into the Common Market is among the most important choices in history, and Christian people must pray that wisdom will guide the making of it.

If the decision is 'yes' the Christian Churches will have immense new responsibility and opportunity to which by God's help we must rise. The contacts between the Churches, Catholic and Protestant, on the Continent and in England will be greater than ever before, and we shall work together in our witness to the Christian foundations of our common life.

Christian influence will help to prevent a united Europe from being introverted and selfish and to lead it to be a Europe which gives all it can to the wider service of a desperately needy world.[2]

The General Synod of the Church of England did not formally debate the issue in 1971, but next June its Board for Social Responsibility published a 24-page report for the Synod's consideration which saw the enlargement of the EEC as 'an exhilarating and spirit-stretching experience for the Church of England as much as for England as a whole. . . . Time and time again, the consideration of the practical involves the ecumenical. If divisions in the Church contribute to human divisions, non-theological factors certainly reinforce ecclesiastical divisions.'

The report went on:

The real challenge, and enormous opportunity for all Christians and other men of goodwill, is to use the unprecedented instrument of supranational institutions achieved within the European Community to grapple more effectively with world poverty because our Lord commands us so to do.

It concluded with a prayer used by the Christian group of European civil servants for over a decade:

We offer up to thee the attempt to create a United Europe. We do not pray that Europe be strong or rich. We pray that her historic peoples may unite in peace

[1] *Observer*, 6 July, echoing the comment of a Labour peer at the time of the vote.

[2] Dr Michael Ramsey, Diocesan News Letter, September 1971.

after being so torn by wars. We pray that the aim and purpose of a United Europe may be the better to serve the other peoples of thy world, the poor and the starving; and that from the new unity may spring a rebirth of the spirit wherein men may acknowledge thee as Lord.[1]

The 'fervent enthusiasm' of the report prompted the *Church Times* to wonder if it would strengthen the old jibe at the Church of England for being 'the Tory party at prayer'.[2]

The British Council of Churches had, in 1967, passed a resolution welcoming the long report presented by its Department for International Affairs[3] and going on:

The Council considers that British membership of a Community which (based as it is on a common understanding of human rights and liberties) counts among its aims the reconciliation of European enmities, the responsible stewardship of European resources and the enrichment of Europe's contribution to the rest of mankind, is to be welcomed as an opportunity for Christians to work for the achievement of these ends.

In August 1971, at the height of the public debate, the International Affairs Department of the British Council of Churches and the Conference of British Missionary Societies published a new 24-page pamphlet by Kenneth R. Johnstone, its former chairman, which essentially summarized the earlier report and also contained a paper written for the Ecumenical Centre in Brussels by a Christian layman in the service of the EEC: 'European moves towards unification do not call for a clericalization of politics, but rather for a confrontation with dynamic Christian social ethics, which are now being put to the test in this field.' Kenneth Johnstone's pamphlet argued that the question of British entry

challenges our deep-rooted insular mistrust of those who speak with other tongues – crude perhaps, but the bulk of our nation are still a good deal less sophisticated in this respect than the rest of us would like to appear. . . . The old disunity which has come so close to ruining us all has somehow to be replaced, in Churches and states alike. . . . Europe is our homeland, the origin of so much that is of lasting value in our culture.[4]

[1] *Britain in Europe: the Social Responsibility of the Church*, pp. 5–10.
[2] 16 June 1972.
[3] *Christians and the Common Market*, SCM, 1967.
[4] Kenneth R. Johnstone, *Britain and the Common Market – A Christian View*, pp. 24, 7, 8.

The pamphlet was circulated, thanks to an outside grant, to the parish clergy or their equivalents in all the member churches of the British Council of Churches, to the parish priests of the Catholic Church in England, and to the secretaries of the 700 or so local Councils of Churches.

The Methodist, Congregational and Baptist Churches felt on the whole that this was not a denominational matter, but one where the free churches should speak together with the British Council of Churches. Thus in the Congregational Church of England and Wales, the Reverend John Huxtable, the Minister-Secretary, declared, 'I feel fairly sure that the arguments for entry cannot be so set out that no sensible Christian could honourably think otherwise', but went on (not, no doubt, without a touch of charity): 'If the Communist Party and Mr Enoch Powell agree as touching anything on earth, I am disposed to think at once that I simply must be on the other side.' He argued:

Those who are aware of the urgent needs of the developing countries are concerned that the increased prosperity which we are led to believe the Common Market will bring to all its member nations should make us careless of the good of the poorer nations. Let us honestly admit the possibility; but let us with equal honesty face the fact that greater prosperity should make it ever more possible for us to give greater aid to the developing nations. If we dedicate our efforts to bringing about that sort of result – and there need be no reason why we should not – then entry into the Common Market could be right from this point of view.

The chief exception to this trend was to be found – temporarily – in the Church of Scotland. In 1967 the General Assembly had decided to 'pray that, if the application is successful, this historic venture may be able to contribute much to the European Community', and in 1968, though rejecting a proposed deliverance approving the government's policy, agreed on one commending study of the Christian principles which underlay the concept of the EEC. In 1970 the General Assembly decided to postpone any decision until it had had a report from its Church and Nation Committee. This was produced in twenty printed pages and concluded rather favourably to entry:

If Britain and Europe go their separate ways, it is a matter for discussion whether they could give independently anything like the amounts in aid which they could give in an economic commonalty. Present evidence suggests strongly that they could not.

It is here on this world scale that the Market has the ability to provide a new context for peace-making among the nations of the world. . . . It is to exercise just this ministry of reconciliation and charity that the Church is called by her Lord.[1]

In May 1971 the General Assembly instructed the Committee to examine the terms and report to the Commission of General Assembly; the Committee reported in the autumn with a deliverance calling on members of the Church 'to accept whole-heartedly the implications of wider European commitment, and in particular to work and pray for the achievement of the aims of reconciliation and peace which are inherent in the vision of the Communities.'

On 21 October 1971, the day the debate of principle began in the House of Commons and just a week before the vote, this deliverance was adopted by the Commission of the General Assembly by 298 votes to 198. But this reflected a remarkable *volte-face* compared with the balance of advice six months earlier: in May 1971 the same body, meeting in General Assembly, had voted by 303 votes to 230 in favour of a motion tabled from the floor warning against the very serious consequences that might arise if entry into the EEC were pursued in defiance of the wishes of the electorate and urging 'Her Majesty's Government to break off all negotiations for entry'. The earlier vote had been taken partly under the influence of the oratory of a powerful figure, the founder of the Iona Community and 'a great gift to the Church – though not everyone always agrees with him', the Very Revd Lord Macleod of Fuinary, a patron of the Safeguards Campaign. He returned to the issue in May 1972, seeking to persuade the General Assembly to reverse its view again. But by then the decision of principle had been taken in London; Lord Macleod's motion was heavily defeated and the Assembly instead decided, 'believing that British membership in the European Economic Community and the maintenance of the Commonwealth are not contradictory but complementary, [to] urge Her Majesty's Government to use its influence in Europe towards bridging the gap between the developed and the developing worlds'.[2]

Numerically insignificant, but not entirely without influence, the Society of Friends was divided on the issue. The Northern Friends Peace Board quoted a Scottish Quaker:

[1] Church and Nation Report to the General Assembly, May 1971, pp. 77–95.
[2] Church and Nation Report to the General Assembly, May 1972, p. 215.

There may be ethical value in a World State, but in what way is a sectional conglomeration of six or more morally superior to a single national state? . . . Friends have pioneered opposition to war, slavery and capital punishment. Would that they might now lead the opposition to the lust for power and gain.

But it also quoted an Irish one:

The structure of decision-making is itself a tribute to Quaker methods. Other Christians, burdened with hierarchic modes of thought and action, do not have the freedom to answer the calls as they come. Let us go forward sure in the Light, knowing how hard a discipline it may be.

Overall its pamphlet *Friends and the Common Market* came out rather in favour than against; it recalled William Penn's 1694 *Essay on the Present and Future Peace of Europe* with its Imperial Diet or State of Europe deliberating in a Round Room with Many Doors (to avoid problems of precedence), and its two-thirds qualified majority voting, and described Jean Monnet 'alongside Dante, Henry IV, Grotius, William Penn, John Bellers and other rare souls, as one of the greatest Europeans of all time'.

One cannot help contrasting these declarations by the radical ecumenical wing of the Church – the one concerned with South Africa, the Third World and race relations no less than with unity between the churches – with some of the more sectarian or conservative groupings, whose views, however, found much less resonance. A pamphlet published by the Protestant Alliance under the title *The Queen and the Common Market*, and distributed at the party conferences, stated:

Unless faithful Protestants stand up and be counted, Europe is about to realize the false anti-Scriptural ideal of One World One Church. The One World is Communist. The One Church is the Church of Rome. The Church of England and the apostate Churches will be swallowed up. *This Common Market in Churches and States is a league with the World, the Flesh and the Devil.*

Just as it had been unfortunate that, at the time of the Messina Conference which decided to set up the Economic Community, there had been a sordid criminal case involving two brothers named Messina, so the fact that the Treaty setting up the Community was signed in Rome psychologically accentuated the fears of ardent Protestants. One of the officers of the Safeguards Campaign advanced the theory that the media of communication were so biased against them partly no doubt because of the pressure of the advertisers, but also because of the long hand of Rome on those who occupied their commanding heights – such as the Editor of *The Times* and the Director-General of the BBC. (Similar arguments were used about such leading pro-Marketeers in the House of Commons as Norman St John-Stevas, Shirley Williams and Maurice Foley, rather forgetting the Catholic rebels on the other side like Anthony Fell and Hugh Fraser.)

More straightforward, however, was the kind of argument presented by Harold Eldred in a letter to *The Times* of 21 July 1971: 'For centuries, Great Britain has held a special place in the world as the repository of Christian truth and the authority of the Bible recognized as the Word of God.' Therefore, he argued:

If Great Britain becomes a member of the EEC she will be allied to countries one of which (at least) is dominated by the Roman Catholic Church from whose yoke we broke free at the Reformation.

To bring us back under the rule of the Papacy would be the most retrograde step and the biggest disaster of all.

Similarly, it was argued at the Safeguards rally in Brighton that no Ulster Protestant could possibly vote for the political unification of Eire and the United Kingdom – though that, of course, was as much a political as a religious argument.

Where the Protestant Alliance feared that entry into the EEC would lead to a *rapprochement* with Rome, and the British Israel World Federation feared the end of the monarchy, thousands of worried and pious individuals writing to the newspapers echoed the view that 'the Common Market with its underlying Treaty of Rome is one of the most evil, totalitarian confederations the Devil ever invented'.

In March 1971 one of the placards at the KBO and WACM rally in Trafalgar Square read 'Amazing Sex Shops Boom – Get Wise and Organize Against European Filth'; and one can see the despair felt at the rising tide of evil about him in the letter to one of the anti-Market organizations of a retired military man:

The Money Power – mostly Jews through the International Monetary Fund – want One World governed by themselves, for themselves. Since money controls everything in this mercenary and materialistic age there has never been any doubt that we would in the end go into the Common Market – for the benefit of the Jews and the destruction of Christianity. . . . Aim at preserving Britain by preserving Christianity. . . . Begin by abolishing evil legislation such as abortion, homosexuality, sex-in-schools, etc. . . . Pray for God's forgiveness, practise penitence. Nothing else of any use.

The CBI and the Farmers' Union

Just as the leaders of the Churches were more favourable to entry than their congregations, so the leaders of organized industry and agriculture were more favourable than those they represented. There was at the outset a very clear contrast between the views of the top echelons of the Confederation of British Industry and the broad opinion of employers and industrialists in the country. In the late 'fifties the leadership of organized industry had come out of the negotiations for a large free trade area in Europe sad at their failure and convinced that they must push for freer trade: they claim the credit for initiating the policy that led to the establishment of EFTA, they were for entry into the EEC in 1961–63, and then increasingly they aimed not simply at free trade but at realizing the notion of an integrated industrial system in Western Europe, in the full knowledge that this implied a political system as well. They wanted to see harmonization of laws, of fiscal systems, of investment inducements, and above all of attitudes – so that, as in America firms do not look for partners in Virginia or in Oregon, but in the United States, so in Europe industry would think and operate on a continental scale.

When the CBI was formed in 1965 (by the amalgamation of the Federation of British Industries, the British Employers' Confederation and the National Association of British Manufacturers) it made its first industrial appraisal of Britain's relations with Europe in 1966, and before that was published at the end of the year had reached three conclusions: first, that there would be 'a clear and progressive balance of advantage to British industry' from membership of an enlarged EEC; second that the Community's method of operation was acceptable given reasonable transitional arrangements; and third that entry should therefore be negotiated as soon as possible.[1] It pressed the Labour government to open negotiations, while at the same time setting out to inform its own members of the importance of the issue, the costs and the benefits.

The CBI felt at this time that their members were perhaps more

[1] For an analysis of the CBI's 1967 consultations with companies see *The Second Try*, ed. cit., pp. 168–70.

EFTA- than EEC-minded. That divergence continued when the issue came alive again after President de Gaulle's departure. According to one report 90% of industrialists in Birmingham were still against entry in summer 1969. There was therefore a major educational campaign to be deployed among the CBI's rank and file. In December 1969 the CBI Council approved two reports published in January 1970: 'Britain in Europe – A Second Industrial Appraisal' and 'Britain in the World – Overseas Trade, Aid and Investment'. Both these reports re-emphasized that the growing interdependence of nations made it an illusion to suppose that national interests could be pursued in isolation, that tariff and other barriers to trade had to be eliminated, and that the enlargement of the EEC was the best policy – subject to two considerations: the Community should eliminate any restrictive arrangements, and there must be adequate transitional periods so as to keep the initial economic strains of adaptation within acceptable limits.

The leadership's personal commitment may be gauged from a briefing on 23 March 1971 in which the Director-General, W. Campbell Adamson, spoke of his

unwavering dedication to the European ideal, and I have found that it is a faith which is widely shared by industrialists up and down the country. . . . What is to be won – or lost – is the opportunity to share in this great enterprise of creating an expanding industrial community. . . . It may only be in the 'eighties that we shall feel the effects of exclusion. . . .

But the dedication was also of a political kind:

In due course some form of political confederation is bound to be involved. . . . Henry VIII would turn in his grave at the thought of allowing the development of a colossus across the Channel which will develop along lines which we are entirely unable to influence. What we want to be part of does not yet exist. . . . It is the prime task of this generation to ensure that Europe's two civil wars are followed, like the Americans', by concord and unity.

John Davies, Campbell Adamson's predecessor, was now a cabinet Minister, but he had taken much the same view. The Deputy Director, John Whitehorn, was well-known for his pro-Market stand. Sir John Partridge and Sir Arthur Norman, successive Presidents, took very much the same line.

With the leadership of the CBI steering this way, it would have needed a focus of opposition somewhere else in the organization to keep it neutral or turn it the other way. But the CBI's leaders met with real opposition in the organization from only two quarters. In ship-building Sir John Hunter took what they thought of as a very personal stand against entry – and he issued a statement in 1971 reiterating his disagreement with the rest of the Council. Some other shipbuilders, however, took the line that they were in such an international market anyway that only wage costs, not the removal of tariffs, would affect their sales. The other sector of opposition or reserve was that of very small firms, who feared their markets might be swamped by large European suppliers, while they themselves were not geared up to seek new markets abroad. Yet the CBI's Smaller Firms Council voted over-whelmingly in favour of entry, though still concerned over the farm system and the loss of Commonwealth preference. (To help such enter-prises prepare for entry, in early 1972 the CBI published a special hand-book on *Small Firms and the Common Market*.)

In early 1970 the CBI set out on two parallel domestic operations. On the one side it set out discreetly to swing its membership and educate it into endorsing its own, as it felt, rather more far-sighted views of the problems. It held half a dozen big regional conferences and meetings up and down the country in which it set out to be seen to be in favour and stress the benefits far more than the government's February 1970 White Paper had done. At no stage was there a poll of members but, with the exception perhaps of Yorkshire, the Council obtained a broad measure of support. On the other side it sought to answer industry's questions, deal with detailed problems like company law and regional incentives, and reassure employers against the prospects of the un-known. The elaborate process of consultation in 1970 and 1971 meant that the favourable attitudes were drawn out and emphasized while the opposition on the whole became converted or muted.

The CBI's Regional Councils reported in early autumn 1971 on their reactions. London and the South-East were clearly in favour, being nearest to Europe; most other regions were favourable, with perhaps the West Midlands (given their important historic trading links) at first rather uncommitted, but then swayed towards entry on the terms negotiated. Apart from the well-known problems of inshore fishing, hill farming and horticulture, where there was some concern, Scottish mining (but not Welsh or Yorkshire mining) was worried, while the motor industry and non-ferrous metals in the West Midlands expected short-term difficulties but also hoped for long-term gains. All over the country there were major industries expecting gains, and in

Scotland textiles, engineering and chemicals envisaged gains also, as did man-made fibres in Northern Ireland.

What the Regional Councils particularly stressed was their concern over the inadequate transport and communications network both within Britain and between Britain and the Continent. Wales and the South West complained of poor air links to the Continent, the South urgently needed a good road link from the Solent to the Midlands by-passing London, London and the South East needed orbital roads around London before any radial development, and the East needed port and road improvements to handle increased traffic to the Continent.

Over and above these consultations individual member firms were invited to volunteer their views if they so wished. About a thousand did so, of which only a tiny proportion were either against or undecided on the issue; the rest were strongly in favour of entry. In spring 1972 the CBI sent a train round the country called 'Impact Europe' with TV cassette briefings, experts appearing in person, and literature packs (including the CBI's own *Europe Briefs* and *Signposts*, a specially prepared desk guide). Nonetheless there were many complaints to be heard from the CBI that industry was not yet taking the likely domestic impact (as against the new export opportunities) seriously enough. But to go into that story would lead beyond the political process into substantive economics.

Relations between the CBI and the government are of course – whichever party is in power – intimate in the extreme. In 1966 the CBI had urged the Labour government to make an application to join the EEC, and in 1970–72 it did what it could to support the Conservative government in the pursuit of this aim. Naturally industry had strong and detailed views on many of the questions raised in the negotiations: the CBI was in almost daily contact with the British delegation or its supporting personnel in the Foreign Office and the Department of Trade and Industry, particularly of course with Sir Con O'Neill and Sir William Nield. The CBI also, however, maintained its links with the Opposition, and at a dinner with some of its leaders in early 1971 did what it could to re-emphasize the importance of entry to industry.

At the same time, the CBI developed its links with the Continent. In London it kept in touch with the embassies of Common Market countries and the EEC's permanent representation, and welcomed EEC and member-state personnel on visits to Britain. It opened a Brussels office with a young economist, Marianne Neville-Rolfe, in charge to make as many useful contacts as possible among the Community's civil servants and national representatives and among its fellow interest groups. It became active in UNICE, the Industrial Federations' Union of the European Community, and cultivated friendships in the industrial organizations of the six member states in their own countries. It used its contacts, prevailing, for example, on its German counterparts to make clear to the German government the heavy resource cost to Britain of the terms envisaged in the earlier stages of the negotiations (and producing a paper on these problems at the Germans' request); building on Anglophile sentiments in Italy and keeping in touch particularly with the 'Young Turk' element in the Italian Industrialists' Federation; seeking to dispel Dutch worries over the future of the Common Agricultural Policy, and the possible disruption and new competition arising out of enlargement. Only its Belgian colleagues seemed at times a little less open to the wider viewpoint the CBI tried to present.

The CBI sought to be, on the subjects that concerned it, at least as well-informed as the Foreign Office, and claimed that its views were given at least as much weight as those of British negotiators in Brussels. With the feed-back the CBI had from these contacts it could go back to the government and offer its advice, query negotiating objectives and consult on tactics. The Europe Steering Committee, presided over by Derek Ezra of the National Coal Board, co-ordinated all this activity; it helped the CBI play a vital role in research and in persuasion, at home in Britain and abroad in Europe.

In January 1963 the annual meeting of the National Farmers' Union had unanimously rejected the EEC terms on agriculture, and appeared to the broad public almost to be hostile to entry as such. In 1966 it had laid all the stress on 'grave consequences for large sectors of British agriculture'.[1] In 1970–71 on the other hand, as the Union itself emphasized, it 'wisely refrained from taking up a pro- or anti-position on the general principle of Common Market membership'. As the President put it:

We have had the benefit of our close and continuing links with COPA – the farmers' organization of the Six – with the farmers' unions in Eire, Norway and

---

[1] For the conclusion of its November 1966 study see *The Second Try*, ed. cit., pp. 165–8.

Denmark and of course with the International Federation of Agricultural Producers, the world farm organization.

Because of these links and the fact that we have been in direct and continuous contact with the Government's negotiators in Brussels we have been able to press our case without having to resort to any special public or press campaigns. We were already at the table. . . . The fact that we are neither in the anti-Market nor pro-Market lobby has, I believe, been of immense advantage in our negotiations with Government, since neither our opposition nor our support can be taken for granted.[1]

Like the CBI, it kept in the closest touch with the government throughout the negotiations – its President, Henry Plumb, with the Minister of Agriculture, Jim Prior, and its Deputy Secretary-General, Asher Weingarten, with Freddy Kearns on the Brussels team and other Ministry officials. So it was also able simultaneously to keep its membership up-to-date on the development of the negotiations and of course to instruct them in the complicated functioning of the Common Agricultural Policy.

Just after the government published its White Paper, the NFU published its own assessment to help members 'reach objective conclusions on the agricultural issues at stake'. The analysis was discussed by members of the Union throughout the country during the summer, and in September the Council reviewed the resolutions sent in from the county branches, which in effect endorsed its own initial judgment. The Council concluded that it had to consider what would happen to British agriculture if Britain stayed out no less than if she went in – and the monetary and trade pressures arising from the Nixon measures in August 1971 were regarded as a relevant omen. The prosperity of agriculture depended not least on the state of the national economy in general. It shared some of its branches' concern over maintaining the stability that the British Agriculture Acts had given the industry, over the future effectiveness of marketing boards, and rather specific questions such as the impact of Continental apple and pear surpluses, the transitional measures for eggs and poultry-meat, and the need to adapt to EEC arrangements for plant and animal health (which were to feature prominently in the implementing legislation in 1972). The Council stressed the need for increased farm investment, for expanded processing capacity, and for what it elegantly called 'the withdrawal of constraints on the development of more positive production and marketing policies'. But having put its various detailed concerns to the

[1] NFU, *British Agriculture and the Common Market*, July 1971, pp. 29 and 3.

government, it came out with a highly positive final overall judgment on the future of farmers' incomes and a clarion call to the industry:

Given the right policies and, above all, confidence, there is little doubt that by the end of the transitional period producers could achieve the Government's forecast of an additional eight per cent in output over and above the expansion that would otherwise have been expected. The total extra production would, it is estimated, result in an extra net saving of imports worth £350–£400 million per annum. . . . There is no doubt that among producers generally, the response to the terms as negotiated by the Government is a positive one. British agriculture for its part is confident of its ability to respond to the challenge presented by membership of an enlarged Community.[1]

The Trade Unions

Things were rather different in the case of the CBI's and NFU's opposite number, the Trades Union Congress. For this there were a number of reasons. For a start the TUC itself thought of many of the intricate problems of the negotiations as outside the immediate interests of its members – as being concerned more with profits and entrepreneurial operations than with wages and working conditions. Secondly, while the CBI had a strong central leadership which was given plenty of scope by its rank and file (who were more concerned with running their own businesses than with affecting public policy), the TUC was a loose confederation of powerful trade union leaders, each of them very much masters in their own house and keenly interested in political action. It was thus difficult for it to act with great cohesion unless the traditional solidarity of the movement could be invoked. So the TUC lacked decisiveness on the issue. Its Council was divided, its General Secretary did not take any strong line, and leaders of the individual unions in the movement differed in their attitudes – from those who were for, via those who were sharply against but were determined to make a go of it if Britain did enter, to those who just felt sullenly or violently hostile to the whole thought of the EEC. The opponents in particular were in something of a tactical dilemma: it was difficult at the same time to be publicly hostile to the enterprise, and also to have an effect on the precise way in which the enterprise was carried out through intimate consultation and contact with those in charge of it. Moreover, the TUC simply did not have (and given its character probably could not have) the sophisticated apparatus of wide-ranging contacts, economic experts and efficient working parties of the CBI: in a highly complex situation

[1] *NFU and the Common Market*, Press Release of 23 September 1971.

with ramifications in ten capitals it could thus hardly be expected to play a really comparable role.

Undoubtedly, however, there were also one or two accidental factors or factors of neglect. The defeat of the Labour Party at the 1970 election resulted in a distinct loss of intimacy with the government. Relations with the new Conservative administration in any case quickly deteriorated as the Industrial Relations Bill was introduced; this made co-operation on other issues seem less attractive, and opposition to the government on any issue that might bring it down a more tempting prospect. In addition, even the Labour government had rather neg-lected to cultivate the TUC on Common Market matters. Of course there were extensive consultations. Nonetheless one way or another there can be no doubt that the unions felt much less involved from the start, and we shall see that in the course of 1969–71 the balance of their influence shifted from tepid support to preponderant opposition.

To look at the membership of the TUC General Council for 1970–71 was not initially to look at a body that was overwhelmingly against entry. Both Vic Feather, the General Secretary, and Lionel Murray, the Assistant General Secretary, were known to be favourable to entry – though the deteriorating relationship between the government and the TUC over the Industrial Relations Bill was making it rather diffi-cult for them to back the government on anything else and must have made them hope that the Conservatives would not last too long in office. The 1970/71 Chairman of the General Council, Lord Cooper of the General and Municipal Workers, its Vice-Chairman, Sir Sidney Greene of the Railwaymen, and Les Cannon of the Electricians were thought to be firm Marketeers.

On the other hand there had been two major changes in union leader-ship since the TUC had approved the government's application. Since Frank Cousins had already turned against EEC membership, his replacement by Jack Jones as General Secretary of the Transport and General Workers' Union altered nothing as far as this issue was con-cerned; but the replacement of Lord Carron as President of the Engineers by Hugh Scanlon was to prove highly relevant. These two unions between them controlled nearly a third of the votes at the Labour party conference, and while the party is far from being Mary's little lamb, it could be difficult for it not to go wherever these two unions went.

The first indication of the way the unions were going came only a week after the Labour government lost office. On 25 June 1970 the

Confederation of Shipbuilding and Engineering Unions, meeting on
the Isle of Man, had voted on a resolution tabled by Clive Jenkins:

This confederation annual meeting is firmly opposed to British membership of
the European Economic Community, believing that the Treaty of Rome will
impose injurious social, economic and political effects. We believe this would
remove control and planning of Britain's economy from our elected Government, react against the trade union movement, strengthen the great international
companies and, by committing Britain to a political power block, would perpetuate the division of Europe and increase world tension.

Though leaders of the Engineers, the Electricians and Plumbers, and the
Clerical Workers opposed the resolution, it was passed unexpectedly on
a show of hands by something like a 3:1 majority.

This reversal proved a harbinger of a battle the TUC General Council
had to fight at the TUC conference in Brighton in September 1970.
Introducing the Council's statement on the subject, Vic Feather
declared that its point was to ensure that Britain's negotiators in
Brussels knew the unions' interests and objectives, and thereby to
influence the course of the negotiations; but only when those negotiations were complete could a balance-sheet be drawn up to assess all the
benefits and costs of joining or of not joining.

The Council's position was opposed from two quarters, one 'pro',
one 'anti' in inspiration, though the first was not overtly favourable in
its text, calling merely for more study and information, while the
second closely followed the Isle of Man resolution, concluding with a
call for immediate union action: 'Congress instructs the incoming
General Council to utilize the full resources of the TUC to inform
affiliates of the effect of Common Market membership and vigorously
to oppose Britain's entry.'

The debate was fairly passionate. Moving the 'neutral' motion, Roy
Grantham, the Secretary of the Clerical and Administrative Workers
(and a vice-president of the Labour Committee for Europe) took a
radical line:

The needs of our children and our grandchildren call for new social and
political authorities, not the outworn system of the nation state which we have
inherited . . . the real price of our not joining the Six is to become the poor man
of Europe. Our opponents are opting to stick to narrow nationalist policies
under a Conservative Government in the name of socialism. . . .

On the other side Dan McGarvey of the Boilermakers declared: 'If we go into Europe we will be signing the death warrant of generations to come, and possibly this generation', while, seconding, Clive Jenkins used typically acid humour: the General Council's statement had the qualities of 'an elderly virgin – uncertain, politely spoken and avoiding any specific proposition' (laughter), and he called the common farm policy 'the most catastrophic failure in agriculture since the Pharaohs'. ('They have created a mountain of rotting foodstuffs equivalent to the combined weight of the entire population of Austria.')

The dissidents – on either side – were not at this stage able to push the TUC off the fence. The General Council's report was approved by 6,073,000 votes to 1,361,000; the overtly 'neutral' but covertly pro-Market motion calling for study of the issues before any decision was taken was rejected by 8,042,000 votes to 700,000; and the motion against entry was rejected by 5,746,000 to 3,215,000 votes. What had thus become clear was that the unions who inclined in favour of the Market – the Clerical Workers, the Civil and Public Services Association, the Inland Revenue Staff Federation and the Transport Salaried Staffs Association – were far outnumbered by the declared 'antis' – the Boilermakers, Scientific Workers, Agricultural Workers, Sheet Metal Workers, Television Technicians, Metal Mechanics and Loco Men. The second biggest union of them all, the Engineers, had a policy-making national committee that rather favoured entry, but did not at this stage want to commit itself. It will be clearest if we run through the attitudes of the major unions in the 1970–72 period in turn in order of size. (The voting figures given in parentheses are those for the Labour party conference of 1971.)

Jack Jones' Transport and General Workers Union (1,000,000 votes) was firmly hostile from an early date. At the turn of 1970–71 its General Executive Council condemned 'great hardships for ordinary families, great increases in prices, and a substantial loss of jobs. No small handful of politicians has the right to inflict such changes on the people' and called for a national referendum before any final decision was made. In June 1971, opening Bevin House in Hull, Jack Jones declared: 'The only people who stand to gain are a tiny number of financial interests, the big money boys who have no loyalty to their country.' On 14 July at the union's biennial delegate conference of 860 delegates in Scarborough only 4 voted against a resolution opposing entry and the terms, which would 'seriously increase prices, increase unemployment, and . . . destroy British economic, political and constitutional independence'.

The tachograph, or 'spy in the cab' (to record hours and speeds and distance driven by lorry drivers) was, under Community legislation, to be compulsory from 1975 for new and from 1978 for all vehicles, and that was one of the specific issues that most exercised the union. It proceeded to launch a campaign of its own to persuade working people generally to oppose entry, with wide distribution of a four-page pamphlet showing a housewife about to be decapitated on Edward Heath's guillotine, and a cartoon of one worker saying to another: 'I can see us ending up being owned by an American firm with a German foreman working for British wages.' So strongly did some of the leading members of the union feel, indeed, that Alex Kitson was to provide a good text in reserve for the pro-Marketeers when, though a member of the National Executive of the Labour Party, he declared on 4 June 1971 on Scottish television: 'I am so dedicated on this issue that I am being honest about it, if it was an issue of for the Market or against the Market, I would vote Tory.'

The second biggest union, the Amalgamated Union of Engineering Workers, consisted in fact of four sections with separate voting strengths: the Engineering Section (881,558 votes) and three smaller component unions, the Foundryworkers (41,720), the Draughtsmen and Allied Technicians (36,967) and the Constructional Engineers (26,100). The old AEU had in 1967 instructed its Executive Council to support Britain's application for membership by a vote of 31:20 in its National Committee. That was in Sir William Carron's day. In 1968 Hugh Scanlon took over as president. As Anthony Sampson puts it:

The most important post is not the secretaryship (held by Jim Conway, a right-wing Labour unionist, dedicated to industrial efficiency) but the presidency; and here the change had been dramatic. For eleven years the president was William Carron, who rose to be Lord Carron – a Catholic turner from Hull who was doggedly loyal to the Labour leaders (first Gaitskell, then Wilson) and with difficulty maintained his position as the right-wing head of a left-wing union. Then in 1967, the outward colour changed overnight, when Carron was succeeded by Hugh Scanlon, who was a member of the Communist Party until 1955, and still has quite friendly relations with the Communists. . . . He was elected to the executive in 1963, impatient under Carron's respectable rule, waiting for his chance. In the mid-sixties the union was turning more militant; Scanlon's rival on the left was Reg Birch . . . who became increasingly Maoist and was rejected by the orthodox Communists; so that Scanlon had his chance, and got the presidency.[1]

[1] Sampson, op. cit., pp. 633–4.

So the balance on the EEC issue also began to shift, though not all that quickly. In 1970 a resolution opposing entry as adverse to the interests of the working people of the country had 26 votes cast in its favour and 26 against; the 1967 resolution supporting entry was then reaffirmed by 27 votes to 23. Jim Conway was writing in favour of entry in the union's Journal in late 1970 (Roy Jenkins contributed a pro-Market article in July 1971), and the union's Research Department put out a discussion paper in June 1971 that was on balance quite favourable. But then in mid-June the four sections together had a day-long delegate conference. By 31 votes to 38 they refused to defer their decision until the terms had been agreed, and then, after Hugh Scanlon had asked for a substantive vote and amid accusations that the anti-Market motion was 'Communist-inspired', they voted 50:19 to oppose entry. One may well argue that the combination of Hugh Scanlon's election in 1968 and the Labour government's loss of office in 1970 made it almost inevitable for both the TUC and the party conference to swing against entry. Certainly, from that vote in mid-June 1971 on, there could be no reasonable doubt left. Jim Conway, on the other hand, was already looking ahead by November 1971, making plans for the aftermath of entry (if entry should occur), and putting out a research paper on trade unions in the Six and their relations with the Community institutions.

Unlike the two biggest unions, the third largest, the General and Municipal Workers (650,000 votes), remained under a rather more conservative leadership. It included a large proportion of the lowest-paid workers, and half its members worked in publicly owned industries. Their votes went against a motion at their Great Yarmouth congress in late May opposing entry and against a motion calling for a referendum. They were the biggest of the pro-Market unions, and without them the Marketeers' showing at the Labour party conference would have been sorry indeed.

Of the main unions outside the Labour Party, the National Union of Teachers had no public discussion of the Common Market at all in 1970–72. On the other hand the National and Local Government Officers' Association had an interesting experience. They were not affiliated to the Labour Party, but like the Teachers they were members of the TUC. In June their conference (representing 400,000 members) overwhelmingly passed a motion 'That this Conference is opposed to the entry of Britain into the European Economic Community unless it can be shown to be in the long-term interests of both Britain and the Community.' On 7 August the National Executive Council resolved by

29 votes to 26 that, though the White Paper published in the meantime did not firmly show it, 'in the light of the public debate which has taken place over the last few months, this committee is in favour of Britain's accession to the European Economic Community', and directed its TUC delegates to vote in favour of entry. The Leeds branch thereupon took the National Executive Council to court and won: Mr Justice Goulding decided that the rules of its Association provided that general policy should be directed by Conference, and that the Council had no power to do anything inconsistent with that general policy. The costs of £1,109 were paid from NALGO funds, and the NALGO delegates voted against entry at the TUC conference.

Neither the Teachers nor NALGO being affiliated to the Labour Party, the fourth largest union there was the Electricians (350,000 votes). In 1967 at its biennial delegate conference at Margate the ETU had carried an Executive Council motion welcoming the government's application to join and taking the view that 'Entry into Europe could be valuable to the nation's economic and social progress, leading as it would to wider industrial and commercial markets for UK products, and also securing a greater degree of influence in the political policies of Europe'. In 1970 – quite apart from the wider context of national opinion – the union suffered the loss of its pro-Market General Secretary Les Cannon. Frank Chapple, the President, who now succeeded Cannon, was certainly an internationalist sympathetic to entry; but he was at this stage much less able to exert influence than his predecessor. There was a substantial change in the attitude of the union's Executive (which paralleled that in the rest of the Labour Movement) as the likely terms emerged. At the end of August 1971 the union balloted all its members and received the largest return ever recorded in its postal ballots: 35,002 members voted in favour of entry, 68,797 voted against, and at the end of October the biennial delegate conference in Blackpool approved the decision to ballot and concurred with the overwhelming opposition to entry shown by members' votes. Its 350,000 votes at Brighton accordingly went against entry.

The National Union of Mineworkers (287,063 votes), meeting in Aberdeen in early July, came out for a withdrawal of Britain's application after only a thirteen-minute debate. Coming when it did, their decision made a majority against entry both at the TUC and at the Labour party conference a virtual certainty. The widespread distribution of a pamphlet on coal mines and the EEC at the pitheads made the

Marketeers feel the case had at least been put, though that was scant comfort.

They had in fact never had any hopes of the miners. On the other hand the attitude of the Union of Shop, Distributive and Allied Workers (284,193 votes) was a disappointment to them: the Trade Union Committee for Europe had at one point counted both on them and on the Railwaymen to support entry. In USDAW's case its annual delegate meeting in Eastbourne in April 1971 did not go into the merits or demerits of entry, but, after the briefest of debates (three speakers, none of them in favour of entry) carried a proposition supporting Vic Feather's call for a national referendum on the issue. On the substance the conference had left it to the Executive to take a decision, and at the last moment the Executive by a very narrow margin came out against entry on the terms proposed. That Walter Padley had ceased to be President was no doubt an important element in the union's change of stance. His influence had been decisive on a number of international questions while he was in office, and the Common Market issue was one on which the union's line shifted when he went.

The Executive Council of the Union of Post Office Workers (186,699 votes) decided on 14 July 1971 that the price of entry was too high, and told its delegates to the special Labour party conference to act accordingly. Tom Jackson, the General Secretary, spoke against entry at that conference, and Norman Stagg, the Deputy General Secretary, did the same at the TUC conference.

The pro-Marketeers had rather counted on Sir Sidney Greene, General Secretary of the National Union of Railwaymen, to deliver the votes of his 159,382 affiliated members on the Market side. At the 1970 annual conference of the NUR, a resolution opposing entry had been lost. At the 1971 conference another such resolution was lost, but an amendment was carried which asked that 'when negotiations are complete, the advantages for entry should be placed before the electorate so that a democratic decision may be taken by them on acceptance or rejection of such conditions before entry'. The effect was that the NUR delegates at the Labour party conference felt able on balance to vote with the Party Executive, which also called for an election.

The National Union of Public Employees (150,000 votes), on the other hand, which had refused to take up any stand since it had, in 1963, decided to await the terms, refused to budge from that position in spring 1971 at its Bournemouth national conference. Then, after a fact-finding visit to Brussels (after which they reported having received 'a

regular deluge of pro-Common Market publications from Brussels'),
they decided in August that membership on the terms negotiated by the
Conservative government would threaten NUPE members' living
standards and called not for a referendum but for a general election.

The Woodworkers (133,000 votes) were another case of the leadership rather in favour, but the annual delegate conference overriding
them. In their case this had already happened in 1970. After a debate
consisting of only four speeches (none in favour of entry) the General
Secretary, G. F. Smith, attempted to have a motion opposing entry
remitted on the grounds that 'We should not put ourselves in the foolish
position of being committed at a time when we still have a lot to discuss
and decide'. But the resolution was carried in spite of his efforts (which
had included the printing of pro-Market matter in the union's magazine
Viewpoint). That decision was binding on the Executive under the rules
of the union.

Clive Jenkins' fast-growing white-collar workers' union, the
Association of Scientific, Technical and Managerial Staffs (120,000
votes) had already taken a firm stand opposing entry at its annual
delegate conference in May 1970, when Russell Kerr for the Executive
Committee accepted a motion which also asked for a national referendum before proceeding further. The union took a notable initiative,
however, in having its Executive Council meet in March 1971 at
Wissant in the Pas de Calais to hear the views of the French trade union
movement on the Common Market. Though they agreed they must
establish closer liaison across the Channel – for example to step up the
campaign to save Concorde – the Executive at the end of the meeting
adhered even more firmly to the view that they should oppose entry to
prevent the British trade union movement being devalued.[1]

The British Iron, Steel, and Kindred Trades Association (91,642
votes) had a meeting of its Executive Council on 16 July – the day
before the special Labour party conference – at which it resolved to
nominate Jim Callaghan as Party Treasurer, support the Party Executive next day on not taking a vote at the special conference, and 'to
vote in favour of entry into the Common Market in the event of such a
decision being necessary'.

The National Union of Agricultural Workers (85,000 votes), though
supporting the NEC at the Central Hall in July in opposing a vote, had
already been mandated by its biennial conference of 1970 to vote
against entry and did so at Brighton in October. Their President, Bert

[1] *ASTMS Journal*, Issue One/Two, 1971.

Hazell, told members that reasonable wages for farm workers would be much more difficult to secure when British farmers could no longer go to the British government to demand price revisions to meet rising costs. The *Land Worker*, however, also printed reports from the national press that 'If there is one British industry which will lick the Common Market into a cocked hat, it is agriculture'. At the 1972 biennial conference they decided to study wages and conditions in the EEC and to make contacts with farm workers' unions of the Six, though one delegate opposing that motion said they wished to have nothing to do with the Six 'because it is a disgusting capitalist-oriented society'.

The Executive of Roy Grantham's Clerical and Administrative Workers (80,530 votes) decided on 11 July 1971 to support entry on the grounds that the terms would have been acceptable to the Labour government. Unions even smaller we need hardly examine in detail.

When the Trade Union Congress met in September 1971, it had before it a detailed twenty-page statement by the General Council on *Britain and the EEC*. The report was hostile to the terms, but not to the principle of entry. The General Secretary, Vic Feather, who had previously made no secret of his mildly pro-entry views, delivered a strong attack on the government, which had failed in the power struggle against France.

The French are on to a good thing, and they know it. No wonder President Pompidou smiles. No wonder he begins to look every day more and more like the Mona Lisa. . . . The British people would have to think twice about signing any treaty – whether the Treaty of Rome or the Treaty of Timbuktoo – if the terms were as bad as these.

The TUC Conference had three motions put to it. One urged a common front with free trade unions in the EEC member states; it was remitted to the General Council for consideration. One, moved by Roy Grantham, accepted the outcome of the negotiations initiated by the Labour government; it was lost by an overwhelming shout without being put to a card vote. And one was moved by Jack Jones:

This Congress opposes the present proposal for Britain to join the Common Market on the terms now known, and believes that a General Election should be held before any decision on entry is taken by Parliament.

Congress therefore calls upon the General Council to launch a public campaign in support of this policy.

The result of the debate was of course a foregone conclusion, as almost all the major unions had reached their positions in the summer before. It was a powerful signal to the Labour Party's own annual conference to be held a few weeks later that Jack Jones' motion was carried overwhelmingly by acclamation.

Members exercising their integrity could destroy the credibility of the whole party

Mrs Judith Hart

The Relevance of the Labour Party

Harold Wilson is almost certainly one of those few men but for whom Britain could not have entered the Community. He rendered a double service. Strategically, it was he who committed the Labour Party to the principle of entry against strong reservations on the part of some of his colleagues. By so doing he ensured that the question of enlargement did not vanish from the Community's agenda in the 'sixties; and he made the task of whatever government might be in power in the early 'seventies a very much less daunting one at home as well as abroad. Had the Labour Party been opposed in principle to entry in 1970, and had it done nothing to prepare at home, in the Commonwealth and on the Continent for the process of accession, then at the very least the timing – and perhaps even the success – of a Conservative application made in the summer of 1970 might have turned out very differently.

Moreover, with the full weight of his political commitment of 1967 in favour of entry, and with his refusal to change his tune fundamentally until a year after the election, Harold Wilson headed off any really massive organized political opposition to entry until after it was too late for that opposition to become effective. (Some people might also wish to add that tactically he rendered a further, if minor, service to the cause by then expressing his opposition to the terms in summer 1971: his change of stance appears to have been a very useful factor in making the bulk of the Conservative Party fall into line behind their leader.) Had Harold Wilson as Prime Minister maintained consistency with his 1962 position, there is little doubt he might well have been able to veto the enlargement of the Community. As it was, his actions particularly in 1966–67 were a major help to the European cause. That is something that Labour Marketeers should not lightly forget under the immediate impression of the events of 1971–72.

Tactically just as relevant as Harold Wilson himself, though of lesser strategic importance, were those Labour MPs who voted in favour of entry or abstained on 28 October 1971 (and also the much smaller number of them who abstained in 1972). No one will ever know whether the forty-one Conservative MPs who refused to vote with the government on 28 October would have stood firm if they had not felt confident that their places would be taken by Labour rebels. If we assume their firmness, however, then indeed only the Labour rebels allowed Edward Heath to take Britain into the EEC. Certainly in one sense the government can claim that on 28 October it provided its own majority: 282 Conservatives voted for entry, while the total vote against was only 244. But the vote against was so low precisely because 89 Labour MPs refused to obey their party whip; had they done so, the motion would have been thrown out. At least on the assumption of unshaken opposition to entry by less than half the Tory rebels, the Labour Marketeers thus proved decisive on the issue.

But whether we make that assumption or not, we cannot leave the Opposition out of the story. Quite apart from the Labour government's role and then the votes in the House of Commons, there were three other influences feeding back into the political process of entry. Firstly, the stand taken by the leaders of the unions and the party can hardly have remained without effect on the electorate at large – however much they were themselves influenced by their view of the attitudes of the electorate. Secondly, there was a possible feed-back into the diplomatic process. As one French negotiator put it: 'Ideally – but this would have been without precedent in diplomacy – we should have liked Harold Wilson's signature as well.' Had the alternative government come out with a clear pledge to denounce the treaty on coming into office, then not even a rock-solid Conservative Parliamentary Party might have prevented certain complications arising in Brussels and Paris at some stages during 1971. Thirdly, Labour's stance clearly matters a great deal for the future evolution of the Community and in particular for the way Social Democratic parties can exert concerted influence within it. But that is a matter, not for contemporary history, but for the future.

In one sense it is a paradox that the party of national pride, the party of tradition and the *status quo*, should have been the party both to make the first attempt to join the Common Market in 1961, and then, a decade later, to achieve that goal. To that extent perhaps it might seem an equal paradox that the majority of the Labour Party should have tended towards opposition to such radical change in both the early 'sixties and the early 'seventies.

Yet Labour had never really been all that internationalist a party, or all that much a party of radical change. 'More Methodist than Marxist', it has in practice again and again had to take account of its founders, the trade unions, and of the union leaders' interpretation of the workers' interests as much as of any theoretical dogmas. Even had it been a radical and internationalist party, the question would still have remained: internationalist with or towards whom, and favourable towards what sort of change? So if it was a Labour government that made the first formal application to join the Community in 1967, a Labour Prime Minister who claimed to be entering it 'at one hell of a pace', perhaps that was in some ways really the more surprising and less characteristic phenomenon.

However that may be, we are still left with explaining an apparent double somersault. When Labour was in opposition in 1961–63, it was on balance hostile to entry. When Labour was in power, it made Britain's first and only unconditional application for entry in 1967 – and did so without any kind of mandate from the electorate even to negotiate. When Labour was back in opposition, by October 1971 it was predominantly hostile to entry on 'Tory terms', or even, it some-times seemed, on any terms at all; and by mid-1972 it looked as if the party might even decide on withdrawal. But then such large generaliza-tions hide internal differences which – as in almost any party of the Left – tend to be not only more interesting but also more obtrusive than the unifying factors. We have to differentiate not only the different levels and segments of the party – the Leader from the Deputy Leader, the shadow cabinet from the National Executive, the unions and the constituency Labour parties met in Conference – but also the ideo-logical strands, the different interest situations, and the clusters of party friends and clients – the *galères* who have been through quite different battles in the past together, and who continue to influence each other through personal affinities. On the face of it, one can argue that the terms made the difference. But the key explanation undoubtedly must be found in the steady and profound distrust of the grass roots of the party towards the EEC, in the switch of the parliamentary leadership from Opposition into government and back again, and in the internal strains within the Labour Movement, including those between the leaders of some of the largest and most active unions on the one side and the parliamentary leadership on the other.

Leaders on Switchbacks

Hugh Gaitskell had started not without some sympathy for the Common Market, but in the last months of his life had swung very decisively against it. At the Brighton party conference in October 1962 it was hardly the terms but the principle itself that Hugh Gaitskell denounced when he spoke of turning our backs on 'a thousand years of British history' and reducing Britain to the status of 'Texas or California'.[1] But greater even than his concern with sovereignty were his fears of a fragmentation of the world between East and West, North and South, and that Britain could get side-tracked from these larger issues by joining an inward-looking Continental bloc at the expense of a worldwide multi-racial Commonwealth association.

It is a macabre and dangerous exercise to try to summon the dead as witnesses in a cause other than that in which they testified: but if anyone had the right to do so, Lady Gaitskell felt that in 1971 he would, on the same criteria, but in the changed circumstances, not have opposed entry, and for herself and in that spirit decided to vote in favour:

A substantial measure of the five conditions spelt out by the Leader of the Labour Party in 1962 have either been achieved or been brought about by changes in the world. . . . I do not often indulge in thinking about what might have been had my husband lived, but I venture to say that I cannot believe that he would not have grasped the hand extended by Willy Brandt at this time.[2]

Harold Wilson had started – well before Hugh Gaitskell came round to that stance – with a highly negative attitude to entry. In June 1962 he denounced the Community as incompatible with the substance of purposive public ownership, with location inducements for industry, and with purposive investment policies; he categorized it as 'anti-planning' in its whole conception. He emphasized 'our opposition to the development of EEC on political lines' and expressed a grave fear of 'the domination of Western Europe by a Paris-Bonn axis, dedicated to an intransigent line in East-West affairs, right-wing, possibly semi-neutralist and, before long, nuclear powered'.[3]

But only four years later, after less than two years at the helm himself, he changed course by 180 degrees, and made the application which, with the 1972 Treaty of Accession, proved successful.

[1] See *The European Common Market and Communities*, ed. cit., pp. 176–80.
[2] Hansard (Lords), 28 July 1971, col. 473.
[3] Hansard, 7 June 1962 (reprinted in *The Second Try*, ed. cit., pp. 83–99).

To explore motives – one's own, after all, no less than those of others – is always a task fraught with difficulty. Harold Wilson's almost unchronicled conversion to EEC entry in 1966, and his much more thoroughly documented – not to say over-publicized – progressive change of tack to the line of 'No entry on Tory terms' during 1971, are cases in point. But whatever relative weights one assigns to them, one can see several possible strands in Harold Wilson's thinking in 1965. It is worth looking at four theories in turn – if only to dismiss one or two of them as subordinate. The first theory sees 1966 purely in terms of personnel policy. The theory is put most baldly by Harold Wilson's friend and close confidant of the time, George Wigg. He first dismisses yet another theory (which indeed is hardly worth discussing):

Wilson told me that his conversion resulted from an article in the *Economist* on October 22nd. I, too, had read the article. I have re-read it often since. I still doubt its influence on Wilson's 'conversion'. Wilson's swing from being a strong antagonist of the Common Market to becoming a protagonist ready to run risks to secure Britain's entry took its place among other historic phenomena exemplified by Paul's conversion on the road to Damascus. The one difference was that, judged by his subsequent actions, Paul's conversion was sincere.

Lord Wigg goes on:

Wilson's conversion was not due to conviction. It flowed from the fact that he had to put Brown and Callaghan in baulk and hold the Cabinet together in the shadow of the July crisis. The Prime Minister had to produce a device that looked and sounded like business.[1]

The Department of Economic Affairs, headed by the Deputy Leader, George Brown, had been set up as a ministry dedicated essentially to economic growth. The July 1966 crisis and the fateful decision not to devalue entailed a decisive switch in priorities from growth to stability – from investment for future productivity to retrenchment in the interests of the balance of payments and short-run world confidence in the pound. As a result George Brown had told Harold Wilson in July 1966 that he would resign, and been only narrowly dissuaded from doing so. Once the Prices and Incomes Bill had passed its third reading, there was every advantage in his moving to a different ministry. As early as 1964 the job he really wanted had been the Foreign Office. He was not in August 1966 in a position to demand it, or to insist – as some commentators have suggested – that an attempt to enter the EEC was

[1] Lord Wigg, *George Wigg*, Michael Joseph, London, 1972, p. 339.

his price for staying in the cabinet. Both he and Harold Wilson agree that the thought of the EEC had in fact been in Wilson's mind before the problem of a reshuffle arose. Harold Wilson's account is not without kindness towards his colleague, and to the reasons for moving Brown away from the DEA he adds: 'We seemed to be drawing nearer to the point where we would have to take a decision about Europe, and George Brown seemed to me the appropriate leader for the task which might lie ahead.'[1] Although George Brown's dynamism was to prove important in the attempt to enter the EEC, that attempt was made for reasons which went far beyond 'keeping George happy'. This first theory, in other words, is not to be taken as more than a very minor ingredient in the causal chain, though once the decision had been taken George Brown's commitment and energy were no doubt a major factor in pushing the application forward with such speed and vigour.

The second theory sees the decision to apply – or at the very least the decision to probe whether an application might be successful – predominantly in terms of domestic party politics. For one thing, it would take people's minds off economic failure at home and provide a stage for showmanship abroad – one of the oldest devices of political management in the world. More specifically, some of his associates remember Harold Wilson feeling, at the turn of the year 1966–67, that a government had at its disposal such means of moulding the public mood that it need never be defeated unless it allowed a debate to arise which could give the Opposition a clear issue on which to claim equality of treatment on the media, and thus to break down the climate of consent. The Common Market might have become such an issue. There are those therefore – Labour anti-Marketeers in particular – who interpret the 1967 application as essentially an attempt to blanket the Opposition, to take the wind out of its sails, and thus effectively to remove a potentially most divisive issue from the arena of party controversy. Even to court a second veto and thereby kill the question, on this theory, was to hurt the Conservatives and Edward Heath far more than the Labour government. The fact that Harold Wilson then began to get interested, decided on his probe round Europe, convinced himself that he could really run the place, and found himself involved in the application much more seriously than as a party ploy was 'just Harold'.

The third theory – going from the more particular towards the more general, and from the later to the earlier set of events – sees the conversion of Harold Wilson above all in economic terms as the result of

[1] Wilson, op. cit., p. 272.

the impact on him of the devastating economic crisis of July 1966. As Richard Crossman put it:

By July 1966 their self-confidence had been shattered. They were subjected to a failure nearly as shocking as the Suez fiasco was for a Conservative government. Less than four months after the electorate had given him a comfortable majority, Mr Wilson found himself facing economic catastrophe, the National Plan in tatters and the Treasury coffers nearly empty.[1]

Yet even before the electorate had given him that majority, and before the whole foundation of growth on which Labour's election programme rested had collapsed, Harold Wilson's attitude had begun to change. His Bristol speech was widely regarded at the time as being unresponsive on the EEC because it accused Edward Heath of rolling on his back like a spaniel at one encouraging gesture from the French government – 'some of my best friends are spaniels, but I would not put them in charge of negotiations into the Common Market'. But the speech was in fact much more anti-Conservative than anti-EEC:

We are ready to join if suitable safeguards for Britain's interests, and our Commonwealth interests, can be negotiated . . . we shall continue and intensify these probings. . . . Given a fair wind, we will negotiate our way into the Common Market, head held high, not crawl in. And we shall go in if the conditions are right.[2]

That pledge was expressly reiterated in the Queen's speech on 21 April 1966, immediately after the election victory. It was thus not a mere campaign gimmick. The dating is important since at that stage, though clearly the economy had not yet turned the hoped-for corner, disaster had not yet struck either, and it suggests a more general reflection – and one not perforce exclusively economic in kind.

So we come to the fourth and most general theory. Michael Stewart had been an opponent of entry in 1961–63: but his experience at the Foreign Office had, before he left it in August 1966, turned him into a convinced and since then unwavering Marketeer. Slowly, if painfully, Harold Wilson was also coming to see the difficulties involved in Britain continuing to play a role as world policeman. Indeed on the

---

[1] Richard Crossman, 'Britain and Europe – A Personal History', *The Round Table*, October 1971, p. 591.

[2] 18 March 1966. The relevant parts of the speech are reprinted in *The Second Try*, ed. cit., pp. 108–12.

very evening of the first Chequers weekend on Europe, in October 1966, seven or eight of the Ministers principally concerned met in the Long Gallery after dinner and reached general agreement – not to be announced until the year after – on an approximate terminal date for Britain's deployment east of Suez. Wilson was moreover profoundly unhappy at the way he was treated by his Commonwealth colleagues in 1965 and 1966 over the issue of Rhodesia, and one has only to read his own account of the September 1966 conference and of his 'cold but controlled fury' to recall just how close to 'the dissolution of the Commonwealth' things had come.[1]

Again, while at the very beginning of his premiership he had had high hopes of his relations with the United States, that 'special relationship' did not really prosper. He is quite clear on the cruder interpretations of some of the difficulties: 'At no time was any link suggested, or even hinted at, between financial help and our policy on Vietnam.'[2] In that sense things were different from the time of Suez, when the mere threat of financial and oil sanctions brought Anthony Eden to heel. But more than one of Wilson's close colleagues did seem to get the impression that understandings had been reached, at least within the financial domain, which did constrict his and the Chancellor's freedom of action on subjects such as devaluation or incomes policy, and that a change in the whole context of some of these problems might be welcome for the enlargement it would afford to his freedom of manoeuvre.

Be that as it may, at the Chequers meeting on Saturday 22 October 1966 to discuss European policy, George Brown and Michael Stewart presented a paper that argued the case for entry into the EEC almost entirely in political terms – as an issue of Britain's whole place in the world. George Brown believed that there was now an open door into the EEC, and moreover that no one would take Britain seriously unless she actually applied. In a judicious if tentative way they had Jim Callaghan's support. There was opposition, however, from Barbara Castle, Richard Marsh, Douglas Jay and Fred Peart. Richard Crossman and Anthony Wedgwood Benn expressed reservations, but they did not resist a tentative approach to the EEC. Some felt that there was really not much alternative, some that an approach was worth making if only to demonstrate that it was doomed to failure. Denis Healey in particular felt sure that de Gaulle would stop the undertaking anyhow, and was later more vigorously to oppose courting such a rebuff.

[1] Wilson, op. cit., pp. 284, 282.
[2] ibid., p. 264.

There was in fact no great conviction anywhere that the economic effects of entry would on balance be clearly beneficial. But the economics of the question were part of the tactics rather than the strategy. The civil servants who spent the morning at Chequers before leaving the Ministers to argue things out in the afternoon had a hard time of it trying to duck economic questions by means of which one Minister after another tried to use them as witnesses to support his particular political case. Two economic difficulties were, however, brought out: those of exchange controls and freedom of capital movements, and those of regional and physical planning through mechanisms like investment grants. It was felt that if by 1968 (the target date for entry in the cabinet papers) the economy was on an upswing, the food price implications of the Common Agricultural Policy could be absorbed without difficulty: if the economy were not recovering, then the country was in trouble anyway. (Mention of the dread word of devaluation appears to have been made at that Chequers meeting, causing predictable emotional upsets to a Prime Minister who had sacrificed the bulk of his electoral programme to maintain the $2·80 parity of the pound.)

Just before summing up the discussion, Harold Wilson sprang on the cabinet his own idea – which he had put to George Brown only that same morning – of a tour of the six capitals to be made by both of them jointly. It was an ingenious concept: abroad it was to impress with the government's seriousness of purpose, while also making it clear that not everyone in Britain was as enthusiastic as George Brown, and that there were doubts to be stilled – some of them doubts which it was up to the West Europeans to answer. At home, the double-headed mission was at the same time to reassure the anti-Marketeers that Brown was not yet being given his head by any means, and yet to demonstrate to the Marketeers that it was more than a ploy to keep him sweet (and out of the country). On the other hand – and this point did not escape those who were sceptical – to give the initiative that much weight was not really necessary if it was intended merely to reconnoitre the prospects. The German Foreign Minister had already proposed a probe through the usual diplomatic channels, and that could have been done without the implied degree of commitment of such a top-level capital-to-capital canvass. Although it was not universally supported at first, the tour was agreed; and in due course it predictably developed a momentum of its own.

On 10 November Harold Wilson announced the government's

decision. His memoirs insist that the statement had been circulated to the whole cabinet, which had gone through it line by line and endorsed it the day before. (Later some cabinet Ministers complained that it was deliberately circulated so late that they hardly had much chance to amend it.)

I want the House, the country, and our friends abroad to know that the government are approaching the discussions I have foreshadowed with the clear intention and determination to enter the EEC if, as we hope, our essential British and Commonwealth interests can be safeguarded. *We mean business.*[1]

The barnstorming around Europe began in December 1966 in Rome. The civil service departments had worked out for these meetings a fat set of briefs full of the difficulties – but sufficiently pro-European to provoke Douglas Jay into writing a vigorous counter-document of his own. The official defence brief in particular was unbending in the extreme, excluding any sort of concessions to Continental points of view – whether on Britain's commitments east of Suez, or her special defence relations with the United States, or any European approach to nuclear problems. To some of his colleagues it began to look almost as if, after the spasm of resolve of November, Harold Wilson had swung back towards finding out first, and deciding whether he meant business afterwards. But the cabinet seems to have encouraged him to keep up the momentum, and once on the Continent he was stimulated and exhilarated by his mission. His speech to the Council of Europe in Strasbourg on 23 January 1967 reflected, and no doubt in turn intensified, a rising political enthusiasm:

We mean business. And I am going to say why we mean business. . . . We mean business in a political sense because, over the next year, the next ten years, the next twenty years, the unity of Europe is going to be forged, and geography and history and interest and sentiment alike demand that we play our part in forging it, and in working it.

The vital stop on their tour was naturally Paris. Paris was the capital at which the Strasbourg speech was particularly aimed, and indeed a copy of it was sent formally to President de Gaulle in advance of Wilson's arrival. We saw in an earlier chapter that Harold Wilson's hope of charming or impressing the General into changing his mind was disappointed. But if he did not impress the General, it seems that Harold Wilson did at least impress himself with Britain's potential role.

[1] ibid., p. 299 (Wilson's italics).

His arguments, it clearly emerged, were overriding political ones. In accordance with a prearranged division of labour, this left George Brown, who had held such political views for a long time, cast paradoxically in the role of a brake on Harold Wilson's movement towards virtual unconditionalism. It was Brown who insisted, for example, in each of the capitals on something more than transitional arrangements for New Zealand unless the period were for a generation. ('I was talking', Harold Wilson observed in castigating the 'Tory terms' later, 'about a generation of human beings, not of hamsters.'[1]) And when the probe was completed with a visit to Luxemburg in early March 1967, Harold Wilson had become so politically involved that no one was in the least surprised when Britain put in a formal and unconditional bid for membership.

This was the period also of exhaustive economic study. One cabinet member of the time recalls the Prime Minister boring the cabinet stiff with a most yawn-making exercise, four red boxes full of papers on Europe, based on a Fabian obsession with economics, and the assumption that there was a crystal ball which – if only you polished it enough – would tell you all you wanted to know. As Harold Wilson himself recalls, 'if anyone had asked for a document on the effect of entry into the Market on British pigeon-fancying, he would have got it'.[2] Meeting roughly twice a week through April, the cabinet then had a second informal weekend at Chequers (30 April 1967) and after that a formal cabinet meeting on Tuesday 2 May to record its official decision.

The cabinet at this stage had two decisions to take, which were intimately, but not very simply, related. Strategically they considered the relative virtues of the EEC, NAFTA and GITA. (NAFTA was the somewhat unrealistic proposal, associated with Senator Jacob Javits among others, to form a North Atlantic Free Trade Area between the USA, Canada and EFTA, which the EEC might then also wish to join.[3] GITA was the alternative of 'going it alone'.[4]) Tactically they had to choose whether to abandon the idea of applying to the EEC, whether to postpone the application until after further soundings had been taken, whether to make a conditional application, or whether to follow the Wilson-Brown line and put in an application to join untrammelled by prior conditions.

[1] Hansard, 21 July 1971, col. 1494.
[2] Wilson, op. cit., p. 287.
[3] Cf. *The Second Try*, ed. cit., pp. 156–64 and 36–40.
[4] Cf. op. cit., pp. 301–5 and 40–4.

The complexity of the relationship between strategy and tactics may be illustrated by several Ministers' positions. Richard Crossman was for an unconditional application, because he thought that only after a sincere and all-out effort to enter the EEC had failed would Britain really settle down to his strategic objective – going it alone, cutting commitments east of Suez, and floating the pound. Richard Marsh was against applying for exactly the same reasons that Richard Crossman was in favour – because he wanted to see Britain more like Sweden. Though not in the cabinet, Harold Lever was also against the application, but for the opposite reasons from Richard Marsh – because he was convinced it had no chance of success: in addition, he felt that by applying at a time when she was not wanted, Britain would be forced to offer a high price which could not be reduced later, when an application might have a chance of success. Ironically enough, since he was in fact openly opposed to entry and a strong champion of the NAFTA solution, Douglas Jay also expressed himself in favour of postponing the application until there might be a better chance of success. Anthony Wedgwood Benn had, in the course of the winter, become a convert to entry in order to plan technology and deal with transnational companies on their own scale, while Barbara Castle, on the contrary, saw in EEC entry an abandonment of Socialist planning and principles, though acknowledging that after the probe the cabinet's hands were pretty well tied.

The line-up in the cabinet therefore was as follows: Harold Wilson, George Brown, Michael Stewart, Roy Jenkins, Anthony Crosland, Gerald Gardiner, Anthony Wedgwood Benn and Ray Gunter were in favour of entry; on the other hand, Douglas Jay, Fred Peart, Denis Healey, Barbara Castle, William Ross, Richard Marsh and Herbert Bowden were against. Anthony Greenwood inclined against, Cledwyn Hughes inclined in favour. That left Jim Callaghan, Patrick Gordon-Walker, Richard Crossman, and (outside the cabinet but involved in its discussions) the Chief Whip John Silkin somewhere in between, in the category of 'maybes' on the strategy, though on the tactics they – like the rest – agreed on the unconditional application being tabled in Brussels. All of them wanted a vigorous and swift follow-up to the application to leave no doubts as to Britain's seriousness and to get the issue decided soon.

So it was the whole cabinet, without any hint or threat of resignation, that supported Harold Wilson when he made his announcement in the House of 2 May 1967 that Britain would apply. Wilson made his own estimate of his colleagues: 'To produce a firm decision without any resignations seemed a near miracle, but perhaps this was assisted by an answer I gave to a question in a television interview on the possibility of resignation[s] – that I felt there might be one, or even two, but that would not stand in the way of a decision whatever that decision might be.'[1] There were of course cabinet Ministers, Barbara Castle and Douglas Jay among them, who privately or semi-publicly made it clear that they were against joining – some of them hoping to reap party popularity in the process. In a sense the absence of any resignation was a pity – the application might have looked even more convincing in Europe if someone had resigned. (It was not until late August that the Prime Minister, largely for other reasons, replaced Douglas Jay as President of the Board of Trade by Anthony Crosland.)

In presenting the application to Parliament Harold Wilson did not lay any particular emphasis on negotiating all the terms in advance: the negotiations, he said, 'ought not to be unnecessarily complicated with lesser issues, many of which can be best dealt with after entry'. This sentiment was by no means shared by all his back-benchers, for he was greeted at this point with noises which Hansard discreetly transcribes as 'Oh'.[2] He re-emphasized the overriding political motive:

The Government's purpose derives, above all, from our recognition that Europe is now faced with the opportunity of a great move forward in political unity and that we can – and indeed must – play our full part in it . . . we intend to pursue our application for membership with all the vigour and determination at our command. . . . This is a historic decision which could well determine the future of Britain, of Europe, and, indeed, of the world, for decades to come.[3]

And the House, approving the application, voted with the most overwhelming majority on a contested issue since the Tichborne case of 1875 – 488 votes in favour, only 62 against. Thirty-five Labour Members voted against, 260 in favour – leaving some 40 or 50 who deliberately abstained. Seven Ministers – including Douglas Jay and Fred Peart – sacked their parliamentary private secretaries for voting against the application.

When, within a week of the British letter of application, de Gaulle put in his 'velvet veto', Harold Wilson came back with the cry 'We will not take "No" for an answer'. George Brown, presenting the

[1] Wilson, op. cit., p. 387.
[2] Hansard, 2 May 1967, col. 311.
[3] Hansard, 2 May 1967, cols 313–14.

cabinet's agreed case to the Six, again stressed the dominantly political nature of the Wilson government's initiative ('the balance of economic advantage for us is a fine one'), and deliberately included the subject of defence:

We want as soon as we can to develop really effective political unity with our fellow West Europeans. . . . We see it, in short, as power for peace . . . exercising influence in world affairs not only in the commercial and economic, but also in the political and defence fields. We shall play our full part in this process.

He promised that 'the British Government and those who will be responsible for the conduct of our negotiations with the Community will spare no effort to bring them to a successful and speedy conclusion' and pledged 'the full determination of my country to succeed in this task. History, I am sure, will judge us all harshly if we fail in this endeavour.'[1]

All these resolutions and promises, some of the former cabinet Ministers now maintain, were just the noises that had to be made to get the negotiations going, which would be stopped either by the French, or else by themselves if necessary. The Labour cabinet was never formally to debate the issue of actually joining, as distinct from that of applying to join. It was, they can of course point out, basically the same ambiguity as that of the Conservative commitment only 'to negotiate; no more, no less'. Both successive Prime Ministers counted on the successful outcome of negotiations so changing the context that a commitment that might at home have looked like one merely to talk would automatically transform itself into a commitment towards the Six to enter once the negotiations were successfully concluded.

In Harold Wilson's case it was not to be. President de Gaulle stripped off the velvet glove of his May press conference and interposed an iron veto in December. Thus Harold Wilson's main strategic foreign policy initiative and eighteen months' campaigning collapsed overnight (as recorded in six lines of his book). All he could do was to dictate a sixteen-point rebuttal and wonder about next morning's papers: 'I enjoyed dictating the sixteen points, though I did not affect to believe that they would have any effect on the General. Nor – though they were generally welcomed by the British press – could I have hoped that they would upstage the news of the Jenkins-Callaghan reshuffle.'[2]

[1] Cmnd 3345, reprinted in full in *The Second Try*, ed. cit., pp. 189–201.
[2] Wilson, op. cit., p. 469.

Nothing more was to happen on the Common Market issue there-after, except for the Soames affair, until after the Hague summit. Then, because they had made a pledge to that effect at the party conference of 1969, the leadership felt bound to issue a White Paper in early 1970, while the Six after The Hague were preparing their negotiating posi-tion on enlargement. Though Foreign Office Ministers wanted to see a political commitment strongly reaffirmed in the White Paper, it was in fact prepared in the Cabinet Office and turned out to be a civil servants' and economists' document. It put the possible balance of payments burden at somewhere between £100 and £1,100 million, and pointed out that some of the effects on the positive side could not really be quantified. It was approved by the whole cabinet, together with the Prime Minister's statement, which promised 'The Government will enter into negotiations resolutely, with good faith', but warned the Six that the conditions to be negotiated would have to be acceptable.

There are good grounds, no doubt, for calling consistency the last refuge of the slow-witted. But since some of the Labour leaders have made great play with the concept and insisted on their own consistency on the Common Market throughout the past decade, it is not one we can totally ignore. (Whether honesty may not sometimes demand an open admission of a change of mind, rather than a charade of consist-ency, is another matter.) The issue divides naturally into three questions: consistency on the principle of entry into a Community of whose essence it is that common laws are made by common institutions outside the national framework; consistency on the economic terms for a few years of transition pending the full application of the Community rules thereafter; and consistency on the procedure by which Britain should take her decision.

In 1972 both the principle and the procedure came into the question of consistency: indeed for some of the former Ministers, it did so even earlier. Peter Shore, who voted for the application in 1967, declared as early as January 1971 that the terms could never be right, which comes as close to rejection of entry on any terms as makes little difference. Anthony Wedgwood Benn came out for a referendum on the Com-mon Market issue before the end of 1970. But, for the bulk of the former cabinet, consistency in 1971 meant chiefly consistency on the terms actually negotiated by the Conservative government with the terms that they would have accepted themselves. Before leaving the record of the Labour government, therefore, we must briefly turn to the kind of terms for the transition period which they hoped to obtain.

That they would ask for no changes on a permanent basis they had already made absolutely clear in 1967.

In 1971 the men most likely to know – the Ministers in charge of the Foreign Office – came out one after another saying that they personally, and in their view the government, would have accepted what came soon to be known as the 'Tory terms'. Michael Stewart, George Brown, George Thomson and Lord Chalfont immediately said so in public. Their leading colleagues at the Treasury – Roy Jenkins, Harold Lever, Dick Taverne – took the same view. At least one former cabinet Minister who voted against entry on 28 October 1971 refused to sign a letter saying that the cabinet would never have accepted these terms. Though he himself would have objected to them, he thought in all honesty that the cabinet as a whole, if Harold Wilson had put the terms to it, would have proved compliant. Evan Luard, who had also been a Foreign Office Minister, and a number of retired Foreign Office officials free to speak, such as Sir Roderick Barclay, the former ambassador to Belgium, also certified publicly that these terms lay within the negotiating position on which they were working.

The argument, when one probes it, in fact takes three different (complementary perhaps rather than incompatible) lines. Lord George-Brown, as Foreign Secretary at the time the 1967 negotiating brief was worked out, later claimed that the 1971 terms were in every particular at least as good or better than the Labour government's fall-back position and in some cases were near the best settlement the Labour government had hoped for. The reply to this was that the cabinet had never agreed any negotiating position in 1967 – after all, the negotiations never actually opened. True, rejoined George Brown, after slightly surprised research: but true only in a technical sense. It was July 1967 by the time all the briefs of the different departments were put together in a single document, and because of the onset of the holidays that compendium seems, by an oversight, never to have been placed formally before the cabinet. But every cabinet Minister had not only approved the brief so far as his own department was concerned, but had also had opportunity to read, and had frequently been consulted about, the briefs of other departments. Having approved all the parts, they could hardly have rejected the whole – and would certainly not have done so.

Other former Ministers can argue on the basis of their knowledge of the 1970 position. It is certainly remarkable that with the election held only twelve days before the opening of negotiations, and Ministers appointed only eight days before, the Conservative government did

not ask for any postponement, but simply picked up the dossier prepared for its predecessor. The Foreign Office did not have to revise its
negotiating position owing to the change in government – they were
able to regard these as bi-partisan issues, only adding a warning about
fish (which might equally well have been added by George Thomson
or any other Labour Minister in charge). To these arguments anti-
Market ex-Ministers can, rightly, reply that in 1970 the terms were
never put before the cabinet either. The Foreign Office Ministers may
be able to say that they would have recommended these terms to the
cabinet, but they cannot guarantee that the cabinet would have
accepted them.

That, however, leads to the third – and in many ways most interesting – line of argument. The very fact that the negotiating brief had not
been put before the cabinet so late before the opening of the negotiations is itself highly significant. It would have had to be approved by
the cabinet before the negotiations opened. It was not approved before
the election campaign, and was not to be presented to it until after the
election. That left at most a week (from cabinet formation after the
result was out on 19 June to a few days before Luxemburg on 30
June) to get the negotiating position through the new cabinet. It was at
Harold Wilson's request that George Thomson and his private secretary, Crispin Tickell (later Anthony Barber's and then Geoffrey
Rippon's private secretary) sat down in a Dundee hotel at the height of
the election campaign to complete the draft of his opening speech
for insertion into the official machinery, swift approval by the cabinet,
and printing for publication. (Barring personal stylistic idiosyncrasies
and changes consequent on the unexpected change of government, it
was this Dundee draft that formed the bulk of Anthony Barber's
presentation in Luxemburg.) We know that cabinet changes were
planned before the election. It is not compatible with normal
political processes that the cabinet should have been constituted in such
a way as to have suffered a major crisis in its first week of existence. One
can only conclude that the distribution of portfolios would have been
governed among other considerations by the first and overriding issue
to be faced, and that at no time would it have been more difficult for
the anti-Marketeers to resist agreeing to a negotiating position than in
that post-election government-forming fortnight in which a victorious
Prime Minister – and the first Labour Prime Minister to have won
three elections running – really would have had all the immediate aces
up his sleeve. There is, we may conclude, little doubt that, had the

election turned out differently, it would have been for Harold Wilson to have collected the prizes for European statesmanship that several foundations lavished on Edward Heath at the end of 1971. What is more, he would have amply deserved them – and, for his earlier historic role, deserves them anyhow.

Settling into Opposition

In its 1970 election manifesto, the Labour Party had been, if anything, more positive about EEC entry than the Conservatives:

We have applied for membership of the European Economic Community and negotiations are due to start in a few weeks' time. These will be pressed with determination with the purpose of joining an enlarged community provided that British and essential Commonwealth interests can be safeguarded.

This year, unlike 1961–1963, Britain will be negotiating from a position of economic strength. Britain's strength means that we shall be able to meet the challenges and realize the opportunities of joining an enlarged Community. But it means, too, that if satisfactory terms cannot be secured in the negotiations Britain will be able to stand on her own feet outside the Community.

Unlike the Conservatives, a Labour Government will not be prepared to pay part of the price of entry in advance of entry and irrespective of entry by accepting the policies, on which the Conservative Party are insisting, for levies on food prices, the scrapping of our food subsidies and the introduction of the Value-Added Tax.[1]

As we have already seen, the issue played little part in the election, and no one could argue that the Labour government's proclaimed determination to press the application was an element in its defeat. When the Parliamentary Party reassembled at Westminster, it had lost 111 former and gained 52 new members. If anything, it emerged from the election slightly more pro-European in composition than at the dissolution. Nevertheless, when the Labour government so surprisingly lost office on 19 June 1970, there were those who immediately hoped or feared that the change of government combined with the narrow Conservative majority would prove the worst of all possible parliamentary configurations for British entry into the EEC. A Conservative government with an ample majority would have risked anti-Market defections. A Labour government, with whatever majority, could have

[1] Now Britain's Strong, Let's Make It Great To Live In (Labour Party Manifesto for the 1970 Election), p. 28.

counted on the bulk of the opposition to vote with it. There were pro-Market Conservatives who foresaw that, on this issue, a Labour Opposition would 'play politics', and be unable to resist the temptation to use a cry popular in the country for getting their rivals out of office regardless of their own convictions on the issue.

As against those fears, the election of the Deputy Leader to replace George Brown (defeated at Belper) gave the Marketeers some comfort. Roy Jenkins won easily against Fred Peart, who was known to be rather unconvinced, to put it mildly, of the wisdom of the Labour government's application. The election was not an endorsement by his colleagues of Roy Jenkins' conspicuous personal commitment to the European cause; but at least it did mark acceptance by the Parliamentary Party of responsibility for the late government's policy even when – as had been the case with Roy Jenkins' Chancellorship – it might have been tempting to disavow the unpopular policies of the past and to throw oneself wholeheartedly into the more delightful and perhaps electorally more rewarding role of total opposition.

In mid-July 1970 Roy Jenkins' victory was followed by the election of the shadow cabinet. And there again, the declared anti-Marketeers did badly: Michael Foot came sixth, while Douglas Jay, Peter Shore and Richard Marsh failed to get elected at all. With Anthony Crosland and Douglas Houghton third and fourth after Jim Callaghan and Denis Healey, and Shirley Williams, Harold Lever and George Thomson further down the list of successful candidates, 'nobody could say', as *The Times* observed on the morrow of the election, 'that this Shadow Cabinet could be easily swung against British entry for crude electoral reasons'.[1]

In this judgment, however, *The Times* had reckoned without two other members of the shadow cabinet – Anthony Wedgwood Benn and Barbara Castle, and without Richard Crossman, who now took over the *New Statesman* as editor. In early August 1970 the *Statesman* came out with a leading article entitled: 'The People v. The Market: Who has the last word?' It argued against Douglas Jay's proposals for a referendum on the issue – Douglas Jay was in any case a Gaitskellite, and thus of little interest to old Bevanites like Richard Crossman – but for converting the Labour Party from its governmental position in favour of entry to the opposite line.[2] 'The reasoning behind it', said the *Sunday Telegraph*, 'is simple and cynical: to climb aboard the anti-

[1] *The Times*, 11 July 1970.
[2] *New Statesman*, 7 August 1970.

Market bandwagon is the best, if not the only chance the Labour Party has of getting itself re-elected.'[1]

But there was in fact far more to it than that. The trade unions, as we saw in the previous chapter, had begun to take a much clearer anti-Market stand as soon as the election was over; and when, at the very end of September 1970, the Labour party conference as usual followed a few weeks after that of the TUC, the defeated former Prime Minister was faced with a situation in which his European policy, never all that popular in the party, was under attack – both from some of the leading trade unions and also from some of his formerly closest and most loyal cabinet colleagues. Peter Shore, on the eve of the conference, came out in total opposition, and when questioned as to how he could square this with his membership of the cabinet that had prepared the negotiations for entry had three things to say: first, that there never was any cabinet commitment beyond negotiating to find out the terms of entry; second, that since then the Common Agricultural Policy had been settled and had come into effect before British entry had been decided upon; and third, that the effort to create a monetary and economic union was tantamount to an additional Treaty of Rome that had not been there before.

Before the party conference itself met there was an attempt, first of all, to prevent any discussion of the issue by using a little-known rule (surely honoured in the breach rather than in the observance) that the same subject may not be debated more than once in three years. That ploy, needless to say, failed as it deserved to do. But the most the National Executive felt it could safely get from the Conference was the meagre reaffirmation of the decisions taken at the previous conference – which had been, in any negotiation for membership of the EEC, 'to insist on adequate safeguards for Britain's balance of payments, cost of living, national health and social security systems, and power of independent decision in economic planning and foreign policy'.

As at the TUC, the Administrative and Clerical Workers moved a motion designed to rally the Marketeers – though here the union was slightly bolder than at the TUC, demanding that negotiations continue to see if acceptable terms could be achieved. The Transport and General Workers Union on the other side brought in a motion opposing entry on any terms that threatened employment, the cost of living, or the independence of political, economic and foreign policies. Moving it, Harry Urwin pointed to the spectre that haunted the leadership – and at

[1] *Sunday Telegraph*, 9 August 1970.

the same time the temptation: only twenty-two per cent of popular opinion were in favour of entry, 'yet no political party represented in the House of Commons is willing to identify itself with the views and fears of the vast majority of the British people'. The National Executive won the vote – but only just. The TGWU resolution was defeated by 3,049,000 to 2,954,000 votes – a majority of only 95,000.

As the year 1970 drew to a close the anti-Marketeers in the party gained further ground, and prepared it to allow the party to move away from its position in government. Anthony Wedgwood Benn, who emphasized at the time that he personally was now on balance in favour of entry, joined Douglas Jay's attempt to outflank both party leaderships with a demand for a referendum. In a 4,500-word letter to his electors in Bristol South-East, he implicitly rejected the doctrines of his illustrious eighteenth-century predecessor, Edmund Burke, on the duty of an MP to exercise his judgment for them: 'If people are not to participate in this decision, no one will ever take participation seriously again. . . . It would be a very curious thing to try to take Britain into a new political unity with a huge potential for the future by a process that implied that the British public were unfit to see its historic importance for themselves.'

The National Executive at this stage voted down the proposal, though Jim Callaghan described it as 'a life-raft into which the whole party may one day have to climb'. All they did in late December was to remit a TGWU resolution calling for a referendum and then vote 15 to 1 (with Harold Wilson absent and Jim Callaghan no longer at the meeting) that there should be a special party conference before Parliament decided on the issue. Denis Healey tried to argue that it would be difficult to find a large enough hall in London to do that, which prompted Anthony Wedgwood Benn to ask, 'Am I to tell my grandchildren that the Labour Party could not pronounce a verdict on the biggest issue of the century because it could not book a hall?' At the same meeting, the Executive voted 12 to 11 against continuing to pay £1,200 per annum to Jean Monnet's Action Committee; Walter Padley, Roy Jenkins and Denis Healey had to attend its meetings thereafter as representatives of the only major democratic party in Europe that enjoyed membership but was not prepared to contribute to the Committee's running costs. Clearly nerves were getting raw, and anything, however undignified, would do as a signal to divide comrades on the Market. The portents for party unity in 1971 were badly clouded that first Christmas back in Opposition.

The first four – nearly five – months of 1971 were, however, still to pass fairly quietly within the party. In January, John Silkin, who as government Chief Whip had been so successful in getting 260 out of 361 Labour MPs to vote for entry in principle on 10 May 1967 (when only 35 voted against), put down an Early Day motion sponsored by *Tribune*, which attracted 108 Labour signatures in 48 hours (though John Rankin withdrew his name almost immediately afterwards): 'That this House believes that entry into the EEC on the terms so far envisaged would be against the interests of this country.' The signatories included 7 members of the Labour Committee for Europe as well as 26 new MPs – half the new Labour intake at the 1970 election – and was to rise to just over 132 as the months went on.

In early May there were signs of strain – Mrs Renée Short attacked 'timid pale pink liberals in the Labour Party' who 'waffled about the dynamic effects' and first had herself reported as referring to Shirley Williams and William Rodgers and then denied any specific references. Denis Healey on the other hand deplored such personal attacks and said it would be criminal for the Movement to tear itself to pieces before they knew the outcome of negotiations: 'Let us conduct our arguments as reasonable men and women. If we cannot demonstrate our brotherhood and sisterhood in our discussions with one another, we cannot expect the world to take our principles very seriously.'

As for the Party Leader, he had been writing his memoirs in the early months of Opposition, and even in 1971 he saw every advantage in keeping his options open and felt it wise not to say anything too categorical until the results of the negotiations should emerge. In February he warned the Six that Britain's economy was strong enough for Britain to be able to stand on her own feet if the terms proved un-acceptable or they used 'highwayman tactics to extract from the British wayfarer into Europe all that is in his purse and more'. (Such warnings are an auxiliary function to diplomacy which any Opposition can perform at home for any government engaged in a negotiation abroad; Harold Wilson was to continue to perform it, to be thanked for it publicly by Geoffrey Rippon, and to acknowledge these thanks in public in his turn.) And at the end of April in Birmingham he warned the government not to rush in on the wrong terms – he was worried in case 'a bouncy negotiator might bounce us into the Market perhaps on the wrong terms' – it was much more important to get the right terms slowly than to get the wrong terms fast.

In all this one has to remember that before early May there had been no breakthrough of any kind in Brussels. There was no evidence yet that Edward Heath would be welcome at the Elysée, and no clear idea as to what might be demanded of him if he ever got there. The whole issue, in other words, might just go away. When Denis Healey had lunched with Wilfred Baumgartner in February, he formed the clear impression that Pompidou would make British accession impossible – and as shadow Foreign Secretary he obviously reported his impressions to Harold Wilson. As on nationalization and on unilateral disarmament, Harold Wilson was no Hugh Gaitskell: he has never seen any need to divide the party over academic or platonic issues on which the party could have no decisive practical impact. So Wilson was not so much sitting on any fence as avoiding the ludicrous spectacle of jumping to one or other side of a fence that might prove not even to be there. Denis Healey might risk – and later regret – jumping off onto the Market side with éclat just after the Paris summit in the mistaken belief that the negotiations would still fail, so that his conversion would remain platonic while gaining him European sympathies; Harold Wilson did not propose to turn the somersault in the opposite direction until there was no other way out.

That moment came almost immediately after the summit and a little too early for Harold Wilson's liking. But first, to exclude the effects of hindsight and establish a fix against which to measure the speed of subsequent events, it is worth quoting what two British political commentators (and not ones to overestimate Harold Wilson's consistency in general) wrote in the first half of May 1971. To begin with the political editor of the *Financial Times*:

If the leader of the Labour Party starts at this late stage to discover a sudden burning indignation on behalf of Caribbean sugar producers, Scottish fishermen and New Zealand farmers, many of us will be quietly sick, but quite a lot of the Parliamentary Labour Party may find it convincing. On balance I still believe
. . . that Mr Wilson has enough concern for his reputation in the history books to want to vote in favour of entry unless his leadership is clearly endangered by doing so.[1]

Three days later, the political editor of *The Times* under the title 'Mr Wilson's Veto' wrote:

The Government know that if Mr Wilson stands firm, at some personal party risk, he is capable of holding rather more than half the Parliamentary Labour

[1] David Watt, *Financial Times*, 7 May 1971.

Party on the course set in 1967, when the Labour Government put in their unhedged application for membership. He would consolidate the European majority in the Shadow Cabinet, and swing behind him a sizable group of uncommitted back-benchers. If he played party politics on Europe by compromising with a free vote, he would give the signal for all but two score or so Labour MPs to butcher the European idea to make a partisan holiday. . . . At that point Mr Wilson's veto would indirectly come into effect. On such evidence as I have, the Birmingham speech did not mean that Mr Wilson is retreating fast to the fence. . . . As Opposition leader he can scarcely be expected to go out campaigning uncritically for entry now, only to find in July that the Cabinet has left him stranded by rejecting the Brussels terms. That is one of his real fears.[1]

Three things are notable in the latter analysis. Firstly that the possibility of a Labour whip against entry was not even envisaged (the free vote was contrasted to a whipped vote in favour); second that even on a free vote only 'two score or so' of Labour MPs were thought to be firm pro-Marketeers; and thirdly that the level of Conservative support for entry was thought sufficiently weak – with the electoral consequences in 1974 of going into the Common Market in 1973 as the main Conservative worry – that even Mr Wilson's allowing the Labour Party a free vote would stop Britain going in: 'Mr Wilson, like Mr Pompidou, has the power to exercise a veto. . . .'

As if to confirm the impression described by the political editor of *The Times*, Harold Wilson, interviewed at length on the BBC's *Panorama* programme that same evening, reiterated repeatedly that his views had not changed at all since 1967, when he led the Labour government's application for entry:

When we made the application I said 'We mean business'. That's right. I agree with that. On the other hand if the terms were prohibitive, you wouldn't join. . . . I still maintain that if the terms are right there is a great gain for Britain. . . . I have not changed my view at all.

In the next morning's *Guardian* the Labour Committee for Europe published a full-page advertisement:

We, the undersigned Parliamentarians, are convinced that the causes of social democracy, world peace, and economic advance in both developed and developing countries would be strengthened by the addition of the United Kingdom, Norway, Denmark and Ireland to the European Economic Community.

[1] David Wood, *The Times*, 10 May 1971.

It was signed by illustrious Continental Socialists, including Willy Brandt, Gaetano Martino, Guy Mollet and Pietro Nenni, as a reminder of the strength of Social Democracy within the Community. But what cut more ice in Britain was that it was signed, in addition, by one hundred Labour MPs ('It was a cliffhanger, but we just made it', the organizers said with a sigh of relief), of whom eight were members of the shadow cabinet (including Anthony Crosland and Denis Healey) and twenty-three more were members of the Opposition front bench selected by the Party Leader himself and (as the press commented to the considerable annoyance of the anti-Marketeers) the 'high-flyers of the future'. The party's problems were beginning to come to a head.

A Sea-change at the Top

A fortnight later the situation was transformed by two events that happened within a few days of each other. There was the Paris summit meeting on 20–21 May. And – from a party point of view no less relevant – there was also a carefully heralded speech in Southampton on 25 May by 'the deceptively bland figure of Labour's "Third Man", Mr James Callaghan',[1] who had asked the press specially to come to hear him and had, it seems, insisted to one journalist who said he could not leave London that night, 'Well, if you want to hear the next leader of the Labour Party, you'd better arrange to be there' – a remark which was reported to Harold Wilson within twenty-four hours though the latter happened to be in Helsinki at the time.

It will give an idea of the briefing given to journalists in advance to read on in Anthony Howard's curtain-raiser for the Southampton speech:

No one else in British public life can muster up quite those same plain man's tones with which to reduce a complex issue to a no-nonsense, down-to-earth matter. But, over and above that, he happens also to be in a position virtually to determine what Labour's eventual attitude to any Brussels terms will be.

The reason is both personal and political – personal because Mr Wilson knows only too well that if he does not come out in flat opposition to whatever terms the Government finally secures, he will forfeit his leadership to a James Callaghan only too ready to do so; and political because, whatever his critics have said against him, no one has ever questioned Mr Callaghan's capacity to sense the predominant mood of the party and then to respond to it. . . .

There is nothing in all this that necessarily divides Mr Callaghan from Mr Wilson (Mr Jenkins, naturally, is a very different case): but it will not, in fact,

[1] Anthony Howard, *Observer*, 23 May 1971.

be Mr Wilson who has called Labour's Market tune. Instead it will be his only surviving rival from the leadership election of eight years ago. For all his recent self-deprecation about having become merely a semi-retired elder statesman in politics, it seems a little implausible that Mr Callaghan has not calculated that some at least in the party will remember that. If, as Harry Truman used to say, 'a statesman is merely a finished politician' there is very little in Jim Callaghan's current performance to suggest that he is yet within sight of qualifying for the title.

So great was the build-up for the speech that the local candidate let it be known that if the speech was to be irrelevant to the by-election he was not sure he wanted it delivered; while if it was an across-the-board challenge for the leadership he would rather Jim Callaghan did not come. As it turned out – with its long passage about sterling – it was certainly not an appeal to the good burghers of Southampton, and the cognoscenti thought they recognized in style and content the hand of Terry Pitt, the secretary of the Research Department and one of the most anti-Market of the Transport House officials.

There can be no doubt that Jim Callaghan was grasping at an opportunity to 'get the Tories out'. He was also clearly concerned to preserve party unity – a concern which implied, above all, that the Parliamentary Party must not get too far out of step with the membership and with the broad mass of voters in the country. It was a concern he showed over immigration issues, where the first reaction of many parliamentarians risked divorcing them from the feelings of working-class and lower middle-class voters. Like Herbert Morrison in the past, who 'had a little birdie sitting on his shoulder better than any Gallup poll', Jim Callaghan understood a good deal of what the rank and file would and what it would not swallow. The fact that, on this issue, there was a ready-made majority within the Parliamentary Party as well, to whom the leadership had not really been responding, both lent additional force to his argument and acted as a bonus in terms of intra-party politics. Moreover, Jim Callaghan was older than Harold Wilson – he would be sixty in 1972: if he was ever to make the leadership this was the time, and the Market the issue. Perhaps he also felt not only a possible vacuum above, but also patent pressure below. He was being challenged for the Party Treasurership by Norman Atkinson representing the Left, and there was a slight feeling of uncertainty in the party that the Left might, in the autumn, capture the NEC and knock some of the present members out of their seats. Jim Callaghan exasperated some of his pro-Market friends at the time by discussing the Market issue solely in terms of intra-party struggles, though it was no doubt meant kindly when he advised one of them to give up his stand and thereby avoid political suicide.

But, whatever his motives, Callaghan was now confronting Harold Wilson with a difficult dilemma: if Wilson stuck to his Market guns there would be a party split with a ready-made alternative leader as well as a large part of the Parliamentary Party, the unions, the conference, and the rank and file against him. If he wobbled, his long-term position in the country (and therefore by a natural feed-back, in the party as well) would not have been improved either. Ronald Butt reported quite explicitly: 'All he will have done is to have irretrievably damaged his own credibility which, I am told (such are the elevated terms in which these great issues are discussed in the Labour Party), had throughout been Mr Callaghan's calculation.'[1]

The division of the party four ways – those who wanted to go in on any likely terms; those who would not go in on any terms whatever; those who were getting worried without quite knowing what to do, and the Leader who said he wanted to see the terms before doing anything – was bound, at this point, to come to a head. And it would be crucial not merely for Harold Wilson's personal position, but for the future unity and electoral credibility of the party as a whole, and therefore for its hopes of achieving everything that it stood for.

The months of June and July thus saw the crystallization of the fronts both on the National Executive and in the Shadow Cabinet. Harold Wilson announced that he would wait for the terms before making up his mind, and that he would not do so until 28 July 1971 – a date that had no significance beyond being that of a shadow cabinet meeting at the very end of the parliamentary session. He would perhaps have liked to defer his decision until the October conference, bringing the tablets of the law down to the full assembly of the people, but Jim Callaghan had jumped the gun, and he could not now afford to leave a void for that long. On the other hand he was not prepared to announce a final decision on 17 July – the date of the special conference – and indeed there was a good deal to be said for him listening, and above all appearing to listen, to what the party had to say then, yet also being firmly in the saddle with a known line of argument before the summer recess.

The issue of a special party conference now became the most contentious item on the National Executive's agenda. The promise made to the party in October 1970 had been for a special party conference if the

[1] *Sunday Times*, 11 July 1971.

parliamentary vote would otherwise occur before the regular October conference. Though the government had decided to defer the parliamentary vote until the end of October, the anti-Marketeers decided to press for a special conference anyway. The Executive was almost evenly split. Ian Mikardo, the Party Chairman, suggested he would conduct it as a balanced debate, and there need be no vote at the end. The Executive took its decision and, by a majority of one, voted for the special conference: one of the Marketeers, Shirley Williams, had voted with the 'antis' on straightforward democratic grounds of maximizing debate – to the amazement and indignation of her friends. 'Her name must be Temple, not Williams', one of the pro-Market union members was heard loudly to declare. When Ian Mikardo then talked of guiding the debate to reflect 'the balance of the party as he saw it' and of allowing a vote at the end, she tried to reverse her previous vote – with the result that she tied Ian Mikardo to the form of conference he had sketched before the Executive vote was taken. Both because it was held at all, and because of the form it took, the 17 July conference was called by some people 'Shirley's Conference'. As it got closer some of her Marketeering friends compared her to the lady of Riga: when the conference turned out, for the Marketeers and for the party, as a great success, some credited her with as much political cunning as they had previously suspected her of treason; both attitudes were, however, over-reactions, symptomatic of the jumpiness of the party at the time.

If Shirley Williams was thus without justification temporarily thought to have ratted, June and July did see two defections from the Market camp that were to be important: Anthony Crosland and Denis Healey. Anthony Crosland had for years been an officer of the Labour Committee for Europe. He had also been campaigning hard all 1970 to be elected for the first time to the National Executive – speaking to smaller groups and in remoter places than at any time in his earlier career. 'Why anyone should be so ludicrously anxious to get himself on that futile body, heaven only knows', one of his colleagues observed – but then after being on that body for a few years it may be easier to be blasé about it. Anthony Crosland consulted various of his friends at length in early summer, and was dissuaded from making a public splash about his retreat from the Common Market cause. He made a private speech to his party in Grimsby, and what he actually said was never reported. But word of the draft reached the *Sunday Times* (probably from anti-Market people in Transport House). The press confronted him with these reports and were told that the Market was not

so important to him, since it was not that important to the man in the
street; that the party was not to be split by an élitist clique who thought
they knew better than the people; and that compared with party unity
and a good many other issues entry into the EEC came low on his
order of priorities. The change of stance thus came out sideways and
– perhaps predictably – rather at half cock. In fact Crosland stayed
away from the House of Commons rather unhappily on the night of
28 October and, though re-elected to the Shadow Cabinet in November 1971, he fell from third to eighth place. When, in April 1972,
Roy Jenkins' resignation triggered off an election for the Deputy
Leadership, Anthony Crosland came third in the first round, having
lost, on some estimates, perhaps forty Marketeers' votes through the
uncertainties of 1971. Had he held their loyalty, there can be little doubt
that he, and not Edward Short, would have been elected Deputy
Leader – with all the longer-term prospects that such a post may open
up.

   The other apparent change of attitude was that of Denis Healey.
Healey had not been one of the original Europeans of the Labour Party
by any means, but in May had come out not only with his signature to
the *Guardian* advertisement, but with a personal confession of faith
splashed over seven columns in the *Daily Mirror* of 26 May:

I've changed my mind too – but in the opposite direction.

   I know it's unfashionable. Some of my friends say it is politically inconveni-
ent too. But the world has changed a lot in the last nine years, and so has the
Common Market. . . .

   The fact is that for other reasons entirely our cost of living went up as much
in a fortnight last month as the worst that could happen in a year through joining the Common Market. . . .

   A Labour man like me is bound to be impressed by the fact that there is not
one Socialist Party or Trade Union in the Common Market which does not
think on the basis of thirteen years' experience that the Common Market has
been good for it, and for its country, and which does not want Britain in too. . . .

   *Britain could be hammered into the ground if she were outside all the main trading
blocs.* . . .

   But failure in Brussels will be a great chance lost for everyone concerned.

   It would mean another quarter of a century in which what happens to all of
us in Europe is decided mainly by the Americans and Russians.

A few weeks later, however, his emphasis was all on the terms: by
13 July 1971, a two-and-a-half-hour BBC debate to which he had been

invited as a pro-European had at the last minute to be strengthened through the participation of Harold Lever, since Denis Healey had moved from the stance so recently declared with so much flourish. (The speed of the change left the BBC somewhat disorganized, so that early editions of the *Radio Times* had to appear without pictures of the politicians invited to take part.)

The Special Conference

The controversial special party conference took place in the Central Hall, Westminster, on Saturday, 17 July 1971, just three days after the Conservative rally held in the same building. There was apprehension on the part of the National Executive and of the pro-Marketeers that the conference might get the bit between its teeth, and, once it had assembled, assert its sovereignty: it might, instead of merely debating EEC entry, insist on voting on the matter and thus forestall the leadership's own decision. There had also been newspaper reports that if that should happen, some of the Labour Committee for Europe members might suggest procedural obstructions – newspaper reports which Geoffrey de Freitas had formally to deny as reflecting the Committee's views in any way.

When the conference met, the Executive proposed to agree on a resolution on 28 July in the light of the forthcoming debate. Alf Morris straightaway proposed the arrangements be altered to allow a vote on a substantive resolution opposing entry and calling for a general election. This was the tensest moment of that day's proceedings. Then Jim Callaghan rose to oppose Alf Morris. He made a low-key speech – and it was not all that difficult to see that he had reluctantly been prevailed upon to stand up for the Executive when in so many ways he must have personally preferred to see the party conference go right ahead and vote. If he really wanted the conference to take his advice, he did not pitch the advice very strongly. But Harold Wilson had been active beforehand in making sure that he had enough union support to keep the debate at this stage a purely consultative one. (As usual at Labour party conferences, half the delegates, representing the unions, had seven-eighths of the votes.) A card vote was demanded, and Alf Morris was defeated by 3,185,000 to 2,624,000 votes. The panic was over. Instead of the tough clash of block votes immediately involving the power balance within the party an intellectual debate could now begin.

The debate was vigorous, hard, but not uncomradely. Ian Mikardo kept his word, in fact called pro- and anti-Marketeers alternately to the point where the Marketeers themselves felt that to viewers watching the debate on television the strength of their arguments must have seemed matched by the strength of their numerical support. They were well organized to put into the shop window the maximum of their assets. There were effective speeches in favour of entry from Bob Edwards of the Chemical Workers, Jack Peel of the Dyers, and Roy Grantham of the Clerical Workers. When Jack Jones reported that in their conference of nine hundred delegates only four had opposed their coming down heavily against the Common Market, Sir Frederick Hayday countered that the General and Municipal Workers agreed with George Thomson that these terms were acceptable.

Of course the balance of view in the trade union movement against the Market came through just as strongly in speeches such as those by Dan McGarvey of the Boilermakers ('we could have a situation where Germany's finger is on the nuclear trigger') and Hugh Scanlon of the Engineers (who denounced the voteless conference as 'an exercise in futility' and wanted the Executive to take 'a definite decision that decisions of party conference are binding on us all and that includes every MP of this party').

But the Marketeers could not complain at the Central Hall: their numerical strength was undoubtedly overstated in the number and in the quality of the speeches. A Knutsford CLP delegate quoted Eric Heffer (1967) against Eric Heffer (1971); Diana Jeuda, the prospective candidate for Macclesfield, anti, was balanced by Helen Brown from Rushcliffe CLP, pro, John Ellis (Bristol North-West), anti, by Arthur Palmer (Bristol Central), pro. In his choice of speeches from the gallery where the *ex officio* delegates sat suspended the Chairman maintained a similar balance. Douglas Jay followed Michael Stewart, and George Thomson ('These terms would have gone through a Labour cabinet') was balanced by an impassioned speech from Peter Shore ('the terms . . . are appallingly bad for the people of this country . . . for people to say that going into Europe will increase the prosperity and rate of growth of this country is flagrantly dishonest').

Various Constituency Labour Party speakers reported that their CLPs were split down the middle and that they had been sent to listen and to demand more enlightenment. A Yorkshire CLP delegate called the British 'a magnificent dolly mixture of European genes and chromosomes. Thus with our exceptional hybrid vigour, we British can undoubtedly provide added stimulus to Europe by our extra brains' and quoted Nye Bevan on the need for a Socialist to be at all times an internationalist. On the other side a delegate from East Anglia speaking as 'a simple soul' feared the day when 'Golden Delicious oust Cox's of England': 'I fought for this country during the war. I do not want to see the Krupp family, or the von Thyssens, I do not want to see the fascists in Italy, who recently got two thousand seats, running the political institutions of this country.'

In a tone that almost suggested no such animal could exist the Chairman called for a pro-Marketeer from Wales; he got a Monmouth delegate: 'I am a Welsh boy. I have been brought up in all the Welsh traditions of the unemployment of the 'thirties. . . . We have had no growth over the last decade. This one can trace at least in part to our exclusion from this dynamic market on the Continent.' On the other side a delegate from Southend recommended 'a very straightforward formula and that is, if the Tories are in favour of it, if Ted Heath is in favour of it, I am against it.' Sporting his braces, a shirt-sleeved Poplar and Stepney delegate (partly in protest against 'a horse race in which the winning post has been removed') called all those unfortunate enough to have sampled Continental beer – 'a sort of polluted washing-up water' – to witness that it would not stimulate growth.

It was not without relief that Marketeers heard the proposal that the debate should finish nearly an hour early, given the heat of the day and the tiredness of the delegates: they might not have been able to keep up the punch of the speeches on their side much longer. So, at 4.15 p.m Harold Wilson rose to deliver one of the two alternative speeches he had prepared for the occasion (the other was planned in case the demand for a vote should, in spite of his efforts, have been successful). As always, he united the conference by a blistering attack on the Conservatives, had his usual dig at the press, and then showed that he for one clearly thought that many of the terms were unacceptable. New Zealand was the issue he stressed particularly and at length. He had already drawn his own conclusion, though others might not:

The negotiations would show whether the Community was a rule-ridden bureaucracy; whether in its motivation it was looking outwards to a Europe-wide unity, or whether it was basically an agricultural welfare complex based on subsidies to high-cost producers, tariffs on imports of cheaper produce, backed by expensive export subsidies to sell high-cost produce to the world at low-cost world prices.

I think the outcome of the negotiations on Commonwealth sugar and on New Zealand tell their own story. Every delegate will decide for himself, every members of the Executive, every Member of Parliament will decide what lesson to draw. I am speaking for myself in drawing that particular lesson.

The debate, however, would continue until October: 'I charge this Movement, as I have the right and duty to do, so to conduct this debate as to respect and honour the views of all members of the party, and indeed of others, regardless of what those views may be.'

Eleven days after the conference, the NEC passed by 16 votes to 6 the resolution it was to put to the Brighton conference in October:

Conference, having studied the government's White Paper (Cmnd 4715), on 'The United Kingdom and the European Communities'; opposes entry into the Common Market on the terms negotiated by the Conservative government; regrets the government's refusal to give the nation the facts necessary for a full appraisal of the continuing costs of entering the Communities against the possible long-term benefits, and in particular the Prime Minister's refusal to set up a select committee to examine the facts available to the government; and further considers that Conservative economic and social policies so weaken and divide the nation that Britain's ability to improve the living standards of our people inside or outside the Market has been undermined; and since, in the words of the present Prime Minister during the election, 'no British government could possibly take this country into the Common Market against the wish of the British people', calls on the Prime Minister now to submit to the democratic judgment of a general election.

It therefore invites the Parliamentary Labour Party, taking account of these factors and the decision of Conference, to unite wholeheartedly in voting against the government's policy.

The six members who voted against were Tom Bradley, Jim Diamond, Roy Jenkins, Fred Mulley, Walter Padley and Shirley Williams.

So far so good. What really did the damage, however, was not so much the special conference as the by-play and immediate repercussions of it. The tactic of the pro-Marketeers up to the Saturday and including it had been a low-profile one: Roy Jenkins even refused to make an expected little address at a lunch in St Ermine's Hotel given by the Labour Committee for Europe for fear of appearing to raise the temperature. The pro-Marketeers at that stage still believed that the Leader's speech at the end of the afternoon would be a fairly balanced one. At the end of the lunch-hour, they saw an advance copy, apparently obtained by a journalist from Harold Wilson's staff: 'That', one

of them later recalled, 'totally threw us off balance.' Harold Wilson
early next week then accused an unnamed pro-Marketeer of having
leaked a copy of his speech to the press complete with rude comments
in the margin. More serious, Roy Jenkins decided to make a carefully
prepared speech at the Monday meeting of the Parliamentary Labour
Party which set out to controvert the Saturday speech in detail and
succeeded so brilliantly and in places with such bluntness that according
o one of his friends people were screaming with delight and banging
fists on tables with applause. From that moment on, many sensed that
'something ghastly was bound to happen' between Harold Wilson and
Roy Jenkins.

The week after, on 28 July, the National Executive decided to launch
a national campaign in support of their resolution, but it also made
clear, as a 'Labour Party spokesman' put it: 'Party members are of
course free – certainly until the annual conference – to express the
views which they honestly hold on the entry terms. They have only
been asked not to make personal attacks or debate with their party
comrades in TV confrontations.'[1]

So, at the end of July, the party leadership had officially swung, while
the conference would not express itself until October. The pro-
Market MPs had clear warning that they were liable to find themselves
in the minority. It remained to be seen how large and how persistent
that minority would be.

The Pro-Market MPs

In the rallying of the Labour Marketeers during this period the conspicuous leading role was clearly played by the Deputy Leader. Had
Roy Jenkins weakened, or had he talked of abstaining on the crucial
vote of principle, the effects would have been very serious on the rank-
and-file Marketeers. Many would have persisted, but others might have
found the strain of standing out against their own party too great. Roy
Jenkins was not universally popular in the Parliamentary Party. He was
regarded as aloof and superior by many of the trade unionists, unwilling
to swill beer with non-intellectuals in the bar and unable to remember
their wives' Christian names or their bodily complaints. During the
spring, summer and autumn of 1971, however, he was available –
'twenty-four hours a day' as one of his friends put it – to any who
wanted to talk to him about the European issue or the difficulties they
faced over it. He did not make many speeches on the subject in public.

[1] *Financial Times*, 4 August 1971.

But he did not have to. His attitude was perfectly well known. It was re-stated in some public meetings organized on his own initiative by the Labour Committee for Europe in the early autumn, culminating in a rally on the eve of the party conference in Brighton.

If anything perhaps his position was over-publicized, even over-dramatized. While he was greeted at the Brighton meetings by shouts of 'Judas', the *Daily Mail* used metaphors comparing him to Jesus Christ. Acres of press speculation were devoted to whether he would resign from the Deputy Leadership, and his friends from the shadow cabinet, before 28 October. This was a possibility he considered in the summer. He felt at the time that perhaps he could not effectively speak against party policy or vote with the government and against the Leader of the party while himself remaining Deputy Leader of the party. Whatever the precise tactical debates between his shadow cabinet colleagues and himself may have been at various dates – and it seems that both Shirley Williams and Harold Lever at one stage wanted to resign – the issue was in the end resolved by as unspectacular a compromise as possible: at the party conference itself none of them spoke, though they made their position absolutely clear in speeches at the fringe meeting on the eve of the conference; in the House of Commons debate in October, again none of them spoke, though Roy Jenkins, Douglas Houghton, Shirley Williams, Harold Lever and George Thomson all voted for the government's motion. None of them resigned, since all of them intended within a matter of weeks to stand for re-election anyway. Roy Jenkins described the procedure of resigning for a few weeks as 'mock heroics' and declined to indulge in them. He had been elected Deputy Leader by an officially pro-Market party, so that he felt his legitimacy was if anything better than that of the Leader who had changed his tune since being elected. Besides, the power-base of the Deputy Leadership was a vital vantage point in the struggle within the party, which he had no right to surrender to the Left unless his position became absolutely intolerable.

His Bevanite opponents found this hard to take: they had all at various times retired or been relegated to the back benches; they did not see why Roy Jenkins should be made of so much finer porcelain that he could not endure sitting there with lesser mortals for a while too – and risk the possibility of not being re-elected. In fact, as we shall see – with the exception of Douglas Houghton, who was re-elected very narrowly – the rest all came back easily in the November elections.

Criticism was not confined to Bevanite sections of the party. One member of the shadow cabinet felt physically sickened that he should have to sit, day after day, at the same table with someone who, throughout their deliberations, reserved the right to flout their decisions, who never argued his case but merely assumed it was so well understood that to say some procedure was 'not acceptable' to him was enough. Others felt that Harold Wilson would have had a tougher time countering Roy Jenkins' open arguments than his manoeuvring friends, and complained that instead of mounting a powerful public campaign in the country or rising as the ex-Deputy Leader in the House of Commons Roy Jenkins had sulked silently in his tent, merely appearing (through journalists like John Harris of *The Economist*) to inspire contemptuous articles about his leader and his colleagues and to feed the press with his discontents. Perhaps the party had to be split anyway – though maybe the Parliamentary Party could have been persuaded to take the pro-entry line and then the Deputy Leader would have been seen to stand up for them against Conference – but at least a resignation by which he would have released himself for an all-out campaign would have made the split a clean one. Whether that would have handed over the party leadership to a section unrepresentative of the Labour electorate is another matter – one which touches on the core of the nature of the party.

The other criticism made of 'Sir Roy and the Knights of the Round Table' – and it was made by pro- as well as anti-Market MPs – was that, with the exception perhaps of William Rodgers' operation, it gave the appearance of a Bloomsbury in-group enjoying each other's company rather than of a broad-based grass-roots campaign. The 'endless little gatherings in Roy's room' (just opposite Harold Wilson's in the narrow and far from sound-proof corridor in which the shadow cabinet breathes, moves and has its being in the Palace of Westminster) put off some people who did not feel welcome in the Holy of Holies. Neither Roy Hattersley nor John Harris were universally popular as its prophets; not everyone in the Labour Movement felt comfortable at working lunches and meetings habitually held in the Reform Club; and whatever the substance, the appearance of a coterie of intimates was not sufficiently avoided: justified or not, this kind of criticism in the Labour Party can be extremely dangerous.

A second key role was played by Douglas Houghton. But where Roy Jenkins was constantly in the public eye, Douglas Houghton was scarcely mentioned in the press until October. This was as it had to be. As Party Chairman, it was his job to conciliate. As a Marketeer, it fell to him to be one of the main channels of communication between the Labour rebels and the inner core of the Conservative government – a job that Roy Jenkins clearly could not afford to do, but which a figure as personally unambitious and as widely respected as Douglas Houghton – a former Minister then in his seventies – could perform. He could 'bump into' William Whitelaw in various quiet places at short notice, providing what might be termed an 'unusual channel' even more over the Common Market issue than over the Industrial Relations Bill, over which the usual channels had broken down. Like other Marketeers, Douglas Houghton impressed on the Conservative leadership the importance of having a free vote. (Since Roy Jenkins was implying that he would vote even against a three-line whip, he could hardly at the same time plead for a free vote and remain convincing.) He failed to persuade the Conservatives to announce a free vote in plenty of time for the Labour Party to follow suit. But, as we have seen, the Conservatives had their own reasons for delaying as long as possible. Given the way the House of Commons operates, with long-standing friendships from school and university days and constant contact in the lobbies, the committee rooms, the tea room and the bar, across the barriers both of parties and of issues, information and speculative scenarios on both the government's and the Opposition MPs' intentions of course flowed freely between all four or five sides throughout this period in any case.

The third key figure among the Labour rebels was William Rodgers. In his early thirties he had been one of the master-minds behind the Campaign for Democratic Socialism in 1960–61 – the campaign to defend Hugh Gaitskell against the Left and, on the issue of unilateral nuclear disarmament, to 'fight, fight and fight again to bring back sanity to the party we love'.[1] He had thus become what the *Statesman* described as 'a practiced hand with round robins, petitions, circulars and card indexes'.[2] He was not a 'European' of the first hour, but had joined the Labour Common Market Committee at the same time as Anthony Crosland in early autumn 1962. At the time of Gaitskell's Brighton speech coming out against EEC membership William Rodgers, like Anthony Crosland, was one of those who refused to join in the ovation to the man whom he had done so much to maintain in his position.

[1] Hugh Gaitskell at the Scarborough party conference, 1960.
[2] Alan Watkins, 'The Non-Threat to Roy', *New Statesman*, 8 October 1971.

William Rodgers did not really at any time play a major role in the
Labour Committee for Europe as such. But, sensing the drift away from
the Market cause in the leadership in May, he engaged in a somewhat
different operation from the Committee's, an operation for which
indeed the Committee was less suited, but which he could run privately,
partly because he had been in the House longer than most of his generation and so could not very well be accused of brashness, partly because
he knew many of the older members of the House rather better than
some of the other young intellectuals, and partly because of his previous
organizing experience. The colleagues on whose judgment and support
he relied were more moderate and in many ways more representative of
the party as a whole than the militants of the Committee. It was the
respect in which the party held men like Ben Ford, Will Hannan,
George Strauss, Ifor Davies, Carol Johnson, Arthur Palmer, Dick
Mabon, Dick Crawshaw and Dick Buchanan that ensured that the
Marketeers should not simply be dismissed as a bright young coterie
cut off from the mainstream of party opinion. At the same time of
course William Rodgers was a close friend of Roy Jenkins, and while
he at no stage attempted publicly to involve the Deputy Leader in
what he was doing, the two men saw each other most weekends in
Berkshire, and their activities were clearly complementary.

Rodgers' first object was to try to obtain a free vote. The demand
for a free vote was also a good way to get people together initially. But
to obtain that he had to show that there were enough people ready to
defy a three-line whip for it to be counter-productive to impose one.
He therefore began sounding out his friends and those who had
expressed European sympathies – members of the Labour Committee
for Europe, signatories of the *Guardian* advertisement and others – to
see if they were for entry on the likely terms, and if moreover they
could see themselves voting in favour even if there were a three-line
whip bidding them vote against.[1] By October, however – indeed perhaps by the end of July – the self-generated momentum of Rodgers
and his friends had led them well beyond the demand merely for a free
vote.

William Rodgers was sharply criticized by some of his friends for

---

[1] In a memo of 30 June Rodgers estimated: 'It is likely that the actual vote in
favour of entry on a free vote with Harold Wilson against is in the range of 75–85.
This compares with perhaps 150 if Harold Wilson is in favour and 50 if there is a
three-line whip against.' (On the afternoon of the vote itself Rodgers' figure was a
majority of 111. The actual result turned out to be 112.)

priggishly excluding from his group any who were unsure of themselves on defying the whips. Why did he not try to persuade them, or
jolly them along – wasn't it moral blackmail just to say: 'I'm sorry, but
then we had better leave you off the list'? His reply was that every MP
was in a special position of his own and had to judge the political and
personal risks for himself – no one could take moral responsibility for
his colleagues. In any case MPs could not be bullied – they had to move
at their own pace: and it was better to have an absolutely coherent
group than to have it contaminated by faint hearts whose possible later
defection might demoralize the rest. That way, looking round the few
brief meetings they had, each could feel sure of the others – and indeed
letting people see the company they were in was the main point of
those meetings.

The group never really had a name. Invitations signed 'W. T.
Rodgers' called it simply 'some of us'. Their number quickly reached
forty or so in June and early July and by mid-July people began volun-
teering, until it became a risk that someone had been overlooked and
would take umbrage at not having been asked. Others regarded being
invited as an honour which they appreciated but explained why,
though they wanted to join, their constituency or other problems were
such that they could not commit themselves that far.

One of the chief dangers to this operation was the plan of a mass
abstention, canvassed among others by James Wellbeloved, a popular
figure in the party, a member of the Labour Committee for Europe and,
incidentally, William Rodgers' room-mate in the House, so that each
was fully aware of the other's operations. The Standing Orders allow
any Member to abstain on deeply felt grounds of conscience, and we
shall see that some twenty Labour MPs did indeed take that course. For
the Rodgers group, however, that was a dangerous because too easy
alternative. Seen from the Continent, it might have allowed the
government to achieve a plurality, but not a majority in favour of
entry. From a Social Democratic standpoint, in particular, to have
entered the EEC on a vote in which no Labour MPs or only a tiny
minority of Labour MPs had voted in favour would be the worst
possible augury for future collaboration. The party – Harold Wilson
included – needed a bridgehead to Europe, which only a substantial
positive vote in favour could provide. Moreover, if the target were
mere abstention, the danger of a division between rebels who would
insist on voting for and those who wanted only to abstain, the danger
of a drift from abstention into a reluctant vote with the party, and the

danger of not getting a free vote by not posing a credible threat to the whips' authority would be too great. In the end William Rodgers challenged Jim Wellbeloved to bring him five people who would otherwise vote against entry but would despite a three-line whip abstain in the interests of broader unity. When not one was forthcoming, Wellbeloved acknowledged defeat and William Rodgers went ahead. Before Parliament rose it was decided to sign a letter to the whips saying simply: 'We feel that you should know that we are amongst those who intend to vote for entry into the Common Market on the terms which have been negotiated.'

It was not surprising that Harold Wilson, at a meeting of the Parliamentary Labour Party in July which was as usual fully reported to the press by its Chairman, Douglas Houghton, lost his temper over what was going on. The *Evening Standard* came out with a headline 'Rodgers' Challenge to Wilson' when a meeting between the two was arranged: but Harold Wilson, asked direct whether he wanted this counting of heads to stop, said no. Nevertheless relations obviously remained strained. At the Brighton party conference, on the night of the vote against entry, William Rodgers slipped enough information to the press for the result of the vote to be almost overshadowed in some of the papers by speculation as to the size of the Westminster revolt against that Brighton decision. The anti-Marketeers in the party were furious at this by no means unsuccessful attempt to steal their thunder.

The most testing time, however, was yet before the rebels. Many of them felt that it was best to face their Constituency General Management Committees shortly before 28 October, and get the painful moment over with before they trod the lobby: most of them had not thought it right to give an absolute commitment to defy a three-line whip before they knew that such a whip would be applied. The weekend of 24 October saw the emergence of constituency problems in more than one case. In several cases, acute difficulties between the Member and his constituency party were never resolved.

The rebels remember this as a time of tremendous friendship and mutual loyalty, a major emotional experience in their political lives. No one who was in touch with the group during that period could fail to note the *camaraderie* of those who chose to treat the EEC issue as a moral or overriding political issue to which party tactics had to be sacrificed. When young intellectuals got jumpy, older trade unionists would steady them. When any one of them was speaking in the debates, the others would try to get into the Chamber quickly to show their support. William Rodgers was a universal aunt and father confessor, discreet but tough. As one of the anti-Marketeers put it: 'He's very good at achieving the aims he sets himself, but making himself popular in the Parliamentary Party is not one of them.' His essential function was to keep people in touch with each other, and, by reassuring them about each other's determination, to turn what might have become a collection of dispirited stragglers into an army confident of its own strength.

Immediately after the conference, William Rodgers, with Ben Ford, Dickson Mabon, Arthur Palmer (a Co-operative Member in his late fifties) and Carol Johnson (a former secretary of the Parliamentary Party in his late sixties and a long-standing European), saw the Chief Whip. It was said that Robert Mellish had had instructions not to receive the round robin from them. This was just as well, since they had already decided not to let him see the names on it. He knew them well enough to believe their figure of over fifty, and also that they thought they could make it over sixty before the vote. But until Tuesday 26 October the whips thought that signing a letter was one thing, and actually voting with the government would be another.

In the week before the vote the rebels got the impression that the whips, in an attempt to spread alarm and despondency, were deliberately rumouring the defection of one rebel after another at the rate of about one a day. These, however, were defections from the *Guardian* advertisement of the Labour Committee for Europe: the Rodgers group kept its list a closely guarded secret and was truthfully able, in each of these cases, to deny that the names in question figured on their letter. Two nights before the vote the whips in effect conceded defeat: they began circulating numbers of possible rebels which could hardly be attained, so that the actual numbers should, on the night, seem more like a victory for them.

When the group held its last meeting in early October, after the party conference but before the Parliamentary Party's decision, William Rodgers had ruled out of order any discussion of what the shadow cabinet members ought to do, or how they should all vote on the implementing legislation, and closed the meeting with the words: 'So we'll meet in the lobby, then.' That was where, in fact (with one exception and four additions) all sixty-six of them did meet. (The exception was Ronald Brown, Lord George-Brown's brother. He was subjected to severe pressures from the extreme Left wing of his rather rough Shoreditch and Finsbury constituency party. Delegates lobbied him with threats on the afternoon of the vote, said they would sit all evening until after the vote to take immediate measures as soon as the vote was taken, and at the last moment secured an abstention which his friends, under the circumstances, saw more in sorrow than in anger.)

This was, as some Marketeers like to put it, a rather pure and disinterested period in British politics – though perhaps some of them saw the positive courage of their friends with greater clarity than the less elevated behaviour of their acquaintances. Of course the Marketeers included people with a vested interest of some kind in Europe – people who enjoyed their trips to the Council of Europe in Strasbourg, or who foresaw more business, or who – even had they wanted to change their minds – had as much to lose in reputation by changing it so late as by sticking to their guns. But there were others, by no means friends of Roy Jenkins or members of any élite circle of intellectuals, who simply felt that this was the right thing to do, and did it without counting the cost. Some were in their last Parliament, and the cost was in personal relations more than in professional life: others felt that they might as well do this and then call it a day. 'Kamikaze pilots' like Ray Gunter and Austen Albu were to carry their support for entry to the length of regular abstention over the implementing legislation. But someone like Pat Duffy, a bachelor of around fifty who had spent years in trying to get back into the House, had nothing to gain and a very great deal to lose. Ivor Richard was warned in advance that he would be unseated if he voted for entry, and was. Dick Leonard declared in the October debate 'in full knowledge of the consequences to myself' that he would vote for; when Norwich North chose a candidate in early 1972 Dick Leonard, whose constituency was redistributed, was, with Ivor Richard, excluded from the short list not least on the grounds of his defiance of the whip.

The sixty-nine who voted for entry had with them the good wishes of the twenty who abstained – and also of another twenty or so who bitterly wished that they could have voted for entry or abstained, but who feared that their situation might have become intolerable. The abstainers included at least one whom the rebels themselves had to persuade not to vote with them. Alan Fitch had resigned from the whips' office over the issue, and his abstention, as more than one put it, was worth several votes against. He was a miner and an older man; had he lost his seat as a result of voting for the motion his personal prospects outside Parliament would not have been something the rebels could have on their conscience.

Those who voted against entry included two whips whom the rebels did not want to see resign their positions: they were of more use to them in the whips' office than in demonstratively leaving it. Robert Mellish, the Chief Whip, was himself at least in theory a Marketeer. He had indicated in early summer that a three-line whip against the principle of entry could be imposed only over his dead body, since he would feel bound to vote for it himself; but he now put party unity and discipline above the EEC issue. Yet perhaps it need not have come to this dilemma for him if he had gauged the state of feeling in the party more accurately earlier in 1971 and had stood up to Harold Wilson for his own convictions on the issue before the party leadership got itself committed the other way. Need there in fact have been a William Rodgers if Robert Mellish had performed more effectively? One could argue that the Parliamentary Party would never have turned against entry, that there would have been a free vote on 28 October, and that there would have been no party crisis in 1972 over the referendum issue if Robert Mellish had been a more sensitive whip and a less accommodating politician. On the morrow of the 28 October vote he declared himself, faced with this failure, ready to resign, though he was re-elected in November 1971.

Like their Conservative counterparts who voted with their party against their real wishes there were others who had been heavily leant on. Shirley Summerskill had appeared both on the Labour Committee for Europe list and in the *Guardian* advertisement, but at the last moment found constituency pressure building up. Walter Padley, with a similar record of European stands, was told by his union that he would not chair the Overseas Committee of the National Executive if he did not toe the party line and indeed might lose his seat on the Executive. Though revolt required considerable courage, particularly in Wales, and Walter Padley was far from well, his vote against entry was a disappointment to the Marketeers. Neither he nor Shirley Summerskill explained their position in the October debate. Leslie Huckfield, who had been first elected at the age of 25 in 1967 and was another Labour Committee for Europe and *Guardian* Marketeer, changed his line during the debate itself. Because he disliked the tone of the White Paper, which seemed to him to be written from the point of view of the Confederation of British Industry and was put forward by a party 'prepared to settle with Smith and in taking the line they have over the sale of arms to South Africa' and because he had other reservations as well, he finally voted against the motion. Sir Arthur Irvine – who had joined the Labour Committee for Europe in the 1961–63 period and signed the *Guardian* advertisement in 1971 – was even more explicit. He had found

a strong feeling in the country, which I cannot ignore, of hostility to the enterprise. . . . It would be arrogance on my part – arrogance and nothing else – to ignore or disregard this condition of public opinion. My intention is either to abstain or to vote against entry, and I still have a little time in which to consider which of these two courses to follow.[1]

He voted against entry, but found himself in difficulties with his local party all the same, on the grounds of not having spent enough time in the constituency. (In the end he was, however, readopted.)

The Brighton Conference

The eve of the conference in Brighton was marked by the usual rallies: one in the afternoon organized by the Labour Committee for Safeguards on the Common Market, one in the evening by the Labour Committee for Europe.

The EEC debate in Conference itself was held on the very first day, with the avowed intention of getting the most divisive issue out of the way as quickly as possible, cutting short any minority activities to oppose the Executive, and leaving plenty of time for the party to close ranks emotionally thereafter. Denis Healey opened the debate with a speech that was scarcely the best in his career, perhaps in part because, though he made it on his own insistence, he seemed embarrassed at making it at all:

I know I may be criticized for this, for reducing a great matter of historical importance to a question of the price of butter. I reject that criticism. I prefer to stand on the position where our greatest Labour Foreign Secretary, Ernie Bevin, stood when he told Conference a quarter of a century ago that he would want his foreign policy to be tested by whether it put an extra pat of butter on the plate of the ordinary man and woman in Britain.

The press cynically interpreted Healey's speech as an attempt to stay on the National Executive, where he occupied the seventh and last seat in the Constituency Party division. If so, he was successful, changing places with Tom Driberg to move up to sixth. But then there is no

[1] Hansard, 27 October 1971, cols 1953–9.

evidence that anyone was greatly helped or harmed in these 1971 NEC elections by their Common Market stand – Shirley Williams, who had herself expected to lose her seat in the women's section, retained it by a margin of a million votes, and only moved to fifth and last position because Eirene White zoomed from fifth to first. In the union division the three most prominent Marketeers, Tom Bradley, Fred Mulley and Jim Diamond, who had received 11·9 million votes between them in 1970, still polled 11·6 million in October 1971, Tom Bradley (who was Vice-Chairman of the Labour Committee for Europe and Chairman of the Trade Union Committee for Europe) recovering from the major setback his Common Market stand had provoked the year before: from 4·9 million votes in 1969 down to 3·2 in 1970 and now back to 3·9 million votes. The two who just did not make it in the Constituency division changed places: Anthony Crosland dropped from 240,000 to 213,000 while Eric Heffer rose from 225,000 to 261,000 votes: both had been Europeans, both by that time appeared headed for the 'No' lobby on 28 October. Certainly in retrospect – perhaps even before the event – there was little reason to believe that Denis Healey would have lost his seat on the Executive whatever his stance had been. On the other hand, in the election of the shadow cabinet in November he dropped from second to twelfth (bottom) place, having presumably lost some of his old friends without making any new ones among his former opponents.

An amendment to the Executive's motion calling for a referendum was moved by Brian Stanley of the Post Office Engineers, but never really discussed: in the afternoon it was heavily defeated by over 4 million to under 2 million votes. On the original full agenda there were motions or amendments for the party to pledge itself, when it returned to power, 'to unilaterally abrogate the Treaty of Rome' (Wandsworth Putney CLP), 'to take Britain out' (Chelsea CLP), or to 'repeal all relevant legislation . . . and withdraw from the Community' (Harrow Central CLP). A prominent trade union leader, presumably wanting to hold in reserve certain *casus belli* for the future, was heard to observe of all the withdrawal motions: 'We don't want that – not this year.' So, as an anti-Market resolution, Composite 35 was the most radical: but what it called for was the withdrawal of Britain's application, not of Britain once she had become a member.

The Clerical and Administrative Workers' Union had submitted a resolution accepting the outcome of the negotiations and recognizing 'that failure by Britain to sign the Treaty of Accession would have most serious consequences and repercussions upon the country, particularly in respect of future investment and employment levels'. The representative of the union, however, went to the wrong hotel for the compositing meeting, and arrived too late for any of this draft resolution to be included. Composite 36, which expressed the pro-Market viewpoint and accepted 'that the terms negotiated are not unreasonable in the circumstances', was in fact lumbered with a Knutsford CLP counter-attack criticizing the Executive for 'committing the party to a financially crippling national campaign' in advance of a conference decision. The Knutsford rider was to prove the composite's undoing. Few pro-Europeans wanted to push their case that far: with the General and Municipal Workers abstaining, the vote would have badly understated support for entry, and at the end of the debate Composite 36 was swiftly withdrawn.

The debate thereafter took a one-sided turn, pretty correctly anticipating in the balance of the speakers the balance of the final vote. Out of some 21 floor speakers, only 4 spoke in favour – Lord George-Brown, Michael Barnes, and two more trade unionists (one of whom unfortunately referred to the 'ECC' throughout his speech). This was not entirely the fault of the Chairman, who had promised that if things became too unbalanced by the luck of who caught his eye, he would selectively redress the balance. Nevertheless the Marketeers claimed to see subtle partisanship in Ian Mikardo's handling of the debate: some of them even regretted the elaborate one-to-one fairness of July, in which they had fired off some of their best guns, and which now justified a more representative selection of speakers. But then Ian Mikardo never pretended to be impartial in his views, and he expressed them both in his opening Chairman's address immediately before the debate (condemning the terms as 'virtually unconditional surrender') and in his comments from the chair thereafter. He insisted on having Lord George-Brown's credentials as a conference member checked before calling him to speak in the latter part of the debate, and later remarked 'George is George and never the twain shall meet' (at which one delegate called out 'Don't be so bloody unkind').

Compared with the Central Hall battle of July, the Brighton debate cannot be said to have taken place at any very high level of logic, relevance or originality. The Marketeers' question-begging pleonasm – if Britain had grown at the same rate as the Six, we would on average be £7 better off – was yet again countered by the expatriation allowance of British war-cemetery workers as proof that German workers were worse off than British. What is good for ICI or British Leyland, a Lambeth delegate proclaimed as self-evident, must be bad for the British worker. Pictures were painted of disarray in the Health Service once consultants took to nipping across to Brussels to perform an operation for a few thousand guineas while the queues lengthened for British patients. The Common Market deserved an entry in the *Guinness Book of Records* as the biggest pig in a poke of all time. Parliament, it was repeatedly asserted, would be reduced to being no more than a county council. ('Go on', muttered an ex-Minister at the side of the hall, 'make it a parish council' and quoted a Jewish proverb: 'If you must eat pig, let the lard really drip off your mouth.') Another speaker did make it a parish council. Perhaps speakers had been looking at the exhibition of Labour publicity material in the bar, with its advice: 'Propaganda is a coarse art: and a mild approach invites a mild response.'

The debate was wound up for the Executive by Jim Callaghan with what one paper described as 'his usual mixture of geniality and guile'. According to several members of the Executive, that body had wanted the emphasis to be laid on the call for a general election, on unity on 28 October, and no commitment to be made for the party when it came to power again: the Executive had not instructed him to suggest the possibility of withdrawal from the Community by a future Labour government. Jim Callaghan's speech certainly succeeded in throwing the whole onus of any and every consequential disadvantage of joining on to the Conservative government. It was his object, as he said afterwards, to make sure that they would have to carry the can all the way. But he also went on to warn the Community that a future Labour government would re-open the very principles which the last Labour government had accepted before it began its negotiations – and without whose acceptance the other five, let alone France, would hardly have conceived a negotiation as being feasible:

If Mr Heath signs the Treaty of Rome to come into force in January 1973, knowing that he does not carry the British people with him, then he must expect the issue to remain open and to be argued about. [*Applause.*]

I should like to indicate what will be the points of the argument. What will need to be reopened will be the test questions that were put to Mr Heath by M. Pompidou and tamely accepted by him. Let me remind you. I have given you two already. 'Do you accept the CAP?' Mr Heath said, 'Yes'. The Labour Party says 'No'.

'Do you accept the unanimity rule that alterations can only be made by unanimous agreement?' In the case of the CAP we do not accept it.

'Do you agree to work for an economic and monetary union?' Mr Heath said 'Yes'. The Labour Movement says 'No'.

'Will you turn away from the open seas and moor yourself to Europe?' Mr Heath said 'Yes'. We say 'No'.

The two votes that were taken on substantive motions showed that, measured by the totals of the union and constituency block votes, there was no majority in the conference for opposition to entry on any terms, but a huge majority against 'entry on Tory terms'.[1] In favour of entry on the likely terms to the point of defying the party executive were only four unions of any size: Lord Cooper's General and Municipal Workers with 650,000 votes, D. H. Davies' Iron, Steel, and Kindred Trades Association with 91,642 votes, Roy Grantham's

[1] The number of delegates, organizations represented, and their voting power was as follows

	Delegates	Number of organizations	Votes
Trade unions	605	59	5,530,000
Constituency Labour Parties	557	548	674,000
Co-operative organizations, Socialist societies and Federations of Labour Parties	23	19	41,000
Total	1,185	626	6,245,000

Votes for Composite 35 (proposed by Liverpool, Walton CLP for withdrawal of application)

For	2,005,000
Against	3,082,000

Vote on Amendment A to Resolution 16 (P.O. Engineers for referendum)

For	1,928,000
Against	4,161,000

Vote for Resolution 16 (proposed by NEC)

For	5,073,000
Against	1,032,000

Clerical and Administrative Workers with 80,530 votes and Jack Peel's Dyers, Bleachers and Textile Workers with 49,000 votes. Between them these four cast just over 811,000 votes. The total of votes cast against the Executive resolution came to 1,032,000 – 221,000 votes coming from other smaller unions and from constituency parties. (The minimum vote per constituency party is 1,000 votes, but 82 of the 630 constituencies were not represented by any CLP at the conference – usually for lack of funds, either to pay their subscriptions, or to send a delegate, or both.) The Labour Committee for Europe issued a statement after the vote claiming that about 40% of constituency parties had voted against the platform – clearly a propagandist piece of psephological interpretation. Other estimates varied from 20 to 33% of constituencies.

At the other end of the scale, the ranks of the 'antis' (who polled 2,005,000 votes for Composite 35) included Hugh Scanlon's Engineering and Foundry Workers with 887,558 votes, Joe Gormley's Mineworkers with 287,063 votes, and Clive Jenkins' Association of Scientific Technical and Managerial Staffs with 120,000 votes. The Agricultural Workers (with 85,000 votes) felt so strongly that they voted for Composite 35 and abstained on the Executive's resolution.

In the middle were those unions that supported the Executive both against Composite 35 and in favour of the NEC's own resolution – with Jack Jones' Transport and General Workers in an intermediate position abstaining on Composite 35 and voting for the Executive on the successful resolution.

But of course it was not simply a debate about the EEC. It was at least as much a debate about the balance of power within the Labour Party and indeed about the nature of the Labour Party itself. In Hugh Gaitskell's time the tension had already become apparent between the well-educated middle-class donnish element in the party – those whom it was easy to imagine sitting in a street café sipping absinthe, as someone had at the time said of Roy Jenkins and Anthony Crosland, and those who, without the experience of early travel and without the comfort (when they did have to travel) of speaking some foreign language, distrusted foreigners, foreign foods and foreign ways. 'And tell me – is there much vice in Strasbourg?', one Labour MP once asked on a visit to the Council of Europe. Of course the educational dimension was not a complete indicator of attitudes. One leading anti-Marketeer who was a former don, so rumour related, always carried his food abroad with him in little plastic bags. But one can see the delegates' point when they were handed at the entrance to the Top Rank Centre a flysheet by a Marketeering MP positively redolent of intellectual lyricism:

For those of us who love the poetry of Victor Hugo, the music of Beethoven or the sculptures of Michelangelo, who share the ethics of Aristotle and the Judaic-Christian ideal that are all part of Europe's heritage, today's artificial divisions seem about as sensible as customs posts on the Pennines to keep out Yorkshire wool.

One could forgive them if they drew the conclusion that for those who did not love Victor Hugo's poetry – might in fact not be quite sure that he had written any – the Channel did not seem all that artificial a division. Thus Eric Hammond of the Electricians union denounced the pro-Market campaign as having displayed élitist contempt for the intelligence of working people: it had been with that same word 'élitist' that Anthony Crosland had dissociated himself from his pro-European friends in the summer.

The issue was put in constitutional terms by Norman Atkinson, Jim Callaghan's rival for the Treasurership of the party, when he swept aside all the certificates issued by Michael Stewart, George Brown, Roy Jenkins and George Thomson that the terms would have been accepted by the Labour government, had it stayed in power. (Privately one or two of them were prepared to admit that the Labour government might well have had to accept worse.) What mattered was not whether a Labour government but whether the party conference would or would not accept those terms. And since on that score there was no doubt (the only doubt being if those opposed to the Executive could even muster a million votes) there followed the second question: would the Parliamentary Party vote as the conference decided? It was the old question that had divided Clem Attlee and Harold Laski in 1945, Hugh Gaitskell and Frank Cousins in 1960. Jack Brooks of the Cardiff South-East CLP addressed himself in the afternoon to 'the Labour Committee for Europe and George Brown in particular' and any MP who might vote for entry: 'I hope there are consequences. If they go into the lobbies and support the most hard-faced bunch of freebooters since the coupon men of 1918, this party will never forgive them. (*Loud and prolonged applause.*)' John Mendelson, not exactly noted for party discipline in the past, delivered much the same message in one of the few good speeches of the debate. And two days later Ian Mikardo, the Party Chairman, spelt out the message at a Tribune Group meeting:

If, as the newspapers are saying this morning, a squalid deal has been done to allow 60 pro-Market Labour MPs to eat their cake and have it – a deal which will make us offensive to our friends and a welcome laughing stock to our enemies – then those 60 constituency parties will have the right, and some of them may exercise it, to pass a verdict on that shabby manœuvre.[1]

So the issue of party discipline, which had simmered away since the late spring, came right out into the open. And it was on the night the Executive motion was passed by a crushing 5 : 1 majority that the Marketeers of the party let it be known that they had commitments from over fifty back-benchers and nearly twenty front-benchers that, come hell or high water, they would vote on 28 October for entry into the EEC.

It was against morning headlines, therefore, such as 'Up to Twenty may quit with Mr Jenkins' (*The Times*) and 'Market could get 70 Labour Votes' (*Guardian*) that Harold Wilson rose to make a fine press-ridiculing and Tory-bashing speech on the Tuesday. He contrived within sixty seconds both to deplore that 'within the Conservative Party, any who hold views opposed to that of the leadership have been subjected to all the pressures, direct pressures, constituency pressures, of which the Chief Whip of Suez is a past master' and also to claim 'the right, I have the duty, to enjoin this movement now to close ranks'. But then there followed an interesting passage:

There is not one Labour Member of Parliament who could have been elected by his own efforts. He is where he is because of the efforts and dedication of thousands upon thousands of those represented by delegates here today. And he is elected to be in his place and to do the job he was sent to do.

Reading about this Conference you would think it's only about one thing. How X or Y or Z is going to vote on 28 October. Conference has declared its voice on that by 'inviting' members to follow its decision.

But 28 October is not an end but a beginning. And the whole Parliamentary Party will fight against the mass of consequential legislation, main legislation, subordinate legislation, statutory instruments, Orders in Council which the Government will endeavour to force through.

I cannot imagine a single Labour Member who, faced with this legislation, will not be in the lobbies against the Government.

While a good many delegates sat on their hands through all these calls to unity, the press was quick to note the distinction implied between a vote on 28 October and opposition to the implementing legislation,

[1] *The Times*, 7 October 1971.

and to sense discreet hints of a compromise with those who could no longer be stopped from voting with the government on the night: that having asserted the principle once, they should then make life so difficult for the government subsequently as to force it out of office if the Conservative anti-Marketeers could be persuaded to abstain or even vote with the Opposition. Some of the press talked of a 'deal' to that effect – a story, of course, vehemently denied in that form by both Harold Wilson and Roy Jenkins, on neither of whom it would have appeared to reflect credit if true and between whom communication had indeed remained almost non-existent except in public. Moreover, anyone familiar with the organizational problems involved (the seventy had never even met in one room) knew that as a group the Marketeers could not physically have accepted such a compromise anyway. On the other hand Douglas Houghton was actively working for a formula of this kind, and since Harold Wilson was confronted with a situation in which unity on the night of 28 October could obviously no longer be achieved, it would have been only sensible for him to try to establish such unity for the long-drawn-out difficult legislative processes thereafter by not insisting too hard on what he could no longer hope to obtain on the 28th.[1]

It was also a shrewd move on his part to force the Marketeers in Brighton to think ahead – a challenge they were unable to meet with any concerted attitude: some of them in the hotel bars and at the Mayor's reception in the Pavilion that night appeared willing to accept the olive branch, some vehemently rejected it on the grounds that, if you will the end, you must will the means, and some talked of abstention on some consequential votes, but not on others. Indeed many of them had only the vaguest ideas as to the form the implementing legislation would take, the procedure the government intended to use, and the number of divisions involved; moreover, there was still that other strategic unknown in the calculation that could make a crucial

---

[1] It is an illustration of one of the dilemmas of any writer on contemporary politics that David Wood, the seasoned political editor of *The Times* whose deep concern for British radical politics emerges normally only in the serious sobriety of his reporting, next morning wrote on the front page: 'I am anxious to make it clear that Mr Wilson has left me in no doubt tonight that he wishes to be regarded as a far simpler interpreter of politics than I. He insists that the words in his speech here on Tuesday should be taken at face value, and that nothing is further from his mind than any attempt to reconcile Mr Jenkins with the party majority at the expense of the Conference decision reached on Monday. I can say only that such an attitude in a party leader bears little relation to the politics I know.'

difference to their attitude: how many of the Conservatives would be abstaining and voting against the government at each stage.

As has already been remarked, the Labour Marketeers had to hope that as many Conservatives would vote with the government as possible so that, the government having provided its own majority in any case, they could not be accused of keeping Edward Heath in power. Their votes would simply be Harold Wilson's reinsurance policy for acceptance of the Labour Party on the Continent after Britain joined. That is why it was part of the tactics of the Rodgers group not to overplay their hand or to show it too soon: it was in their interests that the Tory whips and the constituency parties should help as many Conservative deviants as possible to see the light and pledge themselves to support the government without knowing whether the government could, that night, in fact do without their support. Yet they could not delay in showing their own strength to the party leadership either, if they wanted to try to prevent a three-line whip, stop the leadership from overcommitting itself to reprisals, and avoid accusations of underhand surprise tactics. In fact, as Wilson's speech showed, their timing at this stage was well chosen.

Harold Wilson, however, had also played back skilfully. He rubbed their noses in the unpleasant prospect that they were in for a tactical no less than a moral dilemma. How could the 'men of principle' vote against measures without which entry into the EEC would be impossible – yet how could they vote for them repeatedly over a long period without isolating themselves emotionally and politically from their party? Tactically how could they keep a Tory government in power as its policies unfolded through 1972 – with its social policies, with rising unemployment, and the glimmer of a settlement with Rhodesia as an even nastier spectre on the horizon – yet how could they hope to see Britain enter the EEC if the government fell on a substantive or procedural vote designed to get Britain in? As they left Brighton, it was already less the question of what would happen on the 28th than what would happen in the lobbies in the long nights of 1972 and what that would do to the party and to their own positions that gave the Labour Marketeers grim food for thought.

Edward Heath's decision on 18 October to allow a free vote hit the Labour leadership hard. They seemed not to have reckoned with that possibility. There was jubilation among many ordinary Members in the tea rooms, in the belief that they – and the party – were now off the hook. The news came as the Shadow Cabinet was just adjourning, and it hurriedly reconvened for another brief session. Harold Wilson, at that point, seemed to one or two of his colleagues ready to have a free vote on the Labour side too. But the majority in the Shadow Cabinet found such a late about-turn intolerable. Next day, 19 October, the Parliamentary Party met in a crowded and turbulent meeting. Three votes were taken: each of them surprised the leadership and to some extent even surprised the Marketeers, some of whose supporters were absent. On Michael Stewart's motion for entry on the terms agreed in preference to abandonment of the application the Marketeers polled 87 votes against 151. On Harold Wilson's recommendation to oppose entry on the government's terms 89 voted against, 159 voted for. Thirdly there was a motion for a free vote tabled by William Hamilton. Robert Mellish asked the party to reject it; but he did so in terms that suggested to many that a free vote would in fact be granted, but that it was not for the Parliamentary Party to impose itself on the whips. On this motion 111 Labour MPs voted for, 140 against. As *The Economist*, not without malice but evidently on eye-witness authority, reported:

Mr Anthony Crosland voted both for Europe and a free vote, and Mr Denis Healey against both, though holding up his hand in such a diffident manner it was difficult for many to see what he was doing. Not so Mr Benn. It was his finest hour. With radiant face, the great advocate of participation held up his hand so long that it was still aloft when the tellers came to tell the Chairman the result.[1]

A few hours later the Shadow Cabinet, failing to agree on any amendment that might have allowed the party to vote solidly immediately prior to the now inevitably split vote on the government's motion, left it to the Chief Whip to decide whether to put on a three-line whip. Robert Mellish decided to go ahead as planned, and a three-line whip was duly imposed.

In the great debate that began in the House on Thursday 21 October one after another the Labour Marketeers, doubters, and antis declared their position prior to the vote. But from the point of view of intra-party politics the most interesting speech of all was not made on the floor of the House at all, but at a long-standing lunch date with the lobby correspondents by Douglas Houghton, the Parliamentary Party's Chairman. With Harold Wilson's full foreknowledge he enunciated what became known as 'the Houghton doctrine'. He distinguished

[1] *The Economist*, 23 October 1971, p. 25.

sharply between the vote of principle on the Thursday night and the consequential legislation to follow in 1972, and suggested a 'firm assurance about the future': 'This Government, like all governments, must be able to govern and get their legislation through on their own. From next week they will be on their own.' It was a formula that made explicit, and accepted on his own behalf at least, the very same offer which it had been so hotly denied was implicit in Harold Wilson's Brighton speech. (It soon fell by the wayside as far as quite a few of the pro-Marketeers were concerned, but it was thought necessary at the time.)

In the debate in the House of Lords, meantime, Lord George-Brown explained the change in the Labour leadership's policy. He saw it in internal power terms: 'Let us not be mealy-mouthed that it is largely because of an accidental change in the leadership of a few large component organizations which are forcing decisions on those who now claim to run the party to which I belong.'[1]

The vote of 28 October was only two days away.

[1] Hansard (Lords), 26 October 1971, col. 566.

Newspaper has always had its uses, for table cloths, and wrapping up fish and chips.

> Brother A. Jones

Television and Radio

It is a moot point how far the media of communication – by selection or emphasis, by slanting or tainting the message which it is their business to convey – can themselves sway popular opinion on an issue like British entry into the Common Market. The events they report, the governmental actions and the Opposition reactions which they portray probably account for far more of the fluctuations of the opinion polls than any particular commentator's film script, any particular leading article, or even a steady succession of such persuasive presentations. We shall see in examining the opinion poll figures that sometimes they swung through large arcs without any perceptible changes of attitude and of persuasive effort on the part of the journalists and broadcasters; and that sometimes popular opinion swung in parallel with such efforts.

At the time of the 1961–63 exercise an opinion poll divided readers of the *Express* from those of the *Mirror* – the two biggest newspapers diametrically opposed to each other on EEC entry: the balance of opinion on the issue appeared to be almost the same in both readerships. It is not easy these days to find a sample of people who are representative of the public and yet unexposed to television and radio. At first blush one might think that such a comparison would yield a more significant result. But in their study of *Political Change in Britain* David Butler and Donald Stokes say that

This is not what our evidence suggests . . . the media do give attention to the same issues, events and men; they borrow extensively from each other; and their audiences have many dispositions and beliefs in common. As a result, the experience of following politics by print and broadcast is in many ways more alike than different.[1]

[1] Butler and Stokes, op. cit., Penguin, Harmondsworth, 1971, pp. 280–1.

Where Butler and Stokes, looking at the Common Market issue, did find major correlations between the media and their audience was when they lumped all the media together and simply tested attitudes against exposure to political communication. In 1964 opinion was fairly evenly divided, while by 1966 three-quarters of those who voiced an opinion wanted Britain in Europe.

This change was very closely related to the extent of the voter's exposure to political information. . . . Although the Common Market gained ground at all levels between 1964 and 1966 it was among those who were most exposed to political communication that the most spectacular increase occurred. Indeed the most attentive group swung from an even division in 1964 to a four to one majority for entry in 1966, whereas opinion in the least informed group remained nearly evenly divided.[1]

That this should have happened while those least exposed to political communication were swinging towards Labour, and the Labour Party was swinging towards Europe, is particularly significant:

The key to this difference lies in the demands which the two kinds of problem made on the voter. The appraisal of alternative European policies remained throughout the period a task that was beyond much of the electorate. But appraising the parties . . . was a task that nearly everyone could undertake in some way.[2]

It is a pity that, for the period 1970–72 with which we are dealing, there do not yet appear to be any analogous field studies. Failing them, all one can do is to sketch the efforts of the media on the one side, and the attitudes of the broad public on the other. Precise chains of cause and effect, though sometimes clearly disproved by the sequence of events, cannot be regarded as proven even where the time sequence is compatible with causal relationships. In any case the events themselves, which no journalist or broadcaster could have neglected, government pronouncements and parliamentary exchanges, the campaigns of enthusiasts in the country both for and against, and the thickening air of impending decision were bound to make their impact regardless of the personal views of proprietors (who formed an important ingredient in the demonology of anti-Marketeers), advertisers (whom the anti-Marketeers also made responsible for corrupting the media)

[1] Butler and Stokes, pp. 278–9.   [2] ibid., pp. 279–80.

and communicators (who were seen as smart alecks ready to fall for any new line that made a story, while traditional loyalties were considered old hat).

That having been said, there can be no doubt that if the media had any net influence, that influence would have tended on balance to be heavily for rather than against entry. There are several reasons for that presumption. The first of them is intimately bound up with a very genuine problem for those media, like television and radio, that felt themselves enjoined to keep a strict or rough balance between pro- and anti-Marketeers. The message that if the British went in they would be ruled by foreigners who would put up all food prices was simple and easily transmitted by word of mouth and unsophisticated methods of communication. For a television programme to explore the institutional mechanics of Community rule-making in however objective a way was already to dispel certain of the more naive implications of that earlier message.[1] For another programme to go over lower lettuce, tomato and fruit prices and higher meat and butter prices was already to confuse the black and white sterotype.[2] Whether or not Neil Marten or Peter Shore then appeared in order to debate with Harold Lever or Geoffrey Rippon, the argument had already been lifted on to a different level of information and discourse. Moreover, even to make fears explicit, and certainly to dispel ignorance, was likely if anything to redress the balance of a heavily unfavourable public opinion. In that sense any coverage of events, any background information, any political discussion of the issue was by its very nature, however formally balanced, likely to help the Market cause. Or, as one broadcaster put it, 'silence would have been the only real neutrality'.

Moreover, the very vividness of television or radio presentation could prove an embarrassment to any man or group who has given heavy hostages to fortune (or to videotape) at an earlier stage of a variegated career. The question direct, posed before million of viewers, could drive home a point with an immediacy and resonance no parliamentary exchange ever could. It was one thing for Roy Jenkins to write later, in April 1972, 'This constant shifting of the ground I cannot accept': it was another for Kenneth Allsop a few nights afterwards to play back the sound and picture of Harold Wilson on *Election Forum* less than two years previously – insisting that it was Parliament which must decide whether Britain was to enter the Common Market,

---

[1] ITN *News at Ten*, 29 June 1971.   [2] ITN *News at Ten*, 1 July 1971.

DIPLOMACY AND PERSUASION

and replying to a question on whether he would not at the last minute
allow a referendum:

The answer to that is no. I have given my answer many times, and I don't
change it because polls go either up or down. Heavens, when the polls have been
28 points against me it hasn't made any difference to going on with policies I
knew to be unpopular. I'm not going to trim to win votes on a question like
that. The answer is I shall not change my attitude on that.[1]

Of course there were those, on the government side, who felt that
the elaborate parity systems to which television and radio adhered on
the issue had just the opposite consequences. By continually putting
on the screen a few individuals like Enoch Powell and Neil Marten, was
television not imputing a totally inflated importance to two rather
minor strains of the Conservative Party in Parliament? The fact that
the Labour Marketeers also got their quarter of broadcast time alongside the Labour anti-Marketeers was little comfort. (In July 1971 with
Denis Healey's change of attitude the quadripartite formula in fact
gave way to a quintupartite one, with the Labour 'may-be's' also given
a share of a two-and-a-half hour programme.[2]) But perhaps the net
result of this parity system was to present the Labour Party as far more
split than the Conservatives and thereby if anything to make life less
difficult for the government.

The second reason why the media (in so far as they influenced things)
were more likely to have an influence in favour of entry was that the
communicators were naturally enough on the side of reflection,
criticism and innovation, of internationalism rather than nationalism,
reason rather than sentiment, and that the balance of their views –
there can be no doubt about it – was more favourable to entry than
popular opinion at large. We shall see that the bulk of newspaper
opinion was in favour: on the air, while maintaining the parity formula,
the duty to inform coincided with the inclination to dispel irrational
and to discuss rational objections. Nor would any anti-Marketeer on
the media have thought it possible or desirable to try to minimize
debate on the issue. Where radio and television was concerned, both
BBC and ITV in fact embarked on major programme series to bring
the issue home to the people.

The biggest daily public affairs outlet in the country – probably

[1] BBC *Twenty-Four Hours*, 10 April 1972.
[2] BBC Radio Four, *Your Voice in the Great Debate*, 13 July 1971.

leading the *Daily Mirror* by a short head – was the Independent
Television *News at Ten*. Its daily audience, at a peak viewing hour every
weekday evening, was estimated at up to twelve or fifteen million
people. Nigel Ryan, the ITN's editor-in-chief, was as we have seen a
participant in the 'media breakfasts'. He decided that every day for a
whole month this half-hour programme of solid news should carry a
four- to six-minute item explaining some aspect of the Common Market.
'Every tool of the TV trade we could muster was pressed into service' –
films, interviews, diagrams, animations, and pungent (if at times
technically not quite exact) expositions, with Peter Snow as the anchor
man. 'Stretching our role to the limit, we deemed it to be news, but
with the issue in the air in July, it sat very well with the news and
fitted easily into it.' Though information such as 'the total number of
Italians working in the Common Market outside Italy, which was
554,000 in 1961, went up by only 43,000 to 597,000 by 1968'[1] cannot
have made altogether riveting show business, ITN was pleased
by a very good response in letters and telephone calls (they received
only two letters accusing them of bias). More surprisingly, the ratings
of the number of sets switched to the programme did not fall. Eighteen
such items were broadcast between 28 June and 23 July, on subjects
that varied from taxation and farming to regional policy and sovereignty: altogether they provided eighty minutes' viewing in short
handy packages. If the media had anything to do with the decided
trend in popular opinion between late June and late July (and this cannot be taken as altogether proven), then the intensive effort made by
Nigel Ryan and his team was no doubt one of the largest single new
factors on the scene to which that influence would have to be attributed.

Other independent television companies of course made their own
efforts in addition to the ITN news programmes which they carried.
There were features and debates of various kinds, including some quite
lengthy items – some of them special one-off programmes, some as part
of normal political series. In this the independent channels resembled
the BBC – though the BBC started much earlier and also carried far
more such material. *Panorama*, the weekly political programme,
devoted half an hour to the subject in April 1971, one and a half hours
in May (including the Pompidou interview just before the summit
meeting), an hour in June, part of two more programmes in July, and
after the summer break returned to the subject on 25 October with a

[1] ITN *News at Ten*, 5 July 1971.

film on the car industry's Common Market prospects and a debate along the usual quadripartite lines: Sir Gerald Nabarro and Eric Heffer against, Norman St John–Stevas and John Mackintosh in favour. *Twenty-Four Hours*, a daily weekday programme, produced a Common Market Special on 7 July with videotape animations and political discussions (Peter Shore and Neil Marten, Geoffrey Rippon and Harold Lever); it had already carried Common Market items with debates, opinion poll results, and reports from Luxemburg on 22, 23 and 24 June and was to return to the subject at frequent intervals. There was a special series of six programmes called *The Six and Britain* for the instruction of viewers on 14, 18, 24 and 25 June, the no doubt intolerable gap between these dates being bridged by a repeat of a film called *Europe and the New Zealanders* on 20 June. Two days after *The Six and Britain* finished, lo and behold a new weekly series entitled *Both Sides of Europe* began on 27 June to run on into August.

It all culminated in a three-and-a-quarter-hour programme entitled *The Great Debate* (the diplomacy and politics that went into its production would have made a book in itself – and for all one knows may yet do so). The motion 'that Britain should now join the Common Market' was proposed by Christopher Chataway with Harold Lever and David Steel, and opposed by Barbara Castle, Peter Shore and Edward Taylor. In a mock judicial procedure each side called witnesses to support its case; these witnesses were then cross-examined by the other side. There appeared for entry among others Michael Stewart, Lord Kearton and Andrew Shonfield; against entry Jack Jones, Sir John Winnifrith (formerly Permanent Secretary at the Ministry of Agriculture) and Professor Nicholas Kaldor. In forensic terms, there was little doubt that the cold determined passion and fierce intelligence of Barbara Castle won hands down over the slightly lackadaisical charm of the former television idol Christopher Chataway, who seemed at times not to have done his homework. The experiment of calling foreign witnesses rather backfired against both sides: the argument had become to such an extent a highly-charged, domestic (one is tempted to say incestuous) political one that they seemed scarcely to see where their evidence was meant to fit into the rival *images d'Épinal* so garishly painted by the two sides.

The European Movement had taken strong exception to the BBC's attempt to provide for this marathon programme a sample audience whose reactions had already been tested before the debate: it regarded the BBC's prior questionnaire as clumsy and biased, and doubted whether one could regard any group that had already been interviewed (in this or any other way) as a fair sample to be asked again after the debate – particularly when only a part of the initial sample showed up in the studios. As it happened, some time after midnight the studio audiences in various provincial centres gave their answers to be fed into the computer. 'After the great debate', as Robin Day, its chairman, put it in exasperation, 'the great cock-up.' The computer failed to produce any answer until next morning, when viewers were apologetically informed of a further swing against entry. The suspicion that the computer had been sabotaged by the European Movement, voiced by various wits at the time, was quite unsubstantiated.

In addition to all these special programmes there were the Prime Minister's broadcast on 8 July and the Leader of the Opposition's reply on 9 July; there was an all-party discussion on the same night as Harold Wilson's reply; both the Central Hall meetings – the Conservative Central Council meeting and the special Labour party conference – were given daytime live coverage and evening reports on 14 and 17 July, and the news of course continuously covered the negotiations in Brussels and the political issue at home. Radio also did its bit. Radio Four ran a series entitled *The Road to Europe*, its weekly telephone questions programme *It's Your Line* invited one of the EEC Commissioners, Ralf Dahrendorf (who answered with a much better feel for the British context than the Continental Europeans in *The Great Debate* on television), on another occasion Geoffrey Rippon, and also Enoch Powell (on various subjects). It would be tedious to list the whole gamut of Common Market coverage on the air. Suffice it to say that if the issue was large, complex and difficult, the coverage also was extensive, quite expert, and in its explicit comment politically carefully balanced. There were very few complaints from viewers and listeners that they had not been told enough. The complaint, if anything, was of slightly guilty boredom at what some regarded as well-meaning but possibly officious overkill.

Top People's Papers

There is no doubt that the quality press – among the dailies anyhow – was partisan on the issue. The *Financial Times* had been in favour of British entry for ten years or more, and gave excellent coverage of Common Market political no less than economic news, though its back-page columnist Gordon Tether was scathing about pro-Marketeers and all their works and indeed a signatory of an anti-Market advertisement. *The Times*, too, under its editor William Rees-Mogg, was overtly, massively and sometimes broodingly pro-entry, though its economics editor, Douglas Jay's son Peter Jay, was hostile and did not hesitate to say so on the economic pages. Before there was any 'give' in the negotiations and before the Heath-Pompidou summit meeting had been announced – at a time, in other words, when the prospects of a successful outcome were very far from clear – *The Times* concluded a series of five weighty leading articles on 'The Prospect for Britain' with the stark alternatives, 'Dead Failure or New Start':

Britain will not be 'all right' if the European negotiations fail. That would be a total, disastrous and unmitigated defeat for us, threatening our industry, our currency, our standard of living, our cost of living, our level of employment and even our political institutions with a crisis in the 1970s to which we have no apparent answer.

Referring to the recent bankruptcy of 'a company which was our national symbol *par excellence*, operating in an area of advanced technology which produces vast export returns,' *The Times* continued: 'It used to be said that Rolls-Royce was Britain: if we stay out of Europe, Britain will be Rolls-Royce.' It went on to say that for world manufacturing exports, Britain had now 'little more than stand-by capacity' and yet she could not, like Switzerland, simply live on a few strong export lines: 'It would take a generation to change down to a more limited specialist role. You cannot produce a good lightweight merely by starving an old heavyweight.' The political consequences would inevitably lead to a bad neighbour policy:

Britain out of Europe will reduce her contribution to the world, and withdraw from commitments to European defence and technology. We shall cut foreign aid. These will not be reactions of pique: they will be forced upon us by lack of resources.

Moreover there were risks that the domestic political system would not stand the strain:

Outside the main industrial groupings we should have to make ourselves the ruthless scavengers of world business. There would at some point in the 1970s be a choice between intense national discipline and gross national impoverishment. One may wonder who would be the man for that hour?

The arguments of the Marketeers in the early 'sixties had proved prophetic:

The chief difference between those arguments of 1961, which proved correct at every point, and the argument of 1971 is that the situation is now much worse. In 1961 we were entering the rapids; now we can hear the rumble of the falls.[1]

With this profoundly dramatic view of the alternatives, it was not surprising that by October The Times had little sympathy left for Harold Wilson: 'In 1967 Mr Wilson dismissed people from the fringes of his administration who would not conform to his then belief in Europe. Now he will put the whip on those who do not share his non-belief.' From that analysis there followed root and branch commination:

To put party before country on a matter of preeminent importance is one of the crimes for which a party leader can never be forgiven. . . . His attitude now is that he is prepared to deny the British people an advantage, which as Prime Minister he had found to be essential. He is prepared to deny his country this advantage because he believes, in all probability mistakenly, that to do so will bring him and his party nearer to a return to power. What can one say about such a leader except that he must never be Prime Minister again?[2]

The Daily Telegraph, in spite of the fact that one major section of its traditional readership was instinctively patriotic and suspicious of inno-vation and alien things, was loyal to the party leadership. It did, however, allow Peregrine Worsthorne, a more thoroughgoing Conservative, a good deal of space to put a more reserved viewpoint – though at the time of the summit even he wrote: 'I cannot but be thankful that interests I do not share seem to be prevailing against a scepticism I cannot escape, and that it now looks as if the die is cast. Let us admit it: the Europeans deserve to win. The sceptics have failed to produce an alternative faith.'[3]

The Telegraph gave space to the odd anti-Marketeer for a sustained argument – such as Ronald Bell – but made 'no apology for the fact that the balance is in favour of entry. We have supported entry in principle from the start, and consider the present terms acceptable.'[3] At the time of the Labour party conference, of course, it put the boot in – under the title 'Wobbling Healigans' it attacked Denis Healey and

[1] The Times, 4 May 1971.   [2] 20 October 1971.
[3] Daily Telegraph, 16 August 1971.

Jim Callaghan as 'people who will say anything to please and who in consequence can be trusted neither by friend nor foe, whether in the Labour Party or in the country, or in Europe or anywhere else.'[1] But – unlike so much of the pro-Market press – the *Telegraph* also demanded consistency from the Labour Marketeers:

If Mr Jenkins and his supporters were to content themselves with one fine flight of protest in the parliamentary debate and then proceed to combine with Mr Wilson and the Tory irreconcilables to kill the measure they approve, their conduct will be at least as morally indefensible as Mr Wilson's.[2]

On the morning of the vote of principle it argued that the lack of support in the country was

more apparent than real. Opinion polls, though they suggest that half the population are against entry, tell some strange stories – that people think that entry will be in the country's interests though they are personally against it, that they are against it but would nevertheless leave it to Parliament, and that they would not wish to continue opposition if Parliament decided in favour. Without a doubt a decisive vote for entry tonight will not only give confidence to our prospective European partners but will carry public opinion in its wake.[3]

And its appeal for Parliament to grasp 'The Last Opportunity' as the debate opened saw it in the broadest of terms: 'When they vote next Thursday night they will be passing a judgment on a civilization, a culture, an economic union, a nascent defence capability, above all an idea of Europe which cannot be rejected without grievous results for Europe's future and our own.'[4]

The *Guardian* had been among the first British dailies to take up the cudgels in favour of British participation in the Common Market project and it stuck to this line during the 1970–72 negotiations, arguing that the terms, though not ideal, were adequate, and as good as Labour could have hoped to achieve. Britain, therefore, ought to join.

At the same time the paper habitually stressed two other points. Firstly, it always wanted more frank information than either the Labour or the Conservative government seemed willing to provide. Mark Arnold-Foster in July 1969, for example, took strong issue with Michael Stewart who had told the House of Commons on 23 June 1969: 'It would simply be doing a disservice to the House to try to give

[1] 5 October 1971.   [2] 6 October 1971.
[3] 28 October 1971.   [4] 21 October 1971.

a detailed calculation of the effects of all the factors that would be operating on the balance of payments in the first few years after our entry.' Mark Arnold-Foster caused the government some embarrassment by publishing detailed calculations from an internal enquiry conducted by the Central Statistical Office and the Ministry of Agriculture to show that 'Britain's entry fee . . . would be between £400 millions and £500 millions a year'[1] (after himself previously making an estimate of £600 millions, disregarding a switch from butter to margarine). The Foreign Office, commenting officially on that newspaper report, referred back to Harold Wilson's earlier, and very much lower, estimates (£175–250 millions), but the 'indiscretion' of the *Guardian* may have contributed to the Labour government's promise of the White Paper that was eventually published – with estimates that ranged from £100 millions to £1,100 millions.

The paper's second criticism was both of the Community itself and of Britain's attitude in joining it: the charge that neither Britain nor the Six seemed prepared to be bolder in going forward towards much closer democratic political union – 'without which the Community will be a headless monster'.[2] A long leader previewing the decisive year 1971 argued:

Only five years were needed for the young United States to recognize the weakness of confederate government and to seek a stronger union. Will Europe need a whole generation? . . . Without political direction, Europe is nothing. The Common Market itself will wither and die. . . . To talk of central decisions, direct elections, and a European Parliament with genuine authority is usually regarded as idealistic, unrealistic, or folly. The truth is, though, that unless Western Europe moves on to such a system it will be unable to cope with the Community's own problems.[3]

On the morrow of the publication of the Conservative government's White Paper it returned to the charge on both counts, calling it

a disappointing document. It is politically timid, economically complacent, and vague on some vital points. It fails to recognize the need for political union. . . . But the opportunity is one that Britain ought to seize. Even if the Europe presented in the White Paper seems at times conservative and unprogressive, it can still be the basis of a strong and prosperous Community.[4]

[1] *Guardian*, 14 July 1969.   [2] 8 July 1971.
[3] 28 December 1970.   [4] 8 July 1971.

Being rather on the radical side of British politics – perhaps some would say in spite of that – the *Guardian* found Harold Wilson's speeches in July 1971 'depressing':

The most disreputable aspect of Mr Wilson's speech on Saturday was that . . . it was a denial of what he himself once stood for and a desertion of his earlier good judgment. . . . Labour used to combine pragmatism with idealism, but at present some of its leaders have lost their way. Until it recovers, as it must, it will not have a credible claim to be capable of governing. . . . The irony is that a promise to renegotiate amounts to no more than the Conservative Government intends anyway. On food, New Zealand, and sugar – the key charges in Mr Wilson's indictment – Mr Heath and Mr Rippon have deliberately left a great deal to be decided only after British entry.

The *Guardian* found hope in only one reflection: 'Mr Wilson meant what he said in the 1964 election when he promised to renegotiate the Nassau agreement, but in 1971 Polaris is still with us at the Holy Loch and Faslane.'[1] As one of its writers put it afterwards: 'We didn't particularly enjoy knocking Harold on the head, but it had to be done.'

'Top people' in other words – and the socially mobile aspiring to become top people – were given their daily news, comment and exhortation predominantly with a pro-entry slant: moreover, comment on the Labour Party's difficulties was almost entirely, in those papers, on Roy Jenkins' side and contemptuously anti-Wilson. Only in the intellectual weeklies was that balance reversed.

The weeklies were in fact almost as much protagonists in as recorders of the drama. The *New Statesman* under Richard Crossman's editorship was anti-Market in no uncertain way, anti-referendum, much of the time anti-Wilson, and always anti-Jenkins. It produced a brilliantly argued special 32-page answer to the government's White Paper section by section – optically at first sight indistinguishable from the White Paper itself except for the red cover with reversed and averted lion and unicorn. The author was Peter Shore, one of the acutest critics of entry. The *New Statesman* formed a cudgel within the Labour Party's internal struggle, as of course did *Tribune* at a more popular and explicitly working-class, trade-union, Left-wing level. The *Spectator* was also anti-Market – but from a highly Conservative point of view (which did not prevent it opening its columns to Douglas Jay alongside Enoch Powell and Mercurius Oxoniensis). When, in

[1] 19 July 1971.

April 1972, its editor George Gale concluded that there was no longer any point in arguing the case against entry, he was logical in going 'the whole hog the other way',[1] pledging himself for the next debate to the federalist as against the confederalist side. In counterpoint to the *Statesman, Tribune* and *Spectator,* in effect the Marketeers' own weekly was *The Economist*; its anonymous group-think editorials were staunchly, persistently and often passionately in favour of entry, scathingly contemptuous of Harold Wilson, and at times perhaps excessively partisan in favour of the Jenkinsites (John Harris combined a post on *The Economist* with being one of Roy Jenkins' closest advisers).

The Popular Dailies

But – as a glance at the figures shows – while no doubt these four 'quality dailies' influenced the influential, their combined circulation scarcely exceeded two million; each of the four popular papers by itself exceeded that figure, and the four of them together had a circulation five or six times as large. Among these four popular dailies, it was three in favour to one against – but with a complication in three cases: the *Daily Mirror* and the *Sun*, both traditionally Labour papers, were hotly in favour of entry, while the *Daily Express*, traditionally Conservative, was fervently against.

National Daily Newspaper Circulations, June 1971

Daily Mirror	4,380,000
Daily Express	3,436,000
Sun	2,083,000
Daily Mail	2,007,000
Daily Telegraph	1,455,000
The Times	341,000
Guardian	328,000
Financial Times	168,000

The *Express* concentrated largely on three issues: prices, the sentiments of the people, and national greatness. Typical was its leader on 4 May 1971, 'Scrag-End at the Week-End' ('In the Common Market the week-end joint will be an uncommon luxury') or that on 7 May ('It may be "coffee and cognac" for Mr Rippon. It will be more like bread and water for the rest of us'). 'The Voice of Britain', it boasted in June that it stood alone – with the people – in opposition to entry,

[1] *The Times,* 26 April 1972.

and listed 'Ten Facts to Face in Europe' on 'The Way Your Life could be Changed' including the pay-packet, insurance premiums, health, pensions and so forth. 'Prices are mounting in anticipation of our membership of the Common Market. If we go in they will go through the roof.' And in July: 'Britain's suffering housewives face a staggering £800 million a year leap in food prices by 1978. . . .'

On 7 May 1971 the *Express* had announced 'Europe: It's a Dead Duck', and three days later it was still stoutly maintaining that nothing would come of it:

Just as a mirage lures desert travellers so does the Common Market draw British politicians. Mr Macmillan and Mr Wilson experienced this. Now it is Mr Heath's turn. . . . The Six are too busy squabbling among themselves to consider the claims of candidate members. . . . For Britain that Common Market mirage is about to disappear again.

On 14 May it headlined 'The Great Betrayal' and asserted: 'It's not sugar that Rippon is selling short – it's your way of life.' And when the Prime Minister went to Paris it summarized the issue:

Marriage – French style is what M. Georges Pompidou demands of Mr Heath. . . . And what does that involve? . . . We must dishonour our obligations to our Commonwealth partners. . . . We must obey the dictates of the technocrats of Brussels. . . . Moreover – as M. Pompidou has reminded Mr Heath – the marriage contract is for ever. . . . M. Pompidou may call this a marriage. The British people call it a life sentence.

The success of the talks was 'a victory won by French diplomacy over British interests'[1] and as for the staff who worked for it 'The public will mark it down as the Foreigners' Office'.[2]

After that, attention naturally turned to the domestic front. Already on 20 May the latest Harris poll figures (showing a 20:62 majority against entry) had been headlined: 'Here's your answer, M. Pompidou: NON! and this is the British PEOPLE saying it.' On 25 May it threatened MPs with punishment at the polls: 'The Party Whips will be as nothing to the scorpions of the voters.' In July the *Express* castigated the government's 'Black Paper: How Britain's Greatness will be Surrendered' and, while not spending much time on the internal difficulties of the Labour Party, it reported prominently various unions' decisions against entry and the TUC under the title: 'One great shout

[1] *Daily Express*, 22 May 1971.   [2] 24 May 1971.

says NO to the Six.'[1] As for the Conservative party conference, 'it was more like an American convention than any momentous act of history':

With all the razzmatazz of show-biz – blue balloons and dolly birds dressed in the colours of the Six – the Tory Party marches into Europe. . . . From the stage-managed melodrama of Brussels last June to the super-colossal Brighton Follies yesterday, it's been a great show. . . . 'Enjoy it now, folks, 'cos you're gonna pay later!'[2]

None of this drove the *Express* into support of Mr Harold Wilson. It continued to believe 'Mr Wilson's astonishing gyrations on the Market have gained him naught but contempt among the people. . . . It may be that the tide and time are right for Mr Wilson to sail out of sight.'[3]

On the morning of 28 October, the *Express* predicted a majority of 58 and added: 'If the elected representatives of the people will not speak for the people who elected them the *Daily Express* will continue faithfully to do so.' Next morning its headline a little curiously blamed Labour: 'In by the Left.' Then, the morning after, it abandoned its alliance with those who were determined to fight on in the House of Commons. Though the *Sunday Express* had threatened Edward Heath that 'his present faithful friends will become his equally faithful and unrelenting enemies',[4] Sir Max Aitken himself switched the line:

A mistake – a great mistake – has been made. But it has been made by the House of Commons, and the *Daily Express* accepts the verdict of the freely elected British Parliament. . . . So, if Britain has to go into the Market, then the Market must be fashioned to Britain's will . . . and the *Daily Express* will champion British interests more fervently than ever before. . . . From today onwards the *Daily Express* will discharge its obligations – *by promoting* the British case in season and out, in Brussels, in Bonn, in Rome, Paris or London, wherever it is at hazard. . . . The *Daily Express*, the Voice of Britain, will be stronger than ever when it speaks to foreigners on behalf of Britain.

Diametrically on the opposite side – traditionally Labour in sympathy but pro-Market since May 1961 – stood the *Daily Mirror*. It rammed home facts on Europe's living standards, and true to type it featured Christopher Ward's 'Guide to the Euro-Dollies' (with items such as how they kiss, how Englishmen rate with them, and so forth)

[1] 19 September 1971.   [2] 14 October 1971.
[3] 20 October 1971.   [4] *Sunday Express*, 23 May 1971.

and a series of lavish 'Euro-Dolly' pin-up photographs. But its emphasis was mainly political and the burden of its argument stood summarized in bold type on 8 July:

The *Daily Mirror* says again: Are a people who for centuries were the makers of history – and who can again help to make history – to become mere lookers-on from an off-shore island of dwindling significance? Surely the answer is clear. The terms are known. The prizes are immense. The challenge must be accepted.

Indeed when Prince Philip instanced the Common Agricultural Policy as an example of the bad management of agriculture (and got an accolade from the *Express*: 'Good for Prince Philip: The people applaud his good sense. . . . And wish it were more widely shared by our rulers') the *Mirror* called him 'A Chump'.[1]

In May the *Mirror* ran a Common Market competition for six couples to visit one of the Six and see for themselves (we have already noted the interlocking of journalists between the *Mirror* and the *British European*, and the styles of the two bore marked resemblances). Its emphasis throughout was on historic opportunity. 'Nothing would be more fiercely ironical now, after two Noes from France, if the third No should come from Britain'.[2] As the negotiations seemed to have reached a successful outcome: 'Ten years ago, almost to the day, the *Daily Mirror* took its stand on Europe. . . . Today the *Mirror* salutes an historic occasion.'[3]

It kept to this theme, with a series of clarion calls:

Alerting all *Daily Mirror* readers. And other men and women of sound mind, courage, vision and common-sense. Including MPs of both principal parties. . . . THIS is the historic week. Right here and now. THIS is the week, and Thursday the precise day, when Parliament takes the political and economic decision of our life-time.[4]

The *Mirror* was unashamedly 'élitist' on the Common Market issue:

The public opinion polls in Britain are a joke on this issue. They bring joy only to the anti-Marketeering and bamboozling *Daily Express*. . . . The Tory Party are doing nothing which was not spelt out in their last Election Manifesto – and they won the election. . . .[5]

[1] *Daily Mirror*, 22 July 1971.   [2] 25 May 1971.   [3] 23 June 1971.
[4] 26 October 1971.   [5] 16 July 1971.

And it asked on 10 May:

Are there STATESMEN in the House of Commons or only politicians and careerists? They will have to stand up and be counted. . . . The acid test of personal courage and leadership will soon be thrust on them by the Common Market. . . . For if there is not an affirmative vote in Parliament Britain will be out of Europe FOR EVER. . . . The timid politicians, the time-servers, will assuredly vote NO – moaning that the terms are unacceptable whatever they might be. . . . *Here is Prime Minister Heath's chance of greatness.* . . . The greatest democracy the world has ever known is entitled, surely, to the emergence of three or four statesmen in a decision of historic proportions.

In July the *Mirror* inevitably had to enter the debate within the Labour Party:

. . . the Labour National Party Executive formally and publicly made an inglorious ass of itself yesterday. . . . Oh, as the *Mirror* said on July 16th, the agony of it all. Now, folks, it's official: official twaddle. They have embalmed the double talk. . . . The Wilson line on this occasion is as circuitous as a bent corkscrew.[1]

A few days before the vote it exploded 'four massive myths' for the benefit of the Labour pro-Marketeers – that the government could be brought down on the issue, that an election would help a divided Labour Party, that there would be any chance of another negotiation, and that public opinion really knew what it wanted. On the morning after the vote, the *Mirror* waxed ecstatic, its entire front page being filled with the newsflash:

Dateline Westminster, October 28th
Time: 22.16 hours
The historic decision is made
YES TO EUROPE! ! majority: 112

Perhaps it was not altogether surprising that the *Daily Mirror* provoked some reactions from its traditional readership. Thus Brother A. Jones wrote bluntly in the trade union quarterly *The Way* in September 1971:

A certain daily newspaper that has always hooted like an express train for the Common Market must have gone deaf under a long tunnel and missed the 'but it must be on our terms' part of the statement. For the impact of the full text

[1] 29 July 1971.

seems to have derailed them, they have been hooting like a derailed puffer, for Harold's blood (as they did for the then Mr George Brown), ever since they went around the bend.

For a paper that boasts of representing the people they show a remarkable hostility towards the leaders of the working class. Towards the representatives of the country's two largest Trade Unions (Mr Jack Jones and Mr Hugh Scanlon) they display a show of venom and hatred that all the other Tory newspapers combined have little time or room for.

Newspaper has always had its uses, for table cloths, and wrapping up fish and chips. . . .

The *Sun* was in much the same potentially awkward position as the *Mirror* – except that, having been founded to be very much a Labour paper, one might have expected it to be less strident in its condemnation of Harold Wilson. In fact, as the *Sun* said on the morrow of the October vote, 'The *Sun* has campaigned for this . . . ever since the *Sun* itself began. No other newspaper can claim as much.'[1] It therefore seems to have felt few inhibitions in supporting a Conservative Prime Minister on the issue, and when Prince Philip 'got his royal finger into the Common Market pie' it was the most outspoken of the popular papers:

It is time our sailor Prime Minister told the sailor Prince which way the wind blows. . . . Prince Philip's family farms a lot of acres. But of the 'long-standing agricultural patterns' liable to be 'completely up-ended' in the Common Market, the one the uncommon Prince knows most about is the art of rearing birds to be shot at. . . . That is no basis for shooting down the Market.[2]

Like the *Mirror*, the *Sun* tried to stop Harold Wilson changing course:

The public will not be deceived by political manœuvrings. . . . *They will not respect* those who deny their past commitments in order to dodge and weave from one political foxhole to another. . . . For this is a time of decision. . . . A time for statesmen, not politicians . . . *which will Mr Harold Wilson be?*

Immediately after that conference it condemned the Party Leader as 'the man with a million alibis':

Poor Harold. It seems he has spent his recent years being misunderstood by Most of the People Most of the Time and Some of the People All of the Time. . . .

---

[1] *Sun*, 29 October 1971.   [2] 23 June 1971.

That's what Mr Wilson's excuse-laden performance was all about on Saturday.
. . . It was the *speech of a man with a million alibis*. . . . He knows that in trying to
unite the Labour Party while remaining leader, he is being left stranded by the
tide of history.[1]

When the decision finally came, the *Sun* was harsh in its judgment:

What Mr Wilson's sell-out demolishes is his own standing as a national leader.
. . . If what Harold Wilson claims today is right he conned his Government
colleagues between 1967 and 1970. . . . If what Harold Wilson says today is
wrong then he is trying to con the British public in 1971. . . . The third possibility is that the only person he is conning is himself.[2]

and when the October party conference endorsed that decision the
Sun's verdict was 'an historical blunder'[3] The paper preferred to lay
the emphasis on a constructive role for the party within Europe:

. . . Labour's vital task is to make sure that when Britain joins the Common
Market on January 1, 1973, we do not go in UNPREPARED.
  UNPREPARED to Protect the Regions: The Market has not yet got a
regional policy
  UNPREPARED to insist on fair shares
  UNPREPARED to defend the hard-up
  That is the sort of thing the Labour opposition at Westminster should be
fighting for now. . . . Instead of the abortive struggle to stay OUT, the Labour
Movement should be battling for fair shares when we get IN.[4]

By comparison with these three papers, the *Daily Mail* had a rather
more straightforward task. It could support both the Conservative
Party and the Common Market. It did so, however, in a moderate tone
compared with the shrill emphasis of the other three. Before the Paris
summit, which it described as 'a date with Europe's destiny', the *Daily
Mail* advised: 'The way to play it is the same as poker: sit tight . . .
keep calm . . . and hold your hand up.'[5] Admitting that the Common
Market was far from perfect, the *Mail* claimed it was yet:

the most hopeful project for uniting Europe in our lifetime. . . . The British
public will swing towards Europe only if the terms are fair and are seen to be
fair. . . . All who care for a strong Britain and a strong Europe will wish the
two men well.[6]

On the terms, the *Daily Mail* was satisfied:

[1] 19 July 1971.   [2] 29 July 1971.   [3] 5 October 1971.
[4] 2 August 1971.   [5] *Daily Mail*, 11 May 1971.   [6] 20 May 1971.

If the Commonwealth sugar men are reasonably convinced . . . so is the *Daily Mail*. On this important test case, we believe that the Common Market has shown good will to Britain and good will to the poorer countries of the Commonwealth.

And so – particularly as the Labour leader was coming out against – the *Daily Mail* turned more forcefully in favour, envisaging for Britain a hegemonic role:

The great chance ahead for Britain – a fuller, richer life . . . and a vital role to play.
    NOW WE CAN LEAD EUROPE

Nor was it all a matter of abstract greatness. At the time of the TUC conference, the *Daily Mail* reproved the unions for their faintness of heart:

Now there is a chicken in every pot, a Renault or a Fiat in almost every garage – and a minimum of almost four weeks' paid holiday to tootle around in it. . . . Cheer up, brothers! The water's lovely once you have taken the plunge.[1]

On the other hand the *Mail* as a candid friend admitted that 'Ted Heath's Market line is just not getting over'. 'The great propaganda crusade to join the Common Market has stalled badly with the public.'[2] It regretted the issue becoming a party one as 'a sad end to what should have been a great debate'.[3] Under the headline 'Harold do you re-member?', it flayed Harold Wilson, of course: 'Statesman? Or trick cyclist on the high wire? Will the real Harold Wilson please stand up?'[4] And later it went further: 'Harold Wilson has ratted. . . . In the opinion of the *Daily Mail*, Mr Harold Wilson's great Common Market betrayal unfits him ever again to lead his country.'[5] going on to declare, at the time of the October party conference: 'Like the crab needs its shell, Mr Wilson needs Mr Jenkins . . . as a cover for his own naked opportunism.'[6] A week before the October vote it declared

This time when the division bell rings it will mark the divide between the old and the new Britain. . . . This time there can be no hiding place for abstainers. . . . A Member of Parliament who has not made up his or her mind two hours before midnight on Thursday next does not deserve to sit at Westminster.[7]

As predictable (or more so) as the *Daily Mail* – but of course on the opposite tack – was the *Morning Star*. Its circulation is only around 60–70,000 and its influence is strictly circumscribed by its political

[1] 4 June 1971.   [2] 9 September 1971.   [3] 30 September 1971.
[4] 14 June 1971.   [5] 29 July 1971.   [6] 4 October 1971.
[7] 21 October 1971.

sectarianism; but as the mouthpiece of the Communist Party of Great Britain it is not without interest. Edward Heath to its mind 'represents the Big Business interests who are tied up with their counterparts in the US, who support the Vietnam war and who want to get into the Common Market.'[1] So it came as no surprise to its readers that

like Chamberlain at Munich in 1938, Heath in Paris has been prepared to sign away the national interests of the British people to further the class interests of Big Business. . . . Going in also means strengthening the giant international firms and their power to exploit the workers. . . . It would help those who want to keep Europe divided and perpetuate the Cold War and the arms race.[2]

As for Georges Pompidou, he was 'a former director-general of Rothschilds' Bank. He is a Right Wing soul-mate of the Tories, who has encouraged mergers and capitalist monopoly.'[3] The White Paper it regarded as 'simply an exercise in brainwashing' on the Prime Minister's part:

Despite all its double-talk and special pleading, it cannot conceal the reality — that he is not for Europe, but for the capitalist part of Europe; not for European unity, but for the division of Europe; not for European security, but for NATO and the cold war.[4]

The *Morning Star* always saw entry into the Common Market as part of this much wider world-wide capitalist conspiracy, and also as part of an overall domestic design by the Tories. So Labour MPs who contemplated voting for entry must face up to one central fact:

It is a vote for Heath, the worst Prime Minister for decades; for Carr, the union-basher; for Davies, the UCS butcher; for Home, the cold-war spy-maniac; for Barber, the destroyer of a million jobs; for Amery, the rent raiser; for Thatcher, who turned the children's milk sour. . . . The Labour Movement will never forgive MPs who, whether by action or inaction, help this crew to carry on their wrecking activities. They will be regarded with as much contempt by the Labour movement as were Ramsay MacDonald, Snowden and Thomas when they joined with Baldwin and the Tories in 1931. . . .[5]

Theses of content-analysis will no doubt be written on the attitudes of regional and local newspapers, local radio stations, professional journals and the rest of the media on this issue. But enough is enough. It is time to turn to popular opinion.

[1] *Morning Star*, 21 May 1971.   [2] 22 May 1971.   [3] 25 May 1971.
[4] 8 July 1971.   [5] 28 October 1971.

12   The Views of the General Public

'We do feel unique, don't we?' (*Acquiescent giggles from all*)
SPCR Survey

General Problems and Long-Term Trends

One might almost say that never in the course of British history have so many had to answer so many questions on a single issue as they did on that of entry into the EEC. The answers recorded by half a dozen polling organizations over the last twelve years would be a meal for any data bank. Yet there is unfortunately no single convincing time-series that takes opinion soundings with an identical question right through this period. One can see why this should be so: even an identical wording could, over twelve years, change its connotation and its topicality with changes in atmosphere, terminology and circumstance. Bearing this in mind, the best we can do by way of assembling a series to show a long-term trend is to combine two Gallup questions, the first asked with varying frequency from 1960 to 1967, the second from 1967 onwards. They are set out in Diagram 1, which tells its own story.

There are all sorts of difficulties – most of them well explored – in the use of polling material as evidence of public sentiment. When the issue is of a kind which each citizen usually has to decide for himself, such as how to cast his vote, most are used to deciding; and where actual aggregate behaviour can be used to check sample surveys of intentions or recollections, as in the case of voting, these difficulties are manageable. When on the other hand no action is or will be required of the voter, so that there is not anything like the same sense of personal responsibility; when the issue is one on which, for at least part of the time, all three parties are agreed, so that the normal channels of debate and the normal pulls of party loyalty are suspended; and when the issue is highly complex, with experts paraded on either side in flagrant contradiction to each other – then the interpretation of polling results becomes a very much more problematic affair.

It is easy to poke fun at the overall majority which wanted a referendum, paralleled only by the even bigger majority that did not know what a referendum was; or to see a contradiction between the majority that wanted not Parliament but the people to decide at the same time as the largely overlapping majority which felt that the people did not have the information to decide the issue. But the real problems lay deeper than that. They lay in a genuine sense of bewilderment; a feeling that this issue, while it would profoundly affect people's future, was out of their hands and could not really be put back there – any more than so much else of this modern transnational technetronic world could be brought back into manageable packages under visible democratic control. It was this feeling to which Enoch Powell and Anthony Wedgwood Benn each in his way responded. It was this feeling also which makes it so peculiarly difficult to interpret what often slightly flattered, slightly apprehensive or impatient people said on their doorsteps (or wherever else they found themselves interviewed).

We shall not, therefore, rely on any one poll or any one particular question, but pick out from the mass of evidence what seems most characteristic or significant. The bulk of the data will have to be set out elsewhere.[1]

If, then, we take the opinion polls as certainly not an ideal indicator, but still the best major systematic body of evidence we have about shifts in aggregate views expressed by the public at large on the issue, we find several major reversals in popular attitudes to British membership of the EEC. Depending on the nature of the question, there was if anything a slight majority in favour of entry in the 1960–63 period – and when the question was put with the government's authority staked on the side of entry, the majority could at times become an absolute one. Even – or perhaps especially – after the veto of 1963, considerably more people seemed to want Britain still to try to join than wanted her to abandon the attempt. By March 1965, 57% wanted Britain to try to join, against 22% who wanted to drop the idea. When the Labour government embarked on its probe in autumn 1966, it could look back on the high-water mark of pro-European sentiment – the 71% in favour, 11% against of July 1966. That zenith in the indices preceded any real sign of the government's inclination to try again; but it followed the 'July measures' of financial and mone-

<hr/>

[1] 'Britain and the EEC – Opinion Poll Data 1970–72', *Journal of Common Market Studies*, Vol. XI. Public opinion as seen by the Gallup Poll during the two earlier attempts at British entry is to be found in the same source, Vol. V, No. 1 (September 1966), pp. 49–61, and Vol. VI, No. 3 (March 1968), pp. 231–49.

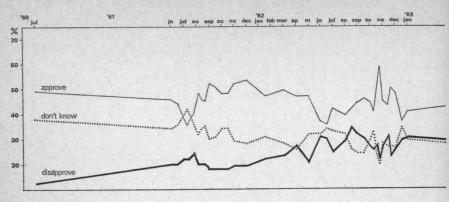

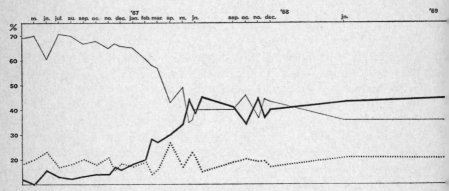

Diagram 1   Gallup poll series, July 1960 to May 1972.[1]

tary restraint. The public clearly thought the grass greener on the other side of the Channel; it was not at this stage responding to any political leadership.

[1] From July 1960 the question asked was: If the British Government were to decide that Britain's interests would best be served by joining the European Common Market, would you approve or disapprove? During May 1967 three questions were asked: (i) The Government has decided that Britain's interests would best be served by applying to join the European Common Market. Do you approve or disapprove? (ii) The Government had decided that Britain's interest would best be served by joining the Common Market and they have applied to for membership. Do you approve or disapprove of their application to join? (iii) Do you approve or disapprove of the Government applying for membership of the European Common Market? Therefore question (iii) was asked on every occasion. Note that since only one poll was taken by Gallup in 1969 the graph has been contracted at this point.

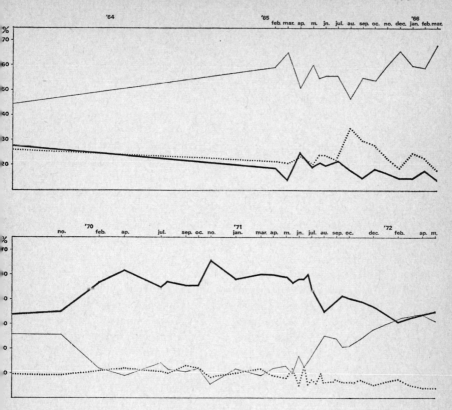

On the other hand, once the government seriously embarked on its European policy, public opinion ebbed quickly away and opposition began to mount – as if there had been something of romantic escapism in the 1966 mood, and a platonic sentiment that could not sustain the harsher realities of what was involved once the issue became a real one. Already in May 1967 – the month of the formal application to join – National Opinion Polls found a 37:41 majority disapproving of the government's decision to try to join the Common Market (as against a 59:19 majority approving only four months before). It is thus perfectly true to say that Harold Wilson's initiative had far wider public support than Harold Macmillan's – at the outset. Yet by the time the initiative failed the Labour government was left with less support for it at home than the Conservatives had enjoyed. A majority disapproving had shown itself first in late 1967, just prior to President de Gaulle's second veto. That majority consolidated itself in the two or three subsequent years. Perhaps the most impressive lesson to be derived from the polls taken up to this point was just how volatile – or from the government's point of view how perverse – public opinion could be.

Just how far removed the political goals of British public opinion were from those of the Six was highlighted in early 1970 by an internationally comparative survey of nearly 11,000 electors in Britain and the Six, carried out by six different polling institutions. (The British survey was taken by Harris Polls.) The questions and the answers to them in the European Community and Britain were set out on page 33. There could hardly be a harsher light thrown on the divergence of political attitudes on the two sides of the Channel – and by implication on the dangers and difficulties of British entry arising out of public opinion. Virtually identical results were still obtained in two Harris polls in February and April 1971 – each showed three-to-one majorities against becoming part of a politically united Europe rather than sticking only to economic ties if Britain joined the EEC (59:20).

Given this brutal contrast in European political ideology or lack of it, most of the British polling organizations not unreasonably concentrated not on the kind of long-run thinking for the Community's future that preoccupied this internationally comparative survey, but on the more immediate problems of whether people favoured entry and of what the disadvantages and advantages would be for them personally and for Britain – the largest unit with which most British electors as yet felt any meaningful identification.

But before we go into a close-up of the 1971–72 polls one further important caveat must be registered. Any study that focuses on a particular problem is liable to mislead as to the state of public opinion

National priorities

Gallup: *What would you say is the most urgent problem facing the country at the present time?*

	1971 Mar.	Apl.	May	June	Aug.
Employment, unemployment	16	15	23	18	28
Prices, cost of living	32	31	31	41	24
Ireland	—	—	—	—	15
Strikes, labour relations	35	26	12	9	8
Common Market	5	4	11	19	13
Most common next problem (pensions, immigration, etc.)	7	9	6	4	5

simply by the very fact of its focus. The first thing, therefore, to make clear is that outside certain circles of passionate or professional 'pros' and 'antis', and of politicians at Westminster (and Labour politicians in particular, for whom the issue became politically and personally so much more critical than for most Conservatives), the country at large throughout this period had a great many other preoccupations. Prices were rising by 10% during 1971, unemployment rose from 700,000 in January to 900,000 in October; there were industrial disputes, unrest in Northern Ireland, and a host of other problems on the public agenda. Perhaps it was not altogether surprising that even in June 1971, when the politicians were in the throes of this issue (with Conservative MPs rallying and the Labour Party moving towards its special conference on this and nothing else), popular opinion saw the issue as by no means the most urgent one requiring the government's attention.

Profile of National Opinion 1970–72

Among the attempts made to get behind the predominantly one-dimensional closed-question for-or-against approach of many polls were the two surveys made for the European Movement. (The first of these was based on an analysis of ten little discussion groups of 85 people in all, held late in 1970; the second resulted from a factor analysis of 2,030 interviews in late February and March 1971.) The small-scale study even then highlighted

some feeling that there is a conspiracy on the part of politicians, media owners and big business to commit Britain to joining the Common Market before the public has had a chance to appraise the pros and cons or to know precisely what is happening. They are confronted with an unusual agreement between all three political parties that Britain should join so that normal political allegiances give them no guidance. They tend to feel that they are fed only the information that is favourable to Britain's joining.

				1972		
Sept.	Oct.	Nov.	Dec.	Jan.	Feb.	Mar.
28	36	32	43	37	27	28
27	22	20	21	18	14	25
17	12	20	12	12	14	17
8	4	5	4	13	33	11
10	13	13	7	5	2	7
6	4	4	5	6	3	5

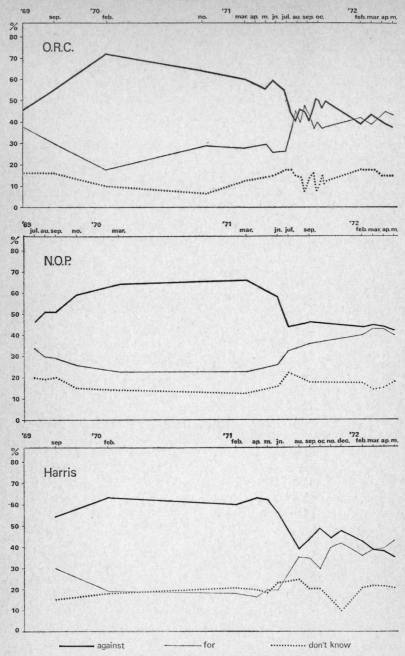

Diagram 2   ORC, NOP and Harris polls, 1969–72

At the abstract level, while joining would 'force us to pull up our socks', it would also involve a threat to national identity – a serious matter in view of what the author called 'complacent attitudes developed by being the head of a large empire': 'Thank God I'm British.' 'We *do* feel unique, don't we. (Acquiescent giggles from all.)' 'Our technicians and craftsmen are the best in the world.' 'We've got more sense of humour.' Considerable sentimental ties with the Commonwealth also emerged: 'They're our family.' 'We're of one blood.' (It should be noted that the Commonwealth was generally seen in the shape of the old white Dominions – very few mentions were made, even in the 2,030 interviews, of the sugar-exporting countries or of the developing countries in Asia and Africa.)

Yet the abstract arguments at the national level were not the decisive ones for personal attitudes:

A striking finding of this project was the distance informants placed between themselves and their problems on the one hand, and the problems facing Britain, on the other. It was almost as if they were talking of a country in which they had spent a package holiday.

What mattered at the personal level were prices, employment, the welfare state, and the possibilities of upheaval and of long-term family security, with short-run sacrifices very much to the fore. As the second study put it: 'Price increases are a painfully familiar phenomenon; economic growth is not. In that sense, the dice are loaded towards a short-term view.'

The clearest and most detailed profile of popular opinion and the swings in it in the summer of 1971 was in fact provided by the series of 'Speedsearch' polls mounted by Opinion Research Centre for the European Movement itself. These were carried out weekly, as part of a larger questionnaire on all sorts of subjects put to a representative quota sample of a little over one thousand people in two rotated sets of fifty different parliamentary constituencies. On pages 360–1 we reproduce the full tables for two of these surveys, taken four weeks apart at the time of the critical swing of opinion in favour of entry which highlight the shifts; pages 366–7 show an abstract of the whole series setting out merely the difference between the percentage of all those (very strongly or not very strongly) for and against, to provide a summary, if rough and ready, way of displaying shifts in opinion in different sectors of British society over the longer period.

The first phenomenon to stand out from the very first column of the first table is one that persisted throughout the series: those who felt very strongly opposed to entry always outnumbered those who felt less strongly opposed; while those who felt very strongly in favour of entry were always outnumbered by those who did not feel so strongly in favour. This phenomenon became less marked with time, but continued in evidence. It was no doubt one reason why, in some of the mini-referenda in which only those who felt strongly took the trouble to participate, the results tended to be much less favourable to entry than the public opinion polls. To the extent that the table on pages 366–

ORC (23–27 June 1971): *How much are you in favour of or against Britain joining the European Common Market?*

	All	SEX		AGE			
		Male	Female	15–24	25–44	45–64	65+
	1085	518	567	187	361	346	191
	%	%	%	%	%	%	%
Very strongly in favour	9	12	6	10	12	9	4
In favour, but not very strongly	18	20	16	24	22	14	12
Don't know	18	15	21	20	16	16	22
Against, but not very strongly	22	18	25	32	23	19	17
Very strongly against	33	34	31	15	27	41	46
All in favour	27	32	22	34	34	23	16
All against	55	52	56	47	50	60	63
Difference	−28	−20	−34	−13	−16	−37	−47

ORC (21–25 July 1971): *How much are you in favour of or against Britain's joining the European Common Market?*

	All	SEX		AGE			
		Male	Female	15–24	25–44	45–64	65+
	1112	539	573	197	360	364	191
	%	%	%	%	%	%	%
Very strongly in favour	18	23	12	15	21	17	16
In favour, but not very strongly	27	25	27	31	26	27	21
Don't know	15	12	17	12	13	14	21
Against, but not very strongly	15	14	17	20	15	14	14
Very strongly against	26	25	27	22	24	27	28
All in favour	45	48	39	46	47	44	37
All against	41	39	44	42	39	41	42
Difference	+4	+9	−5	+4	+8	+3	−5

7 disregards degrees of feeling, it thus simplifies out one element in the total picture. On the other hand, since democratic practice does not normally accord the fanatic extra votes, but counts each vote regardless of the self-assessed strength of the conviction behind it, the simplification is for many purposes justified.

The main curve to fix in one's mind is the average swing in the country as a whole over this period. It is set out as a single line tracing the difference between the percentage in favour and the percentage against entry in each of four polls (Gallup, ORC, NOP and Harris) in

CLASS				PARTY			REGION				
AB	C_1	C_2	DE	Con	Lib	Lab	South	Wales & West	Mid-lands	North	Scot-land
138	245	348	354	332	67	528	429	116	159	284	97
%	%	%	%	%	%	%	%	%	%	%	%
20	15	7	3	15	9	7	11	7	13	8	3
34	22	17	10	25	25	13	18	19	19	18	18
14	15	19	21	18	16	18	14	22	21	24	6
18	21	23	23	20	21	23	22	14	26	22	28
14	27	34	43	21	28	39	36	38	21	28	45
54	37	24	13	40	34	20	29	26	32	26	21
32	48	57	66	41	49	62	58	52	47	50	73
+22	-11	-33	-53	-1	-15	-42	-29	-26	-15	-24	-52

CLASS				PARTY			REGION				
AB	C_1	C_2	DE	Con	Lib	Lab	South	Wales & West	Mid-lands	North	Scot-land
142	242	341	387	381	58	494	437	117	143	320	95
%	%	%	%	%	%	%	%	%	%	%	%
36	18	16	13	33	16	7	21	11	24	15	9
27	36	26	21	35	33	22	29	28	23	27	20
14	12	13	18	13	10	13	13	12	16	16	16
12	12	16	18	7	12	21	12	23	16	16	15
10	23	29	30	12	29	36	25	26	20	25	40
63	54	42	34	68	49	29	50	39	47	42	29
22	35	45	48	19	41	57	37	49	46	41	55
+41	+19	-3	-15	+49	+8	-28	+13	-10	+1	+1	-26

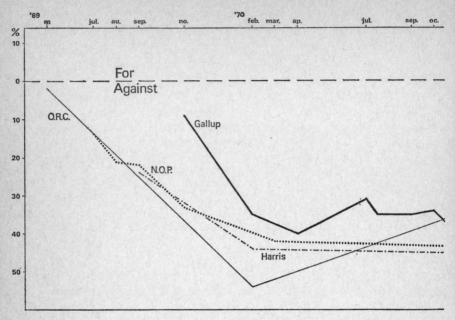

Diagram 3   Composite Graph of ORC, NOP, Gallup and Harris polls.

Diagram 3 and also so far as ORC only is concerned in the first column on page 366. From a plateau of readings near or below – 30% (the minus reading indicates more opposed than favourable to entry) from February until the end of June, all the lines then leapt up suddenly about the beginning of July. As it happened National Opinion Polls had a survey in the field on 6–12 July which was subsequently split by the exact date of interview to see what impact the publication of the government's White Paper had made:

NOP: *Do you approve or disapprove of Britain joining the Common Market?*

	All	**Interviewed on** 6–7 July	8–12 July
	%	%	%
Approve	34	29	39
Disapprove	44	47	41
Don't know	22	24	20

(NOP added: 'This could be a sampling freak, yet in terms of age, class and sex and voting intention those contacted on Thursday [8 July] or later were not dissimilar to those contacted on Wednesday or before.')

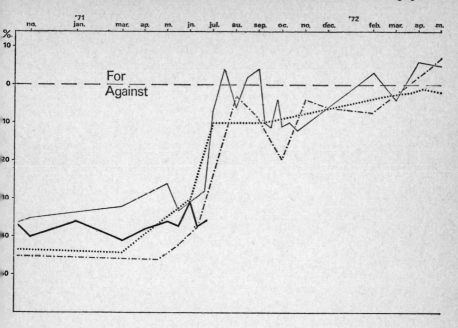

The sudden swing in public opinion towards entry into the EEC is all the more startling if one sees it against the background of voting intentions at that time. Though it was a Conservative government that was urging entry and a Labour Opposition that was shying away, the percentage of the electors who declared they would vote Conservative dropped from 48% in April to 45% in May, 40% in June and 39% in July (according to ORC). Yet between the end of April and the end of July the percentage in favour of entry (again according to ORC) rose from 30% in late April and 26% in late May, to 45% in late July. In no way therefore can the swing towards the government's chief foreign policy have been induced by a swing towards the government as such; on the contrary, the 15% swing towards entry took place in spite of a 10% swing against the government that was advocating it.

However that may be, as from early July the ORC poll after the sudden leap showed a quite different, if still uneven, plateau of opinion oscillating between −10% and +4%, including three positive readings out of four from late July to early September. Then support seemed to seep away somewhat and partially rally again in the further course of that month. It was this sudden shift in the balance by 32 points over a period of four weeks in July that gave heart to the pro-Marketeers, even if the predictions of their optimists that the trend would continue until there was a majority in favour subsequently proved unfounded. The firm trend simply stopped, and the line bobbed about until the vote at the end of October. To explain and expand we must now turn to the various sectional breakdowns of the total population.

The first, and indeed one of the most striking, is that by sex. In every single instance, less women were in favour of entry than men, and though in every single instance as well there were more women 'don't knows' than men, there were still always also more women opposed to entry than men. Often this held good even in the case of those 'strongly against'. Never except in May 1972 were a majority of women in favour of entry. One may hazard the guess that the cost of living arguments were not only the ones most easily understood by the female population, but that they were also the ones to have the most immediate impact on them. The difference between the sexes as measured in this way tended to increase as the summer went on, until in the survey at the end of September 1971 there was a 25% gap between them: the balance of men was $+8\%$, that of women -17%.

The second breakdown to note is that into age-groups. Consistently (with only one exception) the results most favourable to entry were obtained from people between 25 and 45, with the younger age-group from 15–25 close runners-up (and in the lead once, in early September, perhaps because some of them had just come back from roaming the Continent). The over-64s, on the other hand, consistently held the most anti-Market attitudes (though in early July they swung far more than the other age-groups, from a 47% majority against entry to a temporary one of only 5% against by late July). Anxiety as to radical change and fear of higher prices unmatched by bigger long-run prospects beyond their biological reach make a perfectly rational justification for their suspicion and hostility. The 45–65 age-group usually came between the two extremes and swung very much with the average.

The analysis by socio-economic grouping is even more revealing. The upper middle and professional class had a small majority opposed to joining in the beginning of May: by the time of the Paris summit they were evenly split, and in late July there was a 22% majority in favour of entry, though the country at large during those six weeks remained profoundly opposed. The C1 group of clerical, administrative, civil service and supervisory grades started moving in favour, though less decisively, a fortnight after the ABs, and as from early July always had a majority in favour of entry that peaked at 31% in late August, though it then nearly disappeared again at the end of September. The C2s seem to have started shifting in the same direction as the C1s some ten days later; they twice nearly got to an even balance, but fell away again into opposition in September.

The DE group of manual workers started as the most hostile, moving from −40% to −53% between February and early June. Then, in the fortnight to 7–11 July, it was particularly this lowest socio-economic group which swung extensively, just two months after the middle class. Its majority against entry dropped in those two weeks from − 53% to only −10% – the lowest the DE group ever registered. It was a bigger swing even than that of the over-64s. Nevertheless, in every single reading throughout the chart as one went down the social scale, one always found less support for entry and almost always a greater percentage in opposition to it. (With more refined instruments one could perhaps set up models of the time taken for this kind of swing of opinion to filter down from the AB group to the C1 and then the C2 and DE groups. There is a remarkable, if rather crude, one month's displacement in the big shift between the AB and the C1, and then the C2 and DE groups.)

If we turn to the regional breakdown of opinion, there appears to be one outstanding feature: the decided opposition in Scotland early in the year, with 81% opposed as against only 14% in favour of entry (and only 5% of 'don't knows' as compared, for example, with 17% of 'don't knows' in Wales and the West, rising in later polls to 24%). But the Scots, decided as they were, were not immune to the general shift of opinion in July; and then, on top of that, they seem to have had a sizable shift peculiar to themselves at the end of August and in late September (perhaps in response to the very vigorous campaigning on the part, among others, of their Labour MPs). By the end of September the 'pros' had risen from 14% to 43%, the 'antis' were down from 81% to 50%. So the Scots suddenly swung, from their initial extreme opposition, to an attitude much less unfavourable than Wales, the West and the North.

The other regions were less distinctive in their gradient of attitudes. On all the other socio-economic breakdowns it proved simple so to arrange the columns in our tables that within each section support for entry fell, and opposition to entry increased, from left to right consistently; but in the regional section the South, Wales and the West,

ORC: *How much are you in favour of or against Britain joining the European Common Market?*

	All	SEX		AGE				CLASS			
		Male	Female	16–24	25–44	45–64	65+	AB	C$_1$	C$_2$	DE
17–21 Feb. 1971[1]	−32	−25	−36	−21	−24	−34	−51	−4	−14	−35	−45
28 April–2 May[2]	−26	−18	−35	−22	−19	−29	−44	−05	−19	−25	−40
19–23 May	−33	−26	−40	−26	−25	−39	−38	+1	−29	−38	−44
23–27 June	−28	−20	−34	−13	−16	−37	−47	+22	−11	−33	−53
7–11 July	−7	+1	−15	−5	−1	−10	−13	+24	+5	−15	−10
21–23 July	+4	+9	−5	+4	+8	+3	−5	+41	+19	−3	−15
4–8 August	−6	+3	−12	−5	+6	−15	−9	+42	+15	−11	−27
18–22 August	+2	+13	−7	+8	+12	+3	−12	+38	+31	−6	−20
1–5 September	+3	+12	−3	+22	+11	+3	−20	+40	+27	−2	−18
15–19 September	−10	0	−18	+2	+2	−11	−30	+27	+20	−24	−29
24 September	−11										
22–26 September	−4	+8	−17	−2	+6	−8	−16	+46	+2	−13	−28
29 Sept–3 Oct.	−11	−1	−20	−21	−4	−11	−31	+37	+19	−27	−37
6–10 October	−10	−3	−17	−13	−4	−15	−17	+36	+8	−18	−35
13–17 October	−12	−4	−20	−9	−2	−14	−29	+39	+11	−12	−48
3–7 November[3]	−6	−4	−10	−8	+2	−2	−22	+55	+2	−6	−30
2–6 Feb. 1972[4]	+3	+8	−2	+6	+7	+7	−7	+67	+18	−9	−34
1–5 March[4]	−4	+7	−13	−3	+11	−4	−35	+47	+18	−16	−30
5–9 April[4]	+6	+19	−8	+15	+21	+2	−16	+43	+32	0	−24
3–7 May[4]	+5	+7	+3	+11	+16	+8	−20	+49	+33	−9	−20
13–17 September[5]	−9	0	−18	−1	−3	−9	−23	+44	−2	−17	−28

and the Midlands jostled each other out of the left-hand position at various dates, with the South and the Midlands tending to have majorities in favour as from the beginning of July. The North was less favourably inclined than any of the other parts of England, though (until the sudden final Scottish spurt in favour) rather less hostile than Scotland. The polls should not really be regarded as very good evidence on regional swings; though care is taken to make them representative at a national level, they are not always necessarily representative within each region taken separately. But where, as in the Scottish case, other polls with similar questions (like the Harris poll) confirm the ORC findings, the evidence cannot be ignored.

[1] In this poll the words 'or against' were omitted from the question.

[2] In this poll the words 'Britain' and 'European' were omitted from the question.

[3] In this poll the question was: Parliament having decided in favour of Britian's entry into the European Common Market, do you now agree with the decision or not?

[4] In these polls the question was: How much do you approve or disapprove of Britain's membership of the Common Market?

[5] In this poll the question was: Are you in favour of Britain joining the Common Market or not?

PARTY			REGION						
Con	Lib	Lab	South	Wales & West	Wales	West	Mid-lands	North	Scot-land
−20	−17	−39	−27	−19			−32	−30	−67
−8	−31	−47	−22	−11			−23	−33	−48
−12	−23	−43	−30	−28			−32	−26	−46
−1	−15	−42	−29	−26			−15	−24	−52
+30	−8	−28	−2	+3			+3	−15	−35
+42	+8	−28	+13	−10			+1	+1	−26
+37	−18	−31	−5	+3			+5	−6	−31
+36	−24	−24	+16	−14			+11	−2	−35
+40	−2	−24	+5	..	+23	−1	+7	+10	−14
+23	−1	−32	−5	..	−22	−6	−5	−13	−28
+33	−11	−28	+5	..	−19	−22	+5	−11	−7
+32	−14	+3	−16	−4			+15	−11	−43
+27	−1	−36	−5	−19			−11	−11	−26
..	..	..	−12	−8			−5	−15	−20
46	−12	−45	−11	+2			+2	−3	−23
+51	−14	−39	+5	+3			−1	−1	+5
+37	+1	−35	−2	−7			+3	−8	−3
+44	+8	−24	−6	+17			−9	+4	+17
+44	−2	−24	+5	+4			+18	+1	−11
+22	−2	−28	..	..			..	..	..

The picture according to party support is of course of special political significance. In February 1971 54% of Conservative supporters were opposed to entry, and only 34% in favour. (Of these only 10% were very strongly in favour, as against 31% very strongly opposed.) In early May 50% of Conservative supporters were still against entry, with 38% in favour (only 11% very strongly so). But then by 7–11 July – that is, just at and after the publication of the White Paper, but, be it noted, before the Central Council rally in the Central Hall – the picture was transformed: only 28% of Conservative supporters remained opposed to entry, 58% were in favour (23% very strongly so). A fortnight later the 'very strong' supporters had reached 33%, total supporters 68%, while the opponents had withered to 19% (of whom only 12% were strongly against). In other words in just two months at least 30% of Conservatives must have changed their minds. This was a remarkable exercise either of swift political judgment or else of party leadership – or (more probably) a combination of the two.

This shift was contemporaneous with the rallying of the Conservative Parliamentary Party. It would be a wise political scientist who could assign degrees of causal responsibility to the two parallel phenomena for each other. But in so far as Labour supporters in early July swung

in the same direction – and against their own party leadership's trend –
by almost half as much as Conservative supporters, it cannot have been
just Conservative MPs who caused the swing; most if not all of the
swing must have been due to the turn of events, general moods in the
country, and the government's appeal over the heads of Members of
Parliament direct to the people. The MPs, most likely, were shifting
in parallel with these representative samples of their voters (which, up
to a point, is as things ought to be).

The Liberal supporters are a very small group, and not too much
reliance must be placed on any one figure from samples in which one
person interviewed can actually swing two percentage points. The
February–October readings taken together do, however, suggest a
pattern: Liberal supporters came somewhere between Conservative
and Labour supporters in their attitudes, and in spite of their party's
long-standing commitment to the cause did not show themselves
significantly more favourable to entry than the rest of the population.
They may, indeed, have been slightly less favourable than the average
in their class and region.

Of particular fascination in view of what was going on at the top of
their party is the evolution of opinion among Labour supporters. To as
avid a reader of public opinion polls as Harold Wilson, the solidly
above-average opposition to entry displayed by Labour voters up to
the end of June must have been a convincing and weighty consideration. If his course was set for a progressive repudiation of entry (at least
on the terms that were then becoming known), the sudden shift in
early July (by which the percentage of Labour voters who supported
entry rose from 20% to 28%) might not have had such immediate
significance. But thanks to a simultaneous drop in Labour opponents
of entry, the Labour balance against in fact dropped from – 42% in
late June to – 28% in early July. The special party conference changed
nothing there, and the final declaration by the Party Leader against
entry on 28 July could not boost the majority opposed beyond – 31%.
Indeed the majority opposed was down to – 24% a fortnight after
Harold Wilson's public decision – nowhere within shouting distance
of its size before the party had declared its stand and embarked on its
public relations campaign. Moreover the supporters of entry were to
exceed a third of Labour supporters in late August. At no stage
between the end of June and the October vote did even 60% of Labour
supporters declare themselves opposed to entry, though the figures had
been above 60% in each of the previous four polls. It would seem that,

if there was any significant short-term causal relationship here, the chief one was that of the Labour leadership responsive to Labour voters – with the voters then becoming less decided (perhaps in response to the government's campaign) as their party became more extreme in its commitment to opposition.

It is a pity that, since all these are one-shot interviews, we can see only net changes between points in time, and that there is, alas, no real body of evidence relating the opinions of individual members of the general public on the Common Market to their views on other issues over any period. But for the 1963–66 period we do have Butler and Stokes' panel study which brings out several interesting correlations. The most striking of them is concerned with stable attitudes on such issues as the renunciation of nuclear weapons, the toleration of immigration, and the view that unions were not too powerful – all views typically associated with the Left: 'Despite the alignment on the Common Market which the parties assumed under Mr Macmillan and Mr Gaitskell electors who held the "left" position on other issues were more likely to favour *entering* Europe and those who held the "right" position to oppose it.'[1] In other words entry into EEC was seen or felt as a possible banner for the Left rather than the Right, even when the official party leaderships were lined up diametrically the opposite way. But then the issue was not in the forefront of party controversy at that time.

We still find something of the same correlation of attitudes under political circumstances where both parties were simultaneously in favour of entry. The ORC poll of May 1969 shows this clearly, with a 32-point difference between Labour and Conservative support for entry – Labour people on balance in favour, Conservatives on balance against. Only as the Labour party leadership swung firmly into

ORC: *Are you in favour of Britain joining the Common Market or not?*

	Conservatives			Labour		
	May 1969	Dec. 1971	Change	May 1969	Dec. 1971	Change
Yes	36	57	+ 21	52	24	− 28
No	48	29	+ 19	32	64	− 32
(Balance	− 12	+ 28	+ 40	+ 20	− 40	− 60)
Don't know	16	14	− 2	16	12	− 4

[1] Butler and Stokes, op. cit., p. 247.

opposition and the Conservative government declared its support for entry full blast did Conservative voters' support for entry and Labour supporters' opposition to it polarize, with a 68-point difference between them the opposite way from 1969.

In a way the most disturbing table of all is the one showing the very definite profile in the popular view of the sort of people who would benefit, and the sort who would suffer if Britain were to join the Common Market (see below). If the campaign for entry had set out to persuade the country of the benefits, it certainly did not seem to have brought home personal benefits to the bulk of individual voters. Even if the very harsh class differentiation of the summer seemed to be softening a little in the autumn, the issue remained one on which Britain seemed (as on so much else) divided into two nations. Compared with that fact the plethora of other opinion polls seems relatively subsidiary, and is therefore relegated to Appendix C.

Views on Beneficiaries and Victims, 1971 (Gallup)

	BENEFIT			SUFFER		
	Aug.	Sept.	Oct.	Aug.	Sept.	Oct.
Manufacturers, exporters	36	29	29	2	1	1
Financiers, bankers, commerce	26	27	24	1	—	—
Well-to-do people, upper class	13	19	19	1	1	—
Professional people	13	10	9	1	—	1
Working people	8	8	8	39	35	31
Housewives	2	2	2	31	27	28
Old age pensioners	..	..	2	..	..	33
Farmers	8	6	7	22	19	15
Fishermen	1	1	1	22	14	13
Others	9	10	8	17	21	14
Everybody	11	12	10	5	5	8
Nobody	6	4	7	8	8	8
Don't know	18	14	18	12	9	12

It would not be in the interests of the Community that its enlargement should take place except with the full-hearted consent of the Parliaments and peoples of the new member states   Edward Heath

The Vote of Principle

Such was the background in public opinion against which the set-piece debate of principle took place in the House of Commons. It lasted for six days in late October 1971. The motion had been framed with care by the government, after detailed consultation with one or two Labour Marketeers, to ensure that it would muster the maximum possible vote. (The Labour Marketeers wondered afterwards if they should have insisted also on deleting all reference to the government, but were on the whole well content with the wording.) It read: 'That this House approves Her Majesty's Government's decision to join the European Communities on the basis of the arrangements which have been negotiated.'

It was a purely declaratory motion, without legal effect. And of course it was being taken before the text of the Treaty of Accession had been drafted – indeed before the fisheries issue (and quite a number of minor matters) had been finally settled in Brussels. But enough was known of the terms through the government's White Paper of July for the agreements on the bulk of the major subjects to be clearly understood; and, in any case, the agreements reached in Brussels essentially concerned the problems of transition, while what was really at stake now were not so much the next half-dozen years as something much larger: British accession to a Community whose common legislation could override British national decisions and which (though the Coal and Steel Treaty was concluded for only fifty years) has provided in its constitutional texts for no procedure of withdrawal.

Some 180 MPs spoke during the course of the debate – though for the first five days of it the gallery was as usual better filled than the House. For days there had been long queues, and on the final night excited crowds of enthusiasts and dissenters massed at the gates of the Palace of Westminster. Inside, in the diplomatic gallery, escorted by representatives of the Community, sat Jean Monnet, with whom Edward Heath had been in close touch over the past decade or more. Close by sat Jean-René Bernard from the Elysée. When the Lords, after a three-day debate, had taken their overwhelming vote of 451 to 58 in favour, Lord George-Brown came over, squatted on the steps of the Strangers' Gallery, and on a disputed point down on the floor was spotted intervening with a mute gesture – to the delight of some of his cheering ex-colleagues below. It was a parliamentary occasion unparalleled in many years.

The record of the debate is one to be read, not summarized. There was little in it that was new in substance from the government side, though Harold Wilson's formula for re-negotiation was listened to with minute attention in the diplomatic gallery:

I now wish, before coming to a conclusion, to deal with the position of a Labour Government coming into office, after accession to the Community. . . . What we should do – this was made clear by my right hon. Friend – would be immediately to give notice that we could not accept the terms negotiated by the Conservatives, and, in particular, the unacceptable burdens arising out of the CAP, the blows to the Commonwealth, and any threats to our essential regional policies.

If the Community then refused to negotiate, as we should have asked, or if the negotiations were to fail, we would sit down amicably and discuss the situation with them. (*Laughter.*) Well, neither coffee nor cognac, but British beer, at its present standards. (*Hon. Members: 'Oh.'*). . . .

We should make clear that our posture, like that of the French after 1958, would be rigidly directed towards the pursuit of British interests and that all other decisions and actions in relation to the Community would be dictated by that determination, until we had secured our terms. They might accept this, or they might decide that we should agree to part; that would depend on them. That is our position.[1]

Edward Heath wound up the debate, sitting down at 10.00 p.m. While he was still speaking, a frail elderly figure picked its way from the Labour benches over the legs of a House packed to the limit, crossing the floor towards the lobby of the Ayes: John Rankin, a Left-wing MP in his eighties, who feared he would not make the Ayes lobby in the later crush. On the Opposition front bench, Roy Jenkins, Harold Wilson, Denis Healey and James Callaghan sat pressed together in what must have been embarrassing physical proximity. It was the

[1] Hansard, 28 October, 1971, cols 2103-4.

climax of the domestic political battle that had been raging for the previous six months or more, and building up for years before that.

The high drama of the days leading up to 'the 28th' and of the debate that afternoon and evening, the emotions in the Chamber, the lobbies, and in the television studios putting out marathon Common Market programmes that night we have seen reflected to some extent in the chapter on the press. Immediately after the vote was announced Harold Macmillan lit a beacon fire on the cliffs of Dover, to be answered by another beacon from Calais. There was a party of celebration in Admiralty House. The European Movement, the Labour Marketeers, and a good deal of the public felt that victory had gone – by a majority very few would have predicted even a fortnight before – to the pro-Market cause. The voting was 356 Ayes, 244 Noes. The majority of 112 was in fact slightly larger than that by which the French National Assembly had ratified the EEC treaty in 1957:

Ratification Majorities in the Lower Houses of the Six

	ECSC (1951)			EEC (1957)			Euratom (1957)		
	For	Against	Abs.	For	Against	Abs.	For	Against	Abs.
Belgium	165	13	13	174	4	2	174	4	2
France	376	240	11	341	235	..	337	243	..
Germany	232	142	3	Large majorities by show of hands					
Italy	265	98	201	311	144	54	365	144	..
Luxemburg	47	4	1	46	3		45	3	..
Netherlands	62	6	32	144	12	..	120	6	..

The euphoria on the pro-Market side was, however, not matched by corresponding dejection on the part of anti-Marketeers. A vote of principle on a declaratory motion was one thing: the passage through the House of Commons of all the enactments that were the prerequisite of full legal membership was quite another. Leading anti-Marketeers declared with some show of sincerity that they remained convinced that Britain would not in fact enter the Community at all. Public opinion was still on balance against entry – even before all the details had been spelt out. Eighty-nine Labour Marketeers might in a mass make one grand gesture; but even under the Houghton doctrine, quite apart from the pressures which would come from their constituencies, they could not possibly vote with the government and against the majority of their own party night after night after night. With an Opposition that would substantially close ranks, attention would focus on the forty-one Conservatives who had voted against entry on principle or abstained: the government's fate would be in their hands.

If they stood firm, the government could be forced to go to the country; and the electorate would most likely (if only on general economic grounds – unemployment or inflation) put back into power a Prime Minister pledged to 're-negotiate' and if necessary to drop the whole idea. The opposition to entry, in other words, refused to lie down defeated: they were convinced that, though 'the 28th' might have been a battle lost, they had by no means yet lost the war.

The European Communities Bill

In the original member states, the two Rome Treaties on the EEC and Euratom, like the Paris Treaty on Coal and Steel, had, according to their constitutions, been laid before their chambers, debated, and ratified by vote of the legislature. In Britain, however, the treaty-making power is an executive prerogative: ratification is normally by the sovereign, on the advice of her government. It was with affected or genuine surprise that, early in 1972, anti-Marketeers realized not only that the treaty would be signed before it had even been published (the lawyers and translators were still working until the last few days to put its total of over 300 pages into final shape), but also that there would at no stage be any debate in Parliament on the treaty as such.

Clearly, there was no possibility of Parliament amending a treaty negotiated and signed by ten sovereign states. While the debate might have allowed MPs to put their views on the details, these views could not therefore affect the texts: in that sense the only question remained the simple one of to join or not to join. No doubt a debate on the texts would have been much more detailed than the October debate, but in the end the question for decision was still only the simple yes or no to the treaty as a whole. (Suggestions from the Opposition that Parliament might seek amendments from the other nine signatories were given short shrift from the Continent.) In any case Parliament would have to pass a bill to make joining legally possible. This would thus be the form in which Parliament gave its final approval. Ratification by the sovereign would be held over until Parliament had enacted the legislation to give the treaties legal effect in Britain.

It is here that the constitutional difference between the six Continental countries and Britain becomes most relevant. In their case international law quite explicitly takes precedence under the constitution over domestic law: just as their legislatures cannot by simple legislative process amend their constitutions (but can do so if at all only under special procedures involving larger majorities or other safeguards), so once they have ratified an international law binding them to fulfil certain obligations, the national judicial system is legally bound in case of apparent conflict to give the fulfilment of those obligations precedence over national statutes. In Britain, on the other hand, international treaties, not normally being ratified by Parliament, are not part of domestic law. Moreover Parliament, not being bound by any constitution, can enact statutes that conflict with the country's international obligations and yet expect their legal enforcement. (This is one aspect of the famous problem of 'Parliamentary sovereignty'.) Therefore, instead of ratifying the treaty, Parliament would have to translate it into domestic law; without such a statute, the domestic legislative implications of the treaty would remain legally inapplicable in Britain. Its purely international aspects, on the other hand, did not require any statute: which is why neither the trading arrangements with New Zealand nor the changes in fishing limits required parliamentary enactment.

When Labour Ministers had been laying their plans in 1967, they had been advised that they would have to put through Parliament a 'Bill of a Thousand Clauses' which might take up to a year of parliamentary time. Some of them, therefore, were somewhat galled when the Conservative government, a few days after the signature of the Treaty in Brussels, published a single bill of 12 clauses, which even with its attached 4 schedules came to no more than 37 pages.

The government law officers, headed by Sir Geoffrey Howe, had in fact been considering a gamut of possibilities. At one end stood the possibility of two bills, one of a constitutional character and another the 'Bill of a Thousand Clauses' which would have explicitly amended every single statute that might need amending to comply with every single Community instrument – whether on weights and measures or on safety regulations or the proportions of foreign to British films screened in British cinemas, on quality standards in gas meters or the improper breakage of seals. With every single item exposed to parliamentary gaze and voted on (at least in committee), the parliamentary time taken and the hackles raised by one clause after another in one quarter or another would have made this a tedious and – for the government – highly dangerous procedure. At the other end of the range of possibilities stood a single one-clause bill, simply enacting that all present and future Community law would hereby automatically be British law, in case of doubt or conflict superseding Parliament's unilateral enactments. This would have seemed an abdication of parliamentary sovereignty so wholesale and explicit as to have disturbed or affronted quite a few Conservative MPs to a needless and again possibly dangerous degree. What the government settled for was a compromise between the two extremes – though very much on the economical side: a single, two-part bill, of which Part 1 in three clauses dealt with the constitutional problems, including those of finance, and Part 2 in nine clauses dealt with specific matters on which British law had to be changed in the immediate future.

The bill, according to the Explanatory and Financial Memorandum preceding it, was designed to make 'the legislative changes which will enable the United Kingdom to comply with the obligations entailed by membership' and to exercise the rights of membership of the Communities.

Clause 1 defined a Community treaty: not simply the Accession Treaty itself and the three basic treaties and the two supplementary treaties (the one of 1967 establishing a single Council and a single Commission for all three Communities, the other of 1970 amending some of its budgetary provisions), but also the scores of treaties with Latin American countries, African countries, Middle Eastern countries and so forth to be specified as Community treaties by Order in Council; though new treaties were not to be specified as such unless a draft of the Order in Council had been approved by resolution in each House of Parliament – thus in effect giving Parliament a theoretical veto on any domestic obligations arising out of future Community treaties.

Clause 2 was the heart of the bill. Its first subsection gave automatic force of law to such present and future Community law as was self-executing under the treaties. Subsection 2 dealt with Community law which under the treaties needed enactment by each nation state to determine its detailed implementation within each member country. Subsection 3 dealt with Britain's financial obligations to the Community. The most vital parts of Clause 2 of the bill read as follows:

(1) All such rights, powers, *liabilities, obligations*[1] and restrictions from time to time created or arising by or under the Treaties, and all such remedies and procedures from time to time provided for by or under the Treaties, as in accordance with the Treaties are without further enactment to be given legal effect or used in the United Kingdom shall be recognised and available in law, and be enforced, allowed and followed accordingly; and the expression 'enforceable

[1] Parts of bills which are directly financial in character are printed in italics: they are the concern only of the Commons, not the Lords.

Community right' and similar expressions shall be read as referring to one to which this subsection applies.

(2) Subject to Schedule 2 of this Act, at any time after its passing Her Majesty may by Order in Council, and any designated Minister or department may by regulations, make provision –

(a) for the purpose of implementing any Community obligation of the United Kingdom, or enabling any such obligation to be implemented, or of enabling any rights enjoyed or to be enjoyed by the United Kingdom under or by virtue of the Treaties to be exercised; or

(b) for the purpose of dealing with matters arising out of or related to any such obligation or rights or the coming into force, or the operation from time to time, of subsection (1) above;

and in the exercise of any statutory power or duty, including any power to give directions or to legislate by means of orders, rules, regulations or other sub-ordinate instrument, the person entrusted with the power or duty may have regard to the objects of the Communities and to any such obligation or rights as aforesaid.

In this subsection 'designated Minister or department' means such Minister of the Crown or government department as may from time to time be designated by Order in Council in relation to any matter or for any purpose, but subject to such restrictions or conditions (if any) as may be specified by the Order in Council.

(3) *There shall be charged on and issued out of the Consolidated Fund or, if so determined by the Treasury, the National Loans Fund the amounts required to meet any Community obligation to make payments to any of the Communities or member States. . . .*

Clause 3 made sure that Community treaties and instruments would be regarded as proved and treated in legal proceedings in accordance with the jurisprudence of the European Court. Schedule 1 set out certain definitions, while Schedule 2 limited the powers of the government to make subordinate legislation under Clause 2 (2) in various ways, and provided that

any statutory instrument containing an Order in Council or regulations made in the exercise of a power so conferred, if made without a draft having been approved by resolution of each House of Parliament, shall be subject to annulment in pursuance of a resolution of either House.

These three sections with their two schedules were sufficient to cope with the constitutional problems.

Part II of the bill dealt with amendments to British legislation. Clause 4 introduced Schedules 3 and 4 of the bill which listed the acts or parts of acts repealed and the enactments amended – from part of a section of the 1971 Finance Act down to the Coal Consumers' Councils (Northern Irish Interests) Act of 1964 and the dispositions on the grading of fresh horticultural produce laid down in the Agriculture and Horticulture Act 1964. Clause 5 dealt with customs duties, Clause 6 with agriculture in general, Clause 7 with the Sugar Board, Clause 8 with foreign films, Clause 9 brought some aspects of company law into line with Community rules, Clause 10 dealt with restrictive practices, Clause 11 made it a criminal offence to give false evidence before the European Court or disclose classified Euratom information, and Clause 12 allowed statistical information to be disclosed to the Communities. And that was all.

The bill left out the Value Added Tax, embodied in the subsequent Finance Bill, and all those changes in the law which either could be made by the government using its existing powers to make subordinate legislation or else did not need early application on accession. The number of matters already agreed in the negotiations and on which further legislation would be required over the next few years was, however, fairly small: the government thought that not more than four instruments of delegated legislation would be required in 1972, and a dozen in 1973.

The Constitutional Problem

The general problem which the bill was designed to meet had been stated very fairly in the Labour government's White Paper of 1967, *Legal and Constitutional Implications of United Kingdom Membership of the European Communities*:[1]

COMMUNITY LAW

Application by the United Kingdom Parliament

20.   If this country became a member of the European Communities it would be accepting Community law. By 'Community law' is meant the whole body of legal rights and obligations deriving from the Treaties or their instruments, whether conferred or imposed on the Member States, on individuals or undertakings, or on the Community institutions. A substantial body of legislation would be required to enable us to accept the law.

21.   In the first place provision would have to be made for those matters on which the Treaties leave the necessary legislation to be passed by Member States, for example, in the fields of customs duties, agriculture and transport.

[1] Cmnd 3301, reprinted in *The Second Try*, ed cit., pp. 113–32.

For this purpose complex legislation would be needed immediately on joining the Communities; and further legislation would be needed from time to time to give effect to subsequent Community instruments. Legislation of this character poses no new problem. The necessary provisions would be enacted by Parliament, or possibly by delegated legislation issued under Parliamentary authority which could cover future as well as present Community instruments. 22. Secondly, it would be necessary to pass legislation giving the force of law to those provisions of the Treaties and Community instruments which are intended to take direct internal effect within the Member States. This legislation would be needed, because, under our constitutional law, adherence to a treaty does not of itself have the effect of changing our internal law even where provisions of the treaty are intended to have direct internal effect as law within the participating States. The legislation would have to cover both provisions in force when we joined and those coming into force subsequently as a result of instruments issued by the Community institutions. No new problem would be created by the provisions which were in force at the time we became a member of the Communities. The constitutional innovation would lie in the acceptance in advance as part of the law of the United Kingdom of provisions to be made in the future by instruments issued by the Community institutions – a situation for which there is no precedent in this country. However, these instruments, like ordinary delegated legislation, would derive their force under the law of the United Kingdom from the original enactment passed by Parliament.

Impact on United Kingdom Law

23. The Community law, having direct internal effect, is designed to take precedence over the domestic law of the Member States. From this it follows that the legislation of the Parliament of the United Kingdom giving effect to that law would have to do so in such a way as to override existing national law so far as inconsistent with it. The result need not be left to implication, and it would be open to Parliament to enact from time to time any necessary consequential amendments or repeals. It would also follow that within the fields occupied by the Community law Parliament would have to refrain from passing fresh legislation inconsistent with that law as for the time being in force. This would not however involve any constitutional innovation. Many of our treaty obligations already impose such restraints – for example, the Charter of the United Nations, the European Convention of Human Rights and GATT.

Certainly there was a difficulty here which had never presented itself in quite that form to the Six. When the Parliaments of the Six ratified the three original treaties in 1951 and 1957, the ratio of substantive domestic policy to foreign policy content involved in the issue had been low. The EEC treaty was an outline treaty, with its backbone of operational commitments practically confined to tariffs. Everything else was to be settled thereafter – and the treaty was little more than an agreement to agree by certain procedures. But the domestic implications – particularly those of the EEC treaty – had grown immensely over the years. By the time Britain came to join, volumes upon volumes of agreements had been reached: and they had been reached by procedures in which the Six had been represented, but Britain had not. No wonder that the Opposition complained not only that future legislation would be made by procedures that by-passed parliamentary representation, but also that by the simple application of two or three clauses of the bill pre-existing Community legislation was being made applicable in Britain which no parliamentarian would ever have time even to read, let alone debate or vote on.

In two respects the Opposition was here pointing to perfectly valid concerns. The fact that the Community's procedures were essentially inter-governmental and bureaucratic, with little direct control by any directly elected representatives of the citizens affected, was causing dissatisfaction among the Six themselves. (Some of them looked forward to British entry among other reasons precisely because they hoped British parliamentary traditions would shift the balance within the Community in favour of early institutional reform on that front.) Secondly, the degree of control by the British Parliament over delegated legislation – whether concerned with the EEC or with any other subject under the sun – hardly seemed adequate to many parliamentarians in any case. Orders in Council, if the government regard them as important, get at most one-and-a-half hours of debate in the House; if judged by the government to be less important, they are merely laid on the table and taken as approved by the 'negative procedure' unless they are prayed against and thrown out (without debate). So there was a case for improving the British Parliament's procedures on delegated legislation in general – indeed there was a Committee sitting at the time on that very matter – and clearly that case was reinforced by the degree to which delegated legislation would have to be used to implement Community law.

Yet, on the other hand, adopting the common rules was of the essence of joining the Community as it was: and since none of these rules could be amended unilaterally by the British Parliament, debating them all solemnly one by one would have made a mockery of Parliament indeed. Was the Opposition – so the *ad hominem* argument could run – not already complaining anyhow that the government, in urging Members to reject every amendment to the twelve clauses of the bill, was treating Parliament with what Michael Foot called 'full-hearted contempt'? The dilemma was thus inherent in joining the EEC at all. Clause 2 was, as Sir Geoffrey Howe put it, not 'an optional extra'. Parliament had voted in the Second and was to vote in the Third Reading for implementing the Accession Treaty. It could not will the end without willing the means. What is more, the Labour Party could not object to the automatic direct application of present and future Community law in Britain without objecting to the most basic principle of the Community itself – and thus shifting its ground into an opposition of principle, admitting its inconsistency with its own application of 1967 and exacerbating all the strains within its leadership and its ranks.

Nevertheless – as something of an afterthought, a carrot to combine with the stick of a threatened dissolution of Parliament if the Second Reading vote should go against the bill – the government was prepared to give Westminster a certain role. Not only, of course, would Community law have writ in the United Kingdom solely thanks to this Act of Parliament. Not only would British MPs sit in the European Parliament. Not only, as Geoffrey Rippon put it in the Second Reading debate, would no government

proceed on a matter of major policy in the Council unless they knew that they had the approval of the House . . . assuming that a question arose on which there had been strong feelings in this House, *prima facie* it would be a matter in the national interest and a British Minister would have power to insist in the Council of Ministers that it was a matter of major national importance which required a unanimous decision and that he could not be part of that unanimous decision

– suggesting that the Westminster Parliament would have an indirect power of veto under the 'Luxemburg Disagreement' of 1965. But also:

in addition to the traditional procedures, the Government believe that there is a need for the House to have special arrangements, under which it would be apprised of draft regulations and directives before they go to the Council of Ministers for decision. These arrangements should cover the instruments which will be directly applicable and the non-direct instruments.

In order that the details might be worked out in a way which meets the interests of Parliament as a whole, we propose that an *ad hoc* committee of both Houses of Parliament should be set up forthwith to consider what would be the most suitable method of ensuring adequate parliamentary scrutiny of these draft regulations and directives.[1]

[1] Hansard, 15 February 1972, cols 274–8.

Though Peter Shore's first response was to suggest the bill be abandoned until the *ad hoc* committee had reported, the Labour Party in the end refused to accept participation in any such committee. Opposed to entry on the terms obtained, it argued that it should not help to work out how Parliament could best scrutinize the implementing legal instruments. Moreover, the party even raised doubts as to whether it would allow its MPs to go to take part in the European Parliament if Britain did join: and, given the size of the government's majority, that might make it difficult for the government to allow a reasonable number of its own MPs to go to Strasbourg. Conservative members of the House of Lords and a few brave pro-Market Labour MPs might go, but that would hardly be the kind of British parliamentary contingent which the European Parliament would need in the opening years of the Community's enlargement. The Opposition was evidently out to show that, even if the bill passed by some 'wafer-thin' majorities in the House, without the 'full-hearted consent' of the people, Labour had ways of hobbling the government and undermining Britain's position in the Community from the start, not merely by the threat to renegotiate or withdraw, but quite immediately by impairing the functioning of the Community's own institutions.

Questions of Procedure

That implicit addition to the procedure outlined by the bill was, however, yet to come. In the opening weeks of 1972 there were several more immediate problems of procedure to be faced by the government. One of the ideas behind the proposal to table two separate bills had been that one of them, that on constitutional matters, should be taken on the floor of the House, the other, to implement the details, could be sent 'upstairs' to a Committee. While the major constitutional issues obviously had to run the full gauntlet of a committee of the whole House sitting in the Chamber, the detailed matters could then be dealt with more efficiently, more quietly and with greater certitude of a majority for the government on every clause if it was taken in Committee. Conservative anti-Marketeers could be virtually excluded from the Committee by the whips, and Labour pro-Marketeers might be included (and find it easier to be helpful in Committee than in the Chamber downstairs). The problem was whether the government could get a majority for sending the bill upstairs; and then the tacticians recalled that if a motion to send part of a bill upstairs was lost, under Standing Orders the whole of it was automatically sent upstairs.

In the end, however, perhaps particularly on William Whitelaw's advice, it was decided that the bill as it was finally drafted should be taken on the floor. It proved a wise decision, though of course it was not enough to stifle accusations by anti-Marketeers of both parties that the government was railroading the bill through the House.

The Labour Opposition, and some of the Conservative anti-Marketeers, were clearly determined not only to fight the bill clause by clause, but also to table so many amendments of major and minor import that the government would either have to give up trying to get the bill through the House, or else sacrifice the bulk of the rest of its legislative programme to doing so. With a Housing Finance Bill that was particularly distasteful to the Labour Party going through Parliament simultaneously, Labour pro-Marketeers in particular would be pressed hard into helping to obstruct the bill: their colleagues could always argue that obstruction, even if it did not bring down the government, would at least compel it to abandon its divisive domestic legislation. Michael Stewart at one stage threw out a hint to the government that if only they would abandon some of their other contentious schemes, they would find it much easier to get the European Communities Bill through the House.

But the government refused any such bargain. An alternative strategy for the government was to limit any attempts at filibustering that might be made, and if necessary to use the 'guillotine', by which discussion would be curtailed along a previously agreed timetable for votes to be taken on each clause in turn by certain dates and times. But they could be no more sure of obtaining a majority in the House for the imposition of a guillotine than they could be for sending the bill upstairs. Part of the tactics of the early stages thus had to be to allow the House enough freedom to feel fairly treated, and to give the Opposition enough rope so that a majority for a guillotine would slowly accumulate if it should be required. On 2 May 1972 the government did in fact move that only ten more days be devoted to the Committee stage (which had already taken up twelve days). It obtained a majority of eleven.

The government's third concern was over possible amendments actually being passed. There were two quite separate problems here. One was that no amendment should be in conflict with the requirements of the Accession Treaty and the basic treaties of the Community. The adoption of any such amendment would have prevented implementation of the treaties, and thus nullified the object of the exercise.

But there might also have been amendments which were compatible with these treaties, but which simply chose to implement the treaties in a somewhat different way from that proposed by the government. (The proposed *ad hoc* committee might itself, had it been set up, have put forward such modifications.) The government at first appeared very willing to entertain suggestions from the House of Commons of this kind. Once the bill was tabled, however, it became apparent that they were anxious to avoid any single such amendment being passed. This was for purely domestic procedural reasons: there would then have had to be a report stage on the floor of the House before the Third Reading, taking up more parliamentary time and letting the issue drag on until the party conference. They were thus determined to put through the whole bill, and nothing but the bill, in the exact form in which it had been tabled and without any amendment, however insignificant. It is difficult to believe that this second problem of the time-table was quite as vital as the first, that of satisfying the treaty. Had the House been allowed the feeling that there were some matters within Britain's national discretion on which it could alter the bill and engage in a genuine constructive dialogue with the government, a little of the heat might have gone out of the tense parliamentary situation.

Just what was required from the House became the subject of angry clashes as soon as the Committee stage began. As we have seen, Clause 1 of the bill gave a general definition of what a Community treaty was. It was immediately challenged by the Opposition (which in this context soon meant not only part of the Labour front bench, but also a small group of Conservative anti-Marketeers). Some opponents of entry even wanted every such treaty inserted verbatim into the bill, so that every part of each of the treaties could be debated by the House. That was the extreme position. Less extreme views were reflected in many of the amendments. This was not simply a matter of discussing treaties between the Community and Latin American trading partners: it seemed to anti-Market MPs a glaring anomaly that the Brussels Treaty of 22 January 1972 should not itself be subject to amendment by the House. The issue sparked off a two-and-a-half-hour procedural conflict on the very first day of the Committee stage. The Chairman of Ways and Means had selected only 12 of the first 69 amendments tabled, and ruled that all the more important ones not selected for debate had in fact been out of order, on the grounds that 'since this is not a Bill to approve the basic treaties, Amendments designed to vary the terms of those treaties are not in order, and I have no option to rule otherwise.' In the terms of Erskine May, quoted by another Member:

A committee is bound by the decision of the House, given on second reading, in favour of the principle of the Bill, and should not therefore amend the bill in a manner destructive of this principle.[1]

Or, as Sir John Foster put it later in the afternoon:

The House of Commons is not prevented from discussing anything except by its own rules. It is a rule of this House that wrecking Amendments are out of order. . . . If passed they will alter the treaty; and if we cannot bring the treaty into force, that will wreck the whole purpose of the Bill.

In other words the House could reject each and every clause, and in any case there was another chance of throwing everything out all at once at the Third Reading: but having accepted the bill in the Second Reading and sent it to Committee, the Committee stage could not be used to make the bill pass the gauntlet of amendment after amendment, each of which would have negatived its whole purpose.

As against this, the anti-Market opposition on both sides of the House felt that either the bill must in fact be one to approve the treaties, in which case amendments such as Michael Foot's to delay implementation until 1975 instead of 1973 must be in order (indeed surely a delay in implementation was not contrary to the principle of the bill?), or else the government was guilty of having drafted the bill in such a fashion as deliberately to exclude amendment of the terms of entry – some of which, like those of fishing limits – had not even been agreed at the time of the October debate of principle. As Enoch Powell put it: 'The House finds itself in the position, on the Bill, of being unable to debate a whole series of changes in the law of this country which will come about if the bill is passed.'[2] Since the government had promised the House full opportunity for debate just prior to signature, Douglas Jay felt that 'sharp practice has been piled on sharp practice throughout'.[3]

The Opposition first tabled a motion of censure on the Chairman of Ways and Means, which was lost after nearly six hours of debate, by

[1] Hansard, 1 March 1972, col. 455.
[2] Hansard, 29 February 1972, col. 272.
[3] Hansard, 1 March 1972, col. 452.

35 votes; and the House then sat on for another nearly nine hours of procedural wrangling until, at 7.00 in the morning, a few minutes of progress were finally made on the Committee stage of Clause 1 by a compromise behind the scenes. The following week the Opposition tabled a motion of censure on the government itself. The censure was defeated by 47 votes. But it is time to leave the legal and procedural wrangles and return to the politics of the situation in that first quarter of the year 1972. For, on the European Communities Bill itself, the government was by no means able to command such respectable majorities.

The Voting in 1972

There were in fact, in the course of the first seven months of 1972, 104 divisions on matters relating to British accession to the EEC, from the two divisions two days before the signing of the treaty (calling on the government not to sign until the full text had been published and laid before the House) until the Third Reading on 13 July. The government itself was not particularly popular in the country during this period. The Second Reading debate had to be held in emergency lighting thanks to a dispute in the power industry which abruptly raised the already high figure of one million unemployed even further. In the House neither the Liberals nor the Labour Party liked what was happening in Ulster – 13 people had just been shot by the army on 'Bloody Sunday' – and both certainly strongly disapproved of the attempt to reach a settlement with Ian Smith in Rhodesia. The exhausting struggles over the Housing Finance Bill dovetailed and sometimes overlapped with the European Communities Bill, tempers were frayed and feelings running high in the House, where even the official report recorded exchanges like '"The old twister!" Harold Wilson: "Shut up!"', and where the Home Secretary found himself physically assaulted by Bernadette Devlin. The Labour Chief Whip went on record in February as saying: 'I would do anything short of anarchy to bring this government down', and talked of 'smashing them', and Labour Marketeers, at least in February and March, were under constant pressure to vote against the government and their convictions in the hope that just one last shove would actually topple Edward Heath, force an election, and return Labour triumphant. No wonder some of them felt that if only the government were more popular, their policy of entry into the EEC would be seen to have plurality support in the country: it was the government's general unpopularity that seemed to them to be pulling the Market down with it, and making theirs an even more burdensome task.

The two score Conservative anti-Marketeers as they had defined themselves on 28 October were faced with a very different dilemma. On that occasion the government had, for what that was worth, taken off the whips. It may have been a gesture without very much meaning, but it gave the anti-Market Conservatives an argument, particularly in their constituencies, to defend their voting with the Opposition or abstaining. No such lifeline could be thrown to them in the votes on the Second Reading of the bill on 17 February, when the government was fighting for its survival with its back to the wall. The rebels were called in one after another, some of them interviewed by the Prime Minister in person, and told in no uncertain terms where their duty lay. Edward Heath and the whips made it very clear that this was a question of confidence, and that the government would resign if it did not obtain a majority that night. Just in case anyone thought they were bluffing, Edward Heath repeated this as the unanimous resolve of his cabinet in the House a few minutes before the division. The government scraped home with a majority of eight, and the political editor of *The Times* acknowledged: 'Writing from Westminster in the immediate aftermath of the division, I cannot say with certainty that the Government will be able to carry its Common Market legislation.'[1]

The majority of eight represented in fact something of a triumph over the Conservative anti-Marketeers: only 13 Conservatives and 2 Ulster Unionists (of the 39 who had voted against on 28 October) were still voting against the bill; only 6 Conservatives and Ulster Unionists had failed to vote.[2] More than half the rebels had come to heel at the first acid test. But in fact the rest were to keep up their opposition, to be joined from time to time by others, and when in early April the Ulster Unionists announced that in view of developments in Northern Ireland they were withdrawing their general support for the government, anxiety rose even further. The government had to reckon at times with

---

[1] 18 February 1972.

[2] The heroes of the resistance that night (with the total number of times they were to vote against the government in the 104 divisions in brackets as given by *The Political Companion*, No. 12) were Enoch Powell (81), John Biffen (78), Roger Moate (71), Neil Marten (69), Robin Turton (66), Richard Body (65), Sir Derek Walker-Smith (64), Anthony Fell (49), Michael Clark Hutchison (48), John Jennings (28), Ronald Bell (6), Sir Gerald Nabarro (2), David Mudd (1), plus two Ulster Unionists, James Molyneaux (47), and John Maginnis (31).

fully twenty defectors of one kind or another on a nominal majority of less than thirty.

What saved the government, and the European Communities Bill, was almost certainly the devotion to the European cause of a dozen or so people – five of the Liberals and a handful of Labour men who (though none of them ever carried their rebellion to the point of treading the other lobby, as the Conservative anti-Marketeers did) simply refused to vote against their convictions. On the night of 17 February seven Labour MPs abstained or were avoidably absent.[1] The seven Labour men could not have turned out the government. But if we assume nothing would have deterred the Conservative rebels, the five Liberals, had they voted the other way, could have inflicted on the government a defeat by two votes. The Labour Chief Whip, Robert Mellish, had made repeated attempts to get them to vote with the Opposition on the night of 17 February, appealing to them to throw out a government whose policies on Rhodesia, Ulster and unemployment the Liberals condemned as much as the Labour Party did. When the figures were announced, and it was realized that the Liberals' votes had enabled the bill to pass, Robert Mellish called them a 'gutter party' and there were unruly scenes with Jeremy Thorpe being jostled on the floor of the House by one or two angry Labour MPs – an ugly incident not quickly forgotten. While Emlyn Hooson voted against the bill (as he had voted against entry on 28 October), the other five Liberals felt that it would have been outrageous for them to vote against a policy which the Liberal Party had been the first to adopt, long before the Conservatives themselves: five of them in fact voted for the guillotine as well.

On the Opposition front bench, Peter Shore and Michael Foot were the chief spokesmen on the bill. Michael Foot had already effectively collaborated *de facto* with Enoch Powell over the reform of the House of Lords, and just as an implicit alliance between the government and the Labour Marketeers was to become apparent as the bill progressed, so did the mutual support between the surviving Conservative anti-Marketeers and that part of the Labour front bench which carried the

---

[1] The five pro-Market abstainers that night (with their total number of absences or abstentions on the same authority in brackets) were Freda Corbet (102), Austen Albu (98), Carol Johnson (88), George Lawson (82), and Christopher Mayhew (55). Michael Barnes (98) was in Bangla Desh with Hugh Fraser, an anti-Market Conservative; Ray Gunter was in South Africa, and resigned his seat shortly afterwards.

heat and burden of opposition to the bill. The bulk of the Labour Party closed ranks behind its front bench, or rather behind the section of it operative on this issue. It proved to be a long and bitter parliamentary struggle – all the more painful because the Labour Party's champions on the issue felt that they were being betrayed by some of the people sitting on the benches behind them.

The Labour Marketeers were clearly in a difficult dilemma. Up to twenty or so had already decided that on the floor of the House they would vote with their party throughout, and had started by doing so on 28 October. Naturally they took the view that they must now vote against the implementing legislation also. Some had abstained on 28 October with the argument that, since they could hardly vote with the government night after night in 1972, they preferred for consistency's sake not to vote with it on 28 October either. Others took the line – propagated by Roy Hattersley, in an article in the *Guardian* in early July 1971 – that, after one great demonstration on the vote of principle, it was not the job of Labour MPs to help the government with its parliamentary business, and that thereafter they would, therefore, night after night, vote against the implementing legislation that was the inescapable prerequisite for the ends they had on 28 October so fervently approved. (That was the 'Houghton doctrine'.) Still others decided on *à la carte* procedure: where they felt a principle was involved, they would abstain; where they felt there was no principle involved, they would vote Nay. But the line between matters where a principle was involved and those where it was not is in practice not such an easy one to draw.

Politics and the human soul have their own dynamics, and people who started out all set to act on one principle found themselves, as the spring and early summer of 1972 wore on, not always able to stick to their initial resolve. On the one hand the act of voting against what they believed was found by some to be physically nauseating: no one should underrate the emotional strains on people torn between party and principle on either the Conservative anti-Market or the Labour pro-Market side. On the other hand, in the end the bulk of pro-Marketeers usually voted with their party, secure in the knowledge that a handful of their colleagues who had least to lose or who found voting against too repulsive would in fact ensure that the government could obtain a bare majority. That, too, was a possible escape – so to organize as to ensure the passage of the bill while voting against it oneself. The truth of the matter is that there was perhaps no single ethical solution to this impossible dilemma: and that age and prospects, temperament and conviction, forming a different mix in each individual, left each with a differently weighted choice.

The disciplined comradeship of the nearly ninety pro-Market Labour MPs of 28 October thus crumbled completely. But then there was in fact no effort made to sustain it. The pro-Marketeers did not want to become a party within the party and exacerbate the split. They wanted it forgotten as soon as possible. They had no intention of martyring themselves, or of leaving the commanding heights of the party vacant for the Left wing to walk into. Roy Jenkins could hardly have stood for the Deputy Leadership in November if he had not pledged that he would always endeavour to vote with the party except on 'a major central principle' directly contrary to the October decision. The rest could hardly as a body act with greater ideological purity than their leader whom so many of them wanted to have in an official position where he could both help to keep the party together and stand up effectively for their point of view. Moreover, in what proved to number over a hundred divisions spread over five months, they could hardly hope to hold even twenty or thirty of their number to consistent abstention. Only a handful abstained on both readings and for most or all of the Committee stage: they were almost all people who had served their time honourably in the party, and some of them – the 'Kamikaze pilots' – either did not in any case want to fight the next election or decided that their convictions were worth the risk. Most of the rest, at most stages of the proceedings, felt they could not but vote with the party. As one of their leaders had put it in early February: '1971 was a difficult year: 1972 will be a distasteful one.'

The Break

It was this distaste for what was being done and said in their name that finally caused the patience of some of the leading pro-Marketeers to snap. Paradoxically enough, it was the feeling that the proceedings in Parliament were making a mockery of democracy, while the opinion polls were far from showing the full-hearted consent of the people, that triggered off the reaction which then suddenly made things much easier for the government.

Anthony Wedgwood Benn, who had succeeded Ian Mikardo as Party Chairman after the Brighton conference, had made the concept of 'participation' the lodestar of his year of chairmanship. The fact that

President de Gaulle's frequent referenda had hardly satisfied the demands for 'participation' in pre-1968 France he found unconvincing. Though his ideas of a referendum before entry could not even find a seconder in the shadow cabinet in late 1970, he had not abandoned the notion. On 15 March 1972 the shadow cabinet once more turned it down: it would seem that there were only four votes in favour, Harold Wilson having spoken against its adoption. But next day, just before going to visit Edward Heath at Chequers, Georges Pompidou announced that he would submit the enlargement of the Community to a referendum in France. It was a constitutional procedure alternative to that of parliamentary ratification of the Accession Treaty, and it suited the President for domestic purposes (to split his Socialist from his Communist opponents) and also to strengthen his position abroad, especially in the councils of the enlarged Community. (He did indeed greatly embarrass the French Left, though for domestic reasons he obtained only a very limp *oui* in the poll on 23 April. But that was not relevant to this stage of British politics.)

So, in a slightly changed climate, on Anthony Wedgwood Benn's initiative, the National Executive of the Labour Party on 22 March reversed their position. (They did so by a majority of 13 votes to 11, with Harold Wilson, Roy Jenkins and James Callaghan all absent.) While at the Brighton conference they had successfully obtained the defeat of the Post Office Engineers' motion calling for a referendum, they now, less than six months later, called for a referendum themselves. Two days later Edward Heath announced a plan for 'periodic plebiscites' in Northern Ireland. On 29 March, four days before Easter, the shadow cabinet met. Harold Wilson and Edward Short had changed their minds. William Ross and Denis Healey were (it would seem avoidably) absent without leaving word with the Chairman on how they felt. (William Ross was a determined opponent not only of entry, but also of referenda, which could be a useful tool for Scottish Nationalists.) And by 8 votes to 6 the shadow cabinet in turn proceeded to reverse the position it had reasserted only a fortnight before, and to recommend a whipped vote of the Labour Party to follow Neil Marten and Enoch Powell into the lobby in favour of a consultative referendum before entry.

The pro-Market members of the shadow cabinet dispersed for the Easter recess: independently, Roy Jenkins in Berkshire, Harold Lever in the South of France, and George Thomson all came to the same conclusion. They had stood for re-election, after grave hesitation, at the end of 1971 in order not to hand over all the power in the party to the anti-Marketeers and the Left; in order to hold the party to at least advocating entry in principle, even if there was opposition to the transitional measures; and in order to protect their friends against reprisals for their pro-Market convictions. They had voted with a bad conscience against the Second Reading of the European Communities Bill, and brought down on themselves accusations that they had ratted just as much as Harold Wilson, only a little later. And now the shadow cabinet, under a Party Leader who had gone on record over and over again absolutely unequivocally against a referendum, had stood on its head in defiance of Conference's own decisive vote six months before. They had taken all they could stand. They could take no more. The Sunday after Easter George Thomson went out to see Roy Jenkins, and they phoned Harold Lever. On the Monday morning they met with Shirley Williams, who felt she should for the moment stay. At lunchtime Roy Jenkins, George Thomson and Harold Lever resigned.

Roy Jenkins' letter of resignation was long and detailed. The shadow cabinet's reversal of stance was only 'a single incident illustrating and accentuating a growing divergence': the official majority position of the party, which was only one of opposition to the terms of entry, had increasingly become one of opposition on principle. But the bulk of the letter was concerned with the effects of the decision on the Labour Party, within which Roy Jenkins emphatically situated his protest. Firstly, he asked, what would result from Labour men fighting each other publicly in the country over the 'Yes' or 'No' to the referendum – or else, if the pro-Marketeers were muzzled, what sort of a referendum would that be? Secondly – shades of the old 'middle-class élitist' gibes notwithstanding – he condemned referenda as such:

By this means we would have forged a more powerful continuing weapon against progressive legislation than anything we have known in this country since the curbing of the absolute powers of the old House of Lords. Apart from the obvious example of capital punishment, I would not in these circumstances fancy the chances, to take a few random but important examples, of many measures to improve race relations, or to extend public ownership, or to advance the right of individual dissent, or to introduce the planning restraints which will become increasingly necessary if our society is to avoid strangling itself.

Thirdly he could not stomach the inconsistent exploitation of the referendum issue for short-term political advantage:

This, in my view, is not the way in which an Opposition, recently, and soon again I hope, the government of this country, should be run. . . . If Government is born out of opportunism it becomes not merely difficult but impossible. . . . This constant shifting of the ground I cannot accept.

In terms of intra-party power politics, Roy Jenkins, George Thomson and Harold Lever had now seen – perhaps too late, but then a serious politician cannot afford to resign until it is too late to do so – what David Watt put very clearly on the very morning of their resignation:

The stampede is on and, under present management, the herd is not going to be diverted. When it has passed in a month or two the chances are that we shall find that Mr Jenkins and his friends are no longer there. The question of whether they will be grazing somewhere by themselves or lying mangled upon the prairie will have to be answered in the next few weeks.[1]

The Times, the morning after, eulogized Roy Jenkins as 'a man who can be seen to set himself the standards of an earlier and stronger age of British statesmanship', George Thomson and Shirley Williams ('as near to being wholly good people, people of serious moral purpose, as it is decent for a politician to be') and Harold Lever ('the Ulysses of the Labour Party, a man both subtle and wise'), and bewailed the party's fate: 'To lose such people tears at a party's heart'.

There was heavy criticism immediately from various quarters and in various directions. Some felt that it was a pity for Shirley Williams to stay on the Executive (the previous year she had been if anything more ready to resign than some of her closest colleagues), and for Roy Hattersley to take a vacant place on the front bench (even if he wrote a warning letter to Harold Wilson saying he agreed with the men who had resigned, and might have to do the same if Labour policy became any more anti-European).

Other Labour Marketeers argued in the opposite sense: that to resign because personal relationships were getting too unpleasant round the table was a dereliction of political duty. The pro-Market cause could not be strengthened by three of its heaviest guns leaving the National Executive to which their colleagues had elected them. If they had only stayed on three more days, some argued, the vote in the Parliamentary Party on 12 April might well have gone against a referendum: by simultaneously personalizing the issue and resigning the Marketeers had discouraged their friends from going on fighting, and made their

[1] *Financial Times*, 10 April 1972.

enemies vote for a referendum if only as an expression of their distaste
for the Marketeers, or to emphasize unity and solidarity with the
Leader.

In a reply to these critics, George Thomson acknowledged that this
was indeed a matter of personality – for Roy Jenkins, but by implication also for Harold Lever and himself. 'It did not lie in his character to
be able to do so. He could not have lived with himself. . . .' George
Thomson also turned this problem of personal credibility to the long-
run positive advantage of the party:

. . . the public is becoming weary of the cynicism of politics, the acrobatics for
short-term tactical advantage, the statements with as many escape clauses in the
small print as in a hire purchase agreement.

I believe he may find that in relation to the kind of leadership the country
needs and wants the best way to save your political life is to be ready to lose it.[1]

To allow the precarious compact between the Marketeers and the
anti-Marketeers to snap in this way, not least by changing his own vote
on the referendum issue, certainly looked like a critical error on Harold
Wilson's part. Presumably he must have believed that the other three
really committed pro-Marketeers would, like Shirley Williams, be
content with something like a letter warning him that they could not
stay if the rot went any further. Perhaps he felt that they had already
compromised themselves sufficiently to be able to swallow another
humiliation. But for Harold Wilson personally, the replacement of
these three on the Shadow Cabinet by three anti-Marketeers, Reg
Prentice, John Silkin and Barbara Castle, could not be compensated for
even by Michael Foot's defeat in the election for Deputy Leader by
Edward Short, the man whose change of vote on the referendum issue
had signally contributed to the resignations, though the Marketeers'
votes on the whole went to him rather than to Anthony Crosland.
With the Party Chairman, Michael Foot and Peter Shore in the lead, the
'stampede' now resumed, and the next question to arise was whether
Harold Wilson, with no pro-Marketeers to hold any sort of effective
balance for his balancing act, might not sooner or later prove to be
another victim himself.

But from this new situation there were two obvious gainers –
Labour's Left wing (including Anthony Wedgwood Benn), and the
Conservative government. The Left wing's challenge had been framed

[1] 'Why we were right to resign', *Observer*, 16 April 1972.

in a 'heads you lose, tails I win' fashion in any case: the Labour Marketeers had either to lose even more credibility, and even more self-respect, or the Left would win some of the leadership positions vacated by them, and thus tip the balance of influence in the party. Anti-Marketeers of the Centre and Right of the party might worry as to Labour's electoral chances after such a damaging split – the exact obverse of the worries felt in the 1922 Committee less than a year before on behalf of the Conservative Party. But the Left, having used the one issue on which they could get support both from something like half public opinion and from much of the party's Centre and Right, seemed poised to establish their ascendancy. And since they argued that it was the lack of radical Left-wing policies which had caused the downfall of Harold Wilson's government in June 1970, they could be unperturbed on the electoral consequences for the party, and feel that an anti-Market platform would if anything prove a major further asset at the polls.

As for the government, they must for once have blessed the names of Enoch Powell and Neil Marten for their referendum amendment, and the Labour anti-Marketeers who had so overplayed their hand as to provoke the (possibly overdue, but possibly also still avoidable) break at the top of the party. From that Monday lunchtime of 10 April 1972 onwards, the eventual passage of the European Communities Bill was almost assured. One does not resign from the Deputy Leadership of a party, they felt, in order then to allow the measure in support of which one resigned to be defeated in the House. Though Roy Jenkins, Harold Lever and William Rodgers voted against the Third Reading, George Thomson, Michael Stewart, Dick Taverne (in deep trouble in his Lincoln constituency) and some others abstained. Perhaps the Parliamentary Labour Party has two rules, one relaxed, for the majority, and another rigid, for those who still maintain claims to leadership. For the latter to have abstained, they felt, would have diminished their influence in the party for a decade. Their voting record, in the end, was better than that of quite a few anti-Marketeers in the party. But then they were now fairly confident at each stage that the government would in fact be able to do without them.

Nevertheless there was still a very uncomfortable period ahead for the government's parliamentary managers, when they could not be quite sure of their majority on any particular vote. The situation had its farcical aspects – as when the TUC leaders called at No. 10 only to find the Prime Minister and senior colleagues just about to leave No. 10 for a vote in which, by an administrative oversight, they had not been paired. And there are (perhaps apocryphal) stories of various Labour men ringing up to say that there was no need to worry, they knew a dozen would abstain that night, though each of them added apologetically that unfortunately they could not be among that dozen themselves. The signals network of 'unusual channels', cross-party friendships and habitual gossip compared likely rebel voting patterns on both sides, Labour Marketeers warning the government and reminding it of its own responsibilities rather than responding to any appeals to deliver so many votes – which they were not now in any case in a position to do. Partly by luck, mostly by Conservative management, on occasion through Labour's 'total abstainers', the result turned out to be a long series of narrow escapes. The majority for the Second Reading had been eight: it was to fall to that figure again in Committee on 19 April on an amendment to safeguard EFTA interests and, more crucial, in June on Clause 2 standing part of the bill. If that had been lost, according to David Wood: 'there would have been a situation little short of a constitutional crisis.'[1]

On 24 May on an amendment in the names of Messrs 'Powell, Foot, Walker-Smith, Shore, etc', and again on 22 June on the clause embodying some of the prerequisites of the Common Agricultural Policy, the government majority fell to 5, on 3 May on one amendment to 6, on another to obviate freedom of capital movements to 4 (265 in favour of the amendment, 269 against). The odd defeat in Committee on minor matters would not have been fatal: the clause could presumably have been reinserted in a more carefully organized vote at the report stage. But the government was trying to avoid any such stage, and besides did not want to lose face by being defeated on any part of the bill. More important, for the guillotine on 2 May the majority was 11, and by the time it came to the Third Reading, on 13 July, it was up to 17.

The maximum number of MPs who voted in favour at any one time (after 28 October, when the figure was 356) was 309 on the Second Reading. It was 301 on the third. The government could not claim to have obtained the votes of half the House in favour of its implementing legislation. But then on the substance the government could rightly book the tacit consent of the Labour abstainers and some of the Labour men who felt forced to vote against. And for formal purposes it now argues – pace full-heartedness – that a majority of 'one is enough'. The Royal Assent could thus be pronounced on 17 October 1972.

[1] The Times, 15 June 1972.

Inconclusion

It would have been profoundly satisfying to end this book on a conclusive note – with the triumph of a cause, with a great reconciliation
of peoples, with the trumpets sounding as the outer walls of the EEC
fell down to admit four new members, as it entered on new closer
relationships with its neighbours and undertook new responsibilities
towards the rest of the world. Life, alas, is not quite like opera, history
not always as dramatic as the Old Testament, and if there was victory –
as in a sense of course there was – it was victory not by a knock-out but
on points, and a victory that will still require further consolidation.

The government succeeded in their primary aim. They obtained
parliamentary approval of the principle of entry by a large majority,
and they secured – by a hair's breadth – the passage of the implementing
legislation. But they failed to obtain the 'full-hearted consent' of the
British people before entry. They can, of course, argue that their job is
to lead, and that popular opinion will in due course ratify EEC membership once it is an accomplished fact. The people were apprehensive
about decimalization of the currency too; yet now the great step has
been taken no one would dream of going back on it. That may be true.
But, even so, another danger remains. The great unsolved endemic
problems which dogged the British economy right through the 'fifties
and especially the 'sixties could now find in EEC membership a new
alibi. Where overdue radical reforms in Britain are made all the more
urgent by EEC membership, foreign politics and undemocratic Continental bureaucracy could become a scapegoat both for the difficulties
of adjustment to a fast-changing world, and for the failures resulting
from insufficiently radical reform. The major task of rallying the understanding and the will of the country for the domestic changes required
if it is to meet the demands of its citizens remains to be done.

The Conservative anti-Marketeers – a dwindling band of them, at
least – fought the good fight as they saw it to the end of the legislative
road. They failed, but they were clearly determined not to give up the
battle for public opinion. Certainly the anti-Market campaigns as non-
party bodies still felt confident that some of their most telling arguments, some receptive climates of opinion, and some of their biggest
opportunities to hit the headlines and rouse the electorate were yet to
come. Those who believe in the wider Community of nations – within
Europe and beyond it – will have to think harder and work harder to
give greater impetus to the Community in all sorts of fields, and to

make its ordinary citizens feel that what the Community does is good news for them. If they fail in that, they may find that they have over-played their hand, and are in danger of being overwhelmed by a nationalist backlash.

The Labour Marketeers succeeded in allowing the bill to pass, and in maintaining a slender bridge to Continental Social Democracy on which future political co-operation in re-shaping the Community will have to be built. But they failed to hold the Labour Party to its declared policy of entering the EEC in principle; they lost some of the com-manding heights in the party structure and were in danger of being edged into the periphery of party decision-making; and some of them looked as if they might have committed political suicide for the European cause.

Harold Wilson looked like succeeding in the lonely task of holding that turbulent coalition, the Labour Party, together through one of the worst storms of its history, though not without cost to his image with at least a section of the public.

The Labour anti-Marketeers failed to stop British entry. They suc-ceeded in swinging the party officially very close to their own views. But whether that would effectively keep the whole party out of power for several elections, whether it would prove irrelevant com-pared with other issues on the public agenda, or whether it would sweep Labour back to power on a wave of anti-Market sentiment like that which overwhelmed the Norwegian Socialist government, no one could be sure.

For the 'Europeans', 1 January 1973 no doubt constitutes a triumph. In one sense a quarter of a century of work will not have been in vain. The Marketeers have won at the level of the political institutions, of the élite, the leadership of the churches, industry and agriculture. The bill has become an act, entry a *fait accompli*. But though the triumph is far from hollow, it should be muted. The British people is divided in mind, and divided along class lines even on this issue. The onus of proof before the broader British public remains on those who want to see Britain part of a larger Community. The opposition of the bulk of trade unions and of the larger part of the Labour Party membership at the grass-roots level remains a grave liability overhanging the political process of enlargement. The loyalties to such a wider Community, which we noted at the outset were hardly widespread in Britain, remain to be forged. Familiarity may dispel fear, habit may begin to tell on the side of membership, boredom may breed indifference, but that is not the spirit in which the European Movement set out to kindle the enthusiasm of European peoples a quarter of a century ago.

At the same time the Community Britain is entering is a very different thing from the Community envisaged in the hopes and aspirations of the 'forties. Moreover, the challenges of those days have been overlaid with others, to which the Community has hardly yet begun to respond. Its enlargement will bring with it new problems for the Community no less than for its new members.

Though agreement over enlargement has now followed on agreement over completion, the third element in that triptych decided upon at The Hague, the 'deepening', has now to make progress. Economic and monetary union is seen to be rather more difficult than some people at The Hague realized. The problems of sterling were swept from the negotiating table at the Paris summit, but they will not simply go away for that reason. Between all the Community countries differential rates of inflation will continue to produce strains which cannot be papered over by mutual support funds and lofty sentiments. Technological and industrial, regional and social action must become far more of a common responsibility. Resource depletion and environmental deterioration may require a re-direction as well as acceleration in technological advance and economic growth. Defence is a subject on which we have hardly started. Our foreign aid programmes remain puny, our trade policy ineffectual, and our foreign policy aims inchoate.

In the internal structure of the Community there is no agreement on how the Brussels executive and legislative functions are to be brought under less indirect democratic control. The social and psychological problems of the scale of our operations, the complexity of our interdependence, and the accelerating rate of change in our conditions of life have been barely grasped. A summit meeting may point to certain goals. But only a hard struggle of an intellectual and scientific, technical and economic, diplomatic and domestic political nature can bring those goals any nearer.

Both in Britain and in Brussels, then, there are sterner tests ahead, and battles to be fought compared to which British entry was simple.

'Britain entered in 1973. . . .' Whether the future historian will put a full-stop, a semicolon or a comma after that statement, an 'and . . .' or a 'but . . .', it is too early to tell. In large part the decision is ours to determine. Books, mercifully for reader and writer alike, must at length come to a close. But the act of accession on 1 January 1973 is not an end. It is a means, and it is a beginning.

Appendix 1: An Anatomy of Rebellion

On 28 October 1971, in the vote of principle on British entry into the EEC, 131 MPs – fully one in five – rebelled against their party leadership. Nothing of the kind has been seen in British politics since the vote preceding Chamberlain's resignation in 1940. The full vote was:

The Vote on 28 October

	Con & UU	Labour	Liberal	Others	Total
In favour	282	69	5	—	356
Against	39	198	1	6	244
Abstained	2	20	—	—	22
Unable to vote[1]	6	2	—	—	8
	329	289	6	6	630

Disregarding Mr Hooson, the lone Liberal who disagreed with his Party Leader, and taking together, as for most purposes one could, the abstainers and those who voted in the opposite lobby from their Party Leader, there were 41 Conservative and 89 Labour rebels on whom to test some of the journalistic generalizations of autumn 1971.

Almost as interesting, of course, as those who actually rebelled were the two groups of Conservative and Labour MPs who at some stage showed some inclinations to go against the way their party went, but who finally conformed. Thus there were, on the Labour side, 17 MPs who were members of the Labour Committee for Europe, and 21 MPs who signed the *Guardian* advertisement of the Labour Committee (10 of them in both categories simultaneously) but then voted against entry on the terms agreed. That made a group of 28 Labour MPs who might be considered to have been potential rebels, but came to heel.

On the Conservative side people tended to be more discreet in their opinions, to sign less advertisements and to join less committees: yet there were 5 members of the Common Market Safeguards Campaign (and one member who had voted against the 1967 application) who finally voted with the government, and rightly or wrongly observers in their constituencies and at Westminster listed between them over 60 Tory MPs in the spring of 1971 who were regarded as being on the whole dubious or hostile about entry into the EEC. This gave – for what the classification was worth – an analogous group of something over 20 Conservatives who fell into line after showing some signs of a contrary view.

[1] 3 Chairmen, 4 tellers, 1 ill.

Unfortunately, however, statistical techniques cannot go beyond the uncertainty of the data. Should the man who later claimed he was drunk when he signed one of these documents be regarded as a waverer? Should the man who went round saying he resented not being asked to sign the same document but then voted the opposite way be counted? Where did one reckon the MP who was simultaneously on the notepaper of the Safeguards Campaign and of the Committee for Europe? The next appendix supplements the precise statistics on the actual rebels with impressionistic comparisons of the less clearly definable wavering conformists on the Conservative side.

Even in the case of the actual rebels one was of course dealing with very small numbers. In the case of the Conservatives one man's action would shift $2\frac{1}{2}$ percentage points. Rather than peddle percentages, therefore, it seems better to compare the rebels with a representative sample of the same size drawn from each party. (Rounding to the nearest unit will occasionally make the representative sample slightly larger or smaller than the rebel group.) Such a comparison will at least show the sort of weight to be assigned to the argument in each case.

Let us, to illustrate, take the hypothesis that the rebels tended to be the deadbeats, with nothing more to hope for in politics, while the young aspirants avidly conformed. Principle, on this hypothesis, is the luxury of old age, careerism the requirement for the under-forties. There is, of course, also the contrary hypothesis as far as the Labour Party is concerned: that the Marketeers were the bright young things, while the old carthorses of the party remained insular, backward-looking, and hidebound in working-class solidarity.

The computer immediately gives the lie to both these simplifications. If there were any significant deviation from the average, it would be that there were more youthful rebels on the Tory, less on the Labour side: and more rebels than average among the old Labour MPs – including men like John Rankin (aged 82) and Douglas Houghton and George Strauss (both in their seventies).

Age

	Conservative		Labour	
	Rebels	Representative sample	Rebels	Representative sample
Under 40	9	7	14	16
40–49	9	15	27	27
50–59	15	14	23	25
60 and over	8	6	25	20
	41	42	89	88

There is no evident direct correlation between the Market vote and religious denomination – though it is not always easy to know what real personal significance nominal membership of a religion has to each MP. No doubt there were fervent Protestants who saw the Treaty of Rome as a popish plot – though the six out of eight Ulster Unionists also had other reasons for joining Bernadette Devlin and Gerald Fitt in the 'Nays' lobby (where the Rev. Ian Paisley was also to be found). In a Parliament with the unprecedented number of 37 Roman Catholics (20 of them on the Labour benches), Norman St John-Stevas, Shirley Williams and Maurice Foley may have been active on the Market side, but Anthony Fell and Hugh Fraser voted against both their party and accession to the Treaty of Rome, while Bob Mellish applied the whip against.

As far as Jewish internationalism goes, of the 40 Jewish MPs exactly 20 voted for, 20 against, an anti-Market deviation from the parliamentary average accounted for by their much greater representation on the Labour benches. The only significant deviation there lay in rebelliousness as such: 3 Tories and 14 Labour men crossed the floor in the division, making it a 43% index of rebellion among Jews, as against 19% for non-Jewish MPs. None of them abstained.

It has also been said that a university education led to greater openness to entry into the EEC. The Conservative figures give no support to that belief. The Labour figures, on the other hand, while not supporting it either as far as other universities are concerned, highlight a correlation between particularly an Oxford education and pro-European rebellion: not only the Rodgers-Taverne-Williams group that ran the Labour Club in the late 1940s, but also the more recent vintages. Of the 14 Labour rebels under 41, Barnes, Mac-Lennan, Marquand, Richards, Roper and Whitehead were all Oxford men, while only Dalyell hailed from Cambridge.

University Education

	Conservative		Labour	
	Rebels	Representative sample	Rebels	Representative sample
Oxbridge	19	21	34	22
Other	6	5	26	26
None	16	15	29	41
	41	41	89	89

This seems to chime in with the trend already noted in the late 'fifties:

> On every question except civil liberties Oxford members behaved differently from the rest of the party . . . within each age-group, so far as can be ascertained, Oxonians were more European, more internationalist, and more humane than their opposite numbers from Cambridge.[1]

[1] S. E. Finer, H. B. Benington and D. J. Bartholomew, *Backbench Opinion in the House of Commons 1955–59*, Pergamon, Oxford, 1961, p. 119.

The low proportion of rebels among the Labour MPs without university education may, however, be in part a product of trade union influence. Quite a few sponsored MPs who wanted to vote for entry had their arms twisted in no uncertain way – unless they came from a union like the General and Municipal or the Clerical Workers, which were in any case in favour of entry. Some of them compromised by abstaining. The next table, therefore, segregates the 'Ayes' from the abstainers among the Labour rebels.

Trade Union Sponsorship

	Ayes	Representative sample	Abstainers	Representative sample	All rebels	Representative sample
Not sponsored	50	36	5	10	55	46
Sponsored by GMWU	2	3	5	1	7	4
Others sponsored	11	26	9	8	20	34
Co-op sponsored	6	4	1	1	7	5
	69	69	20	20	89	89

One could refine these figures: thus 4 of the sponsored rebels came from the Transport Salaried Staffs Association and the National Union of Railwaymen, both unions which went against entry by very narrow margins. With such adjustments, the implication would stand out even more strongly. To look at it the other way round: the Transport and General Workers had 18 MPs, but only one rebelled; the Mineworkers had 20, but only 2 rebelled, one of them by abstention.

It does look on the statistics alone as if it was difficult to vote against a sponsoring union's decision. Thus trade union sponsorship – and indeed, more generally, relations with the nominating body within one's own party – seems to have been a rather more important factor than the size of the parliamentary majority. If fewer Labour men with very safe seats rebelled, this is likely to be associated with the tradition of working-class solidarity with whatever the majority decides, and with the same solid working-class background of which trade union sponsorship and absence of university education tend to be ancillary indicators.

It certainly does not look as if very many would-be rebels were deterred by the size of their electoral majority – though one or two MPs could be quoted who were no doubt not entirely uninfluenced by that consideration: three of the Labour Committee for Europe members who voted against on 28 October, and two of the Safeguards Committee Conservatives who voted for, had

Size of Majority

	Conservative		Labour	
	Rebels	Representative sample	Rebels	Representative sample
Under 1,000	1	3	9	7
Under 3,000	4	6	13	14
Under 5,000	8	5	20	14
Over 5,000	28	28	47	53
	41	41	89	89

majorities under 3,000. Indeed, there were cases where a small majority – at least on the Conservative side – could give an MP additional leverage against his constituency association: if he were to be refused renomination he could threaten, by standing as an Independent, to let in the other party instead.

What appears to have acted as much more of a deterrent to rebellion was the imminent redistribution of seats, which forced a great many sitting members to face a fresh nomination procedure against other comers. (That consideration loomed even larger in some Tory minds after the Chelmers report and may have helped erode opposition in early 1972.) It took extra courage from men like Dick Leonard and Ivor Richard, whose constituencies were disappearing, to burden themselves with the handicap of defiance of the whip in their search for new seats. (One or two others, however, regardless of age, were resigned to pursuing their careers elsewhere after the next election.)

A rather more striking correlation, at least on the Labour side, was that indicating that new members may have found it more difficult to rebel than those who had acquired the self-confidence, the credit with their constituencies, or at least a more rounded political image than those whose first distinction would otherwise have been that of voting against the party that had just sent them to Westminster. The Labour rebels included only 5 new members, as against the 20 new members a representative sample of the party would have contained. Curiously enough this clearest of all the departures from the norm on the Labour side was not matched among the Tories; ten of their rebels were new members, which is exactly what a representative sample would have included. Lt-Col. Mitchell may have faced greater dangers in his life, but young men like Toby Jessel and David Mudd (or Peter Fry, first elected in late 1969) cannot have found it altogether easy to stand out against the party line – indeed, on the second reading of the Accession Treaty only 3 new members were still voting against the government.

Which brings us to the last, and perhaps the most significant of all our deviations: the fact that while, of the Labour MPs who had not held cabinet office in 1964–70, only 28% rebelled, of the former cabinet Ministers 61% refused to toe the party line. Of 23 cabinet Ministers in the outgoing cabinet, only 9 voted against entry.

No doubt one could, with further data, establish other, more conclusive correlations: first experience of the Continent (or of foreign *au pair* girls), linguistic ability, business connections, general traditionalist or innovatory temperaments – but alas, the data of political science do not contain these perhaps equally or even more relevant tit-bits. Perhaps the conclusion from this exercise is twofold. First, it explodes various current myths. Second, it puts anecdotal material into perspective, reducing the alleged typical case on occasion to the only possible instance.

Beyond that, statistical tabulators are no substitute for old-fashioned piecemeal history, treating each MP as an individual with his own fairly unique conjunction of problems: for in the last resort, the rebels were the men and women who wanted to rebel, and had the guts for it – or those who, whether they wanted to rebel or not, had boxed themselves in by their earlier declarations. Actuarial tables or political science correlations are useful in their way: but only documents and interviews can give us the feel of events, and of just what compound of heroism and villainy individual human beings are made.[1]

[1] The bulk of this Appendix first appeared in New Society, 4 May 1972; the editor's permission to reprint it here is gratefully acknowledged.

Appendix 2: The Timing of Conservatives' Decisions

In Chapter 6 we looked at the problems within the Conservative Parliamentary Party first through the eyes of the official party managers, then through those of the Conservative Marketeers, and lastly through those of the rebels. Thanks to the careful work and the canvassing skill of Norman St John-Stevas and several of his colleagues in the Conservative Group for Europe we can, however, also attempt to look at these problems, with hindsight, in somewhat more 'objectively' measurable terms not usually available to the political scientist.

A correlation of the January estimates made for the Conservative Group for Europe with the voting of Conservative MPs in October is revealing. It shows that, even if the 'doubtfuls' of all shades are treated as not having been subject to any prediction, 75% of the votes in October were predicted correctly nine months earlier. If one took the 'doubtful +' category as predicting a vote in favour, and the 'doubtful –' as predicting abstention or a vote against, the percentage of correct prediction nine months in advance would rise to 86%. On that interpretation 281 out of 326 members' behaviour would have been correctly predicted nine months in advance. Of the remaining 45, the 19 'middle doubtfuls' split 16 to 3 in favour, while a great many of the other 25 – classed as rather hostile – publicly announced a 'Damascus' which in effect confirmed the reliability of the assessment at the time it was made.

Unless in each of a great many individual cases the Conservative Group for Europe erred in the same direction as intentions later changed, we may draw several interesting conclusions: firstly, the unofficial whips' assessment was remarkably good – indeed better than that of the party whips themselves. We shall see that much the same turned out to be true on the Labour side. The explanation may take several forms. Government whips may think it their duty to err on the side of caution – though when it comes to the crunch, excessive caution could discourage a Prime Minister (if he is more concerned with the party's overall control of the country than with any specific policy measure) from pushing through a policy against over-cautious advice. Secondly, perhaps, the party whips are concerned with a great many other issues, while the enthusiastic amateur can concentrate on one. Thirdly, the whips are an official channel, invested with a certain aura of authority, and part of a continuing relationship vital to each MP's future. He may, therefore, be more discreet with them than with an ordinary fellow-member, and the whips may for their part overcompensate in discounting that discretion. In other words, they may not always believe a man will vote with them when he intimates as much. Fourthly, of course, the gifted amateur can sometimes beat the professional at any game by

Correlation of CGE Estimates with October Votes

	Number of MPs				Percentage			
October votes	Pro	Doubt-ful	Anti	Total	Pro	Doubt-ful	Anti	Total
ALL MPS					Correctly predicted: 75%			
Voted For	217	63	5	285	64	21	2	87
Rebels	1	12	28	41	—	4	9	13
Total	218	75	33	326	64	24	11	100
NEW MEMBERS					Correctly predicted: 67%			
Voted For	48	21	3	72	58	26	4	88
Rebels	—	3	7	10	—	4	9	13
Total	48	24	10	82	58	30	11	100
MEMBERS RETURNED AFTER ABSENCE					Correctly predicted: 77%			
Voted For	15	4	—	19	68	18	—	86
Rebels	1	—	2	3	5	—	9	14
Total	16	4	2	22	73	18	9	100
CONTINUOUS OLD MEMBERS					Correctly predicted: 78%			
Voted For	154	38	2	194	69	17	1	87
Rebels	—	9	19	222	—	4	9	12
Total	154	47	21	28	69	21	9	100
MARGINAL SEATS					Correctly predicted: 77%			
Voted For	40	10	2	52	72	18	4	95
Rebels	—	—	3	3	—	—	5	5
Total	40	10	5	55	72	18	9	100
MAJORITIES OVER 2,000					Correctly predicted: 74%			
Voted For	177	53	3	233	65	20	1	86
Rebels	1	12	25	38	—	4	9	14
Total	178	65	28	271	65	24	10	100
SCOTS					Correctly predicted: 69%			
Voted For	14	3	2	19	64	14	9	86
Rebels	1	1	1	3	5	5	5	14
Total	15	4	3	22	69	19	14	100

trying hard enough. It was no accident that in Eldon Griffith's sweepstake on the majority on 28 October William Rodgers – the Marketeers' unofficial whip on the Labour side – won by coming within one vote of the correct total and

Norman St John-Stevas came second by being within two. (John Silkin recalls having got it exactly right but had not entered. But then he was a player turned gentleman.)

The second conclusion is rather more important. It does very much look as if voting inclinations were fairly well defined in the Conservative Parliamentary Party in January 1971 – four months before the Paris summit, six months before the terms were known, and nine months before the October vote. There was only one error in the 225 names classified as 'doubtful+' or better – and that error was queried at a very early stage. (This was the CGE member who voted against entry, William Clark; apparently he did not change his views, but had just not been sounded out properly.) Omitting him, the most remarkable feature of this table is that 28 out of the final 39 votes against were accurately spotted nine months in advance of the vote – and that the 'doubtful–' and 'against' categories, comprising 62 members at the time, contained 37 of the 41 rebels at the end of the day. Of course, inclinations are not necessarily firm intentions, and there remained a job to be done in bringing all those who were already favourably inclined actually into the government lobby on a concrete set of terms. But for the rest, the 'doubtfuls' and worse consisted of 81 MPs, of whom perhaps two dozen were hopeless cases. The battle could thus in effect be concentrated on the other 50 or 60 members.

The third conclusion is as to the timing of the decision in the case of those members. Nothing happened between late January and late April, except that the Conservative Group for Europe consolidated its membership from within the group of those who were in favour in any case. Accuracy in identifying rebels and supporters did not really progress in these three months: the April estimate contained 38 out of the final 41 rebels in a pool of 63 members listed as 'doubtful' and 'against'. There was no significant change in MPs' views – neither between doubtfuls and those favourable, nor between doubtfuls and antis. Those whose judgment was suspended quite naturally kept an open mind while time passed without the negotiations showing any progress.

The big change came about after the summit, as negotiations were concluded, terms announced, the government opened its overt campaign of persuasion in earnest and Harold Wilson started shifting decisively against entry, thus making the issue a party battle. Then suddenly, by the end of July, accuracy was quite remarkable: 279 out of the 284 who voted for were named correctly, and, if 'persuadability' is an elastic term, there was in fact little persuasion over the summer, for all but 5 of those listed as 'persuadable' or 'against' proved indeed to be rebels. (The overall figures reported on 1 August were thus spot on – 284 in favour, and 284 voted in favour on 28 October; 41 others – and 41 rebelled.

The five who were thought persuadable and did vote with the government were James Allason, Wilfred Baker (who was concerned about fishing and voted with the government on the understanding that a reasonable solution would be found for that problem), Sir Edward Brown (sometimes displayed by the party as an authentic working-class member, who has great loyalty to the party), Hamish Gray and Fergus Montgomery. Their places were in effect taken by five thought to be 'all right' – William Clark, Donald Kaberry, and Robert Taylor (who were wrongly thought to have shifted out of the 'against' into the 'favourable' category), Peter Fry and Colin Mitchell who had (as it proved, wrongly) been moved from the doubtful on to the favourable list.

In other words the evidence suggests a fourth conclusion: that whatever patterns the anti-Marketeers saw in the events of July, August and September, and though there may have been several cases of people who moved out of a position of hostility into one of compliance with the party during the summer, this does not seem to have been a large-scale phenomenon. The ranks had rallied by late July, and if there was 'skulduggery' it must have taken place before the House rose for the summer recess. It is possible that there was constituency pressure in June and July – but it is doubtful that there can have been much of it before mid-July, and unlikely that it produced such startling effect within a fortnight. It is possible that there was pressure from the whips on the 'doubtfuls' and the weaker brethren among the antis – though the stronger antis were, it seems, never troubled by the whips. But we may guess that, whatever the general arguments about giving Parliament time, the whips who thought that a vote of principle in late July or early August would have resulted in an 'un-acceptably unfavourable' result were wrong, at least as far as Conservatives were concerned, and that the recess probably did not yield even a handful of further Conservative votes for the government.

It is not difficult, on publicly known data, to build up an *a posteriori* picture of what kind of MPs actually rebelled: it would also be possible to describe who showed various signs of rebellion at certain moments. At the risk of letting the evidence bear conclusions to the very limit, however, we can now also, from these tallies, try to go further and test certain notions as to what factors were at work in some Conservative MPs who were initially more undecided, or more open to conversion, than others.

It has been suggested, for example, that new members are less likely to rebel than established ones. The evidence of the vote on 28 October does not bear out this hypothesis: the percentage of new members who actually rebelled against the party is to all intents and purposes the same as that of old members, and that of members who returned to the House after a period of absence. On the other hand there is a significant difference between new and old members if we take the January assessment of inclinations. Had they split in the same proportions as old members, seven less would have been 'doubtful' and eight more would have been 'pro' in January. It may be that the Conservative Group for Europe whips knew the new members less well, and were, therefore, more inclined to class them as doubtfuls. In fact, however, this seems not to have been the whole explanation. It is, after all, not surprising that new members are more agnostic in their political attitudes than more experienced ones, and it may well also be that, given the cross-pressures of public opinion on the one side and government policy on the other, they were indeed less certain what they would do before the issue had taken on concrete form, as it did in the course of June and July.

There is also a contrast when we divide up members between those in marginal constituencies and those with majorities of over 2,000 votes. Here there is a slight difference in intentions as perceived by the CGE in January: had the marginal members divided in the same ratio as those with safer seats, four less would have declared themselves pro. We may also notice here the fact that, had they voted in the same proportion as the non-marginals, not only would 4 less have voted for, but 7 or 8, not 3, would have voted against. Again the absolute totals are small: but the figures are compatible with the very opposite of that *a priori* notion that people in marginal constituencies did not want to declare themselves too early, when in January the tide was running against the Market; and that, being more sensitive to popular opinion, they were more inclined to vote against entry than those holding safer seats.

The numbers of women, of Scots and Welshmen, and of Ulster Unionists are too small to prove any generalizations different from those applying to the party as a whole. But they can explode some widely held impressions. Certainly the hypothesis that the Scots, frightened of being neglected on the periphery of the larger economic unit, voted disproportionately against entry is flatly belied by the facts. Nor did proportionately more of the 14 women change their minds than of the 311 men.

If there were major correlations between social, geographical or other categories of members and their openness or timing of decisions, they must have been of a subtler kind. The odds are that on the whole people decided as and when they wanted to. The cases we have picked out in Chapter 6 were thus leading examples of the twenty-five people classified as 'doubtful' or 'anti' rather than typical instances of the Parliamentary Party as a whole.

Appendix 3: Further Polls of Popular Opinion

Logically prior to attitudes on the issue – though not necessarily psychologically so – is the problem of how informed the public was – and felt itself to be. The level of factual knowledge about the EEC was deplored by many, not least by the general public itself. Thus, NOP asked in the first half of June 'Do you happen to know which European nations are full members of the Common Market? If Yes, which?' As usual, men, the upper middle class, people in their thirties and forties, and in this case Conservatives, appeared the best informed: but overall only 13% seemed able to name the six member states correctly. (These findings correspond to those of the poll taken by Social and Community Planning Research earlier in the year, when less than one person in five could, even with the aid of a list, identify the six member states of the EEC.) But then the simple test of asking which countries belong to the Common Market may not be the only or even the best way of judging how far the electorate's understanding of the political issues went.

When it came to comparisons between Britain and the EEC, ORC found that at least half their sample could usually, already in late April 1971, get any particular comparison right, and no more than one in six or so would get things the wrong way round:

ORC: *Which – Britain or the Common Market – would you say has the . . .*

	Britain	Common Market	Same	Don't Know
Higher cost of living?	13	73	4	9
Higher wages?	18	52	8	22
Faster growing prosperity?	11	62	5	22
Longer holidays for workers?	15	45	7	33
Higher level of unemployment?	58	11	7	24

while where the answer was more subjective, people felt that British was best:

	Britain	Common Market	Same	Don't Know
Better standard of living?	49	26	9	16
More influence in the world?	42	31	8	19
Better social services?	78	6	3	13

(which, in the case of social services, rather depends on one's definition).

The Social and Community Planning Research Poll threw up a broadly similar picture – with perhaps on the whole less people claiming to know the answers, but where answers were given by guesswork or wrongly they tended to be in Britain's favour – such as the 28% who thought Britain's family allowances bigger than those of EEC member states, as against 10% who got that comparison right. What the latter survey added was evidence of a fairly accurate comparison between two of the EEC countries – Germany and Italy (though here again less than half actually ventured a view).

Advantages and Disadvantages of Common Market Entry

Gallup: *What do you think would be the advantages to Britain if we join the Common Market? Any other advantages or arguments* for *joining?*

	Nov. 1969	1–4 July 1971	6–11 Oct. 1971
British industries/agriculture will benefit/expand	16	20	20
Better wages/working conditions	7	8	7
Keep down cost of living/cheaper goods	8	6	6
Closer *political* links with Europe	11	6	7
Full employment will be maintained	6	4	13
Less travel restriction in Europe	10	4	6
Wider range of goods in shops	12	4	6
Closer *military* links with Europe	6	4	6
Social/medical/education services will improve	3	1	3
Goods for the Commonwealth	4	1	2
Other advantages	7	9	16
No advantages	32	36	28
Don't know	21	16	16

Gallup: *What do you think would be the disadvantages for Britain of joining the Common Market? Any other disadvantages or arguments* against *joining?*

	Nov. 1969	1–4 July 1971	6–11 Oct. 1971
Cost of living/prices will go up	67	68	67
Commonwealth will be affected	12	12	9
More unemployment/labour imported	11	10	12
Loss of political identity/sovereignty	10	9	9
British industry/ agriculture will suffer	11	8	5
Too close *political* links with Europe	5	3	5
Increased competition for British industry	8	2	6
Social/medical/education services will suffer	5	2	4
Cut in wages/poorer working conditions	5	1	3
Too close *military* links with Europe	4	1	2
Other disadvantages	7	7	11
No disadvantages	5	5	11
Don't know	15	9	4

When we turn from factual knowledge to the arguments in the debate, in February 1971 only 12% claimed to ORC that they understood the advantages and disadvantages very well, another 32% answering 'quite well'; 38% confessed 'not very well', and 18% 'not at all well'. That did not, however, mean that particular strands of the total argument were not readily expressed. Gallup repeatedly asked about advantages and disadvantages: the results are set out on page 412. (The sensitivity to the employment arguments for entry – and to Continental competition and employment repercussions as an argument against entry – seems, not surprisingly perhaps, to have increased considerably during the autumn as unemployment figures rose.)

At least the short-run effects of entry seem to have been fairly well understood, though the degree of harmonization entailed by joining the Community may have been overestimated – for example in the case of social security benefits. Gallup asked in August, September and October 1971 whether working hours, holidays and social security benefits would increase or decrease, and only 4%–12% thought that things would deteriorate in these respects, with 24%–40% thinking they would improve, and typically around 40% thinking there would be no difference. On the other hand, 28% consistently thought that the level of unemployment would fall and 28%–29% that it would rise, with only a quarter thinking there would be no difference. (In the September Gallup poll, 45% simultaneously thought the level of employment would rise, only 16% that it would go down. Clearly macro-economic concepts like the relationship between employment and unemployment are more difficult to handle than matters like prices and holidays.) In September not even 1% were under any illusion that food prices might fall, and 94% thought they would rise, 71% thinking the rise would be 'a lot'. Over half, however, also thought wages would go up, nearly half that taxes would go up; less than 10% thought that either of these items would fall.

Yet Gallup also found that it was thought by 40 : 25% that the British economy would be strengthened by entry, and by 43 : 20% that general living standards would be better if we joined than if we did not. Since it is hardly likely that these expectations determined attitudes, the degree to which attitudes shaped economic expectations is illustrated by two NOP questions asked in September:

NOP: *If we join the Common Market, do you think that Britain's exports would go up or down?*

	Approve of application	Disapprove of application	All
Up	77	35	47
Down	7	24	15
Same	8	23	16
Don't know	8	18	22

NOP: *If we join the Common Market, do you think that British industry would become more efficient or less efficient?*

	Approve of application	Disapprove of application	All
More	79	34	46
Less	5	26	16
Same	8	23	17
Don't know	8	17	21

Interesting differences arose when one made distinctions between the short and the long run, between the present and the next generation and between personal attitudes and judgments of the national interest. ORC on 11 February 1970 asked 'If it becomes clear that we would be better off in the Common Market in the end, but that the cost would be high at first, would you then be in favour of joining?', and obtained a balance of 49 : 38% who would. In March 1971 ORC asked 'If Britain joins the Common Market, do you think it will benefit or harm the next generation?', and twice in the autumn 'Do you think that Britain's entry into the European Common Market would be in the national interest or not?'. The answers are set out on pages 416–17. As in the case of the straight questions of for and against entry, sex, age and class, political and regional differences are strikingly marked, with opposition increasing and support decreasing as one goes from males to females, up the age scale, down the social and leftwards along the political dimension, and, generally speaking, northwards in the United Kingdom.

The extent to which the issue had become one of social class is clearly seen just before the October vote in the replies to this question, too. The upper middle class split 67 : 23, the lowest social class 27 : 54 in their judgments of Britain's national interest over the issue. The 15–24 age group tended to be less favourable in their judgment than the 25–44 (it was not more hostile, but understandably had a greater proportion of don't knows). Over and over again the data highlight the same gradients: men of the southern upper middle class in their thirties (particularly if they tended to vote Conservative) were the archetypal Marketeers: old Scottish working-class women, particularly if Labour voters, bore all the marks of the antis. The original chasm on this issue between the Scottish Labour MPs who supported entry and their constituents could hardly have been greater.

The national orientation throughout this period was still a little more towards the Commonwealth than towards Europe, but with interesting systematic variations according to age, social class, sex, region and party preference. Three ORC polls taken over six years show a decisive rallying of the 'don't knows' to the belief that Britain's future lay with Europe once Parliament had taken the decision of principle and was embarked on the legislation – though how far the

ORC: *Where do you think the main future of Britain lies in terms of trade and economics – with America, Europe or the Commonwealth?*

	1966	Feb. 1971	Feb. 1972
America	12	13	8
Europe	37	27	52
Commonwealth	39	37	33
Don't know/none in particular	13	24	7

question was interpreted as normative and how far as merely predictive it is difficult to say.

Europe was to the fore in the minds of those under 45, of the upper middle classes, and – at least after July 1971 – the Conservatives: the Commonwealth still seemed more important to the older, to the semi-skilled and unskilled working class, and to Labour supporters.

There was not much confidence in the notion, still occasionally proclaimed by 'Europeans', that Britain could prove the leader if she joined the Community: the 9% who thought so in November 1969 had shrunk to 5% in Gallup's repeat of that question in October 1971. 39% on the first occasion, 36% on the second rather thought Britain would take a back seat, while the number of those who saw the Community as a group in which all are equal rose from 36% to 46%.

The government's assurances on the preservation of Britain's national identity may in the autumn of 1971 have had some rather marginal success. The Gallup question 'Will we lose a lot of our national identity, a little, or none at all?' secured the following responses:

Gallup: *Will we lose a lot of our national identity, a little, or none at all if we join the Common Market?*

	29 July–1 August	September	6–11 October
A lot	27	27	31
A little	35	30	28
(Lose some	62	57	59)
None at all	27	34	28
Don't know	11	10	14

When it came to the processes by which the country's decisions should be taken, popular opinion certainly never felt hostile to the government's negotiating 'to see what terms we can get'. In February 1970, the month of the Labour government's White Paper, 67 : 28% replied to an ORC poll that it should. In late April and the first couple of days of May 1971 – before the Heath–Pompidou summit was announced – 48 : 24% said that if the negotiations were successful,

Detailed Breakdown of Three ORC Polls

ORC: *If Britain joins the Common Market, do you think it will benefit or harm the next generation?*

3–7 March 1971

	All	Male	Female	15–24	25–44	45–64	65+
		SEX			**AGE**		
Benefit a lot	12	14	10	11	13	14	6
Benefit a little	22	24	21	31	26	18	14
(Total benefit	34	38	31	42	39	32	20
Harm a lot	29	29	29	23	29	30	34
Harm a little	15	16	15	14	14	16	17
(Total harm	44	45	44	37	43	46	51
Don't know	21	17	25	21	18	22	28
(Difference	− 10	− 7	−13	+ 5	− 4	−14	−31

ORC: *Do you think that Britain's entry into the European Common Market would be in the national interest or not?*

29 September–3 October 1971

	All	Male	Female	15–24	25–44	45–64	65+
Yes	47	52	43	48	55	44	35
No	34	34	34	32	33	35	37
Don't know	19	14	23	19	12	20	25
(Difference	+13	+18	+ 9	+16	+22	+ 9	− 2

13–17 October 1971

	All	Male	Female	15–24	25–44	45–64	65+
Yes	43	48	39	44	50	42	33
No	41	40	42	37	37	43	49
Don't know	15	11	10	19	13	15	18
(Difference	+ 2	+ 8	− 3	+ 7	+13	− 1	− 16

they would accept the terms (an odd formulation not above suspicion of circularity, but one used both by ORC in April–May and by Gallup in late May 1971). In late May 35% said they would accept them, 18% said they would not, while 28% gave the (perhaps logical) answer that it would depend on the terms. In both polls, as was to be expected, Conservatives, those between 25 and 44, men, and – in the first of the two polls – the upper middle class were the ones most willing to accept the terms.

	CLASS			PARTY			REGION				
AB	C_1	C_2	DE	Con	Lib	Lab	South	Wales & West	Mid-lands	North	Scot-land
18	15	12	8	16	12	9	14	12	9	13	7
32	29	20	18	25	33	21	23	24	27	20	20
50	44	32	26	41	45	30	37	36	36	33	27)
21	23	35	30	23	27	33	26	25	32	31	36
14	12	13	19	15	13	15	18	12	14	12	23
35	35	48	49	38	40	48	44	37	46	43	59)
14	21	20	26	22	16	21	19	27	18	25	15
+15	+ 9	−16	−23	+ 3	+ 5	−18	− 7	− 1	−10	−10	−32)
67	59	42	35	66	46	33	49	47	56	46	29
17	20	41	44	15	34	51	31	40	29	29	54
15	21	17	21	19	20	16	20	12	15	24	16
+50	+39	+ 1	− 9	+51	+12	−18	+18	+ 7	+27	+17	−26)
67	55	43	27				49	42	45	37	38
23	31	42	54				37	39	39	45	51
10	14	15	19				14	19	15	17	10
+44	+24	+ 1	−27				+12	+ 3	+ 6	− 8	−13)

From mid-1969 onwards, at any rate, a broad majority of the country anticipated British entry into the EEC. In mid-July 1969, after Pompidou's election
to the Presidency, 57 : 22% of respondents told NOP they thought Britain
would be successful in joining the Common Market. By November 1969 and
March 1971 69 : 19% and 73 : 18% thought it was very likely or quite likely that
Britain would join in the next five years. In early 1971 the impasse in the negotiations somewhat reduced those figures, until by late April and the first two

days of May ORC found only 40:34% thought they would succeed – with Conservatives obviously more optimistic about their party's leaders achieving their objectives than Labour supporters. The Harris Poll on 17 May – just before Edward Heath's visit to President Pompidou – found that 93% of those who favoured entry, and 81% of those who opposed entry, thought Britain would in fact join: but because those who were not sure where they stood on the issue also had a high percentage of those who did not know if Britain would join, the overall figures came down to 82% thinking Britain would join, 7% thinking she would not, with 11% don't knows.

From July to October the Gallup figures for those who thought she would not join fell to 6%–8%. These figures were broadly confirmed by a NOP poll on 24 September, which showed 83% thought Britain would, 10% thought she would not join.

Gallup presented its respondents with four alternative procedures before Britain should finally join or reject the Common Market:

	May 1971	1–4 July 1971
Party vote in the House of Commons	6	7
Free vote in the House of Commons	14	20
General Election on the issue	27	29
National Referendum	42	36
Don't know	11	9

No one really seemed to think much of a party vote in the House – though that was what the government appeared to insist, until the last moment, on demanding, and what the Labour Party unsuccessfully tried to make it on 28 October – and nearly succeeded, in early 1972, in obtaining. Even in the case of Labour supporters there was a clear 2:1 majority in the October 1971 Gallup poll against pro-Market Labour MPs having to toe the party line:

	All	Con	Lib	Rest	Lab
Free vote	72	85	82	71	60
Follow Labour Party policy	16	6	7	8	27

But a free vote meant, it would seem, freedom from the party whip, not a vote according to an MP's own convictions. Gallup did not find much understanding of Burke's concept of representation. Asked in October 1971 what an MP should do whose own views differed from those of his constituents, only 28% thought he should follow his own judgment, as against 62% who felt he should vote according to his constituents' views.

Two of the polls did explore the problem of a general election on a specific issue as seen by the electorate. In April 1971 Harris asked how people would vote in a general election in which the Tories and Liberals supported entry, while Labour opposed it. They arrived at the following result:

Would vote	All voters	Favouring entry	Opposed to entry	Con	Lib voters	Lab
Conservative	30	54	21	68	6	3
Labour	46	23	60	12	35	85
Liberal	3	9	2	—	41	1
Other	3	1	1	1	1	1
Would not vote	4	3	4	5	4	1
Uncertain	14	10	12	14	13	9

It is difficult to know how far the response to such a very hypothetical question posed in cold blood would bear any relation to voters' decisions at the end of a hard and emotionally fought campaign. (If any of the Labour leadership thought that there was any close correspondence, these figures must have encouraged them to press for a general election on the issue, which would have held out hopes of a landslide victory.) Those opposed to entry were further asked how likely it was that, in such an election, they would vote for an anti-Common Market Independent candidate: 17% of them thought they definitely, a further 17% probably, would, though the party breakdown made moderate nonsense of the original hypothesis, with Labour voters (whose party the question assumed would be anti-entry) more inclined than Conservative voters to desert their party for an anti-Common Market candidate.

In July 1971 Gallup asked simply: 'If there was a general election on the issue and you disagreed with your party's policy on British entry would you still vote for the party or not?' and found that 49% would still vote for their party right or wrong on that particular question; in the last week of February 1972 Gallup offered various specific alternatives, and it would appear that then only one in seven would actually vote for another party, the rest abstaining or not knowing what they would do.

	All	Con anti-Marketeers	Lab pro-Marketeers
Still vote for party	48	41	54
Vote for other party	14	19	13
Would not vote	22	25	17
Don't know	16	15	16

Various polls asked questions about a referendum – notably Harris, which secured in February 1971 a majority of 70 : 17% for a referendum on the question 'Do you think we should have a national referendum to decide whether to join the Common Market, or should the Government make the decision?' In late April 1971 the same question got much the same response – 70% for a referendum, 20% for the government deciding. NOP in September 1971, on the other hand, asked: 'Do you think the public as a whole has enough information on which to vote in a referendum on whether or not Britain should join the Common Market?', and only 17% replied that the public had enough information, while 80% felt that they did not. These responses are compatible with either a demand for yet more information, or with the cynical view that no one had enough information (not even the government), or else that information is irrelevant anyhow.

More thorough work on this question was undertaken by ORC, which asked a quota sample of 1,005 people a battery of five questions in late March and early April 1971. The majority did not claim to know what a referendum was: 41% of men and 68% of women said they did not know. On the other hand, 'Do you think it would be a good idea if the Government asked the people to vote Yes or No before it decided on whether we should go into the Common Market?' obtained an overwhelming 82 : 14% in favour. ORC then generalized the issue with interesting divergencies according to the form of the question (the third part being in fact asked second), and according to the party preferences of the respondents, as set out below.

ORC: (i) *Do you think the people should have a direct vote on every important decision that faces the government?*

(ii) *Who do you think should take important decisions – the elected government or the people?*

(iii) *If a political party makes certain promises about its policies and is then elected, do you think it should go back to the people to get approval again or just go ahead?*
(31 March–4 April 1971)

		All	Conservatives	Liberals	Labour
(i)	Yes	42	30	45	55
(ii)	The people	33	22	31	47
(iii)	Go back to the people	27	15	24	38
(i)	No	49	62	44	36
(ii)	Elected Government	59	72	64	44
(iii)	Go ahead	66	80	75	53

Put in these ways the demand for referenda on important issues was not in general a majority demand, though the call for a referendum on entry into the EEC was: the public did see this as a special and overriding issue. Throughout the table there was a steady differential: the Conservatives were happier to leave things to the government (which was, of course, at the time a Conservative one), while Labour supporters championed direct popular decision-making more than the Liberals.

The referendum was not, at that time, on the programme of any party – indeed the Labour party conference was to reject it by a decisive majority in early October 1971. We have already noted the swing towards entry among Conservatives once Harold Wilson had shown that he was going to come out against it in summer 1971, and it is another measure of the extent to which people decide such issues in party terms that as soon as the referendum became a partisan question it immediately lost popular support–the dramatic loss occurring almost entirely among Conservative supporters. Harris asked the question in February 1972 – before either the French President had announced his referendum or the Labour Party had come out with any such demand – and then again in April 1972:

Harris: *Do you think we should have a national referendum to decide whether or not to join the Common Market, or should the government make the decision?*

	All voters			Conservatives			Labour		
	Feb.	April 1972	Change	Feb.	April 1972	Change	Feb.	April 1972	Change
Should have referendum	75	64	– 11	69	46	– 23	79	78	– 1
Government should decide	20	31	+11	28	50	+22	16	17	+ 1
Don't know	5	5	—	3	4	+ 1	5	5	—

It almost looks on these figures as if a cause formally espoused by the Labour Party at this time received – if not the kiss of death – at least a sizable set-back in terms of total popular appeal.

As far as the substantive decision itself and the resulting political situation is concerned, this was largely accepted once the major debates seemed to be over and the second reading had taken place:

Gallup: *Do you think it would be a good thing or a bad thing for this country if the government failed to get the support of Parliament for its Common Market policy?* (last week of February 1972)

	All	Conservative	Labour
Good thing	25	12	34
Bad thing	51	70	39
Don't know	25	18	27

On this showing even a plurality of Labour supporters seemed at this stage to think it would be better for the implementing legislation to go through. But by this time (as we saw on pages 356–7) public attention had largely shifted elsewhere, with unemployment, the cost of living, Ireland and industrial disputes regarded as far more urgent problems facing the country. The great debate, as far as the general public was concerned, was over, for good or ill. And as we saw in Diagram 3, in spring 1972 people seemed to drift into accommodating themselves, at least temporarily, to their fate, in effect ratifying *ex post* the decision that had been taken by Parliament.

Index

The only institutional provision that needed rather more elaborate adaptation (but the solution had long since been agreed informally) was the re-jigging of the voting strength of each member state in the Council of Ministers. Under the Rome Treaty this had broadly fulfilled three criteria when the vote was on a proposal from the Commission:

(a) it had prevented a veto from any one country even in conjunction with Luxemburg;
(b) it had allowed a veto by any one big country in conjunction with any other country except Luxemburg, and
(c) it had not given a veto to the three Benelux countries (whose combined populations were only half that of any of the big countries).

These three criteria had been satisfied by giving France, Germany and Italy 4 votes each, Belgium and the Netherlands 2 votes each, and Luxemburg one vote: a 'qualified majority' then consisted of any 12 of these 17 votes, or to put it the other way round 6 votes were required to exercise a veto on proposals from the Commission.

The voting rules for the new Community, assumed to be one of ten states, were

(a) to give the new members, if they were unanimous, a veto against the old,
(b) to give any two big countries, or any one big country combined with both Belgium and the Netherlands a veto and
(c) to give the smaller countries, even without Luxemburg, a veto against the four biggest.

These conditions were in due course satisfied by Article 14 of the Treaty of Accession, which amended the Rome Treaties as follows:

Where the Council is required to act by a qualified majority, the votes of its members shall be weighted as follows:

Belgium	5
Denmark	3
Germany	10
France	10
Ireland	3
Italy	10
Luxemburg	2
Netherlands	5
Norway	3
United Kingdom	10

For their adoption, acts of the Council shall require at least:

—forty-three votes in favour where this Treaty requires them to be adopted on
a proposal from the Commission,
—forty-three votes in favour, cast by at least six members, in other cases.

Slightly more difficult, but also resolved as negotiations progressed,
was the problem of the length of the transition period during which the
applicant states would progressively undertake the full duties of membership and obey all the rules of the Community in full: notably of
course how quickly they would abolish their tariffs against other
member states of the Community, and how quickly they would move
to applying the Common Agricultural Policy. The British asked for a
three-year transition for industry (where they hoped to export to the
Continent soon), a six-year period for agriculture (where they hoped
to delay application of the rules for as long as possible), and a still
longer period for the financial contribution they would have to make
for the Community – a brash attempt to pick out the plums first and
pay up later. In December, Geoffrey Rippon agreed that 'adequate
parallelism' should mean a five-year period of transition for industry
and agriculture alike: but he maintained that the financial aspects, as
well as sugar and milk products, would still need longer transition
periods. (For Euratom, the Atomic Energy Community, no one
objected to a much shorter transition period before the rules became
fully applicable to the United Kingdom.) The final rhythm by which
the adaptations were to be made did not, however, get settled for some
time. In the case of tariffs, the system as finally embodied in Article 32
of the Accession Treaty was that there should be five equal reductions,
each of a fifth of the tariff, on trade between each new member and the
other members of the Community – the first on 1 April 1973, the others
on 1 January of 1974, 1975 and 1976, ending in free trade within the
enlarged Community as from 1 July 1977. The new members would
also adopt the common external tariff in stages to be completed on that
last date.

The negotiations were, of course, to deal with an enormous
mass of disparate material. A brief glance through the Treaty of Accession (let alone the forty-two volumes of secondary legislation) is a
reminder of just how much more than the setting up of a 'customs
union with a common agricultural policy' was involved. We shall
return to the enlarged EEC's relations with certain overseas Commonwealth countries; that little could be done for Canada and Australia,

and that India, Pakistan and Bangla Desh, Ceylon, Burma, Hong Kong and Singapore could not become Associates in the same way as the African countries was never questioned. The protocols on, for example, the Channel Islands and tanning extracts of wattle, the application of the Generalized Preference Scheme by new members and the exchange of information on nuclear energy, and the declarations on base areas in Cyprus and on the definition of 'nationals' all bear witness to the diversity of themes on which agreement had to be reached. But the major political rows were to take place over six key issues: Britain's budget contribution, her application of Community preference, New Zealand dairy produce, cane sugar, sterling, and finally, ludicrously, fish.

The Negotiations Reach Deadlock

The financial contribution was the first to become a principal bone of contention. The nub of the issue arose out of a *de facto* asymmetry between the fund-raising and the money-spending of the Community, as planned for the final system. The Community's own resources were to be raised in three ways: firstly from the common external tariff, secondly from the variable import levies on the import of agricultural produce, and thirdly from up to one per cent of value added in each country as collected by the value added tax. The last element is one that is roughly proportionate to national income. But in its other two elements of fund-raising, the Community taxes not so much flows of income as flows of import expenditure; and with over 90% of its own spending it helps in the first place one industry only, namely farming.

In a Community which is psychologically and politically, economically and monetarily integrated that may be an unexceptionable transfer of funds from one section of the community to another along perfectly clear 'objective' lines of policy. But for the British, coming in at a late stage, the calculation of what would flow not between urban and rural, but between British and non-British populations seemed very pertinent. And looking at it in national terms, of course, one could easily caricature the actual upshot of the policy. One could argue that the EEC raised the bulk of its funds from those countries that were the big importers (of industrial goods no less than of farm products) from outside the Community; and it then spent the bulk of its funds in those countries which were the largest producers of foodstuffs. This asymmetry proved tolerable – not much more than that – within the

Community of the Six. It involved as things stood a net transfer from Italy and Belgium to Holland and France – plus a very major contribution from Germany to France and Holland. It was from the French point of view a device for milking the German industrial 'miracle' for the benefit of the French peasants – and justified from the German point of view by the political advantages of belonging to the Communities rather than standing isolated in Europe. Some might call it a form of delayed war reparations. From the Community's point of view a certain transfer from the richest regions – such as the Rhine-Ruhr area – to the poorest farming regions in the Massif Central and the South-West of France would also be justified, though the Common Agricultural Policy was a rather inefficient and approximate method of doing it. But what was tolerable for Germany was not necessarily so for Britain. Britain imported almost as much in absolute value from outside the Community as Germany, and would therefore become liable to make a gross financial contribution that would be analogous: but since her farm sector was a very much smaller one than the German, she would get very much less back – thus paying a substantially larger net contribution to the Community than the Federal Republic, whose gross national product per head was by 1971 a third larger than the British. Any such arrangement would have seemed *a priori* inequitable – a sort of penalty for the delay in joining (a delay of which the first five years may have been Britain's, but the next nine years at least were in large part other people's fault). And it would also be very dangerous for the Community itself, for it would set up additional balance of payments strains for Britain that could result in serious disturbances of the economic balance within the enlarged Community.

It was not so easy to solve this problem. For a start, the French had made it a condition of the opening of negotiations that precisely the internal financial arrangements of the Community should be all sewn up before talks with the candidates began: and the Community as a whole was agreed that the *'acquis communautaire'* – the settlements already achieved – could not be called into question in the process of enlargement. Moreover, the whole concept of a 'net contribution' was anathema to Community thinking. It had to be so: for if each calculated what he put in and what he got out of any policy, that would corrode the whole foundation of the Community concept. When the notion of a 'fair return' was introduced – by the French – into the financing of Euratom, it sounded the death-knell of that organization's useful life. Indeed in raising the problem in terms of a net contribution, how-